Devan Shepherd

**SAMS**
# Teach Yourself
# XML

# in 21 Days

## SECOND EDITION

**SAMS**

*A Division of Macmillan Computer Publishing*
*201 West 103rd St., Indianapolis, Indiana, 46290 USA*

# Sams Teach Yourself XML in 21 Days, Second Edition

## Copyright © 2001 by Sams Publishing

International Standard Book Number: 0-672-32093-2

Library of Congress Catalog Card Number: 00-111798

Printed in the United States of America

First Printing: August, 2001

04   03   02   01      4   3   2   1

## Trademarks

All terms mentioned in this book that are known to be trademarks or service marks have been appropriately capitalized. Sams Publishing cannot attest to the accuracy of this information. Use of a term in this book should not be regarded as affecting the validity of any trademark or service mark.

## Warning and Disclaimer

Every effort has been made to make this book as complete and as accurate as possible, but no warranty or fitness is implied. The information provided is on an "as is" basis. The author and the publisher shall have neither liability nor responsibility to any person or entity with respect to any loss or damages arising from the information contained in this book.

**EXECUTIVE EDITOR**
Michael Stephens

**ACQUISTIONS EDITOR**
Carol Ackerman

**DEVELOPMENT EDITOR**
Heather Goodell

**MANAGING EDITOR**
Matt Purcell

**PROJECT EDITOR**
Natalie Harris

**COPY EDITORS**
Kim Cofer
Karen A. Gill

**INDEXER**
Sandra Cannon

**PROOFREADER**
H. Stanbrough

**TECHNICAL EDITORA**
Frank Neugebauer
Robert Gonzales

**TEAM COORDINATOR**
Lynn Williams

**INTERIOR DESIGNER**
Dan Armstrong

**COVER DESIGNER**
Aren Howell

**PRODUCTION**
Stacey Richwine-DeRome
Ayanna Lacey

# Contents at a Glance

# Contents

# Contents

# Tell Us What You Think!

As the reader of this book, *you* are our most important critic and commentator. We value your opinion and want to know what we're doing right, what we could do better, what areas you'd like to see us publish in, and any other words of wisdom you're willing to pass our way.

As an executive editor for Sams Publishing, I welcome your comments. You can fax, e-mail, or write me directly to let me know what you did or didn't like about this book—as well as what we can do to make our books stronger.

*Please note that I cannot help you with technical problems related to the topic of this book, and that due to the high volume of mail I receive, I might not be able to reply to every message.*

When you write, please be sure to include this book's title and author as well as your name and phone or fax number. I will carefully review your comments and share them with the author and editors who worked on the book.

Fax:      (317) 581-47770
E-mail:   feedback@samspublishing.com
Mail:     Michael Stephens
          Sams
          201 W. 103rd Street
          Indianapolis, IN 46290 USA

# Foreword

I'm sure we've all experienced the excitement of purchasing a new piece of software, only to be disappointed with the documentation provided. Haven't you wondered how an amazingly talented person or creative team can conceive of and develop such a great new product, yet manage to consistently fail so miserably at telling people how to use it? After all, it is those technicians who presumably know their product best and who also understand the types of business problems their product was developed to address.

As president of a company that was on the leading edge of XML training, I began to better understand what was happening in such situations. Many professional programmers/developers, while quite good at solving technical problems, are not particularly good at telling others precisely what they're doing; they tend to skip steps and assume knowledge that their audience does not necessarily possess. Although much has been made of the difficulties of hiring personnel with good technical skills, for our company the challenge was to find people who had both the requisite technical abilities *and* the communication skills to effectively explain complicated concepts relating to an emerging technology.

To survive in the technical education/training business, you must be willing to accept responsibility for the students' learning. It's not enough to just deliver the material and concepts; you have to make sure the information is conveyed in a manner that enables students to successfully apply the technology to solve business problems unique to their companies. Instructors must be articulate, entertaining, quick-witted, intelligent, and able to quickly demonstrate how the tools and technology can be properly used in a variety of situations. Individuals with these qualifications are extremely difficult to find.

I first met Devan Shepherd at a Comdex show where he was a speaker, having heard of him previously by reputation. Since working closely with Devan, I have become even more impressed with his technical skills, his understanding of the learning process, and his knowledge of the proper place of technology in the workplace. When we worked together, we regularly encountered people who were enamored with XML and its potential, but who all too often regarded it as something that could do some "cool" things rather than as a business tool that could solve useful business problems. In other words, these people were interested in technology for its own sake, missing the point that it was the solution to specific business problems in which their management was interested, much more so than fancy programming tricks.

Devan's students benefit greatly from his ability to bring technical, instructional, and business skills to the classroom. In this instructional text on XML, Devan offers readers an informative step-by-step manual of the state of the art as it relates to this important technology. He provides detailed and tested code examples with easy-to-follow sample problems that readers can easily generalize to their own business situations. An important addition is the list of Web sites and other resources where additional information can be found for various XML-related topic areas. By following the text and exercises in this book, readers should truly develop a significant understanding of XML, related technologies, and how this information can be of benefit across a broad range of business circumstances. After all, if you're reading this book, isn't that the point?

—*Bryan Snyder*

Bryan Snyder is the former president of Architag International, a training and consulting organization specializing in XML services and integration. He has significant experience in consulting, corporate finance, and strategy, and is now working for a high-tech plastics manufacturer.

# Introduction

XML, the Extensible Markup Language, is the *lingua franca* of the Internet. With XML, you have a completely extensible, easy-to-learn, and richly featured universal format for structuring data and documents that can be exchanged efficiently over the Web.

Even though the "M" in XML stands for "Markup," XML is not, strictly speaking, a markup language. Rather, it is a sophisticated "Meta" language used to describe highly structured and uniquely specialized markup vocabularies.

Whether you are championing a new era of electronic publishing and content management, designing sophisticated e-commerce solutions, or delving into interoperable scientific data exchange, XML offers you an opportunity to create an industrial-strength, self-describing, data-driven solution. In many cases, the tools at your disposal are built in a vocabulary expressed in XML syntax. By mastering XML, you are learning a family of specialized technologies that coexist in an elegant symbiosis, in a variety of architectures, on a multitude of platforms. The XML family of technologies offers media and platform independence that is ideally suited to delivery of data to an infinite array of user agents, including applications, browsers, Web-enabled wireless devices, and tools we have not even conceived of yet. XML may well be *the ultimate enabling technology* to come about at this stage of the Internet evolution.

*Sams Teach Yourself XML in 21 Days, Second Edition* covers everything you need to know to "hit the ground running" with XML and several of its most important related standards (including XSL, the Extensible Stylesheet Languages; Xpath, the Extensible Path Language; Xlink, the Extensible Link Language; Xpointer; XML-Data Reduced; and XML Schema, to name a few). You will see many working code examples of these technologies and be able to use what you have learned immediately.

## Who This Book Is For

XML is arguably one of the most revolutionary new computer technologies to come along since the Web was conceived in the early 1990s. You probably already know Hypertext Markup Language (HTML) and have created Web sites of your own. This book assumes that you are a seasoned developer, proficient with a variety of technologies and languages. Some of the working code examples in this book make use of JavaScript, VBScript, Java, databases, Active Server Pages, and object-oriented programming techniques, to name but a few. The goal, however, is not to teach you any of those languages, but rather to demonstrate how XML can be elegantly woven into the fabric of real-world solutions that assimilate the inherent strengths of component technologies. If you aren't a "heads-down, 24/7, coder," don't let that discourage you from continuing with this book. The many working-code examples and detailed line-by-line analyses will give you everything you need to know to use the code immediately and learn along the way.

# Conventions Used in This Book

Throughout this book, several uniform conventions are used that serve to distinguish different styles of information presentation. For instance, examples of code, commands, statements, and any text that you type or see displayed on a computer screen appears in a computer typeface. Here is a code listing as an example:

```
<?xml version="1.0"?>
<mybook>
    <title>Sams Teach Yourself XML in 21 Days, Second Edition<title>
    <author>Devan Shepherd</author>
    <publisher>
        Sams Publishing, a Division of Pearson Education, Inc.
    </publisher>
    <ISBN>0-672-32093-2</ISBN>
    <year>2001</year>
</mybook>
```

Most of the code listings in this book are thoroughly analyzed, many on a line-by-line basis. To make it easier for you to follow along with written descriptions of the code, line numbers are provided for complete code listings, like this:

```
 1: <?xml version="1.0"?>
 2: <mybook>
 3:     <title>Sams Teach Yourself XML in 21 Days, Second Edition<title>
 4:     <author>Devan Shepherd</author>
 5:     <publisher>
 6:         Sams Publishing, a Division of Pearson Education, Inc.
 7:     </publisher>
 8:     <ISBN>0-672-32093-2</ISBN>
 9:     <year>2001</year>
10: </mybook>
```

Partial code listing and snippets of code are typically not numbered unless they are quite long.

When you create your own documents based on the listings provided, you do not enter the line numbers. These are just provided as a reference.

You will also see a variety of icons throughout this book that flag special sections of information. For instance, you will see

**Tip**

Tips that provide special information to you about such things as testing, debugging, performance, and good programming practices.

**Note**

Notes that offer supporting information, references from Web sources, quotations, and so on.

**ANALYSIS**   Analyses follow most of the code examples to provide a "walk through" of any new concepts, features, functions, grammar, syntax, or styles being introduced.

The following typographic conventions are used in this book:

- Code lines, commands, variables, and any text you type or see onscreen appear in a `computer typeface`, as you saw in the example listings.

- Placeholders in syntax descriptions appear in italic computer typeface. Replace the placeholder with the actual filename, parameter, or whatever element it represents. For example, if the syntax in the book looks like this: `<XML src="`*URL*`" />`, you would replace the characters *URL* with a valid URL to satisfy the syntax.

You can find supporting source code for the chapters in this book at `http://www.samspublishing.com`.

# PART I

# The Basics of Markup

# DAY 1

# An Overview of Markup Languages

Welcome to *Sams Teach Yourself XML in 21 Days, Second Edition!* During the first day, a very brief history of the Internet will establish the evolutionary nature of the World Wide Web (the Web) and the role played by the World Wide Web Consortium (W3C).

Today you will learn

- The role that XML will play in the e-business world
- Some of the limitations of the Hypertext Markup Language (HTML) that currently predominates markup on the Web
- What SGML (the Standard Generalized Markup Language) is and the relationship that exists between SGML, XML, and HTML
- Seven characteristics of XML
- How to start creating your own XML documents with self-describing markup elements

# The Web Is a Revolutionary Phenomenon

In a very few years, the Web has grown from a novelty to become the world's library. At the heart of this global repository is the empowering concept of "hypertext," a term first coined by Ted Nelson in 1965 to describe a means of connecting streams of data from disparate computers.

 **Note**

> Ted Nelson presented these ideas in *A File Structure for the Complex, the Changing, and the Indeterminate*, 20th National Conference, New York, Association for Computing Machinery, 1965. For more on Ted and his Xanadu project you can refer to `http://jefferson.village.virginia.edu/elab/hfl0155.html`.

In the late 1960s Doug Engelbart created a prototype "oNLine System" (NLS) that comprised hypertext browsing, editing, e-mail and other components that we now associate with the Web.

But the Web has become so much more than that. The rich tapestry of multimedia presentation with video, graphics, sound, and audio has surpassed the original intent of Tim Berners-Lee, acknowledged inventor of the Web, who in 1989 proposed

> a universal linked information system, in which generality and portability are more important than fancy graphics—from `http://www.w3.org/History/1989/proposal.html`.

Berners-Lee began, in 1980, with a notebook program called "Enquire-Within-Upon-Everything," conceiving a myriad of hyperlinks that would provide virtual interconnections between disparate computer repositories of information. He later (October 1990) settled on referring to his creation as the World Wide Web. Although he started with somewhat grand, ethereal visions (the Web, after all was meant to hold the entire universe of mankind's information), the approach to delivering this knowledge was quite practical and somewhat simplistic.

The methodology he developed while working at the CERN (Conseil Européene pour la Recherche Nucléaire, or in English, the European Organization for Nuclear Research) was designed to permit document exchange over TCP/IP (Transmission Control Protocol/Internet Protocol). Berners-Lee proposed the following:

- A new universal Internet document addressing method, called the *URL* (Universal Resource Locator)
- A new TCP/IP protocol, to be known as *HTTP* (the Hypertext Transfer Protocol)
- A new document description language, which was named *HTML* (the Hypertext Markup Language)

All of this reached the world in the form of a functional range of software tools (browsers), originally programmed on the NeXT platform in Objective C and later ported to C to work on other platforms.

 **Note**    You can read a brief but quite interesting summary of the developments that characterized this Web revolution at http://www.w3.org/History.html, in an article entitled "A Little History of the World Wide Web."

What this tells us is that beneath all of the colorful banners, smooth moving animations and real-time audio/video streams that characterize the modern Web are collections of simple text documents (primarily in HTML and related technologies), capable of being transferred efficiently and reliably from one computer to another across the Internet.

# Why Do We Need Another Markup Language?

It might seem as though the Web Revolution has progressed rapidly enough relying primarily on Web site markup using HTML. With HTML, a Web programmer can certainly create simple hypertext links that work. From the focus of one HTML page, a link can be actuated (for example, when the end-user initiates a mouse-click over a provided HTML hypertext anchor on a page) to download the content of a different page.

HTML provides portability that doesn't exist, inherently, in other technologies. Portability is one of several principal objectives in the underlying design of the Web.

There is a relatively shallow learning curve associated with HTML. Everyone from young schoolchildren exploring hobbies and common interests through grandparents sharing pictures of their grandchildren can be published on the Web with very little effort. Editors and Graphical User Interface (GUI) HTML development tools are affordable or freely available for download from the Web. Browser interfaces are inexpensive, powerful, and easy to use.

Why then, if HTML has all of this to offer, might you consider learning XML at all?

One of the reasons lies in the fact that HTML suffers from serious and compelling limitations. What started as a data markup language has been bent and molded into a Web presentation tool. However, as a presentation tool, HTML is weak, offering little control over the placement and management of "white space" on the page, for instance. HTML has problems with character spacing, justification, and hyphenation. Dealing with multiple columns of data, such as those in a newspaper, is problematic for HTML.

When HTML was first created, issues of style were not intended to be included in the language. Event tags for such commonplace styles as italic (<I>) and bold (<B>) were added to the language later. These styles typically are used to denote emphasis, and the intent was for inclusion of an emphasis tag in the language that would be styled by a separate process if and when styles were applied. This separation of content from style is characteristic of XML. XML is a metadata-centric language that defines markup for data, and not for style. Issues of style are handled separately from the data. You will learn to add style to data markup in a variety of different ways. On Day 14, you will see how to add cascading stylesheets (CSS) to XML documents, in much the same way you might add them to an HTML 4.01 page. On Day 15, you will learn about the Extensible Stylesheet Language (XSL) and its rich Formatting Object (FO) components. On Day 16 you will use Extensible Stylesheet Language Transformations (XSLT) to transform XML documents into HTML.

As a data markup utility, HTML lacks flexibility. There are only a limited number of pre-defined tags with no capability of extending beyond that pre-designated set. As new versions of HTML have been developed over the past few years, new functionality has been added, but seldom in a consistent fashion. Oftentimes, new tags have been introduced that are only supported by a single vendor's browser, thereby breaking the cardinal rules of Web markup that say all applications should be interoperable and data delivery should be platform independent.

The W3C intends to stop the release of new versions of HTML. The current version (4.01) is meant to be the final version. Perhaps you have read about XHTML and wondered what it is. XHTML is HTML reformulated as an application of XML. You will read more about the rules of XML today and tomorrow. In particular, you will see that HTML *can be* XML if it follows the syntax rules for XML. In fact, XHTML 1.0 and HTML 4.01 are quite similar, but the elements of each are bound to different namespaces, or collections of acceptable elements. You will learn about namespaces on Day 8.

HTML does not readily support the modularity or reusability of coding that is customary in other languages. In object-oriented languages such as C#, C++, Visual Basic and Java, there are classes that provide for the sharing and reuse of objects and methods between

1

multiple programs. You will learn on Day 18 about XInclude, a new technology that promises to provide code reusability functions to XML programmers. During Day 10 you will explore a similar concept using an embedding technique available to XLink-aware applications. However, HTML has none of these capabilities.

HTML has inconsistencies that permit what might best be called "bad" code to be written and publicly disseminated. XML enforces "good programming practices" through a consistent application of syntax rules. You will learn many of these rules today and tomorrow, but by way of example, some versions of HTML do not always require an end tag marking the completion of certain forms of markup. Browsers had to support the mixed rule sets that became characteristic of HTML. For instance, in HTML a paragraph begins with a <P> tag. Early versions of HTML did not require the programmer to terminate a paragraph with a corresponding </P> tag. Browsers had to effectively "turn off" a paragraph markup instruction by determining where, in the stream of text, the markup was complete, rather than precisely where the document author wanted the paragraph to end. The latest standard, HTML 4.01, requires that a paragraph, and in fact all tags, have corresponding terminating tags at the close of markup. However, browsers still support the hundreds of millions of Web sites that include poorly formed HTML, and therefore do not enforce or validate the HTML 4.01 standards.

You will learn about well-formed XML documents on Day 2 and see that the syntax constraints for XML are strict and rigidly enforced. However, these same rules provide a level of flexibility to the programmer that is simply unavailable to HTML authors.

## Seven Facts You Should Know About XML

The acronym XML stands for the eXtensible Markup Language, but in some ways, the name is misleading. XML ought to refer to the eXtensible Meta Language, because it is a standardized, yet highly flexible means of creating other languages. Perhaps more accurately, XML permits the authoring of dialects of languages that follow precise and exacting rules for structure, syntax, and semantics as established by the World Wide Web Consortium (W3C). You will learn some of those rules today and see the importance of others as you read on and complete the exercises in the book.

**Note**

The World Wide Web Consortium (W3C) is the official standards organization responsible for promoting the development of interoperable technologies (specifications, guidelines, software, and tools). It was founded by Tim Berners-Lee, acknowledged inventor of the Web, as a means of sharing consistent information.

> **Tip**
>
> The W3C Web site (http://www.w3.org) offers one of the best sources of information on many XML and related technologies.

In this section, you will learn seven statements that serve to characterize XML. The W3C has a section that describes XML in ten points (http://www.w3.org/XML/1999/XML-in-10-points), but three of these are left as placeholders for future characteristics. The seven characteristics are as follows:

1. XML offers a method of putting structured data into a text file.
2. XML looks a bit like HTML.
3. XML is machine readable, but human intelligible.
4. XML comprises a family of technologies.
5. XML is verbose.
6. XML is relatively new, but has honorable roots.
7. XML is license-free, platform-independent, and well supported.

## 1. XML Offers a Method of Putting Structured Data into a Text File.

When you think of traditional programs used to create, manipulate, and maintain data, typically those data are stored in some binary, often proprietary format. Commercial word processors, databases, and spreadsheets might have the capability of producing text data, but they are designed for optimal use of binary data formats that differ from one program type to another and often from one vendor to another. Because of this, the process of sharing data is cumbersome, at best, and sometimes the proprietary nature of certain data formats makes it impossible.

You might have experienced this kind of predicament if you have had occasion, for instance, to exchange a document created in a particular version of Microsoft Word with someone who is using Corel WordPerfect. A document saved in the native binary format offered by one product is not readable by the other and vice versa. In order to exchange the documents, you need to take extra steps to first save the document in a format that is accessible to both products. Often, in so doing, you might even need to compromise some of the rich formatting features that derived from using the package in the first place.

XML provides for the storage of data as simple text. Any application, or human being for that matter, that can read a text file can read an XML document. You don't need the originating software program in order to access the data. This makes correcting a problem in an information systems environment as simple as launching any available text editor to review and modify the document. Most operating systems provide at least one free text editor as part of the accompanying tool distribution. Other editors, perfectly adept for such a job, are freely available on the Internet.

You'll note that statement 1 reads, "XML offers a method of putting *structured* data into a text file." XML is a set of rules for creating text formats that are easy to generate and easy for computers to process. The resulting text files are structured such that they are

- Unambiguous
- Extensible
- Platform independent

**Note**

> The *"X"* in XML stands for *Extensible*. Extensibility means that the language can be advanced or stretched to meet specific needs. Because XML is not based on a finite set of tags, you can create descriptive tags that fit your requirements.

Even though any simple text editor can be used to create and manipulate XML documents, you will read about several specialized tools over the course of the next three weeks and be given information on obtaining them if you choose to use them for your own XML work.

By convention, generic XML files typically have a `.xml` file extension, as in `mydocument.xml`. Specialized dialects created using XML often employ a notable file extension. A very few selected examples include

- `.xsl`   Extensible Markup Language File
- `.xsd`   Extensible Schema Definition
- `.xdr`   XML Data Reduced Schema
- `.mml`   Mathematical Markup Language (MathML)
- `.cdf`   Channel Definition Format

## 2. XML Looks a Bit Like HTML.

There are quite a few similarities between XML and HTML. If you are already familiar with HTML, you already know some of the syntax rules that also happen to apply to XML. Consider the markup in Listing 1.1. Is this snippet of code an example of HTML or XML?

**LISTING 1.1**

```
<P>
    Here
    <EM>m
    prese
</P>
```

The answer ...................................................... snippet of either HTML
or XML. It ................................................................. lages. You'll learn
more about ...

XML was, h........................................................ flaws that characterize
HTML. The .......................................................... predefined set of
tags like there ........................................................ r own tags, you can
choose names ......................................................... graph with a <P> tag,
you might cho......................................................... e more meaningful
for you to mar......................................................... their meaning or
relevance. For .......................................................... ent, you might
decide to have ...

- <introdu
- <summary>
- <sales_in
- <address>
- <descripti
- <etc>

With regard to similarities, then, you can see that both HTML and XML comprise
markup tags that are bracketed by < and > symbols. In markup languages, a simple element includes a start tag, element content, and an end tag, as shown in Listing 1.1.

**LISTING 1.1**   An XML Document with Only One Element

```
1: <title>Sams Teach Yourself XML in 21 Days</title>
```

This single element constitutes a simple, well-formed XML document. The name of
the element is title, and it appears in the start tag (<title>) and the end tag
(</title>) of the element. The entire string (<title>Sams Teach Yourself XML in 21
Days</title>) from the beginning angle bracket of the start tag to the ending bracket on
the end tag is called the *element*. The text data contained by the tags is called the *element
content*.

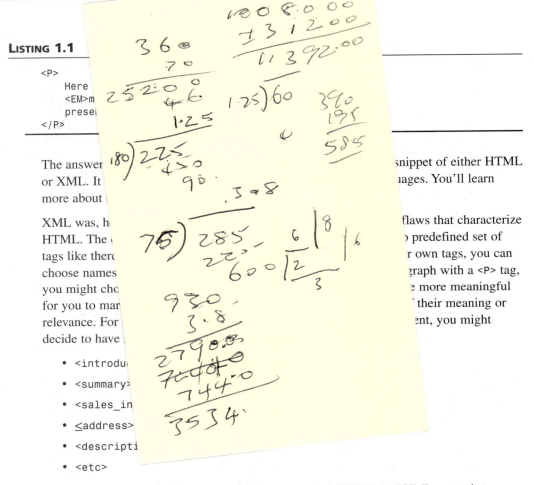

**Tip**

> The data contained by the tags of an element are content of that element. This is called *element content*, or simply *content*. However, the term *element content* is also used by some of the schema languages you will learn about later in this book.

**Tip**

> All elements in XML must be terminated. Non-empty elements must have a start tag and an end tag. Empty elements must be properly terminated.

XML elements in markup are the building blocks of the language, analogous to nouns in a spoken language. They are objects, places, and things in markup. XML can also have attributes, similar to attributes in HTML that serve to modify or qualify the elements, just like adjectives modify nouns in a spoken language. Attributes, if present, are always placed in the start tag of the element. Listing 1.3 shows a slightly more complex element that incorporates attributes and includes other elements as its element content. When an element contains child elements, the child elements are said to be *nested*.

**LISTING 1.3**   XML Document with Nested Child Elements and Attributes

```
1:  <account type="checking" currency="U.S. Dollars">
2:      <name>Smith</name>
3:      <balance>34,576.89</balance>
4:  </account>
```

**ANALYSIS**   Lines 1–4 are the entire account element. Two attributes modify the account element, analogous to the way that an adjective modifies a noun, by providing additional information about the element. The attributes are type and currency with the values checking and U.S. Dollars, respectively. The values of attributes are always placed in either single or double quotes. The account element contains only element content (lines 2–3). In other words, the account element does not contain character, or text, data, but rather it contains child elements, name, and balance (lines 2–3). Each element, name, balance and account has a start tag and a corresponding end tag with a forward slash (/) in the end tag. All XML elements must be terminated.

**Tip**

> Attribute values in XML must be enclosed in single or double quotes.

Deciding between the use of an element or an attribute to characterize your information is sometimes a difficult process. If you can think about information acting like an adjective modifying a particular noun, such as a checking account, or U.S. Dollar currency, chances are you are dealing with attributes. On the other hand, if information has real data value, it might be better marked as an element. Elements can have child elements and attributes cannot. Therefore, any entity that is a container of other elements is likely an element. These are not hard and fast rules; in fact, no rules exist. You will need to examine each markup project uniquely to determine what works best in each situation.

XML elements can contain text content, other elements, any combination of text and other elements, or be empty elements. An empty element is one that does not have content between a start and end tag. In HTML, the `<IMG SRC="`*`filename.ext`*`">` is an example of an empty element. The syntax of an empty element is this:

```
<element_name />
```

Listing 1.4 shows an example of an empty XML element.

**LISTING 1.4**  Example of an Empty XML Element

```
1:   <date month="September" year="2001"/>
```

The `date` element is an empty element. The terminator (`/`) is within the start tag. This is a short-form equivalent to writing `<date month="September" year="2001"></date>`. Even though the two are functionally equivalent, it is good programming practice to use the short form of the empty element in XML programming. Even though this element has attributes, with values, it is still considered empty because no data is present between a start and end tag.

Note that this particular element has an attribute. You might wonder just how an element can be considered empty if it has attributes with values. Attribute values, after all, are data, so why would we consider such an element to be empty? An empty element is one that does not markup content. Content only appears between the start and end tag. Attributes are not considered content even though they provide qualitative information about elements. On Day 12, you will learn about the Document Object Model (DOM), which provides a programmatic means of accessing individual parts of an XML document. You will discover that attribute data occupy a different part or "node" in the structure represented by the XML document than do content data.

So far, you have seen some syntactic similarities between HTML and XML, both comprised of elements and attributes. One of the fundamental differences between the two is characterized by the ability you have as a programmer to create your own self-describing elements in XML. Compare the two code examples in Listing 1.5 and Listing 1.6.

**LISTING 1.5** An HTML Code Snippet

```
<HTML>
    <H1>Invoice<H1>
    <P>From: Devan Shepherd</P>
    <P>To: Sally Jones</P>
    <P>Date: 26 July 2001</P>
    <P>Amount: $100.00</P>
    <P>Tax: 21 %</P>
    <P>Total Due: $121.00</P>
</HTML>
```

**LISTING 1.6** A Comparable XML Code Snippet

```
<Invoice>
    <From>Devan Shepherd</From>
    <To>Sally Jones</To>
    <Date year="2001" month="July" day="26" />
    <Amount currency="USD">$100.00</Amount>
    <TaxRate>21</TaxRate>
    <TotalDue currency="USD">121.00</TotalDue>
</Invoice>
```

Looking at these two examples, ask yourself the following questions:

- Which document has more relevant value?
- Which captures the most useful information for a processing application?
- Which listing offers the most potential uses?

You can see that XML, with its self-describing elements and attributes, offers a richer markup. If an application required invoice data, the HTML snippet in Listing 1.5 would not be able to provide anything other than a series of paragraphs. To differentiate the content of one <P> element from another would require extensive programming, scripting, or pattern-matching logic. On the other hand, the XML in Listing 1.6 offers us data components with meaning, somewhat like disparate fields in a flat-file database. XML is metadata-centric, preserving the intelligence and useful information about the data it marks up.

Consider the structure of a markup document. A single element contains all of the other elements in the document. This single document, at the highest level of the document structure, is known as the *root element*. In an HTML page, the root element is always the HTML element. In an XML document, you decide the name of the root element. In the example shown in Listing 1.6, the root element is Invoice.

**Tip**

A well-formed XML document must contain one and only one root element containing all others.

Another key difference between XML and HTML is that HTML mixes content and formatting in the same markup stream. For instance, the purposes served by the <H1> tag in HTML are to mark a particular string of data as a heading level 1, but also to inform the browser that anything so marked should be rendered in a larger type face in the browser.

XML is based on the premise that content and appearance, or style, should be kept separate from the markup encoding of data. XML relies exclusively on style sheet languages such as Cascading Style Sheets (CSS) or the eXtensible Style Sheet Language (XSL) for rendering or for transformation of documents from one structure to another. Your will learn to apply CSS and XSL for browser-side rendering on Days 14 and 15. On Day 16, you will build on that knowledge to use the XSL transformation language (XSLT) to convert XML documents into HTML as part of middle-ware scripts for platform-independent delivery of XML data via the Web.

## 3. XML Is Machine Readable, But Human Intelligible.

You have seen that self-describing elements provide an opportunity for XML documents to be intuitive by nature. The actual semantics of data are preserved as intelligence that is delivered in XML along with content and attribute values. Nonetheless, XML is computer code. It is read and used by XML processors. Tomorrow you will learn about one form of processor, known as a parser, which interprets an XML document a line at a time.

## 4. XML Comprises a Family of Technologies.

There are several important component technologies in the XML suite. Table 1.1 lists these technologies along with an expansion of the acronym for each and when you will read about them in this book.

**TABLE 1.1**  XML Technologies

| Chapter | Technology | Description |
|---------|------------|-------------|
| Days 1,2,3 | XML Version 1.0 | Technical Recommendation for XML |
| Day 4 | DTD | The Document Type Definition (a schema) |
| Day 5 | XDR | XML Data Reduced (Microsoft schema) |
| Day 6 | XSD | XML Schema Definition (W3C schema) |
| Day 8 | Namespaces | A method for qualifying element and attribute names |
| Day 9 | XPath | XML Path Language |
| Day 10 | XLink | XML Link Language |
| Day 11 | XPointer | XML Pointer Language |
| Day 12 | DOM | Document Object Model API |
| Day 13 | SAX | Simple API for XML |
| Day 15 | XSL | eXtensible Style Sheet Language |
| Day 15 | XSL-FO | XSL Formatting Objects |
| Day 16 | XSLT | XSL Transformation Language |
| Day 18 | XInclude | XML Include Syntax |
| Day 18 | XBase | XML Base URI Syntax |

As you read about each of these component technologies and experiment with the code examples provided, pay attention to the text describing the W3C status of each technology. Some of these components are still in early working draft forms and will change considerably in the months and years to come. XML processors support other members of the XML family differentially as of the date this chapter was written. There is a great deal of anticipation in the XML programming community surrounding the standardization of some of these components. For instance, the final version of a W3C schema language will serve to reduce the number of schema options that exist currently, making development and support easier for XML programmers.

## 5. XML Is Verbose.

Because XML files are text documents with tag delimiters, they are almost always larger than comparable binary files. This characteristic was considered seriously at the time that XML was designed. The members of the W3C charged with creating the XML standard chose to make XML verbose, thereby providing ample room for extensibility and element/attribute self-description.

The designers of XML realized that storage space is a commodity that continues to become cheaper over time and so file size wasn't considered a design concern. Additionally, inexpensive, often free, compression software is widely available for use on multiple platforms. Applications such as GZIP and ZIP are fast and efficient.

Finally, XML is optimized for transport over the Internet via the HTTP/1.1 protocol which, by implementation, compresses text data strings on-the-fly, thereby saving bandwidth.

## 6. XML Is Relatively New, But Has Honorable Roots.

XML was first conceived in 1996 and became a W3C standard on February 10, 1998. XML is based on the Standard Generalized Markup Language (SGML), which was created ten years earlier. SGML is also a meta-language used to create other languages. One of the applications of SGML is HTML. You might be confused by this relationship, but just remember that XML is a subset of SGML and that HTML is an application of SGML. XML and HTML are not peers. Figure 1.1 depicts this relationship and lists several applications of SGML and XML. You will learn about some of the popular XML applications during Day 19 as part of a discussion about integrating XML into a business model.

**FIGURE 1.1**

*The relationship between SGML, XML, and HTML.*

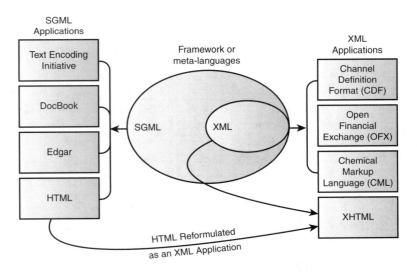

You might have read about the eXtensible Hypertext Markup Language XHTML and wondered what it is and where it fits within the context of other markup languages. XHTML, strictly speaking, is the reformulation of HTML as an application of XML and is meant to offer some extensibility to HTML. The W3C offers a great deal of information about XHTML at its Web site `http://www.w3.org/MarkUp/`. XHTML brings the rigor of XML to Web-based rendering.

## 7. XML Is License-Free, Platform-Independent, and Well Supported.

No one owns the exclusive rights to XML. It is free of licensing issues and available for all implementations. The associated component technologies are also in the public domain.

The platform-independent nature of XML makes it ideal for use on and over the Web. New e-business models are driving the need for transparent exchange of transaction-based data over the Internet.

Most of the major software development corporations have contributed to the XML collective through creation of tools, promotion of standards, and delivery of example-based solutions. As such, they tend to offer considerable support to XML developers.

# The Role of e-Business

It is evident that the user experience has been enriched by multimedia methods of data presentation, and that this has ushered in an era of significant change in the "look and feel" of the Web. However, the demand by business for sophisticated information delivery has provided the necessary financial resources required for the rapid acceleration of universal and far-reaching Web-based development. In fact, the ways in which we do business have changed dramatically as commercial entities have embraced delivery of business data in electronic form.

When the business community began to support the use of the Web to conduct commerce, the expectations of Web customers increased exponentially. Static Web pages were incapable of providing timely data, giving way to dynamic content models. The business world required new tools and technologies to deliver not only legacy data, but also a new style of information in response to the growing sophistication of Web-savvy customers. You might already be using Web-based banking services or making travel arrangements over the Internet.

Individualization and personalization of content followed so that Web sites could "recognize" a visitor and customize the information delivery experience to the unique needs of a single person. You have likely made a repeat visit to a Web site where you have been greeted by name. Perhaps you have even been to an e-commerce site that is "aware" of the last purchase you made, such as a book or audio CD. The site might offer suggestions of items you might be interested in based on your previous purchases, such as a book by the same author or music in the same genre. Maybe you have visited a Web portal site that provides the local time, current temperatures, and a weather forecast for your neighborhood. These are all examples of content personalization.

New business models are contributing to rapid advances in delivery technologies. Electronic syndication of data is a case in point. Consider the weather forecast example. Most sites offering such a service collect your ZIP code or postal address and then store a small reference ID number, known as a cookie, on your computer. When you return to the site, a program retrieves the cookie ID and searches for your record in the visitor database. It matches your location with forecast data from an extensive online database, thereby creating a customized Web page for you. The data used is typically obtained from a syndicated service that delivers the same basic weather information to all its subscribers, much like a cartoon syndicate delivers the same version of a cartoon strip to newspapers all over the country on the same day.

Micropayment models offer another example of Web-based innovation in the business world. You are able, for instance, to visit an online bookstore and purchase only those chapters of a book that interest you rather than the book as a whole. The information exchange required to effect such a transaction could be automated on a Web site that might even help you to choose similar chapters from several books to construct your own customized reference document on a particular topic. This is already becoming popular in the music industry where creating and purchasing a CD packed with your favorite songs is only a few mouse clicks away.

Off-Web examples of e-business transactions have also helped to promote technological advances. Consider the electronic transactions that take place when you choose to pay for gasoline by using a credit card at the pump. In this case, you insert your card into a reader that collects your credit card account number and other data stored on the magnetic strip and passes that data to a processing service bureau, known as a clearing house. The clearing house validates the card and ensures that the account has sufficient credit to permit a purchase. After the card is validated, an acceptance transaction is returned to the pump to turn it on. While you are filling your tank, other transactions are exchanged between the gasoline vendor and your bank with final tallies being calculated, closing entries being exchanged, and a receipt being printed when the pump stops.

By reading this book and working through the programming examples provided, you will learn how XML is ideally suited to create solutions for these and many other business problems. During the next three weeks, you will manipulate XML technologies, create customized documents using your own self-describing data elements, and explore parsers and application interfaces. You will also learn how to transform markup from one language to another, use XML in conjunction with databases and server-side processing, and integrate a suite of technologies to create real-world solutions. *Sams Teach Yourself XML in 21 Days, Second Edition* will provide you with all of the resources and hands-on exposure you need to achieve mastery of these exciting and powerful technologies.

# Creating Your First XML Document

You have seen that XML is composed of intuitive, self-describing elements, contained within one root element. There are still a few simple rules to master, but you'll cover those tomorrow. At this point, you know enough to create your first XML document. Here are the tools you will need to complete this exercise:

- A text editor ( Notepad, SimpleText, and so on). You can use any editor that can save ASCII text documents, but if you use a word processor be careful that you don't save your document in a binary format.
- The Microsoft Internet Explorer browser (version 5.0 or above) will be used a number of times throughout the book. If you don't already have a copy loaded on your machine, you can download one at `http://www.microsoft.com/ downloads/search.asp`.

The document you create will be a simple document containing your first name, last name, and a joke. Call the first name element `<first>` and the last name element `<last>`. The joke can be any one-line string of text in an element called `<joke>`. Start by launching the editor of your choice and then creating the XML document. Don't forget to have one root element and an element for each separate data component in your document. You must decide the name for the root element. You also must terminate each element; in this case, you will terminate with an end tag.

When you have finished, save your document as `me.xml` and then launch Microsoft Internet Explorer and browse the result. If you don't save your document with a `.xml` extension, you might not get the desired results, so be sure to do so.

To view a document in Internet explorer, enter its full path and filename into the address field on the browser window. When a document is viewed in Internet Explorer, the browser application passes your XML document through a special processor, called a *parser*. The parser checks to make sure that your document conforms to the syntax rules for well-formed XML. If your markup is correct, the parser then transforms your document into a form that is easy to read with markup tags in a color that is different from the text the tags contain. This process of transformation is known as an *Extensible Stylesheet Language Transformation* (XSLT). You will learn more about XSLT on Day 16.

Listing 1.6 offers one potential solution, but yours will likely have different structure, with your own element names, perhaps different nesting, and hopefully a funnier joke.

**LISTING 1.6**    A First XML Document

```
< data>
    <name>
            <first>Devan</first>
            <last>Shepherd</last>
    </name>
    <joke>ASCII silly question, get a silly ANSI</joke>
</data>
```

Figure 1.2 shows the result of displaying this simple XML document using the styles built into the Microsoft Internet Explorer browser. IE does this transformation automatically for you if the document is well-formed.

**FIGURE 1.2**

*The rendered result of Listing 1.4.*

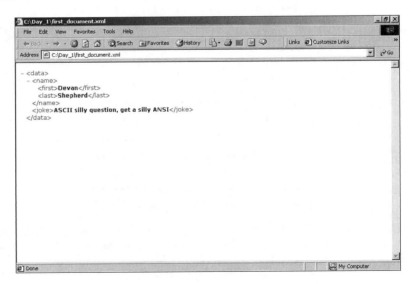

As noted earlier, the Microsoft Internet Explorer browser shows the element names in one color and the element content in another. This is done by transforming the XML into an HTML page, contained in memory, with an associated stylesheet. The stylesheet is built into the distribution that comes with IE.  In fact, the browser has an XML processor, called a *parser*, built in. You will learn more about parsers tomorrow.

# Summary

Today, you were introduced to XML as a framework or meta-language used to create other languages. You learned a bit about the importance of markup in the world of e-commerce and how the business community has helped to promote a rapid acceleration of Web technologies. You studied the seven statements that characterize XML and learned a few of the syntax rules that constrain the standard. You finished by creating your first XML document and parsing it with Microsoft Internet Explorer. Tomorrow, you will learn a great deal more about well-formed XML and appreciate some of the benefits that XML offers you as a Web programmer.

# Q&A

**Q How has the business community played a role in the development of the Web?**

**A** Business has fueled an accelerated development of Web technologies by providing not only the necessary funds, but also by creating new models for e-business and data exchange.

**Q Why do we need another markup language?**

**A** Strictly speaking, XML is not exactly a markup language, but it is needed in part to provide a means of programming for the Web beyond the inherent limitations of HTML.

**Q Is there anything that HTML does well?**

**A** It provides a means of creating executable hypertext. It is easy to learn and therefore has enjoyed large-scale proliferation across the Web. It is supported by a wide array of cheap yet powerful browser interfaces.

**Q Can I view my document in Netscape or another browser?**

**A** Netscape version 6.0 is a browser that provides support for XML documents. You can view an XML document using Netscape, but the document will not appear in the same form that it does using Internet Explorer. You should, in fact, try viewing your document in another browser to see the differences between that and the view provided by Internet Explorer. Remember that IE is providing a transformation from XML into HTML for the purpose of styling your document with markup symbols. This transformation is done using an Extensible Stylesheet Language Transformation (XSLT) with a default stylesheet that is built into IE. You will learn about XSLT on Day 16.

**Q  Why is HTML a concern?**

**A**  HTML lacks flexibility due to its limited, predefined tag set. It can't be easily extended and it suffers from inflexible built-in styling.

**Q  What are the seven characteristics of XML?**

**A**  The seven statements are

1. XML offers a method of putting structured data into a text file.

2. XML looks a bit like HTML.

3. XML is machine readable, but human intelligible.

4. XML comprises a family of technologies.

5. XML is verbose.

6. XML is relatively new, but has honorable roots.

7. XML is license-free, platform-independent, and well supported.

# Exercise

The exercise is provided so that you can test your knowledge of what you learned today. The answer is in Appendix A, "Answers to the Questions."

Create an XML document that depicts your name, home address, e-mail address, and date of birth. Use attributes for the date. When you are finished, save your document and view it with Microsoft Internet Explorer 5.0.

# DAY 2

# XML Syntax Explored in Detail

Yesterday you learned a little about what XML is and where it came from. Today, you will explore the construction rules for an XML document.

Today, you will learn

- The syntax of a well-formed XML document instance
- Methods for checking a document instance to ensure it is well formed

## Authoring Your Own XML Elements

During Day 1 you saw several XML document listings. XML documents comprise elements and attributes using names that you can create. Today, you will explore those constructs in more detail and create some XML documents. You will start by creating what is known as "well-formed" XML.

> **Note**
>
> The term *XML instance* is synonymous and can be used interchangeably with *XML document*. You will see both used throughout this book. A document is, in fact, an *instance* of the markup language being used. For clarity, when referring to HTML code, the phrase *HTML page* will be used rather than HTML document or HTML instance.

For an XML document to be considered "well formed," it must comply with all of the basic syntax rules for XML. You learned some of those rules on Day 1 and will discover others today. If any of the basic syntax rules are violated, your document is not well formed and cannot be used by XML processors. In fact, the XML processor will report an error, which in many cases will help you to correct the problem by pointing you in the direction of the error.

# XML Software Tools

Because XML documents are just simple text files, you can create and manipulate them with almost any simple text editor. A variety of more sophisticated editors are available that check the syntax of your documents for you as you enter data. some of these editors are available as free downloads from the Internet, such as the Architag X-Ray editor (`http://www.architag.com/xray`) and commercially available products, such as Altova's XML-Spy (`http://www.xmlspy.com`) or Tibco Extensibility's XML Authority editor (`http://www.extensibility.com`). An extensive listing of software tools can be found online at (`http://www.oasis-open.org/cover/publicSW.html`). Almost every operating system and hardware platform has options available. For the purpose of following along and completing the exercises in this book, you will need only a simple editor most of the time.

In addition to a text editor, many of the exercises require that you load your XML documents into a *parser* to check for errors. A *parser* is software that is aware of XML syntax rules and can report to you any problems encountered when your document is read into memory. If you do not already have a copy on your computer, it is recommended that you download Microsoft's Internet Explorer (IE) browser, version 5 or greater. This browser has an XML parser built in. The IE browser is available in versions for Macintosh, Unix, and Windows operating systems. It can be obtained as a free download from `http://www.microsoft.com`.

## Platform, Software, and Operating System Dependencies

Unfortunately, even though the goals for XML technologies include complete platform, software, and operating system independence, many of the useful individual tools and processors are not yet universally available. Some of the code examples you will work through in this book will only, for instance, work on a Microsoft platform, or by processing with a Netscape browser, or will rely on a particular implementation of a Java-based parser. This means that you might need to be somewhat selective about the solutions you choose to implement. Web developers, for example, are aware of many issues related to browser specificity that limit the tools and features they can incorporate on Web sites if they want users—regardless of their chosen browser—to be able to access their data. Throughout this book, alternative solutions, platforms, and options will be mentioned wherever possible. Sometimes, the examples will be provided using one base technology, such as a Microsoft platform, but the concepts will typically transfer well to another platform. On Day 12, for instance, you will learn to create JavaScript programs to access the Microsoft implementation of an Application Programming Interface known as the Document Object Model (DOM). This Microsoft implementation is widely supported and has the largest installed base of any DOM solution. However, if your own architecture requires the use of another solution, you will find that there alternate DOM implementations in PERL, Java, Python, and several other popular languages, with support for a variety of platforms. In such cases, Web links will be provided to source alternative tools.

# XML Syntax Rules

In this section, you will read about some of the syntax rules of XML and have an opportunity to see how the parser handles XML documents. To get the most out of this explanation, you might want to create each of the examples provided and parse them yourself.

Launch your favorite text editor and use it to create an XML document. The document you will create will use XML to mark up a recipe for bean dip. Start by thinking about how a typical recipe is structured. Figure 2.1 shows a recipe on an index card. Most recipes have a title, to distinguish one from another. A list of ingredients and the quantities of those ingredients is essential, as is a set of instructions for preparation. You will also include some serving suggestions.

> **Devan's Bean Dip**
>
> 1 can refried beans
> 1 can burrito sauce
> 8 oz. Cubed jalapeno cheese
> 1/2 cup sour cream
> In medium sauce pan, heat beans and burrito
> sauce until bubbly. Add cubed cheese and
> stir until melted. Remove from heat and stir
> in sour cream.
> Serve as a dip with corn tortilla chips

When you create an XML file based on an existing document, you need to examine the original closely to understand the construction of the instance to be marked up. This is known as document analysis and it is a necessary part of the markup process. To mark up the bean dip recipe, you will keep the analysis step relatively simple. Start by identifying the components of a recipe. You learned on Day 1 that the basic building blocks are called elements. Elements are declarative, like nouns in a spoken language, and act as containers for information that can include data or other elements. You'll learn later a few other things that can be contained by elements.

To understand the elements for the bean dip recipe, consider what it is that you want to wrap with element tags. In the case of each major component of the recipe, you will need to determine the following:

- What the element will be called
- Where the element starts, corresponding to the start tag of the element
- Where the element ends, so that you know where to place the end tag
- What precisely is contained by the element
- What the relationship is between the element and other elements in the recipe

In Figure 2.2, a typical recipe is shown as a block diagram. From the diagram, you can see that a recipe `element` contains a `title` element, an `ingredients` element, a `preparation` element, and a `serving` element. The `ingredients` element contains `item` child elements and corresponding `quantity` child elements.

Another useful depiction of XML documents is shown in Figure 2.3. This shows the recipe in a tree structure, which offers a useful and significant model for XML.

**FIGURE 2.2**

*A block diagram depicting a bean dip recipe.*

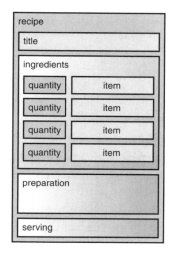

**Note**

On Day 12 you will learn about an Application Programmer Interface (API), known as the Document Object Model (DOM) for XML. This API deals with all XML instances as a tree of nodes and provides you, the programmer, with a means of querying, adding, deleting, and modifying nodes and their content.

**FIGURE 2.3**

*A tree diagram for the bean dip recipe.*

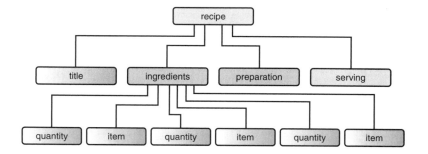

The tree diagram shows the same relationship between elements as the block diagram. We have one and only one root element, called `recipe`, and it is a container for all of the other elements. Take a close look at the `ingredients` element—it contains the child elements `quantity` and `item`. For the XML instance to be considered well formed, the child elements of the root element and all sub-elements must be sequential or nested without any tags overlapping. You will learn a simple technique for verifying proper nesting later today, but first, create an XML document for the bean dip recipe by entering the code described in the following steps using a text editor.

**Tip**

> A well-formed XML instance must contain one and only one root element containing all other elements. Elements contained within the root element can have child elements, but child elements must be properly nested. All of the elements contained by the root element are child elements of the root element.

1. Start by creating a root element called `recipe`. It should begin with a `<recipe>` start tag. Terminate the `recipe` element with a proper end tag in the form `</recipe>`. It is a good programming practice to terminate your elements as you go go.

2. The root `recipe` element will contain all other elements. Enter the start and end tags for each of the child elements of `recipe`, namely the `title`, `ingredients`, `preparation`, and `serving`.

3. Next, place the start and end tags for each of the `quantity` and `item` elements in pairs between the root element tags for the `recipe` element. Four pairs of these are contained within the ingredients element.

4. With all of the element tags in place, fill in the appropriate data between each tag pair, from the index card depicted in Figure 2.1.

5. Save your document as `bean_dip.xml`. It should look like Listing 2.1. If you view this listing in IE, you should see something like Figure 2.4.

**LISTING 2.1**   An XML Recipe Document—bean_dip.xml

```
 1: <recipe>
 2:   <title>Devan's Bean Dip</title>
 3:   <ingredients>
 4:     <quantity>1 can</quantity>
 5:     <item> refried beans </item>
 6:     <quantity>1 can</quantity>
 7:     <item>burrito sauce</item>
 8:     <quantity>8 ox</quantity>
 9:     <item>cubed Jalapeno cheese</item>
10:     <quantity>1/2 cup</quantity>
11:     <item>sour cream</item>
12:   </ingredients>
13:   <preparation>In medium sauce pan, heat bean
14:       and burrito sauce until bubbly. Add cubed
15:       cheese and stir until melted. Remove from
16:       heat and stir in sour cream. </preparation>
17:   <serving>Serve as a dip with corn
18:       tortilla chips</serving>.
19: </recipe>
```

FIGURE 2.4

*The bean dip recipe as a well-formed XML document created with a text editor and viewed using Internet Explorer.*

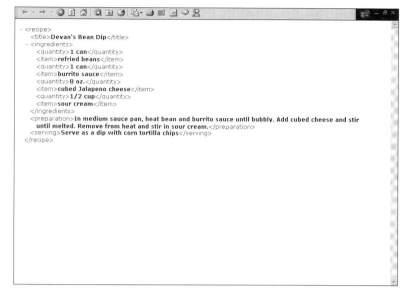

On Day 1 you learned the parts of an element and that an element comprises a start tag and an end tag and might also have element content. XML tags are case sensitive, unlike those belonging to HTML; therefore, the start and end tags of an XML element must be written in the same case. In some instances, an element is empty, in which case it has no element content or data between the start and end tag. The angle bracket (<) in the start tag is also known in markup languages as the Markup Declaration Open, or MDO. The closing angle bracket (>) in the end tag is called the Markup Declaration Close, or MDC. Consider the element

```
<item>sour cream</item>
```

The parts of this element could be described as shown in Table 2.1.

**TABLE 2.1**  Anatomy of Your `item` Element

| Markup | Description |
|---|---|
| < | Markup Declaration Open |
| item> | Element name |
| sour cream | Element content |
| </ | Element termination |
| item | Element name being terminated |
| > | Markup Declaration Close |

The indentation of lines that you saw in listing 2.1 represents a good programming practice. By indenting child elements, it is easier to see the levels of nesting in an XML document. The extra whitespace is ignored by most XML processors and doesn't cause problems.

> **Tip**
>
> Whitespace between elements in an XML document is normalized, or reduced, after one character by many parsers. However, unlike HTML, XML passes whitespace characters to the XML processor as they are encountered. It is the job of the processor to decide how whitespace will be handled.

As you learned during Day 1, the Microsoft Internet Explorer browser (version 5.0 or above) is capable of allowing you to view an XML document on the screen using different colors to depict the element names and their content. This is because the Internet Explorer browser has a special XML processor, called a "parser," included in the browser application code. The parser checks your XML document to ensure that it is well formed. If it is, it associates a built-in stylesheet with the XML instance and then performs a transformation using XSLT. You will learn about XSLT on Day 16.

Launch Internet Explorer and point it at your saved copy of bean_dip.xml. You should get a result similar to that shown in Figure 2.5.

**FIGURE 2.5**

*The MSXML processor built in to the Microsoft Internet Explorer browser creates a tree structure for the* bean_dip.xml *instance.*

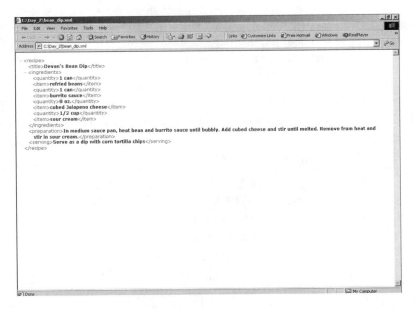

After the Microsoft Internet Explorer browser is installed on your system, the Microsoft implementation of an XML parser is available to you. An XML parser is software that is aware of the rules of syntax for XML version 1.0, as established by the World Wide Web Consortium (W3C). The parser is capable of processing an XML document to ensure conformance with these standards. XML parsers throw exceptions and cease processing if any of the syntax rules is broken.

All XML parsers check to see if a document is well formed. You will learn tomorrow about parsers that can also check to see if a document is valid in addition to being well formed. Validity involves an extra set of constraints that the programmer enforces through creation of a schema defining the explicit structure of an XML document. In this way, the programmer can specify the order of elements in an XML document, the presence of required elements and, in some cases, validate the data types for element content. More on that tomorrow!

## Proper Nesting of Elements

The "No Crossed Lines" test for proper nesting ensures that elements are either sequential or nested without overlap of start and end tags. An XML document that does not adhere to this rule makes no sense to XML processors. You might be aware that HTML does not impose the same constraints. In HTML, as it is interpreted by most modern browsers, the following code examples will render the exact same results:

```
<B><I>This text will be bolded and italicized</I></B>
```

```
<B><I>This text will be bolded and italicized</B></I>
```

The first snippet is well formed with the italic element `<I>...</I>` appropriately contained as a complete child of the bold `<B>...</B>` element. The second code snippet has the bold element end tag `</B>` preceding the italic end tag `</I>`, which is inappropriate and poorly formed. If you drew one line between the `<B>` and `</B>` and a second from the `<I>` to the `</I>`, they would intersect in the case of the second code snippet—an indication of improper nesting.

Tip

> If you draw a line from the start tags of all elements to their corresponding end tags in any XML instance, the lines should never cross.

Figure 2.6 shows the `bean_dip.xml` instance with lines drawn between the start and end tags of all elements. None of the lines intersects, indicating proper nesting.

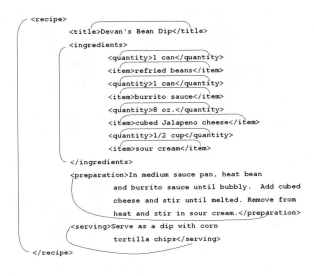

**FIGURE 2.6**

*The "No Crossed Lines" test for proper nesting applied to the* bean_dip.xml *document.*

# Naming Conventions in XML

The names you used for the recipe document were simple and descriptive. Even though XML is computer readable, it is also human intelligible. You must adhere to a few rules for element names in XML, such as

- An XML element name must begin with a letter, an underscore, (_) or a colon (:)
- After the first character, the element name may contain letters, digits, hyphens (-), underscores(_), periods (.) or colons(:)
- Element names cannot begin with "XML" or its variants because these names are all protected by intellectual property rights held by the W3C

# XML Declarations

You have created several simple XML documents that are well formed and that can be parsed by Microsoft Internet Explorer 5.0. Although IE accepted this XML as is, it is a good programming practice to include a declaration that the document is XML. In fact, some parsers *require* this processing instruction, or XML declaration.

Add an XML declaration to your bean_dip.xml document before the start tag for the root element <recipe>. It will look like

```
<?xml version="1.0"?>
```

The complete `bean_dip.xml` code listing should now look like the code shown in Listing 2.2. Note that the XML declaration is the first line of the document. Modify your recipe markup and save the new document as `bean_dip2.xml`.

**LISTING 2.2**  An XML Declaration—`bean_dip2.xml`

```
 1: <?xml version="1.0"?>
 2: <recipe>
 3:     <title>Devan's Bean Dip</title>
 4:     <ingredients>
 5:         <quantity>1 can</quantity>
 6:         <item>refried beans</item>
 7:         <quantity>1 can</quantity>
 8:         <item>burrito sauce</item>
 9:         <quantity>8 oz.</quantity>
10:         <item>cubed Jalapeno cheese</item>
11:         <quantity>1/2 cup</quantity>
12:         <item>sour cream</item>
13:     </ingredients>
14:     <preparation>In medium sauce pan, heat bean
15:         and burrito sauce until bubbly. Add cubed
16:         cheese and stir until melted. Remove from
17:         heat and stir in sour cream.</preparation>
18:     <serving>Serve as a dip with corn
19:         tortilla chips</serving>
20: </recipe>
```

The XML declaration on line 1 tells an XML processor that the document being parsed is XML. Although some processors do not require this declaration, it is good programming practice to include one in XML documents.

The syntax of an XML declaration is a little different than that of an element. This declaration is a processing instruction (PI) that provides special information to the XML parser informing that the document that follows is an XML document coded in version 1.0 of the Extensible Markup Language. The XML declaration PI, if included, always resides in the prolog of an XML document as the first line. You will learn about other processing instructions on subsequent days. Table 2.2 shows the component parts of the XML declaration statement.

**TABLE 2.2**  Anatomy of an XML Declaration

| Markup | Description |
| --- | --- |
| <? | Markup Declaration Open (MDO). In XML, PI statements always begin with this MDO.xml XML Processing Instruction. |
| version="1.0" | Required version information There is only one version of XML; therefore this attribute always has a value of 1.0. |

**TABLE 2.2**   continued

| Markup | Description |
| --- | --- |
| encoding="" | Optional character encoding declaration. |
| standalone="" | Optional `standalone` attribute with values of either "yes" or "no". |
| ?> | Markup Declaration Close (MDC). |

In the XML processing instruction Open phrase, XML must be in lowercase letters for the PI to be acceptable to XML parsers. You will see that all XML declarations currently indicate use of XML version 1.0. This is because there is only one version of XML. It is conceivable that this will change at some point in the future and for this reason, the version is a required attribute in the XML declaration. The encoding attribute is used to indicate character coding that is neither UTF-8 nor UTF-16.

**Tip**

> UTF-8 and UTF-16 are standard character encoding schemes for data. UTF-16 is also known as "Unicode with byte order marking" by encoding professionals. Discussion of different encoding schemes is beyond the scope of this lesson, but excellent information about encoding can be obtained at the W3C Web site (http://www.w3.org) or at http://msdn.microsoft.com/xml/articles/xmlencodings.asp.

The standalone attribute tells the XML processor whether or not an external Document Type Definition (DTD) is to be associated for the purpose of validation of the instance. You will learn all about validating XML during Day 3. For the most part, XML that is only well formed doesn't need to use a Standalone Document Declaration. Such declarations are there to permit certain, albeit negligible, processing advantages.

# Adding Comments to Your Code

As is the case in most programming, XML has a provision for the inclusion of comments in markup. Unlike comments in some languages, XML comments might also be exposed to XML processors. In other words, as you will learn on Day 12 when you discover the Document Object Model, you can, under program control, interrogate and manipulate comments in an XML document or use them as part of your processing.

Comments in an XML instance take the same form as they do in HTML, such as

```
<!-- This is a comment -->
```

Using your editor, place a comment in your `bean_dip.xml` document to remind yourself that hot sauce can be added to spice up the bean dip. Place the comment before the serving element and then view the results in Microsoft Internet Explorer 5.0 (IE5). Add the following comment just before the serving element in your code:

```
<!-- For extra spicy bean dip, add your favorite hot sauce to the mix -->
```

Figure 2.7 shows the result of viewing your code using Internet Explorer. Note that the XML parser in IE5 presents the actual text of the comment in a different colored type after it performs the XSL transformation for you. You will learn during Day 3 and Day 12 that the text of the comment resides in a comment "node" as part of the XML instance.

**2**

**FIGURE 2.7**

*Adding a comment to the* bean_dip.xml *document.*

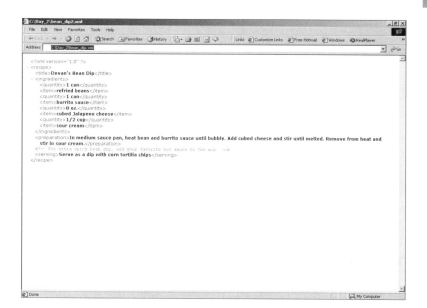

# Placing Attributes in Your Well-Formed XML Instance

Your learned during Day 1 that attributes are like adjectives in a spoken language in that they modify elements, which are analogous to nouns. In XML, attributes are always located in the start tag of the element they are providing additional information about.

Using an editor, modify your `bean_dip.xml` document so that the title is an attribute of the `recipe` root element and each of the quantities becomes an attribute of the item they are modifying. When you are finished, you document should still be well formed. The syntax for an attribute on an element is

```
<element_name attribute_name="value">content of element</element_name>
```

Attributes are always declared in the start tag of the element being qualified. You can have any number of attributes on an element and each will reside in the start tag. For instance

```
1:  <element_name
2:          attribute_name1="value"
3:          attribute_name2="value"
4:          attribute_name3="value">content of element</element_name>
```

Sometimes, when markup becomes long, your code can be made easier to read by using line feeds and indenting to align similar items. All four lines of the multiple attribute example still correspond to just one element, even though they span four lines of a document. In XML, the extra "whitespace" characters are normalized after one. That is, they are omitted or ignored by the processor that skips over the extra spaces.

**Tip**

> Remember, you can verify that your document is well formed by parsing it with Microsoft Internet Explorer 5.0.

Listing 2.3 shows code with attributes.

**LISTING 2.3**  Well-Formed Attributes in an XML Instance Document—bean_dip3.xml

```
1:  <?xml version="1.0"?>
2:  <recipe title="Devan's Bean Dip">
3:      <ingredients>
4:          <item quantity="1 can">refried beans</item>
5:          <item quantity="1 can">burrito sauce</item>
6:          <item quantity="8 oz.">cubed Jalapeno cheese</item>
7:          <item quantity="1/2 cup">sour cream</item>
8:      </ingredients>
9:      <preparation>In medium sauce pan, heat bean
10:             and burrito sauce until bubbly. Add cubed
11:             cheese and stir until melted. Remove from
12:             heat and stir in sour cream.</preparation>
13:      <!-- For extra spicy bean dip, add your favorite hot
14:             sauce to the mix -->
```

**LISTING 2.3** continued

```
15:     <serving>Serve as a dip with corn
16:          tortilla chips     </serving>
17: </recipe>
```

Note that each of the attributes is, indeed, within the start tag of the element it modifies. Note also that the attribute values are in quotes. Single quotes or double quotes can be used, but for the instance to be well formed, all attribute values must be enclosed in quotes.

XML parsers are unforgiving of syntax rule violations. To prove this, remove the first quote from one of your attribute values in your `bean_dip.xml` document. After you have made the change, parse the document by loading it into the Internet Explorer browser. For instance, if you remove the first quote on the `quantity` value on the `item` element in line 4 of listing 2.3, you will receive an error from Internet Explorer that looks like this:

```
A string literal was expected, but no opening quote character was found.
Line 4, Position 18
  <item quantity=1 can">refried beans</item>
-----------------^
```

Next, replace the first quote around the attribute value and remove the end quote from the same value. The message that is reported by IE is different in this case. Because the parser did not find a closing quote for the attribute value before it encountered the next Markup Declaration Open character (<), it determined that there was a problem with the attribute value. If you get stuck trying to replicate this error, see Figure 2.12, which shows the error with a quote missing from the first quantity attribute value. To be well formed, the offending line of code should read

```
<item quantity="1 can">refried beans</item>
```

# Summary

Today, you learned about the syntax rules that characterize well-formed XML. You discovered that Microsoft Internet Explorer 5.0 and above have XML parsers built in that can also check to ensure that your documents are well formed.

Tomorrow, you will learn about valid XML and how you, as a programmer, can control the structure of an XML document beyond mere well-formed constraints.

# Q&A

**Q  How are XML and HTML different with regard to basic syntax rules?**

**A**  For an XML document to be well formed, it must comply with all of the syntax rules established by the W3C as part of the XML version 1.0 specification. An XML document that is not well formed is considered "broken" and cannot be completely processed by a parser or browser. In HTML, although syntax rules exist, browsers don't rigidly enforce all of them.

**Q  What tools do you need to create well-formed XML documents?**

**A**  All that is required is a text editor and a parser to ensure conformance with well-formedness constraints.

**Q  Why is the analysis step important to XML developers?**

**A**  It is essential to understand the elements of a document structure to ensure that it can be marked-up correctly. The developer needs to know where each element begins and ends, the purpose of each element, the content to be contained within the element, and the relationship among all of the elements in the XML instance.

**Q  What are the basic syntax rules that characterize well-formed XML?**

**A**  The most important rules include

1. An XML document has one and only one root element that contains all other elements and their content.

2. XML element names are case sensitive and the start and end tag names must, therefore, be case identical.

3. Elements contained within the root, or within other elements, must be sequential or properly nested.

4. Attribute values in XML must be enclosed within single or double quotes.

**Q  What is the syntax of a comment in an XML document?**

**A**  `<!-- This is a comment -->`

# Exercise

The exercise is provided so that you can test your knowledge of what you learned today. The answer is in Appendix A.

Listing 2.4 presents a poorly formed XML instance. The intent behind this document is to list two music albums with some details about each. Based on all that you have learned about the syntax of XML, correct this document using an editor. Test your corrections by parsing the document with Microsoft Internet Explorer 5.0.

**LISTING 2.4**    A Poorly Formed XML Document

```
<?XML version=1.0?>
    <cd number="432>
    <title>The Best of Van Morrison</Title>
    <artist>Van Morrison</artist>
    <tracks total=20">
    <cd number=97>
    <title>HeartBreaker</title>
    <Subtitle>Sixteen Classic Performances</subtitle>
    <artist>Pat Benatar</Artist>
    <tracks total=16>
    </CD>
```

2

# DAY 3

# Valid XML Instances

You now know the syntax rules that characterize well-formed XML. Today, you will explore the concept of valid XML.

You will learn

- What validity means in XML
- Why validity is important when exchanging data with others
- How XML deals with data structures and document structures
- Some of the common misconceptions about valid XML

## Why Should You Care About Valid XML?

You have learned that the use of XML requires strict adherence to syntax and that the parsers and processors used for XML will deal harshly with any violation of the rules. In fact, your document is considered "broken" by an XML parser if it has even the smallest of syntax errors. With such an exacting degree of constraint over XML, why do you need a more complex system of rules?

Validity in XML has to do with the structure of the document. You learned on Day 1 that XML provides a method of placing structured data into a text file. However, structure implies much more than syntax. An XML document, for instance, might be syntactically perfect, but include elements in the wrong order or exclude elements that might be required by a processor to complete an e-commerce transaction or to solve a particular business problem.

By way of example, imagine marking up this book in XML. You would probably have elements such as `title`, `author`, `publisher`, `ISBN`, `date`, `toc` (table of contents), and so on just for the front matter of the book. Within the body of the book, you might include markup for `chapter`, `section`, `paragraph`, `emphasis`, `note`, `tip`, `table`, and perhaps many more. You can see that the markup could become quite complex and elaborate. For purposes of this discussion, consider only the front matter elements just listed.

Listing 3.1 depicts an XML document that marks up sample front matter for this book.

**LISTING 3.1**    Front Matter Marked Up in XML—`MyXMLBook.xml`

```
 1: <?xml version="1.0"?>
 2: <!-- listing 3.1 - myXMLBook.xml -->
 3:
 4: <book>
 5:    <title>Sams Teach Yourself XML in 21 Days, Second Edition</title>
 6:    <author>Devan Shepherd</author>
 7:    <publisher>SAMS Publishing</publisher>
 8:    <isbn>0-672-32093-2</isbn>
 9:    <date>June 2001</date>
10:    <toc>
11:       <day number="1">An Overview of the Internet and Markup Languages</day>
12:       <day number="2">XML Syntax Explored in Detail</day>
13:       <day number="3">Valid XML Instances</day>
14:    </toc>
15: </book>
```

**ANALYSIS**    The book root element (lines 2–13) contains `title`, `author`, `publisher`, `isbn`, `data` and `toc` child elements. All are well-formed with start and end tags shown in matching case. Child elements are properly nested in parent elements with no start and end tags overlapping. The `toc` element has three-day child elements with text content. The `number` attributes on the `day` elements serve to modify `day` elements in the same way that an adjective modifies a noun in a spoken language.

Not only is the XML document shown in Listing 3.1 well-formed and logical machine-readable code, but it truly is human intelligible. The structure of this document could be represented with a simple tree diagram, like the one shown in Figure 3.1. However, you have no rules in place yet to enforce that structure.

**FIGURE 3.1**

*Tree structure for the Sams Teach Yourself XML in 21 Days, Second Edition front matter XML example.*

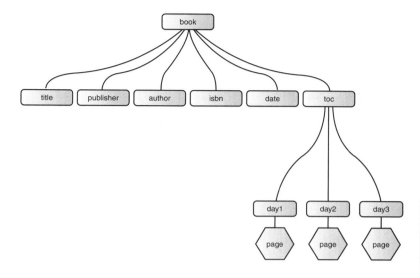

Now examine the document in Listing 3.2. This is also a well-formed XML document. You can prove that by running it through an XML parser. Note that Microsoft Internet Explorer does not report errors and shows a formatted listing of the instance, as shown in Listing 3.2. Remember that this is because Internet Explorer has a built-in parser. Even though the document is well-formed, it no longer bears much resemblance to the structure diagrammed in Figure 3.1 and wouldn't serve to mark up the front matter of this book.

**LISTING 3.2**   Well-Formed But Poorly Structured XML Document— mixed_front_matter.xml

```
 1: <?xml version="1.0"?>
 2: <!-- listing 3.2 - mixed_front_matter.xml -->
 3:
 4: <book>
 5:   <toc>
 6:     <day number="1">An Overview of the Internet and Markup Languages</day>
 7:     <title>Everything You Ever Wanted to Know About XML</title>
 8:     <title>XML an Why Cats Chase Laser Pointers</title>
 9:     <date>July 2001</date>
10:     <date>June 2001</date>
11:     <date>August 1908</date>
12:     <author>Devan Shepherd</author>
13:     <publisher>Sams Publishing</publisher>
14:     <title>Sams Teach Yourself XML in 21 Days, Second Edition</title>
15:     <day number="1">An XML Overview of the Internet and Markup
Languages</day>
```

**LISTING 3.2**    continued

```
16:      <title>Sams Teach Yourself XML in 21 Days, Second Edition</title>
17:      <date>June 2001</date>
18:      <day number="2">XML Syntax Explored in Detail</day>
19:      <isbn>0-672-32093-2</isbn>
20:      <day number="3">Valid XML Instances</day>
21:    </toc>
22: </book>
```

The well-formed instance in Listing 3.2 contains multiple dates and titles and an illogical order of elements, and it no longer makes intuitive sense. For instance, the toc element contains dates and other elements that are not typically part of a table of contents. This is not at all what was intended when you set out to markup the front matter for the book.

You need a mechanism to ensure constraint beyond well-formedness. If you are describing this book using XML markup, it makes sense to use a mechanism to enforce some simple constraints. In many cases, the constraints enforce document content rules, business rules or stricture that determines the order of elements, the presence of elements and attributes, and an indication of the number of occurrences expected. For the book's front-matter instance, you might want to establish structural guidelines, such as

- There is one and only one book element—the root element—that contains all others.
- The book element contains one each of title, author, publisher, isbn, date, and toc elements in that order.
- toc should contain as many day elements as needed.
- Each of the day elements has a required number attribute indicating which day is being encoded.

These simple content rules can be incorporated into a schema that acts to define the structure of the XML instance. Think of a schema as being like a contract that you enter into with XML to ensure that the desired structure is maintained. As a programmer, you will create a schema to apply to your document that maps well on the business problem you are addressing, or perhaps you might be able to select one from a public repository of schemata. Most schemata, like other parts of the XML family, are extensible by nature. Therefore, if a preexisting schema is only 80% right for your business, you might choose to extend it to make it fit your specific needs. Then, when you share data with others, you can include your extended schema to ensure that they adhere to the structure of your XML data stream.

**Tip**

It is not always necessary to create a unique schema. There are large repositories of public schemata maintained on the Web for use by particular industries.

There are several forms of schemata that are used in XML programming. During Day 4 you will learn to create, use, and interpret Document Type Definition (DTD) schemata. The DTD approach originated with SGML and has carried over to XML, but suffers from some shortcomings with regard to data type constraints and a syntax that is not the same as XML. On Days 5 and 6, respectively, you will learn about the very powerful XML Data Reduced (XDR) Schema dialect of XML and the XML Schema Definition (XSD) Language recommended by the W3C. All three of these technologies offer a means by which you can enforce the business rules that define the structure of your document. Each approach has advantages and disadvantages, but in time, the disparate methods should be coalesced into a single standard by the W3C and widely supported by industry and software tool developers.

**3**

**Note**

Data Type Validation enforces the classification of data values. Data Type Validation provides a means for a computer to make distinctions between such types as integers, percentages, floating point numbers, dates and strings, to name only a few.

# Data Type Validation—Another Reason for Validity

The need for document validity certainly transcends the simple needs shown by the preceding book markup examples. Imagine if you were conducting business-to-business (B2B) transactions over the Internet with a business partner. One of the principal advantages of XML for B2B is that it is platform independent. Therefore, you can do business with someone over the Web regardless of the operating system they run, or the programming and database languages they support. This is only effective, however, if you can guarantee (or perhaps enforce) the structure of the documents you exchange. You might need to ensure not only the structure of the transaction regarding element order and construct, but also regarding data type validation.

Elements and attribute values that are as simple as dates might be prone to error without careful validation. If your business partners are located in another country, they might, by convention, represent date values in a format that is different from your own. All of the date formats shown in Table 3.1 are used somewhere on the planet to represent October 9, 2001. Even though four digit years (including the century) are now more typical by convention, two digit years have been shown here to further highlight the potential for confusion.

**TABLE 3.1**  Sample Date Formats from Around the World for October 9, 2001

| Format | Value |
| --- | --- |
| mmddyy | 100901 |
| ddmmyy | 091001 |
| yyddmm | 010910 |
| yymmdd | 011009 |

To ensure integrity of data transactions with business partners, you might need to enforce one and only one format in a schema. You can see how the numeric values alone really hold very little information and could be easily misinterpreted, resulting in inaccurate processing.

You will learn to control data types with some of the schema approaches presented in this book, such as XDR and XSD. The DTD schema methodology, on the other hand, does not provide easy mechanisms for validating data types. This is one of the differences between DTD schemata and other approaches. You'll read about other differences on Days 5 and 6. Then, when creating your own schema you will be able to choose the methodology that best suits your own needs.

**Note**    It is possible to describe data types in a limited fashion using notations in conjunction with DTD schemata; however, this approach is not ideal.

Table 3.2 provides a few examples of data types that might require validation, depending upon the nature of information being exchanged. You have probably used data type validation in other forms of programming.

**TABLE 3.2** Examples of Data Types

| Data Type | Description |
| --- | --- |
| Boolean | 0 (false) or 1 (true) |
| Char | Single character (for example, "C") |
| String | Series of characters (for example, "CIST 1463") |
| Float | Real number (for example, 123.4567890) |
| Int | Whole number (for example, 5) |
| Date | Formatted as YYYY-MM-DD (for example, 2001-10-09) |
| Time | Formatted as HH-MM-SS (for example, 18:45:00) |
| Id | Text that uniquely identifies an element or attribute |
| Idref | Reference to an id |
| Enumeration | Series of values from which one can be chosen |

3

Data Typing is used to qualify the nature of particular data elements. Structure in a document is a separate consideration. Structure is a scheme for organizing related pieces of information. The order and placement of elements in XML is often part of the defined structure of the XML instance document. In the next section, you will read about some of the issues related to structure in XML.

# How Do You Recognize Data Structure?

The XML document listings you reviewed today, particularly Listings 3.1 and 3.2, shared many of the same elements, but characterized different structures. The order of the elements was not identical even though the element names were. As a result, one of the documents was intuitive and easy to follow (Listing 3.1), and the other (Listing 3.2) was not particularly representative of the desired markup.

## Structure in the Recipe Markup Language

In XML, you will need to examine your documents very closely and understand the data structures, quite apart from any concern you might have for rendering the data in a browser. During Day 2 you reviewed the structure of a recipe and created two models to depict that structure. One was a block diagram (Figure 2.5) and the other offered a tree depiction of the recipe (Figure 2.6). You chose which items on the recipe card were important enough to warrant being dealt with as separate chunks of data. You eventually created the `bean_dip3.xml` file, shown in Listing 3.3.

**LISTING 3.3**  bean_dip3.xml

```
 1: <?xml version="1.0"?>
 2: <!-- listing 3.3 - bean_dip3.xml -->
 3:
 4: <recipe title="Devan's Bean Dip">
 5:   <ingredients>
 6:       <item quantity="1 can">refried beans</item>
 7:       <item quantity="1 can">burrito sauce</item>
 8:       <item quantity="8 oz.">cubed Jalapeno cheese</item>
 9:       <item quantity="1/2 cup">sour cream</item>
10:   </ingredients>
11:   <preparation>In medium sauce pan, heat bean
12:       and burrito sauce until bubbly.  Add cubed
13:       cheese and stir until melted. Remove from
14:       heat and stir in sour cream.</preparation>
15:       <!-- For extra spicy bean dip, add your favorite hot
16:           sauce to the mix -->
17:   <serving>Serve as a dip with corn
18:       tortilla chips</serving>
19: </recipe>
```

The process you undertook to map the structure of the recipe document was to create a model, a tree, something almost like a roadmap to the information contained on the recipe card. Then you defined element and attribute names that were self-describing and intuitive. You processed the information in a parser, thereby proving that it was machine readable and then had a look at it with your own eyes, to show that it was human intelligible. This is a fairly typical example of the approach you might take the next time you create an XML instance based on a document with a known structure. To add validity, you need only consider the rules that are associated with that structure and then author an associated schema to enforce those rules when the document is parsed. For the final recipe markup language you might have rules such as these:

- There is one and only one `recipe` element—the root element—that contains all others.
- The `recipe` element includes a required `title` attribute.
- The `recipe` element must contain one each of `ingredients`, and `preparation` elements in that order, plus an optional `serving` element.
- `ingredients` must contain at least one, and might contain any number of, `item` elements.
- `item` elements have a required `quantity` attribute indicating the amount of each item needed.

# You Might Already Be Using Structured Data

In business, you might already have document structures in place. In fact, some of these might even be rigidly enforced by either convention or policy. Like many companies, yours might have guidelines for correspondence, memoranda formats, invoice formats, and so on. Good document structure is typically more obvious than good data structure. When thinking about data structure, consider databases and the rigid structure enforced by integrated data dictionaries. This is a good analogy because the rules regarding database data structures, like those in XML, are more concerned about the characterization of the data than they are about how those data might be rendered in a form or a report. Dealing with output from a database requires the use of a report generator or another application, function, or query that is separate from the storage and validation of the data itself. The same is true with XML—XML on its own is all about the data and it requires the use of complementary, ancillary, technologies to produce output.

3

When you concern yourself with validity in XML, you are effectively concerning yourself with data structure, rather than presentation. Web developers have, for some time, had to consider the structure of e-content and the impacts of storage, retrieval, maintenance, and transfer of that material rather than merely how those data might be rendered in a browser window. Technical writers, documentation specialists and, to some degree, even attorneys creating contracts and legal briefs have had to deal with complex sets of predefined and stringently enforced document structures for many years. XML offers a means of codifying structures and sharing them with business partners and other users of information.

As noted, however, XML is all about the data. XML on its own has nothing to offer with regard to rendering of those data. So unlike a document structure that typically maps readily onto an output device designed to create paper reports, XML data structures are only meant to encapsulate the kernels of data themselves. When it comes to rendering, you'll use a variety of different, but complimentary approaches including, perhaps, cascading stylesheets, the Extensible Stylesheet Language (XSL), a part of XSL known as the Extensible Stylesheet Language Transformations (XSLT), and scripting to render data stored in XML structures. You will have an opportunity to master many of these techniques as you read the remainder of this book.

**Tip**

The fact that XML has the characteristic of keeping data structures separate from style and content is part of what makes XML interoperable by nature. The same XML instance can be used to ultimately generate paper reports, create CD-ROM storage media, and present data to browsers, Web-enabled cellular phones, personal digital assistants, and a variety of other *user agents*.

What then is the difference between document structure and data structure? Document structure provides a reader with an organized means of quickly following the path of information delivery desired by the author. When you write a memorandum to a colleague, you typically indicate to whom it is addressed, along with your own name as the author, the date, and perhaps a subject line or priority, followed by the body of the message. The recipient perusing the document can use the document structure to quickly determine all of these components and then follow along without getting lost or distracted by details that can be scanned quickly. Data structures reflect the content and provide computer applications with a roadmap, not unlike a keyword index, to the data stored in various containers and sub-containers within the context of the whole document. In data structure, there is no qualification of the importance of one document component over another. All are equally relevant and it is up to the application or XML processor to determine how to use the data obtained from each container.

## You Can Use XML to Add Structure to Unstructured Information

XML offers you an unlimited mechanism to use structured data for information transfer. In fact, with XML it is easy to mix and match structured and less structured data, including text, numeric data, and strings to produce highly customized output streams to solve particular needs. You could accomplish the same end by using a variety of programming techniques, but XML was ideally designed with this kind of need in mind.

Table 3.3 is an extract from a database that contains courses offered by an XML training organization. The format of the database table has records for each course and fields that include Course_Number, Course_Name, and Instructor.

**TABLE 3.3**  Course Listings Database Table

| Course Number | Course Name | Instructor |
| --- | --- | --- |
| XML111 | Introductory XML | Bob Gonzales |
| XML333 | Advanced XML | Devan Shepherd |
| XMT222 | XMetal Core Configuration | Gene Yong |

If the data in this table were stored in a comma delimited text file, the result might look something like the document shown in Listing 3.4.

**LISTING 3.4**   Comma Delimited Text Version of Database Records

```
Course_Number,Course_Name,_Instructor
XML111,Introductory XML,Bob Gonzales
XML333,Advanced XML,Devan Shepherd
XMT222,XMetal Core Configuration,Gene Yong
```

XML provides a means to supplement these data with additional information that might be of value to humans or to computers. For instance, Listing 3.5 shows the same data included with additional information that could be used to produce a press release about upcoming course offerings.

**LISTING 3.5**   Highly Structured Data Obtained from a Database Combined with Additional Information in XML

```
 1: <?xml version="1.0"?>
 2: <!-- listing 3.5 - courses.xml -->
 3:
 4: <announcement>
 5:   <dist>For Immediate Release</dist>
 6:   <to>All Potential Students</to>
 7:   <from>Devan Shepherd</from>
 8:   <subject>Public Course Offerings in August</subject>
 9:   <notice>ACME Training is pleased to announce the following
10:     public courses, which are offered on a monthly basis.</notice>
11:   <contact>For more information, or to register for any of these courses,
12:     please visit
13:   <Web site>http://ACME-Train.com/university</Web site></contact>
14:   <courses>
15:     <course id="XML111" instructor="Bob Gonzales">
16:     Introduction to XML</course>
17:     <course id="XML333" instructor="Devan Shepherd">
18:     Advanced XML</course>
19:     <course id="XMT222" instructor="Gene Yong">
20:     XMetal Core Configuration</course>
21:   </courses>
22: </announcement>
```

The XML output is now infinitely more useful than the comma delimited text version of the data, not only because of the added information, but also because of the use of attributes within the course elements. This XML source can be used to create an e-mail message, a newsletter, or other printed document. The same data can also be transformed, under program control, into another markup language for use by a commercial advertising service. Using XML technologies, you could also create output from the same source file for Web-enabled wireless devices, such as cellular phones, Personal Digital Assistants, pagers, and so on.

You will learn on Day 14 to use cascading stylesheets (CSS). On Days 15 and 16, you will learn the Extensible Stylesheet Language (XSL) and the subset of XSL, Extensible Stylesheet Language Transformations (XSLT), to style output like this for use in a browser or other user agents, devices and processors.

> **Note**
>
> Valid XML guarantees the integrity of data structure, as though a contract has been established with the XML instance. Automation of content delivery is simplified because of this guarantee and can be affected using XSLT.

# You Can Parse for Validity

You have already used a parser in the exercises you have completed to this point. The Microsoft Internet Explorer browser includes the MSXML parser in distributions of the product at version 5.0 or above. You have, therefore, checked your documents to ensure well-formedness utilizing the MSXML parser. However, you have really only used the parser to prove that your documents are well-formed. Parsers can also be used to validate your XML against a schema, such as, DTD, XDR, XSD, or another schema language document, provided the parser is programmed with the rules for those languages. Figure 3.2 depicts this. In the figure, *yes* refers to documents that are considered valid, whereas *no* indicates those that are not.

**FIGURE 3.2**

*An XML document with an associated schema is passed to a validating XML parser.*

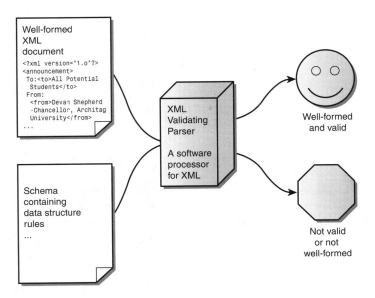

**Tip**

> A valid XML document is also well-formed; however, there is no guarantee that a well-formed XML instance is also valid.

A validating parser will first check an instance to ensure that it conforms to basic XML syntax rules, or is well-formed. Then it will confirm that all of the document content rule constraints characterized by the schema that you associated with it (or schemata, because you might associate more than one with your document) are completely satisfied, thereby guaranteeing validity of your document. In other words, validating parsers confirm syntax and data structure.

A parser is just a software application that interprets text a single character at a time, unless it is instructed by a programmer or schema author to skip over particular sequences of data. XML provides you a means to use these parser programs to comprehend the semantic intent of the markup being applied to the text.

**Note**

> The W3C refers to a parser as an XML processor in the official specification for XML 1.0: "A software module called an XML processor is used to read XML documents and provide access to their content and structure." (Please see the XML Technical Recommendation at http://www.w3.org/TR/1998/REC-xml-19980210 for further details.)

After the parser has interpreted the XML document and checked for well-formedness and validity, it then exposes the data in the form of a document tree structure to other applications for further processing. You have explored the use of IE5 in this regard, which uses the tree structure returned by the MSXML parser to display a structured document in the browser window showing that everything is as it should be. Recall that IE uses an XSLT process to assign a default stylesheet to the XML document at the time that you view it in the browser window. That is why you get things like the colored markup display in IE. Alternately, IE catches an error thrown by the parser and displays that, along with a snippet of code at the point in your document at which the error occurred without listing, or transforming for the purpose of formatting, the entire XML instance document.

This prevailing concept of documents built as tree structures is one of the reasons that you learned to represent a document in this fashion on Day 2 (recall Figure 2.6). You will revisit the concept of a document tree many more times throughout the course of the next few weeks. On Day 12 you will learn to use the Document Object Model (DOM) API to manipulate the individual nodes of your XML trees.

# Is Validity All That You Need?

You have seen that validity ensures structural constraints, but does that guarantee that those you exchange information with will know how to use your data? Not necessarily! All that validity ensures is the structure of the data in your XML instance, it is up to the application to determine how those data will be manipulated or processed further. Even if you publish your schema along with your XML document, those two pieces alone are not sufficient to complete an application of those data to solve a business problem.

Another typical misconception is that a schema is essential to conducting business over the Web with XML. A schema is a good method, but not the only method of ensuring the integrity of data that is generated for use by XML. One major advantage to using schemata in conjunction with XML documents to help control machine-generated content, improve searching, or validate data structures is that they are designed for that purpose. On later days, you will use programming techniques to manipulate data without having to build the logic pertaining to validity if a schema is associated with your XML documents.

# Summary

You have learned that a schema can be used effectively to ensure that the structure of the data being marked up is what you expect it to be. In particular, with measures in place for validity, you can do the following:

- Enforce the use of a predefined set of tags.
- Ensure that the elements and their attributes are in the precise order required by your document content or business rules.
- Control data types (provided you employ a schema approach that facilitates data type constraints).
- Control data integrity for optimal transaction-based exchange of information over the Web.
- Enforce all of these rules, controls, and constraints.

# Q&A

**Q  What is the difference between well-formed and valid XML?**

**A  Well-formed XML is syntactically perfect—it conforms with the basic rules for all XML documents. Valid XML is well-formed and it complies with the constraints imposed by an associated structural schema.**

**Q  What are some of the constraints that a programmer can impose by creating a schema for an XML document?**

**A**  A schema enforces the name and structure of the root element, including specification of all of the child elements. The programmer can ensure the exact order and quantity of each element and predetermine which elements are required or optional. The schema can dictate which elements have attributes and determine the acceptable values for the attributes, along with any defaults. As in the case of elements, attributes can be made to be required or optional.

**Q  What schema languages are in use by XML document authors?**

**A**  Several forms of schema languages are in use currently. The Document Type Definition (DTD) language has survived from the days of SGML and will be covered tomorrow. Microsoft has released the XML Data Reduced (XDR) language as a schema dialect of XML (to be covered on Day 5). The W3C is working to coalesce the XML dialects of schemata into a single working form called the XML Schema Definition (XSD) language, which will be presented on Day 6.

**Q  Is it possible to use schemata to control data types in an XML data stream?**

**A**  XDR and XSD have ready means for constraining data types. The DTD approach can't handle data type rules as easily. Programmers determined early in the life cycle of XML evolution that data type validation was essential for XML to be used in e-commerce and e-business transaction models.

**Q  What is the difference between document structure and data structure?**

**A**  Document structure provides a reader with an organized means of quickly following the path of information delivery desired by the author. Data structures reflect the content and provide computer applications with a roadmap, not unlike a keyword index, to the data stored in various containers and sub-containers within the context of the whole document.

**Q  What is a parser and what does it have to do with validity?**

**A**  A parser is a software application (known by the W3C as an XML processor) that interprets a text document one character at a time. There are two generic types of parsers used with XML. One, a non-validating parser, is only capable of ensuring that a document is well-formed; that is, it satisfies the basic XML rules for syntax. A validating parser ensures that a document is well-formed and then applies the document content or business rule constraints defined by any associated schemata to ensure that the document is also valid.

## Exercise

The exercise is provided so that you can test your knowledge of what you learned today. The answer is in Appendix A.

At the end of Day 2, the exercise called for you to correct a poorly formed XML document and make it well-formed. The document described two albums in a music collection with elements for cd, title, artist, and tracks. You would like to create a valid music collection markup language, which you will refer to as MCML. Based on the well-formed solution to the previous exercise, create a tree diagram for MCML and write down some of the business rules that might be used to enforce validity.

# DAY 4

# The Document Type Definition (DTD)

You have learned that an XML document is valid if it has an associated schema and if the document complies with the constraints expressed in that schema. Today you will learn about one type of schema, the Document Type Definition, or DTD.

In particular, you will learn

- What a DTD is and how it is associated with an XML document
- How to write an internal and external DTD
- How to declare elements and attributes in a DTD
- How to use entities in DTDs
- The difference between validating and non-validating parsers
- Some of the shortcomings of DTDs and why it was necessary to create other forms of schemata

# Where Did DTDs Come From?

Recall that the association of a schema with an XML document means that the document may be shared independently of an application. The schema adds constraints about the XML document that ensure the inclusion of required elements and attributes, their specific order, and, to some extent, their valid content. With these constraints in place, you can exchange your data with others and a common schema can be used for validation. In fact, you will learn that a schema can be built in to an application to validate an XML document used to provide data for other purposes. A parser is just such an application. A parser validates an XML document by assuring that it is well-formed and then checking and testing the constraints provided in an associated external (or internal) schema.

The DTD is a form of schema that originated in the SGML world. When XML was first introduced, it was intended to be some kind of a DTD-less SGML. In some ways, this is true because you can certainly have well-formed XML without any associated schema, but the schema (the DTD), as you already know, is a powerful means of adding valuable constraints for data exchange based on consistent data structures. You can have XML without a DTD or schema; that is what well-formed XML is, but schemata add validity for document content and business rules.

 **Tip**

> A DTD (or any XML schema, for that matter) provides a template for document markup that indicates the presence, order, and placement of elements and their attributes in an XML document.

You have already learned that an XML document can be depicted as a tree of elements that contain data, other elements, and attributes. The DTD can be thought of as a structure that also defines a tree, but there are some differences between a DTD tree and an XML document tree, even if the XML document conforms to the DTD.

A DTD tree does not, itself, have any repetition of elements or structure. However, its structures provide for repetition of elements in a conforming valid XML instance. Consider the XML document in Listing 4.1 (you saw something similar to this during Day 3).

**LISTING 4.1**  A Course Listing Announcement as a Well-Formed XML Instance—
`courses.xml`

```
1: <?xml version="1.0"?>
2: <!-- listing 4.1 - courses.xml -->
3:
4: <announcement>
```

**LISTING 4.1**   continued

```
5:      <distribution>For Immediate Release</distribution>
6:      <to>All Potential Students</to>
7:      <from>Devan Shepherd</from>
8:      <subject>Public Course Offerings in August</subject>
9:        <notice>ACME Training is pleased to announce the following
10:       public courses, which are offered on a monthly basis at its
11:       headquarters.</notice>
12:       <more_info>For more information, or to register for any of these
➥courses,
13:       please visit <website>http://ACME-
➥Train.com/university</website></more_info>
14:     <courses>
15:       <course id="XML111" instructor="Bob Gonzales">Introduction to
➥XML</course>
16:       <course id="XML333" instructor="Devan Shepherd">Advanced XML</course>
17:       <course id="XMT222" instructor="Gene Yong">XMetal Core
➥Configuration</course>

18:     </courses>
19: </announcement>
```

On line 14 of the listing is the `courses` element, which contains other `course` elements. With that in mind, a document tree diagram to depict this instance might look something like the one shown in Figure 4.1.

**FIGURE 4.1**

*Document tree for the Press Release* `courses.xml` *document.*

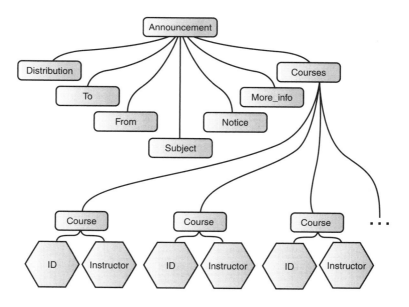

The document tree in Figure 4.1 shows multiple course elements, each with id and instructor attributes. A DTD tree would list the course element only once, but would include a special + operator to indicate that more than one was possible. You will learn more about the plus sign and other special DTD operators later today. Figure 4.2 shows one possible DTD tree for the courses.xml document.

**FIGURE 4.2**

*A DTD tree for the Press Release* courses.xml *document.*

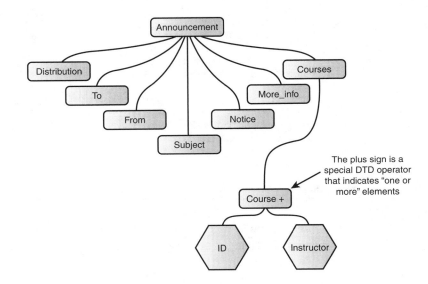

You will learn to create and read simple DTDs today that could provide the constraints represented by DTD trees. There are tools available to help with this process, including some that will interrogate one or more well-formed XML documents and generate DTDs that validate those documents. (For example, an online program that does this is located at http://www.pault.com/pault/dtdgenerator/. If you prefer to run a DTD generator locally, you can download the SAXON distribution of tools from http://users.iclway.co.uk/mhkay/saxon/saxon6.0.2/index.html.) But first, you should learn to code some simple DTDs by hand.

# Understanding the Rules

DTDs deal with the elements in an XML document as either container elements or as empty elements (that is, placeholders in the document structure). The container elements can house data (for example, text), child elements, or a combination of both. The DTD provides syntax for strictures (or constraints) to control these content models.

**Tip**

> The declaration of element or attribute content in a DTD is called the content model for that particular element or attribute.

## Basic Element Type Declaration Syntax in a DTD

The elements in any XML document are the fundamental structures that are pieced together to create the instance. Each element must be declared in a DTD with element type declarations.

Element type declarations take the form

```
<!ELEMENT    element_name    ( content model )>
```

**Note**

> The examples that follow build on one another. You are encouraged to create each example as it is presented, by writing the corresponding code for each listing using a text editor. Later today you will parse some of these examples to prove that they represent valid XML. Save each new version of your document as a separate file, named `message01.xml`, `message02.xml`, and so on.

## A Simple Element with Text Content

Consider the short XML document in Listing 4.2 as an example of a simple element. In fact, this is a very simple XML document that comprises only a single element, `note`. Create this document and save it as `message01.xml`.

**LISTING 4.2**   A Short, Well-Formed XML Instance—`message01.xml`

```
1: <?xml version = "1.0"?>
2: <note>Remember to buy milk on the way home from work</note>
```

The element `note` contains only text and nothing else. You could validate this document by creating a DTD that had an element type declaration specifying that `note` contained only #PCDATA, a DTD reserved keyword for "Parsed Character Data," or text. PCDATA is just text data, but it is text data that is read by an XML parser and processed appropriately. Therefore, if you have markup in the PCDATA, it might affect the parsing of the document. This can be either a desirable or an undesirable event. Later, you will learn ways of preventing text from being interpreted by the parser using a type of data called

CDATA. CDATA is just text, but it is text that the parser does not attempt to process; markup characters, such as angle brackets, are ignored in CDATA segments, but resolved in PCDATA segments.

Because DTDs offer a means of validating the structure of documents, they contain the rules for content. Each element or attribute has an associated content model in a DTD that declares and defines what is contained. For instance, an element might contain text data or other elements, or it might be empty. All of these content models are encoded differently with a DTD. DTDs can be provided in separate documents and associated by a special instruction in the XML instance document, or they can be included as inline encoding. Today, you will see the inline form first and the external approach shortly thereafter.

**Tip**

The reserved keyword #PCDATA in a DTD is always in all uppercase characters.

Listing 4.3 shows the XML document with a DTD embedded. Create this document and save it as message02.xml. Line 3 is the element type declaration and will be explained more fully.

**LISTING 4.3**   A Short, Well-Formed, and Valid XML Instance—message02.xml

```
1: <?xml version = "1.0"?>
2: <!DOCTYPE note      [
3: <!ELEMENT note      ( #PCDATA)>
4:                     ]>
5: <note>Remember to buy milk on the way home from work</note>
```

**ANALYSIS**   Line 1 is the standard XML declaration that you have used in all other exercises. It declares that this is an XML version 1.0 document—there is nothing new in this line.

Line 2 is a special document type declaration, placed in the prolog of an XML document that associates the DTD with the XML document. You will learn to use the Document Type Definition to indicate either an inline DTD (known as an internal subset) or one that resides in an external DTD document on its own (called an external subset). The syntax for the two different approaches varies slightly and will be explored in detail today. The Document Type Definition always starts with <!DOCTYPE and ends with a >

symbol. The word DOCTYPE must be all in uppercase characters. The first few lines of an XML document before the line containing the root element is often referred to as the *prolog* of the document. The prolog contains the processing instructions for the document, such as the XML declaration (<?xml version="1,0"?>) and a DOCTYPE declaration if a DTD is used. You will learn on Days 5 and 6 that other forms of schemata are associated with XML document instances using different information in the prolog, or as attributes on the root element start tag.

The document type declaration in line 2 tells the XML processor (for example, the validating parser) that a declaration exists called note and that anything inside the square brackets ([ ]) comprises the inline DTD. In other words, line 2 starts the internal subset DTD called note. In this case, note is the root element.

Line 3 provides an element type declaration for the element note. In particular, it declares that note is an element that contains only text, or #PCDATA. The part of the declaration that is contained within parentheses is known as the content model, or content specification. It is within the content model that you will tell the XML parser what to expect as content for each XML element in your document. In some cases, your will declare that an element is empty. In other cases you will declare a container element that holds other elements. Some elements will hold data and still others may have mixed content, including text along with other elements. Examples of each kind of content model follow.

**Tip**

> The DTD keywords DOCTYPE and ELEMENT must be in uppercase.

Line 4 marks the close of the inline DTD and tells the XML processor that the XML document follows.

Line 5 contains the note element with its text (#PCDATA) content.

## An Element That Contains Another Element

Elements can be containers for other elements. The root element of an XML document is typically such an element. Listing 4.4 shows the note element with a message element as content. Create this document and save it as message03.xml.

**LISTING 4.4**  An Element Containing Only a Child Element—`message03.xml`

```
1: <?xml version = "1.0"?>
2: <note>
3:     <message>Remember to buy milk on the way home from work</message>
4: </note>
```

This time, in order to create a DTD for this XML document, you'll need to indicate that the note element has element content, namely message, rather than #PCDATA. However, you will then have to declare the message element as having #PCDATA content because all elements in the instance must be declared—that is part of the stricture that will be enforced by your DTD. Listing 4.5 shows the XML document, complete with an internal subset, or inline DTD. Create this document and save it as `message04.xml`.

**LISTING 4.5**  A DTD Declaration for an Element Containing a Child Element— `message04.xml`

```
1: <?xml version = "1.0"?>
2: <!DOCTYPE note      [
3: <!ELEMENT note       ( message )>
4: <!ELEMENT message    ( #PCDATA)>
5:                      ]>
6: <note>
7:     <message>Remember to buy milk on the way home from work</message>
8: </note>
```

**ANALYSIS**  Line 3 declares that the element note contains a message element. Line 4 goes on to declare that the message element contains #PCDATA. Lines 6 through 8 constitute the well-formed and valid XML instance. As you can see on line 7, the message element is properly nested within the note element (that is, message is a child of the note element.) The indentation, or tab spacing, of the message element is offered only for clarity. Indenting your code is a good programming practice that makes it much easier to read at a later time. Spacing like this is not required in XML. You will learn later today how XML processors deal with extra space characters.

## Declaring an Empty Element

Empty elements are typically used as placeholders, or to provide required attribute values that do not properly modify other elements. You'll learn about attribute declarations in DTDs later today. On line 3 of Listing 4.6, an empty element number has been added to the XML document. Create this document and save it as `message05.xml`.

**LISTING 4.6**   An Empty Element in an XML Document—`message05.xml`

```
1: <?xml version = "1.0"?>
2: <note>
3:     <number />
4:     <message>Remember to buy milk on the way home from work</message>
5: </note>
```

Listing 4.7 shows the internal subset DTD that properly declares the new empty element. Create this document and save it as `message06.xml`.

**LISTING 4.7**   A DTD Declaring an Empty `number` Element—`message06.xml`

```
 1: <?xml version = "1.0"?>
 2: <!DOCTYPE note      [
 3: <!ELEMENT note       ( number, message )>
 4: <!ELEMENT number        EMPTY>
 5: <!ELEMENT message     ( #PCDATA)>
 6:                    ]>
 7: <note>
 8:     <number />
 9:     <message>Remember to buy milk on the way home from work</message>
10: </note>
```

**ANALYSIS**   Line 3 indicates that the `note` element now contains a `number` element, followed by `message` element. The comma (,) between the elements in the content model indicates that an element is followed by another element in the order declared. The XML processor interprets line 3 to mean that the element `note` contains a `number` element, followed immediately by a `message` element, in that order. An XML instance with a `message` element before a `number` element would not be valid according to this DTD.

Line 4 uses the keyword `EMPTY` in the content model of the element `number` to declare it as an empty element. According to the DTD, `number` may not contain text or other elements.

**Tip**   The DTD keyword `EMPTY` is always written in uppercase.

## Using the DTD Keyword ANY

Sometimes you might know that a particular element is not empty (that is, it contains elements or text or both), but you are not certain what the precise content model should be. The DTD keyword ANY can be used to declare the content for elements that are characterized in that manner. To understand how ANY affects the definition of an XML structure, you will add elemental content to make the structure more complex. Then, by encoding the content model with the ANY keyword, you will remove constraints on that model.

Consider the XML instance shown in Listing 4.8, in which the child element date has been added to the note container element. Create this document and save it as message07.xml.

**LISTING 4.8**   Adding Another Child to the note Element—message07.xml

```
1: <?xml version = "1.0"?>
2: <note>
3:     <number />
4:     <message>Remember to buy milk on the way home from work</message>
5:     <date />
6: </note>
```

You could expand the declaration of the note element on line 3 of Listing 4.7 to include the new date element. If you did, it would look like

```
3: <!ELEMENT note       ( number, message, date )>
```

While it is not very precise and offers much less in the way of validity, you could also choose to use the keyword ANY to indicate that the element note may contain any type of content, including text or other elements, without regard to their specific names or order. Listing 4.9 shows the DTD with such a declaration included. Create this document and save it as message08.xml.

**LISTING 4.9**   The note Element Is Permitted ANY Content—message08.xml

```
 1: <?xml version = "1.0"?>
 2: <!DOCTYPE note      [
 3: <!ELEMENT note      ANY>
 4: <!ELEMENT number    EMPTY>
 5: <!ELEMENT message   ( #PCDATA)>
 6: <!ELEMENT date      EMPTY>
 7:                     ]>
 8: <note>
 9:     <number />
10:     <message>Remember to buy milk on the way home from work</message>
11:     <date />
12: </note>
```

Line 3 provides the ANY declaration for the element note. For the document to be valid, however, also requires the addition of line 6, declaring the EMPTY content of the date element. Without line 6, the XML document would not be valid. Line 4 offers the same constraints for the number element. You may not have elements in your XML instance that are not declared in the DTD.

**Tip**

> The DTD keyword ANY is always written in uppercase.

## Mixed Content Models

There may be times when you want to establish a rule to permit an element to contain text or other elements in some combination. A mixed content model provides this capability. Listing 4.10 shows an XML instance with some #PCDATA included in the root element along with the child elements you created earlier today. Create this document and save it as message09.xml.

**LISTING 4.10**   Mixed Content in the note Element—message09.xml

```
1: <?xml version = "1.0"?>
2: <note>This is an important note
3:      <number />
4:      <message>Remember to buy milk on the way home from work</message>
5:      <date />
6: </note>
```

The root element, note, on line 2 contains a text string This is an important note. Listing 4.11 shows a DTD that validates this instance. Create this document and save it as message10.xml.

**LISTING 4.11**   Validation of an Element with a Mixed Content Model—message10.xml

```
1: <?xml version = "1.0"?>
2: <!DOCTYPE note       [
3: <!ELEMENT note       ( #PCDATA | number | message | date )*>
4: <!ELEMENT number     EMPTY>
5: <!ELEMENT message    ( #PCDATA )>
6: <!ELEMENT date       EMPTY>
7:                      ]>
8: <note>This is an important note
9:      <number />
```

4

LISTING **4.11** continued

```
10:     <message>Remember to buy milk on the way home from work</message>
11:     <date />
12: </note>
```

**ANALYSIS** Line 3 declares the mixed content associated with the `note` element. An XML processor would interpret that line to indicate that the `note` element may contain any combination of text or the elements listed. This is actually a fairly complex statement. The pipe (|) character means "or" in the DTD language. The content specification says the element `note` may contain `#PCDATA` or `number` or `message` or `date`. The asterisk (*) near the end of the content specification means that the items in the parentheses may be used any number of times or not at all. Therefore, using the same DTD means that the XML document in Listing 4.12 is also valid.

LISTING **4.12** Another Valid XML Instance Using the Same Mixed Content Model for the `note` Element—message11.xml

```
 1: <?xml version = "1.0"?>
 2: <!DOCTYPE note      [
 3: <!ELEMENT note      (#PCDATA | number | message | date)*>
 4: <!ELEMENT number    EMPTY>
 5: <!ELEMENT message   ( #PCDATA)>
 6: <!ELEMENT date      EMPTY>
 7:                     ]>
 8: <note>This is an important note
 9:     <number />now we can no longer control the occurrence of
                    each content type
10:     <number />
11:     <message>stuff</message>to remember
12:     <message>Remember to buy milk on the way home from work</message>
13: </note>
```

If you examine the differences between Listings 4.11 and 4.12 you will see that both contain the same internal subset or inline DTD. However, Listing 4.12 does not have a `date` element and the document is still considered valid because the mixed content model requires the (*) operator to qualify the optional nature of the content model. Line 10 shows a second empty `number` element and line 11 a new `message` element, both of which are permitted by the mixed content model. Text (#PCDATA) shows up in several places within the `note` element (lines 8, 9, and 11).

By using a mixed content model, you lose a lot of control over the declared structure of the document. You will still need to use mixed content models from time to time, but it is a good idea to avoid them, if you can, when the business problem being solved calls for tighter controls over the data structure of your document.

## Element Content Models in Summary

So far, you have learned to use a DTD to declare several different types of content for an element. Table 4.1 summarizes these content specifications and shows the syntax used for each.

**TABLE 4.1** DTD Content Specifications for Elements

| Content | Syntax | Interpretation |
|---------|--------|----------------|
| Element(s) | `<!ELEMENT name (child1, child2)` | This element contains only child elements. |
| Mixed | `<!ELEMENT name (#PCDATA | child)*>` | This element contains a combination of text and sub-elements. |
| EMPTY | `<!ELEMENT name EMPTY>` | This element contains no content. |
| ANY | `<!ELEMENT name ANY>` | This element may contain either text or element content. |

# Declaring Attributes in a DTD

Suppose that you decide that the empty elements `number` and `date` make better sense as attributes of the `message` element because they modify the `message` element. Remember that attributes modify elements, similar to the way adjectives modify nouns. The next example will take the empty elements `number` and `date` from Listings 4.8 and 4.9 and make them attributes of the `message` element. This is shown in Listing 4.13.

**LISTING 4.13**   An XML Instance with Attributes—`message12.xml`

```
1: <?xml version = "1.0"?>
2: <note>
3:     <message number="10" date="073001">
4:         Remember to buy milk on the way home from work
5:     </message>
6: </note>
```

Line 3 now contains `number` and `date` as attributes of the `message` element. The DTD will need a special mechanism for the declaration of attributes. The `ATTLIST` keyword is used for this purpose.

Attribute declarations take the form

```
<!ATTLIST   element_name   attribute_name1 (type) defaults
                           attribute_name2 (type) defaults>
```

There are three fundamental types of attributes that are declared within a DTD. These are

- Strings, indicated by the `CDATA` keyword
- Tokenized attributes, indicated by declared tokens
- Enumerated attributes, in which a choice of valid values is provided

Attribute defaults are declared to permit document authors to control the valid values for attributes. You'll see examples of each of these default declarations later today. The three default types implemented by DTDs are shown in Table 4.2.

**TABLE 4.2**   DTD Attribute Defaults

| Value | Interpretation |
|---|---|
| #REQUIRED | Specifies that the attribute must be provided. |
| #FIXED | Provides a constant declaration for an attribute value. If the value is other than the one declared the document is not valid. |
| #IMPLIED | The attribute is optional. That is, if the attribute does not appear in the element, then the processing application can use any value (if it needs to). |

## String Type Attribute Declarations

Listing 4.14 shows a DTD that validates the XML instance provided in Listing 4.13.

**LISTING 4.14**   A DTD with a Simple ATTLIST Declaration—message13.xml

```
 1: <?xml version = "1.0"?>
 2: <!DOCTYPE note      [
 3: <!ELEMENT note       ( message ) >
 4: <!ELEMENT message   ( #PCDATA)>
 5: <!ATTLIST message
 6:             number  CDATA    #REQUIRED
 7:             date    CDATA    #REQUIRED>
 8:                     ]>
 9: <note>
10:     <message number="10" date="073001">
11:         Remember to buy milk on the way home from work
12:     </message>
13: </note>
```

**ANALYSIS**   Line 5 declares that the message element requires a number attribute and a date attribute. Both of the attributes are of the CDATA type, which permits any string to be included as data. The CDATA keyword allows any characters to be included in the string, except <, >, &, or ". The #REQUIRED keyword indicates that the number and the date attributes must be provided for the message element.

Line 10 assigns the value "10" to the attribute number and the value "073001" to the attribute date, both of which modify the message element.

## #FIXED Attribute Declarations

Listing 4.15 shows a new attribute from with a value "Kathy Shepherd". Using the #FIXED keyword, you can ensure that an attribute value is what you expect it to be. For the current exercise, you will ensure that all messages are from Kathy Shepherd.

**LISTING 4.15**   A New Attribute, from, Introduced to Modify the message Element— message14.xml

```
 1: <?xml version = "1.0"?>
 2: <note>
 3:     <message number="10" date="073001" from="Kathy Shepherd">
 4:         Remember to buy milk on the way home from work
 5:     </message>
 6: </note>
```

The DTD declaring the fixed attribute value is shown in Listing 4.16.

**LISTING 4.16** A Valid XML Instance with a #FIXED Attribute Value—message15.xml

```
 1: <?xml version = "1.0"?>
 2: <!DOCTYPE note       [
 3: <!ELEMENT note       ( message ) >
 4: <!ELEMENT message    ( #PCDATA)>
 5: <!ATTLIST message
 6:            number  CDATA  #REQUIRED
 7:            date    CDATA  #REQUIRED
 8:            from    CDATA  #FIXED      "Kathy Shepherd">
 9:                    ]>
10: <note>
11:     <message number="10" date="073001" from="Kathy Shepherd">
12:        Remember to buy milk on the way home from work
13:     </message>
14: </note>
```

Line 8 declares that the attribute from must contain the value Kathy Shepherd and can contain nothing else. For example, if line 11 were like this

```
11:     <message number="10" date="073001" from="someone else">
```

the document would be considered broken by the XML processor and an error would be generated indicating that it was not valid.

## #IMPLIED Attribute Declarations

Listing 4.17 shows an #IMPLIED attribute. Attributes that are implied are optional, and validity is not affected by their presence or absence.

**LISTING 4.17** A Valid Document with an #IMPLIED Attribute—message16.xml

```
 1: <?xml version = "1.0"?>
 2: <!DOCTYPE note       [
 3: <!ELEMENT note       ( message ) >
 4: <!ELEMENT message    ( #PCDATA)>
 5: <!ATTLIST message
 6:            number  CDATA  #REQUIRED
 7:            date    CDATA  #REQUIRED
 8:            from    CDATA  #FIXED      "Kathy Shepherd"
 9:            status  CDATA  #IMPLIED>
10:                    ]>
11: <note>
12:     <message number="10" date="073001" from="Kathy Shepherd">
13:        Remember to buy milk on the way home from work
14:     </message>
15: </note>
```

Line 9 declares an #IMPLIED attribute, status, in this document. Since it is implied or optional, the document instance is valid without the inclusion of the attribute in the message element. If line 12 included a status attribute, such as

```
12:      <message number="10" date="073001" from="Kathy Shepherd"
status="urgent">
```

the document instance would still be valid.

## Tokenized Attribute Types in DTDs

With tokenized attributes, you can impose certain constraints on attribute values, but these constraints are limited, as you will see. The tokenized options do provide a means of constraining the values permitted for attributes. For example, you may want to have a unique ID for each element or only permit an attribute to have one or two different values. Table 4.3 lists the four different tokenized attribute types available with DTDs.

**TABLE 4.3**   DTD Tokenized Attribute Types

| Value | Interpretation |
|-------|----------------|
| ID | Uniquely identifies an element |
| IDREF | Points to elements that have an ID attribute |
| ENTITIES | Refers to an external unparsed entity |
| NMTOKEN | Value consists of letters, digits, periods, underscores, hyphens, and colon characters, but not spaces |

## Using ID and IDREF Attributes

Listing 4.18 shows an example of an XML instance that could be validated using ID and IDREF attribute types. In this example, the note XML document has been extended to include several new message elements with qualifying attributes that ensure that each is uniquely identified by a number attribute and outcome elements that are associated with the notes via a msg attribute. The XML instance is well-formed.

**LISTING 4.18**   The note XML Document Extended—message17.xml

```
1: <?xml version = "1.0"?>
2: <note>
3:     <message number="a1" from="Kathy Shepherd">
4:         Remember to buy milk on the way home from work
5:     </message>
6:     <message number="a2" from="Greg Shepherd">
7:         I need some help with my homework
8:     </message>
```

**LISTING 4.18**    continued

```
 9:        <message number="a3" from="Kristen Shepherd">
10:            Please play Scrabble with me tonight
11:        </message>
12:
13:        <outcome msg="a1">
14:            milk was past due date
15:        </outcome>
16:        <outcome msg="a1">
17:            went to a different store
18:        </outcome>
19:        <outcome msg="a2">
20:            homework finished early
21:        </outcome>
22: </note>
```

To clarify the intent of this XML document, imagine a scenario in which an application stores short messages that are received throughout the day, via cellular phone, pager, or e-mail. Each message is assigned a unique ID (for example, the number attribute). The same application stores outcome elements that may or may not be recorded (that is, they are not #REQUIRED). If these optional outcome elements are indeed recorded, however, they must be associated with a particular message (via the msg attribute) so that they can be processed, perhaps matched up, later.

This provides a fairly complex validation problem, but one that is easily handled with a DTD, using the ID and IDREF attribute types. Listing 4.19 provides a DTD validation for this scenario.

**LISTING 4.19**    Validation Using ID and IDREF Attribute Types—message18.xml

```
 1: <?xml version = "1.0"?>
 2: <!DOCTYPE     note      [
 3: <!ELEMENT     note      ( message+, outcome+ ) >
 4: <!ELEMENT     message ( #PCDATA)>
 5: <!ATTLIST     message
 6:                    number    ID      #REQUIRED
 7:                    from      CDATA   #REQUIRED>
 8: <!ELEMENT     outcome (#PCDATA)>
 9: <!ATTLIST     outcome
10:                    msg       IDREF   #IMPLIED>
11:                        ]>
12: <note>
13:     <message number="a1" from="Kathy Shepherd">
14:         Remember to buy milk on the way home from work
15:     </message>
```

**LISTING 4.19**   continued

```
16:        <message number="a2" from="Greg Shepherd">
17:           I need some help with my homework
18:        </message>
19:        <message number="a3" from="Kristen Shepherd">
20:           Please play Scrabble with me tonight
21:        </message>
22:
23:        <outcome msg="a1">
24:            milk was past its best before date
25:        </outcome>
26:        <outcome msg="a1">
27:           went to a different store
28:        </outcome>
29:        <outcome msg="a2">
30:            homework finished early
31:        </outcome>
32: </note>
```

**ANALYSIS**   Line 3 contains a different content model than those shown earlier. In particular, there is a plus sign (+) after the message and the outcome child elements in the content specification for the note element. This is an occurrence indicator that means the child element must exist one or more times within the container element. In this case, line 3 is interpreted to mean that the note element contains one or more message elements, followed by (remember that the comma always enforces order) one or more outcome elements.

Line 4 declares that the message element contains text, #PCDATA .

The declared attribute list for the message element begins on line 5. On line 6 the declaration states that the required attribute number is of the type ID. ID means that each number attribute must be unique. If any number value is repeated in any other element, the document will fail to validate.

**Tip**

> An ID type attribute must begin with a letter, colon (:), or an underscore (_). Only one ID type attribute can be included in any single element.

Line 7 is carried over from previous examples and indicates that element message must have a from attribute comprising a string.

Line 8 declares outcome to include text.

In line 10, the `msg` attribute of the `outcome` element is declared as an `IDREF` type attribute. This means that the value of the `msg` attribute in the `outcome` element is associated with the value of the corresponding `number` attribute in the `message` element. In the example, message number `"a1"`, `Remember to buy milk on the way home from work`, is associated with the outcomes `milk was past its best before date` and `went to another store`. In a similar fashion, the `outcome` element, `homework finished early`, with an attribute `msg="a2"` is associated with the `message` element that has a `number` attribute value of `"a2"`, `I need some help with my homework`. You may notice that there is no `outcome` associated with `message number="a3"`. This is an acceptable situation because on line 10, `msg` was declared as `#IMPLIED`, or optional.

## Using ENTITY Elements in a DTD

Elements are considered containers in markup. Entities are replacement strings that resolve to another form. Readers who are familiar with HTML will know about some of the entities that are commonly used by that language, such as the entity `  ` is resolved in the browser by the inclusion of a single non-breaking space character. XMLhas several types of entities. The first one you will consider allows the substitution of string in an XML document. The declaration and definition of the entity takes place in a schema. When an XML processor encounters an entity, it resolves the entity by substituting whatever is defined for that entity. The processor knows it has encountered a character entity in an XML document when the & character is located. All character entities take the following form:

`&entity;`

The leading ampersand and the trailing semi-colon demark the string that corresponds to the entity reference. The parser will find the reference in the DTD, read the entity string to which it corresponds, and expand or resolve the entity appropriately.

On Day 7, you will explore the use of entities in XML in detail. Entities can be used in several ways. You'll see how to use an entity to reference a stored variable in a DTD. Listing 4.20 shows an entity declaration used to represent a date string.

LISTING 4.20    Entity Substitution in XML Using a DTD—`message19.xml`

```
1: <?xml version = "1.0"?>
2: <!DOCTYPE    note      [
3: <!ELEMENT    note      ( message+, outcome+ ) >
4: <!ELEMENT    message ( #PCDATA)>
5: <!ATTLIST    message
6:              number    ID    #REQUIRED
7:              from      CDATA #REQUIRED>
8: <!ELEMENT    outcome (#PCDATA)>
```

**LISTING 4.20**　continued

```
 9: <!ATTLIST    outcome
10:                   msg        IDREF #IMPLIED>
11: <!ENTITY    today     "073001">
12:                    ]>
13: <note>
14:     <message number="a1" from="Kathy Shepherd">
15:         &today; - Remember to buy milk on the way home from work
16:     </message>
17:     <message number="a2" from="Greg Shepherd">
18:         &today; - I need some help with my homework
19:     </message>
20:     <message number="a3" from="Kristen Shepherd">
21:         &today; - Please play Scrabble with me tonight
22:     </message>
23:     <outcome msg="a1">
24:         milk was past its best before date
25:     </outcome>
26:     <outcome msg="a1">
27:         went to a different store
28:     </outcome>
29:     <outcome msg="a2">
30:         homework finished early
31:     </outcome>
32: </note>
```

**ANALYSIS**　Line 11 shows the entity declaration for the entity today, which contains the string "073001". When a parser encounters the entity reference &today; in lines 15, 18, and 21, it substitutes the string.

Figure 4.3 shows the entity substitution using Microsoft Internet Explorer to parse the document.

## Using NMTOKEN Attributes

Few data type constraints are available in XML. NMTOKEN provides some limitation on the acceptable characters in XML content. In particular, NMTOKEN limits data to the same rules used for XML element name conventions, which is not very restrictive at all. Nonetheless, the name token attribute type or NMTOKEN restricts values to those that consist of letters, digits, periods, hyphens, colons, and underscores. Listing 4.21 depicts the use of the NMTOKEN attribute type.

**FIGURE 4.3**

*A parsed document with an entity substitution.*

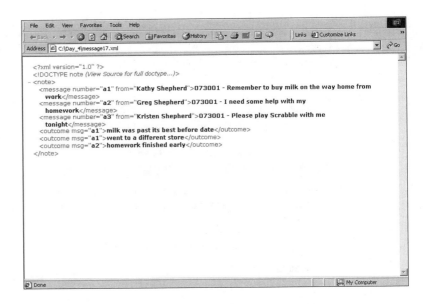

**LISTING 4.21**    An NMTOKEN Attribute Type in a DTD—`message20.xml`

```
 1: <?xml version = "1.0"?>
 2: <!DOCTYPE    note     [
 3: <!ELEMENT    note     ( message+, outcome+ ) >
 4: <!ELEMENT    message ( #PCDATA)>
 5: <!ATTLIST    message
 6:              number   ID        #REQUIRED
 7:              from     CDATA     #REQUIRED
 8:              phone    NMTOKEN   #REQUIRED>
 9: <!ELEMENT    outcome (#PCDATA)>
10: <!ATTLIST    outcome
11:              msg      IDREF     #IMPLIED>
12: <!ENTITY     today    "073001">
13:                       ]>
14: <note>
15:     <message number="a1" from="Kathy Shepherd" phone="720-555-6382">
16:         &today; - Remember to buy milk on the way home from work
17:     </message>
18:     <message number="a2" from="Greg Shepherd" phone="720-555-1234">
19:         &today; - I need some help with my homework
20:     </message>
21:     <message number="a3" from="Kristen Shepherd" phone="720-555-4321">
22:         &today; - Please play Scrabble with me tonight
23:     </message>
24:     <outcome msg="a1">
25:         milk was past its best before date
26:     </outcome>
```

LISTING 4.21    continued

```
27:      <outcome msg="a1">
28:          went to a different store
29:      </outcome>
30:      <outcome msg="a2">
31:          homework finished early
32:      </outcome>
33: </note>
```

Line 8 declares the phone attribute of the message element as an NMTOKEN attribute type. The document is valid as shown; however, if the value of the phone attribute on line 15 were changed to this

```
15:      <message number="a1" from="Kathy Shepherd" phone="720 555 6382">
```

the document would no longer be valid because space characters are not permitted by an NMTOKEN declaration.

## Enumerated Attribute Types in DTDs

Enumerated attribute types describe a list of potential values for the attribute being evaluated. In order for validity to be satisfied, the attribute must have a value included on the list; anything else is considered to be invalid. Enumerated values are separated by a "pipe" character (|), which is interpreted as a logical "or" by the XML processor. Listing 4.22 shows an enumerated attribute alert on line 8, with three possible values (low, normal, and urgent) and a default value (normal) declared.

**LISTING 4.22    An Enumerated Attribute Type—message21.xml**

```
 1: <?xml version = "1.0"?>
 2: <!DOCTYPE    note      [
 3: <!ELEMENT    note      ( message+, outcome+ ) >
 4: <!ELEMENT    message   ( #PCDATA)>
 5: <!ATTLIST    message
 6:              number   ID      #REQUIRED
 7:              from        CDATA  #REQUIRED
 8:              alert    ( low | normal | urgent) "normal">
 9: <!ELEMENT    outcome  (#PCDATA)>
10: <!ATTLIST    outcome
11:              msg        IDREF  #IMPLIED>
12: <!ENTITY    today     "073001">
13:                        ]>
14: <note>
15:      <message number="a1" from="Kathy Shepherd" alert="low">
```

4

**LISTING 4.22**  continued

```
16:        &today; - Remember to buy milk on the way home from work
17:     </message>
18:     <message number="a2" from="Greg Shepherd" alert="urgent">
19:        &today; - I need some help with my homework
20:     </message>
21:     <message number="a3" from="Kristen Shepherd">
22:        &today; - Please play Scrabble with me tonight
23:     </message>
24:     <outcome msg="a1">
25:        milk was past its best before date
26:     </outcome>
27:     <outcome msg="a1">
28:        went to a different store
29:     </outcome>
30:     <outcome msg="a2">
31:        homework finished early
32:     </outcome>
33: </note>
```

**ANALYSIS**  Lines 15 and 18 declare values of low and urgent, respectively, for the alert attribute. You can imagine how an application might be designed to deal with the message elements differently based upon the value of the alert attribute. The message element beginning in line 21 will be processed by the application as though it had an alert value of normal, the default value for this attribute.

Line 8 could be changed to exclude the default value and replaced with a #IMPLIED keyword:

```
8:        alert     ( low | normal | urgent) #IMPLIED>
```

In this case, the alert attribute is not required by the application and if it is not present, no default value is assumed.

# Occurrence Indicators and Sequence Declarations in DTDs

Although they were not referred to directly, you have already learned some of the occurrence indicators and sequence declarations that are part of the DTD grammar in the examples presented today. If you have been typing along with the exercises, you have begun to familiarize yourself with their placement and syntactical relationship with other components in the DTD. You have seen, for instance, the effects of plus signs (+), asterisks (*), vertical bar or "pipe" characters (|), and commas (,) in content model descriptions. Table 4.4 shows all of the special DTD indicators for sequence and occurrence.

**TABLE 4.4**   DTD Sequence and Occurrence Indicators

| Symbol | Example | Interpretation |
|---|---|---|
| , | (a,b,c) | This sequence operator separates members of a list that requires the sequential use of all members of the list (a followed by b, followed by c). |
| \| | (a\|b\|c) | This choice operator separates members of a list that require the use of one and only one member (a or b or c). |
|  | date | The lack of a symbol indicates a required occurrence (one and only one date). |
| ? | subject? | This symbol designates an optional occurrence (zero or one subject(s)). |
| + | paragraph+ | This symbol indicates a required and repeatable occurrence (one or more paragraph(s)). |
| * | brother* | This indicates an optional and repeatable occurrence (zero or more brother(s)). |

Sequence indicators are sometimes called connectors because they serve to connect or establish a direct relationship between two or more elements. Listing 4.23 shows an XML instance with a DTD that makes use of all of the sequence and occurrence indicators.

**LISTING 4.23**   A DTD Using All of the Sequence and Occurrence Indicators—
message22.xml

```
 1: <?xml version="1.0"?>
 2: <!DOCTYPE    note          [
 3: <!ELEMENT    note          ( message, source?, outcome)+>
 4: <!ELEMENT    message       (#PCDATA)>
 5: <!ELEMENT    source        EMPTY>
 6: <!ELEMENT    outcome       (action*)>
 7: <!ELEMENT    action        (#PCDATA)>
 8: <!ATTLIST    message
 9:              number   ID    #REQUIRED
10:              from    CDATA  #REQUIRED>
11: <!ATTLIST    source
12:              delivery (phone | inperson | email) "email">
13:                       ]>
14: <note>
15:     <message number="call_01" from="Kathy Shepherd">
16:         arrived for lunch date
```

4

**LISTING 4.23** continued

```
17:      </message>
18:      <source delivery="inperson"/>
19:      <outcome>
20:          <action>went to restaurant</action>
21:          <action>drove in my car</action>
22:      </outcome>
23:      <message number="call_02" from="Kristen Shepherd">
24:      </message>
25:      <source delivery="phone"/>
26:      <outcome>
27:          <action>returned call</action>
28:      </outcome>
29:      <message number="call_03" from="Kathy Shepherd">
30:      </message>
31:      <source />
32:      <outcome>
33:          <action>reply to E-Mail</action>
34:      </outcome>
35:      <message number="call_04" from="Greg Shepherd">
36:          reminder to book fishing trip
37:      </message>
38:      <outcome>
39:      </outcome>
40: </note>
```

**ANALYSIS**  Line 3 defines the content for note to be one or more sets of message, source, and outcome elements in that order. However, the set of elements may not contain a source element. If the source element is present, there can be only one of them. In fact, there can be only one each of message, source, and outcome in each set. There must be one set in the instance, but there can be any number beyond one as well.

Line 4 indicates that message contains only parsed character data. Line 16 shows an example of the #PCDATA contained within one such message element.

Line 5 declares source to be an empty element. You can see on lines 18, 25, and 31 that the source elements are indeed empty.

On line 6, you see that the outcome element may contain any number of action elements or none at all.

The action element comprises text data, according to the #PCDATA declaration on line 7.

Line 8 begins the declaration of attributes for the message element. There are two: number and from. Line 9 declares that number is required and is an ID attribute type, meaning that each number value must be unique. Line 10 declares that the from attribute has a required value that is unparsed character data.

The declaration of the `delivery` attribute of the `source` element begins on line 11. Line 12 indicates that the valid value for each `delivery` attribute is one of `phone`, `inperson`, or `email`. If a `delivery` attribute is not coded in a `source` element, it is assumed to possess a default value of `email` by the processing application.

Lines 14 through 40 comprise a valid XML instance that satisfies all of the constraints imposed by the DTD. You can see that the `message`, `source`, and `outcome` elements are repeated throughout the document, except in the last set, where the `outcome` element is absent. This absence is permitted by means of the question mark (?) after `source` in line 3.

On lines 18 and 25 the `delivery` attributes of the corresponding `source` elements are declared as `"inperson"` and `"phone"`, respectively. No `delivery` attribute is coded in the `source` element on line 31, so the application will assume that the `delivery` attribute in this case has a default value of `email`.

# Parsing Valid XML Instances

Starting on Day 2, you parsed your well-formed documents by viewing them with the Microsoft Internet Explorer browser, version 5.0 or above (IE5). This worked because IE5 has an XML parser built in. Next you will load several of the documents you created today into IE5 and view the results. Start with the document you saved as `message19.xml` (Listing 4.20) and see if you get the result shown in Figure 4.3. You will recall that this example demonstrated an entity substitution. If you do not get the exact same result as shown in the figure, check your code a line at a time against the listing to see if you can determine and correct the problem. When you are satisfied with the results obtained by browsing `message19.xml`, try a few more of the files you have created today.

On Day 2 you saw the results of trying to parse a document that was not well-formed using IE5. In particular, IE5 produced error messages indicating the nature of the problem, such as a mismatched start and end tag, a missing angle bracket, or an improperly formed element. All of the examples you have created today that include DTDs are both well-formed and valid. Therefore, you will create an invalid XML instance on purpose to view the results in IE5. Load your saved `message15.xml` document in an editor and modify it to match the instance presented in Listing 4.24. If you didn't save `message15.xml`, copy the code in Listing 4.24 into your editor now.

**LISTING 4.24**  An Invalid XML Document—`message23.xml`

```
1: <?xml version = "1.0"?>
2: <!DOCTYPE note      [
3: <!ELEMENT note      ( message ) >
```

**LISTING 4.24** continued

```
 4: <!ELEMENT message    ( #PCDATA)>
 5: <!ATTLIST message
 6:            number    CDATA    #REQUIRED
 7:            date      CDATA    #REQUIRED
 8:            from      CDATA    #FIXED      "Kathy Shepherd">
 9:                      ]>
10: <note>
11: <!-- fixed value for attribute from s/b "Kathy Shepherd"   -->
12:    <message number="10" date="073001" from="someone else">
13:       Remember to buy milk on the way home from work
14:    </message>
15: </note>
```

The changes you will make to message15.xml include modifying the value of the from attribute in the message element on line 12 so that it no longer has the #FIXED value of "Kathy Shepherd" as dictated by the DTD. Change the value to "someone else" or a different value of your choosing. It really doesn't matter as long as it is no longer the exact value declared on line 8.

Add the comment shown on line 11 so that you can easily track the changes made, when you view the results in IE5. Once you have finished, save this new document as message23.xml and parse it with IE5. When you load your document into IE5 you should see something similar to the image depicted by Figure 4.4.

**FIGURE 4.4**

*An invalid XML document (message23. xml) rendered in IE5.*

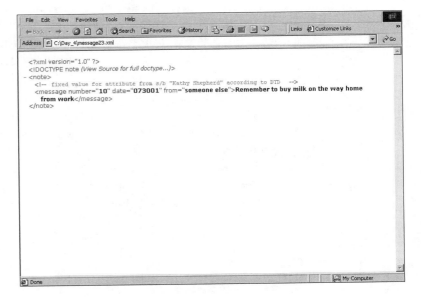

Given that you know there is a validation error in your document, is this the result that you expected? Probably not! In fact, since you know that the value for the `from` attribute of the `message` element on line 12 is invalid, didn't you expect an error message to that effect from IE5? You did not get such an error message. In fact, it appears from the result that the document you parsed is just fine. The comment you added to the instance offers the only indication that something is not quite right.

What does this tell you about the parser that is built in to IE5?

This exercise proves that IE5 does not contain a validating parser for all forms of schemata. IE does not validate XML against a DTD, but rather ignores the DTD. The version of the MSXML parser bundled with IE5 reported that your document was okay by presenting a tree depiction of your document. In fact your document is well-formed, but not valid according to the DTD that is imbedded within it. IE5 failed to validate the document against the DTD; it merely reported back that your document is well-formed.

Therefore, to check the validity using DTDs for your XML documents, you will need to acquire a validating parser. Such a parser is included as a COM object, bundled with the IE5 distribution, although it is not used by the browser. To access this validating parser you need to instantiate the parser object in an application or through simple scripting (for example, using JavaScript or VBScript). You will learn to write some scripts to access the MSXML parser on Day 12. In the meantime, you can download an HTML page containing either JavaScript or VBScript that performs the task for you. To do this, point your browser at the Microsoft Developers Network Web site (`http://msdn.microsoft.com/downloads/samples/internet/xml/xml_validator/`) and follow the instructions to download and install a copy of the XML Validator scripts. The download includes a VBScript and a JavaScript version of the XML Validator, either of which can be launched from IE5. When you point your browser at the script of your choice (`validate_js.htm` or `validate_vbs.htm`), you should see a screen like the one shown in Figure 4.5.

Before attempting to validate any of the instances you have created today, move the `validate_js.htm` or `validate_vbs.htm` script file into the same directory that you saved your work in today. This will allow you to simply type in the name of each file relying on the relative path to nearby documents, rather than having to explicitly indicate the fully qualified path to locate your files on your computer.

Once you have the validation script `.htm` file in the same directory as the XML instances you created today, parse some of them to see the results. Figure 4.6 shows the results of parsing the `message19.xml` file created in Listing 4.20. To return the level of detail shown in Figure 4.6, you will need to expand each node of the document by clicking on it. Expansion reveals child element content and text data. When the entire instance is expanded, the structure on the screen roughly corresponds to a tree structure describing the document.

**FIGURE 4.5**

*The XML Validator script from Microsoft Corporation as it appears in IE5.*

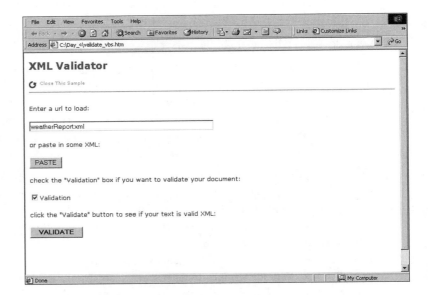

**FIGURE 4.6**

*A valid XML instance (message19.xml) successfully parsed by the Microsoft XML Validator script.*

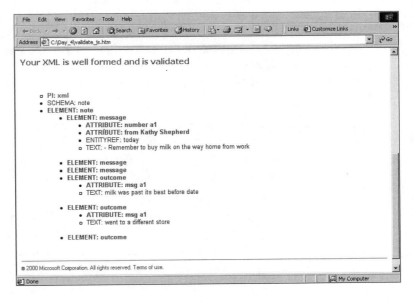

Now that you have seen the results of parsing documents that you know to be well-formed and valid, try parsing the document you created that included an error, shown in Listing 4.24 (saved as `message23.xml`). Figure 4.7 shows the result of this exercise.

**FIGURE 4.7**

*An invalid XML document (`message23.xml`) parsed by the Microsoft XML Validator script.*

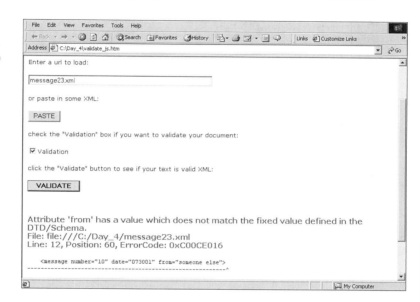

The error message produced by this validating parser indicates that the attribute `from` has a value that does not match the fixed value (`"Kathy Shepherd"`) that you declared in the DTD. You already know that this is precisely the error coded into the instance. The document remains well-formed, but is no longer valid according to the strictures enforced by the DTD.

Continue to experiment with some of the other documents you created today and break a few to learn the ways in which the parser notifies you of errors.

# Declaring External DTDs

Today you have seen how to create a number of powerful constraints using internal DTDs. Next you will learn the changes required for the document type declaration to associate an XML document with an external DTD document. The DTD can be nearly identical to any of those you created today. The major difference is that it will be saved in its own file separate from the XML instance. A validating parser that is able to negotiate the file relationship between the XML document and the DTD can ensure that the constraints imposed by the schema are satisfied. To make things simple, you will place the XML documents, DTDs, and the parser scripts in the same directory on your computer.

The document type declaration you have used so far today follows this syntax:

```
<!DOCTYPE root_element [
<!ELEMENT root_element ( content model )>
                        ]>
```

Anything within the square brackets ([...]) comprises the internal DTD subset. External DTD subsets typically reside in a separate file with a .DTD extension. The whole DTD for an instance is considered to be the combination of the internal subset and the external subset, if both exist. In other words, if you have an inline DTD as well as an external DTD document associated with the XML document instance, validity will be based on the combination of both DTD subsets.

In order to reference an external DTD, the document type declaration should be modified to include either a SYSTEM or PUBLIC keyword followed by the URL for the DTD document. The PUBLIC keyword is typically only chosen when the DTD is widely available or is in the public domain and is shared with a large number of users. PUBLIC DTDs are typically named and stored in a DTD library or repository. If you found yourself working on a particular XML project, you might turn to a repository to see if there was already a PUBLIC DTD available for you to use. SYSTEM DTDs are not typically available from these repositories. As you author your own DTDs, you will usually refer to them via the SYSTEM keyword in the document type declaration, using the following syntax:

```
<!DOCTYPE root_element SYSTEM "myrules.DTD">
```

Earlier today, you reviewed the course-listing announcement document created on Day 3. If you followed the instructions, then you saved the document, as shown in Listing 4.1, in a file called courses.xml. You will need to modify the instance to include an appropriate document type declaration for a DTD. Listing 4.25 shows courses.xml with a DOCTYPE declaration added on line 2.

**LISTING 4.25**   The courses.xml Document Modified to Include a DOCTYPE Declaration

```
1: <?xml version="1.0"?>
2: <!DOCTYPE announcement SYSTEM "courses.dtd">
3: <announcement>
4:   <distribution>For Immediate Release</distribution>
5:   <to>All Potential Students</to>
6:   <from>Devan Shepherd </from>
7:   <subject>Public Course Offerings in August</subject>
8:     <notice>ACME Training is pleased to announce the following
9:     public courses, which are offered on a monthly basis at its
```

**LISTING 4.25** continued

```
10:     headquarters.</notice>
11:     <more_info>For more information, or to register for these courses,
12:     please visit <website>http://acme-train.com/university
        </website></more_info>
13:  <courses>
14:     <course id="XML111" instructor="Bob Gonzales">
                Introduction to XML</course>
15:     <course id="XML333" instructor="Devan Shepherd">
                Advanced XML</course>
16:     <course id="XMT222" instructor="Gene Yong">
                XMetal Core Configuration</course>
17:  </courses>
18: </announcement>
```

Once you have made the necessary addition, save the file as `courses02.xml`.

In the next exercise you will create an external DTD, called `courses.dtd` as referenced in line 2, and then parse the result to show that the document is valid. Recall that Figure 4.2 shows a DTD tree depicting the business rules for this instance. Using a text editor, create a DTD like the one shown in listing 4.26 and save it as `courses.dtd`.

**4**

**LISTING 4.26** A DTD to Validate `courses02.xml`

```
 1: <!ELEMENT announcement ( distribution, to, from, subject,
                             notice, more_info, courses ) >
 2: <!ELEMENT distribution ( #PCDATA ) >
 3: <!ELEMENT to           ( #PCDATA ) >
 4: <!ELEMENT from         ( #PCDATA ) >
 5: <!ELEMENT subject      ( #PCDATA ) >
 6: <!ELEMENT notice       ( #PCDATA ) >
 7: <!ELEMENT more_info    ( #PCDATA | website )* >
 8: <!ELEMENT website      ( #PCDATA ) >
 9: <!ELEMENT courses      ( course+ ) >
10: <!ELEMENT course       ( #PCDATA ) >
11: <!ATTLIST course
12:             id          CDATA    #REQUIRED
13:             instructor  CDATA    #REQUIRED >
```

**ANALYSIS** Line 1 defines the announcement element as a container element containing distribution, to, from, subject, notice, more_info, and courses child elements. Each of these elements, in turn, is declared to contain text data (#PCDATA). Lines 12–13 declare the id and instructor attributes on the course element.

Using one of the Microsoft XML Validator scripts, parse `courses02.xml` to produce a result similar to the one shown in Figure 4.8. All nodes have been expanded in the result.

**FIGURE 4.8**

*A valid XML document (`courses02.xml`) with an external DTD (`courses.dtd`) parsed by the Microsoft XML Validator script.*

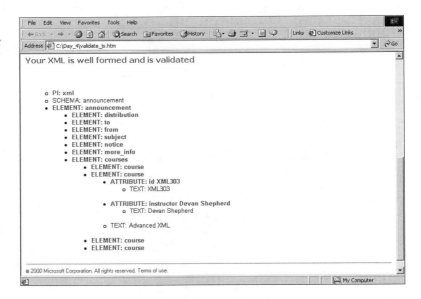

You have seen examples of internal and external DTDs. The decision of which to use is largely left to the document author. Sometimes it is advantageous to use an external DTD if that DTD defines a class of documents and can be reused multiple times. If you have collections of documents that are validated against a set of DTDs, keeping the DTDs in separate files—perhaps stored within a particular DTD directory on your server—might make sense. On the other hand, using an internal DTD, especially within a small, one-time, XML instance document, ensures that the DTD is in view if you review the document in an editor. You will need to weigh these options and decide the approach that best suits your needs.

## Summary

You have learned how to create internal and external Document Type Definition (DTD) schemata today from the ground up. You have mastered element and attribute declarations and seen many examples of increasingly complex applications of DTD strictures. You experienced the difference between validating and non-validating XML parsers and know when each may be used.

In order to complete the exercises today, you needed to learn a completely new language, one that had only a passing resemblance to XML. It shared constructs and basic grammar rules with XML, but used a completely different syntax.

On Days 5 and 6 you will use two different schema languages to validate XML documents. These will have significant advantages over DTDs. For one thing, each will use the same syntax as XML; in fact, the schema documents themselves will be XML instances. They will also introduce more sophisticated controls, including datatype validation constraints and other features not available to DTDs.

# Q&A

**Q  Where did the Document Type Definition approach originate?**

**A  DTDs** came from the SGML world, where they have been used successfully for years.

**Q  What exactly does a DTD do in XML?**

**A  A DTD** (or any XML schema, for that matter) provides a template for document markup that indicates the presence, order and placement of elements and their attributes in an XML document.

**Q  What are some differences between a document tree and a DTD tree?**

**A  A DTD** tree does not, itself, have any repetition of elements or structure. However, its strictures provide for repetition of elements in a conforming valid XML instance.

**Q  What does a document type declaration provide to an XML instance?**

**A  A document** type declaration, placed in the prolog of an XML document, associates a Document Type Definition (DTD) with the XML document. As soon as an XML processor encounters this declaration it reads the DTD and validates the XML instance on the basis of the constraints defined in the DTD.

Be careful not to confuse the terms *document type declaration* and *Document Type Definition* (DTD). They sound alike, but clearly are different.

**Q  What are some DTD keywords that can be used to define different types of element content in XML?**

**A  ANY** allows any type of element content, either data or other elements. Mixed content permits elements to contain parsed character data (text) or a combination of child elements and text. The keyword EMPTY declares that the element contains no content. Element content can be declared for container elements in the XML document.

4

**Q  What are two types of parsers used with XML?**

**A**  Validating and non-validating are two common distinctions made with regard to XML parsers. A non-validating parser is capable only of determining if an XML document is well-formed; that is, it adheres to the basic syntax rules for XML. A validating parser goes a step further and ensures that a document is not only well-formed, but that it complies to the constraints imposed by an associated schema.

## Exercise

The exercise is provided so that you can test your knowledge of what you learned today. The answer is in Appendix A, "Answers to the Questions."

Yesterday, you created a tree structure diagram and listed some of the validity rules for your Music Collection Markup Language (MCML). Based on what you have mastered today, create a DTD to validate MCML files.

# DAY 5

# The XML Data Reduced (XDR) Schema

You have learned how to create Document Type Definitions (DTDs) as a means of enforcing validity constraints or strictures for your well-formed XML document. Today you will learn about a different type of schema, the XML-Data Reduced (XDR) Schema, one of several special varieties of XML schemata. In particular, you will learn

- What an XDR schema is and how it is associated with an XML document
- The difference between DTDs and non-DTD schemata, such as the XDR approach
- How to write and interpret an XDR schema
- How to declare elements and attributes in an XDR schema
- How to use data types in XDR schemata
- Some of the real-world uses for XDR schemata and why they are significant to XML developers

# Why Are There Different Dialects of Schemata?

During Day 4, you learned to create DTDs as a means of providing validity constraints for XML documents. You, in fact, learned to create descriptive passages that served to define and document the structure, semantics, and content of your XML instances to enforce content and business rules by adding stricture and constraints that pertained to each instance. In fact, the addition of constraining rules applied via a DTD or other form of schema is one way to take an XML instance from being merely well formed to a higher level of validity wherein it conforms to business rules or satisfies a paradigm associated with the XML instance.

Further, you discovered a means of not only constraining attribute content, but also specifying default values to be used if values were not explicitly defined in the XML instance. You also learned how to declare parsed entities, which could, in turn, be referenced within documents as a means of including specified content. You discovered that validating parsers, also known as XML processors, used this documentation to enforce strictures that characterized certain business rules.

The validation process of adding constraints that help to map a document's semantics to address a business problem has enormous potential for information sharing in e-business and other forms of electronic communication. After all, if business rules for document and data structure are enforced and validated, then separate XML processors that are given a document and a DTD will agree on the validity or non-validity of the document; this will ensure that each is sending/receiving precisely what is expected for a transaction to take place. You might imagine, for instance, two applications used by business partners exchanging e-commerce data over the Internet. For the transactions exchanged in this relationship to be reliable, the rules of the business model will undoubtedly need to be rigidly enforced. By imposing rigor on the data elements at the document level by requiring validation against a schema, the applications generating and accepting transactions can be optimized for performance; the equivalent of field and record validation will be handled at the instance level.

Developers can define and agree to the structure and vocabulary of data to be exchanged over the Internet and use DTDs or other schemata as a means of enforcing those rules. Similarly, developers can use schemata as a foundation for the conversion of data among various automated systems, providing a validated mapping function from one schema or data dictionary to another. In this way, schemata offer a framework for large-scale data exchange. Applications that accept or generate the data to be exchanged must still be developed, but at least the structure of data can be established such that independent development of applications and tools is possible. This helps to preserve corporate investments in existing processing models and to immortalize valuable legacy data repositories that might not need not to be redeveloped, but instead adapted to generate or accept data in accordance with predefined structural constraints.

On Day 4, you learned that a DTD is a form of schema. The approaches you will explore today and tomorrow also constitute schemas. All of these approaches have advantages and disadvantages. DTDs are relatively good at what they were designed to do, but they suffer some serious limitations when compared with other forms of schemata. You discovered yesterday, for instance, how to employ DTDs as a means of ensuring document-structure conformity. However, doing so required that you learn a completely different language that was not expressed in XML syntax. This offers a serious disadvantage to those learning these technologies for the first time. Therefore, one advantage of the schema approach you will explore today and the one you will learn tomorrow is that you already know much of the basic syntax and structural rules because these involve the creation of well-formed XML. In other words, the schema languages you will learn today and on Day 6 are expressed in XML syntax.

**Note**

Both XML and DTDs can be described using an Extended Backus-Naur Form (EBNF) grammar to explain their respective syntax rules, but each is expressed in a different dialect or vocabulary. DTDs use the EBNF grammar, whereas non-DTD XML schemata use an XML syntax (including elements and attributes, opening and closing tags, and so on), making them XML documents in their own right.

EBNF grammar was developed by scientists in the late 1960s to rigorously express the syntax rules for computer languages and other precise language structures. Nicklaus Wirth, the developer of the Pascal and Modula 2 languages, popularized the use of EBNF. By way of example, the following simple statement expressed in EBNF summarizes XML syntax.

```
[1] document ::= prolog element Misc*
```

This single statement can be interpreted to mean "An XML document must include a prolog, followed by an element, followed by zero or more miscellaneous elements."

5

We have discussed one of the most significant shortcomings of the DTD approach, although others exist. In particular, some of the problems with DTDs include the following:

- As you have seen already, DTDs are not XML instances; therefore, they require the developer to learn a completely different language that uses a fairly complex and symbolic syntax.

- In addition, DTDs are not as easily created, maintained, or validated using XML editors and utilities; however, special tools are available for the creation of DTDs.

- Furthermore, DTDs do not provide much control over data types beyond simple text or document data types, which presents significant problems for validity enforcement in applications that rely on other forms of data, such as financial transactions, date transactions, scientific data exchange, and so on.

- Because DTDs are not XML instances, they may not be as easily extended, searched, or transformed into other markup languages—such as HTML or XHTML—as other XML documents.

- DTDs do not provide support for XML namespaces that allow you to mix elements from different document structures in your document. (You will learn about namespaces on Day 8.)

- With regard to the automated processing of XML documents, more rigorous declaration of validity constraints is required than is possible with DTDs alone.

For all of these reasons, an alternative to the DTD, which may be expressed in XML syntax, is desirable. Standardizing such an alternative is one of the aims of the W3C XML Schema Working Group. On May 2, 2001, the W3C formalized a final standard known as the XML Schema Definition (XSD) Language, which you will have an opportunity to explore in more detail on Day 6. This Working Group had, as a task, the responsibility of coalescing several submissions that were offered by various interest groups and commercial vendors. XDR, the subject of today's lesson, is based on one such submission to the W3C: XML-Data. In the interest of clarity, XML-Data is the full name of the Microsoft schema language, and XML-Data Reduced (XDR) is a subset of the full recommendation. Although the W3C has formalized XSD, XDR continues to be used by a large number of applications. Many products—not just those coming from Microsoft—offer support for XDR. You might find it useful to become familiar with DTD, XDR, and XSD syntax. Tools, such as XML-Spy (http://www.xmlspy.com), can take a schema written in one dialect and convert it into another, using a transliteration approach. This conversion can be a useful timesaver; however, you must still evaluate the post-conversion result to ensure that data types and other specifics were dealt with appropriately.

The Working Group considered the following submissions:

- **DTDs**: Document Type Definitions originated along with SGML and have carried over for use by XML. The XML specification includes significant reference to DTDs.

- **XML-Data / XML-Data Reduced**: Microsoft and its business partners submitted a proposal to the W3C for XML-Data, in January 1998, before the XML 1.0 standard was even completed. One of the strengths of this approach is its rich collection of data types. Complete support for XML-Data is built into Microsoft's XML parsers.

- **Schema for Object-Oriented XML (SOX)**: SOX was developed by VEO Systems, which was later acquired by CommerceOne. SOX (submitted to the W3C in September, 1998) has gone through several versions, with version 2 being the latest offering. One strength of SOX is its easy-to-use functionality for XML structure inheritance.

- **Document Content Description (DCD)**: Microsoft and IBM collaborated on the creation of DCD (submitted to the W3C in August, 1998), which borrows heavily from concepts in XML-Data and a syntax known as Resource Description Framework (RDF).

- **Document Description Markup Language (DDML)**: Formerly known as Xschema, this approach was developed by members of the XML-dev mailing list intended to encompass a subset of DTD functionality expressed in XML syntax. Work on DDML has declined because of the creation of the W3C Schema Working Group. Nonetheless, in January 1999, DDML was submitted to the Working Group for consideration.

Because the W3C created what effectively might be considered a best-practices solution based on the submissions it received, it is important to understand where XSD came from. The earlier list provides an outline of the approaches and players that have collaborated toward an ultimate solution. XSD is meant to be that final solution. However, a number of solutions are being delivered that use other schema languages. The XML-Data Reduced language, for instance is integral to BizTalk, a leading technology used for e-commerce, e-business, e-procurement, supply chain management, and so on.

5

You might wonder whether it is important to learn more than one schema language, or whether you should choose one over another. If the XSD language were a finalized standard in e-business with years of implementation behind it, then perhaps it would be the only language you might need to know. This is far from reality at this stage. Support for XSD is still somewhat limited. Consequently, many legacy systems have been built using DTD and XDR schemata, or other approaches. Microsoft has committed to supporting both its own XDR schema language and XSD, but the fact remains that the pioneers of e-commerce, business users, government, and educational solution providers have already invested billions of dollars in delivery of solutions that rely on DTDs, XDR schemata, and various other standards. It will take some time before the world is able to truly standardize on a single approach to enforcing validity constraints on XML documents. You are well advised to have at least a general knowledge of the structure of several schemata.

**Tip**

If you invest in learning just one schema language thoroughly, then tools can offer assistance in conversion to other schemata. Commercial products include XML Authority and XML Spy. In addition, vendors sometimes offer transformation utilities. Microsoft has a freely available program to convert an XDR schema into an XSD schema. Be aware, however, that translation of schemata from one dialect to another is prone to error. As with any auto-mated code-generation process, you might still need to extensively rework the result of a conversion routine to get the desired results.

The W3C Schema Working Group produced a requirements document for the XML Schema Definition (XSD) in early 1999, and the specification for XSD is now a Recommendation. You will understand the differences between XDR and XSD after working through the material in today's and tomorrow's exercises.

# XML-Data Reduced (XDR) in Detail

The XML-Data Reduced (XDR) dialect is a subset of the full XML-Data specification submitted by Microsoft to the W3C. On Day 4, you downloaded and used a validation script that instantiated the Microsoft XML Parser (MSXML). The schema implementation in that parser is based on the XML-Data Reduced language specification, although the parser also validates DTDs and XSD schemata. Although MSXML is fairly complete, it has some limitations, including a lack of support for inheritance or other object-oriented design features. These issues will be discussed in more detail tomorrow. Furthermore, although considerable support exists for a variety of schema languages in many parsers that ship from SUN, Apache, IBM, and others, you might want to ensure that no hardware or operating system platform issues arise from your choice of schema language. Luckily, as discussed earlier, parsers and validation options are available for almost every platform and operating system.

**Tip**

To use XDR to validate an XML document, a parser that understands XML-Data Reduced is required. The Microsoft MSXML parser is the best choice currently available. As of this writing, the latest version of the MSXML parser is version 4, which has support for XSD as well as XDR.

Like DTDs, XDR schemata define the elements that can appear in an XML instance and any attributes that can be associated with specified elements. For validity to be satisfied, each element in an instance must be declared in a corresponding schema. The absence of an element in a schema predetermines its absence in a valid, conforming, XML instance.

The relationships among elements are also defined in an XDR schema; therefore, all child elements contained by specified elements are declared and further defined with regard to their own content. This includes the sequence in which child elements can appear along with the acceptable number of child elements.

The schema determines whether an element is empty or contains text data, other elements, or some combination of text and other elements. The schema might also define default values for attributes.

# XDR Element and Attribute Declarations

You will begin a study of XDR with a look at how XDR enforces constraints on the elements and attributes in your XML document. These constraints are encoded using elements and attributes that belong to the XDR dialect. This can be confusing. An element or attribute in one language (XDR) is used to define the business rules that add stricture to another language—your markup language.

XDR schemata are XML instances, and as such, they are composed of XML elements and attributes. The XDR language comprises certain predefined XML elements and attributes in accordance with the schema that validates all XDR schema instances. In other words, because XDR schemata are well-formed and valid XML documents, they must comply with a set of rules established by a schema for the schema language. Nonetheless, XDR schemata are extensible, and you'll learn more about that later today.

Because XDR schemata are validated against a schema, certain rules or constraints are placed on their construction. For instance, the root element of an XDR schema is always the Schema element, and it always contains an xmlns attribute specifying the default namespace for the Schema element and the elements it contains.

**Note**

> You have encountered some mention of namespaces on several occasions and might be wondering what they are. You will explore them in detail on Day 8, but this book will refer to them many times before then. Briefly, a namespace is a means of identifying or qualifying an element or attribute as belonging to a prescribed set. The elements and attributes in a particular schema language are bound to the set described for that schema language.

This means that you will typically write an XML instance document that conforms to a schema document that, coincidentally, must conform to yet another schema. Luckily, you only need to be concerned with two out of three of these documents: your XML document and the schema to validate that document. Today, you will explore some of the syntax and usage of the XML-Data Reduced schema language through an introduction to that language. You will get a chance to create several simple XDR schemata and validate them using an MSXML parser. The objective is for you to be able to create simple schemata, understand some of the syntax of typical elements and attributes in XDR, and know where to go should you need more information that is beyond today's scope.

## `ElementType` Declarations

Consider the simple XML document depicted by Listing 5.1. You might recall that this document was first shown on Day 4 and modified along with the concepts you learned about DTDs. You will follow the same learning path today by using a variety of XDR schemata to validate the document as it evolves. Create the document in Listing 5.1 using a text editor and save it as `message01.xml`.

**LISTING 5.1**    A Simple XML Document That References an XDR Schema—`message01.xml`

```
1: <?xml version="1.0"?>
2: <note xmlns = "x-schema:message01.xdr">Remember to buy milk on the way
   home from work</note>
```

**Note**    If you created your XML document using an editor that validates as you go, then this document will be invalid because the XDR file does not yet exist; you will create it next. If you are just using a simple text editor, this will not be an issue.

The root element of the `message01.xml` document includes an `xmlns` attribute with a value of `"x-schema:message01.xdr"`. This tells a validating XML processor that the schema associated with the default namespace for this XML document is in a file called `message01.xdr`. At the time of this writing, the MSXML parser suite available from Microsoft was the only viable XDR parser available.

You will create an XDR schema for this document that includes a `Schema` root element and an `ElementType` element to constrain the `note` element in your XML instance.

The `Schema` root element in an XDR schema contains the elements and attributes that correspond to all the constraint rules for an XML document instance. The definitions in an XML schema are contained within the top-level `Schema` element. The `Schema` element definition must come from the namespace `xmlns="urn:schemas-microsoft-com:xml-data"`. The namespace declaration is an XML-processing instruction.

The `Schema` element in an XML schema document should also contain namespace declarations for other schemas, such as the namespace that defines the built-in data types for XML Schema. Data types are used to constrain data strings to predefined syntax sets, such as dates, numeric values, floating-point numbers, and so on. The data type namespace for an XDR schema is `xmlns:dt="urn:schemas-microsoft-com:datatypes"`.

Therefore, the `Schema` root element of an XDR schema almost always looks like this:

```
<Schema name="myschema" xmlns="urn:schemas-microsoft-com:xml-data"
                         xmlns:dt="urn:schemas-microsoft-com:datatypes">
 <!-- all other declarations are contained within the root element -->
</Schema>
```

The `ElementType`, `AttributeType`, `Entity`, and `Notation` element types are used to declare the major components of the structure of conforming XML document instances. In other words, the `ElementType` element, for example, is the predefined element in XDR that is used to define the constraints pertaining to an element in the corresponding XML instance.

The `ElementType` Element in an XDR Schema has the following syntax:

```
<ElementType
  content="{empty | textOnly | eltOnly | mixed}"
  dt:type="datatype"
  model="{open | closed}"
  name="idref"
  order="{one | seq | many}">
```

Each of the attributes has special meaning with regard to the element being described. The `content` attribute is an indicator of whether the content of the element being declared must be empty, contain only text data, only other elements, or can have a mixed content model. The `dt:type` attribute declares the data type for the element. The valid data types—date, number, time, and so on—will be covered in more detail later today. The `model` attribute is an indicator of whether the content can include only what is defined in the content model or can contain content not specified in the model. When the model is defined as open, the element can include additional elements or attributes not declared explicitly in the content model. When the model is defined as closed, the element cannot include elements and cannot include mixed content not specified in the content model. The DTD uses a closed model. The `name` attribute is required to identify the element being defined. Note that if this element type is declared as a child, then the name resides in an `element` element. You'll see examples of that shortly. The `order` attribute establishes the order of child elements. The value `one` permits only one element of a set of elements to be included, `seq` requires the elements to appear in a specified sequential order, and `many` permits elements to appear, or not appear, in any order. These attributes are summarized in Table 5.1.

5

**Note**

In an XDR schema, when the model is defined as open, the element being defined can include additional elements or attributes not declared explicitly in the content model. When the model is defined as closed, the element cannot include elements or mixed content not specified in the content model.

Listing 5.2 shows the `message01.xdr` schema. Using your text editor, create the document shown and save it as `message01.xdr`. You can follow through the line-by-line analysis provided.

**LISTING 5.2**   An XDR Schema to Validate the message01.xml Document—Saved As
`message01.xdr`

```
1: <?xml version="1.0"?>
2: <Schema
3:     name="message01"
4:     xmlns="urn:schemas-microsoft-com:xml-data"
5:     xmlns:dt="urn:schemas-microsoft-com:datatypes">
6:     <ElementType name="note" model="closed" content="textOnly"
       dt:type="string"/>
7: </Schema>
```

**ANALYSIS**   Review the document in Listing 5.2 a line at a time. Because an XDR schema is an XML instance, line 1 declares it as such. The start tag for the `Schema` root element of the XDR schema begins on line 2. The start tag, in this case, includes three attributes. The `name` attribute on line 3 serves to document the name that you gave this particular schema. This is an optional attribute; however, including it constitutes a good programming practice.

On line 4, the default namespace for the XDR schema is defined with a URI (`"urn:schemas-microsoft-com:xml-data"`), which identifies to the MSXML validating parser that the XML-Data Reduced language is being used. This is the URI that is always used by XDR schema. The default namespace will be assigned for all elements contained within the root element `Schema` unless a proxy to another namespace otherwise declares them (see Day 8 for more on namespaces). An XML namespace *Uniform Resource Identifier* (URI) serves merely as a unique label for the subject namespace that it identifies. This URI is nothing more than a series of characters used to differentiate names. As you know, URL is an abbreviation for Universal Resource Locator. A URL serves as a global address to a remote resource or document. Namespace declarations can contain a URI string that appears to be a URL because it looks like a Web address;

however, this is just a means of ensuring that the namespace is unique. You will learn more about this on Day 8. URIs can also contain Universal Resource Names URNs. URNs are names that are also meant to be unique; however, they do not typically resemble URLs.

> **Tip**
>
> A URI used in an XML namespace is nothing more than a label, or a string of characters, which uniquely identifies the namespace. It makes no difference what, if anything, a URI points to; a URI merely serves as a unique moniker for the collection of element type names and attribute names it characterizes.

Line 5, the last line in the start tag of the `Schema` root element, declares a namespace for data types that are declared in this schema. This instructs the parser to validate any element throughout the rest of the XDR schema that includes a `dt:type` attribute on the basis of data type rules established by Microsoft. You'll learn more about data types today.

Line 6 provides the declaration for the only element in the XML instance `message01.xml`, the `note` element.

```
<ElementType name="note" model="closed" content="textOnly" dt:type="string"/>
```

Line 6 also includes attributes that further describe the `note` element. The `name` attribute provides the name of the element in the XML instance that is being declared. In this case, the `name` attribute designates the `note` element. Attribute `model` has a `closed` value, indicating that a conforming XML document will only contain elements declared in this particular schema. In other words, if the XML instance included elements that were not declared in this schema, the document would be considered invalid. The `content` attribute indicates that the `note` element contains only text data, which is the meaning of the value `textOnly`. You will learn about other values for this attribute later today. The `type` attribute belongs to the data type namespace as indicated by the `dt` proxy. In this case, the valid data type for the `note` element is a `string`. This corresponds to a `CDATA` type in a DTD.

To prove that the XML instance, `message01.xml`, is well formed and valid, use the script you downloaded yesterday. Figure 5.1 depicts the expected results of this test.

The `ElementType` element permits the declaration of several pre-defined attributes. These are summarized in Table 5.1.

**Figure 5.1**

*Results expected from the MSXML parser script applied to message01.xml.*

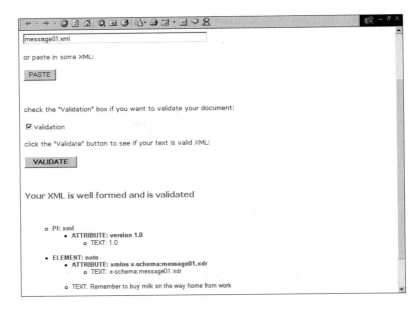

**Table 5.1**  Predefined Attributes for the `ElementType` Element

| Attribute Name | Description |
| --- | --- |
| name | This required element declares the element's name. |
| content | This attribute describes the element's content. The valid values for this attribute include `empty`, designating an empty element; `eltOnly`, indicating that the element is a container for other elements only; `textOnly`, designating text-only content; and `mixed`, indicating that the element can have elements or text. This is the default for `content`. |
| dt:type | This attribute defines the data type of the element. The dt: provides a proxy to the declared namespace for the data type URI. |
| model | This attribute has values of open or closed, indicating whether elements not defined within the XDR schema are permitted in the XML instance. |
| order | This attribute declares the order of child elements in the conforming XML instance. The valid values for the `order` attribute include `one`, meaning that exactly one child element is expected; `many`, indicating that elements can appear in any order and quantity; and `seq`, declaring that child elements must only be in the order presented in the XDR schema. |

## Nested `ElementType` Declarations

As with DTDs, nested elements indicated in an XDR schema must be declared and defined. In Listing 5.3, the `message01.xml` document is modified to include a nested element, `message`, and a child of `note`, the root element. Using your preferred text editor, create a document (or modify one of your existing documents) to create an XML instance that corresponds to the code in Listing 5.3.

**LISTING 5.3**  Adding a Nested Element—`message02.xml`

```
1: <?xml version = "1.0"?>
2: <note xmlns = "x-schema:message02.xdr">
3:     <message>Remember to buy milk on the way home from work</message>
4: </note>
```

Listing 5.4 shows an XDR schema to validate `message02.xml`. Create this XDR schema and save it as `message02.xdr`.

**LISTING 5.4**  An XDR Schema for the `message02.xml` Document— `message02.xdr`

```
 1: <?xml version="1.0"?>
 2: <Schema
 3:     name="Untitled-schema"
 4:     xmlns="urn:schemas-microsoft-com:xml-data"
 5:     xmlns:dt="urn:schemas-microsoft-com:datatypes">
 6:     <ElementType name="note" model="closed" content="eltOnly">
 7:             <element type="message"/>
 8:     </ElementType>
 9:     <ElementType name="message" model="closed" content="textOnly"
        dt:type="string"/>
10: </Schema>
```

**ANALYSIS**  Lines 1–5 are almost the same in this XDR schema as they were in `message01.xdr`. Line 3, however, refers to the name of this schema as `"Untitled-schema"`. The name is optional.

Lines 6–8

```
<ElementType name="note" model="closed" content="eltOnly">
        <element type="message"/>
</ElementType>
```

indicate that the `note` element contains only other elements (`content="eltOnly"`). The `message` element is declared as a child of the `note` element.

Line 9 defines the `message` element as containing a `string` of `textOnly` content. The `textOnly` value refers to the content of the element and not the datatype of that element. This distinction is sometimes confusing because the term *textOnly* implies a qualification on the type of data that comprises the string. In fact, it just means that the element contains data (of any type) and not other elements.

Note that the `message` element appears twice in this schema, once on line 7, where it is declared as a child of the `note` element, and again on line 9, where it is fully defined. When you created DTDs yesterday, you dealt with child elements in a similar fashion, first declaring them and then defining them.

The `element` element is a valid child element of the `ElementType` element in an XDR schema. Child elements can be included in an `ElementType` element. These are summarized in Table 5.2.

**TABLE 5.2**   Child Elements of the `ElementType` Element

| Element Name | Description |
| --- | --- |
| element | Declares a child element |
| description | Provides a description of the `ElementType` |
| datatype | Defines the data type for the `ElementType` element |
| group | Describes the order and frequency of elements that are related |
| AttributeType | Defines an attribute |
| attribute | Specifies the details of an `AttributeType` for an element |

## Empty Elements

You will recall from your reading over the past several days that empty elements in an XML instance are those that do not contain data or other elements. Empty elements might still have attributes, but will contain nothing between a start tag and an end tag of an empty element. This does not mean that empty elements do not convey information. In fact, many have attributes that carry detail; others serve as placeholders. In either case, they have information value without having content. As a consequence of the fact that nothing resides between the two tags, XML permits a short-form syntax for an empty element that looks like this:

```
<element_name />
```

The end tag is eliminated and the terminating slash character is incorporated into the start tag of the element.

Building on your `message02.xml` file, next you'll add an empty `number` element to the instance. Then you'll see how to encode a constraint for that element in an XDR schema.

Listing 5.5 shows an XML instance that contains an empty `number` element on line 3.

**LISTING 5.5**   An XML Document with an Empty Element—`message03.xml`

```
1: <?xml version = "1.0"?>
2: <note xmlns="x-schema:message03.xdr">
3:     <number />
4:     <message>Remember to buy milk on the way home from work</message>
5: </note>
```

You can see that the instance is still quite simple. Although it might seem that the addition of an empty `number` element doesn't add much value, you will have a chance to modify this instance later and make the number an attribute of the message element rather than an element. When you are creating XML documents and schemata, it is often quite difficult to decide whether a particular data object should be encoded as an element or an attribute. You considered this on Day 2 when you created well-formed document instances. No definitive rules dictate when a value should be an element versus an attribute. This decision is largely up to you as the document author. A few things you might consider revolve around the utility of elements and attributes in markup. For instance, elements typically carry information that is valuable as data, whereas attributes often carry adjectival information—such as metadata—which serves to qualify elements in the same way that an adjective qualifies a noun. Elements can have child elements, whereas attributes cannot.

For now, you will encode `number` as an empty element to show the syntax for that form of constraint in XDR. Later, attributes will be added to qualify the element.

To constrain the `number` element to an empty content model in the XDR schema, you'll need to declare the element empty by using the `content="empty"` attribute on the `ElementType` element for that declaration. Recall that `empty` is one of the available values for the `content` attribute. The syntax for the new declaration and definition will include an `element` element that must be added to the `note` `ElementType` element to indicate that the `number` element is contained by the root element. The syntax looks like this:

```
<element type="number"/>
```

Then a new `ElementType` element must be added to declare the new element empty. It looks like this:

```
<ElementType name="number" model="closed" content="empty"/>
```

**5**

The complete XDR schema depicted by Listing 5.6 now validates the `message03.xml` document. Create this schema and save it as `message03.xdr` in the same subdirectory as the XML instance document. You can then validate the document or any of the remaining examples today by loading the XML document into the XML Validator as described earlier.

**LISTING 5.6**   An XDR Schema to Validate an Instance with an Empty Element—
`message03.xdr`

```
 1: <?xml version="1.0"?>
 2: <Schema
 3:     name="Untitled-schema"
 4:     xmlns="urn:schemas-microsoft-com:xml-data"
 5:     xmlns:dt="urn:schemas-microsoft-com:datatypes">
 6:     <ElementType name="note" model="closed" content="eltOnly" order="seq">
 7:         <element type="number"/>
 8:         <element type="message"/>
 9:     </ElementType>
10:     <ElementType name="number" model="closed" content="empty"/>
11:     <ElementType name="message" model="closed" content="textOnly"
        dt:type="string"/>
12: </Schema>
```

ANALYSIS  Lines 6–9 declare the `note` element, which contains elements only, particularly `number`, followed sequentially by `message`. The `order` attribute of the `note` element has a value of `seq`, indicating the sequential ordering of the child elements. As noted earlier today, the `order` attribute can only have values of `one`, `seq`, or `many`.

# Validating Attributes in an XML Instance with XDR

In the previous example, you declared the message number to be an empty element. This gave you a great opportunity to experience the syntax for empty element declaration in XDR, but the value of that encoding is questionable in the context of the messaging scenario that is being used. In the next example, you'll remove the empty `number` element and replace it with a `number` attribute on the `message` element. In this case, you are using good programming practices to change an element that really didn't hold much data value on its own into an attribute that might better serve to qualify the related element. This is a good example of the way in which an attribute is somewhat analogous to an adjective modifying a noun (in this case, an element). You will find as you develop XML solutions, this trial-and-error approach is to be expected even if you have done a good job of analysis prior to coding. Don't be put off by having to change your mind about whether some construct is best encoded as an element or an attribute.

Listing 5.7 shows the message XML instance with an attribute added on the `message` element. Make the necessary modifications to your document and save the result as `message04.xml`.

**LISTING 5.7**   An Attribute Added to the Message Document—`message04.xml`

```
1: <?xml version="1.0"?>
2: <note xmlns="x-schema:message04.xdr">
3:     <message number="10">
4:       Remember to buy milk on the way home from work
5:     </message>
6: </note>
```

Because you have added an attribute to the XML instance, you will need to encode a constraint for that attribute in the XDR schema. Attributes are declared in XDR schemata using the `AttributeType` element. The syntax for an `AttributeType` element is as follows:

```
<AttributeType
    default="default-value"
    dt:type="primitive-type"
    dt:values="enumerated-values"
    name="idref"
    required="{yes | no}">
```

The attributes of the `AttributeType` element are summarized in Table 5.3.

**5**

**TABLE 5.3**   Attributes of the `AttributeType` Element

| Attribute | Description |
| --- | --- |
| default | Default value for the attribute. The default value must be legal for that attribute instance. For example, when the attribute is an enumerated type, the default value must appear in the values list. |
| dt:type | Specifies the data type for this attribute type. An attribute can take one of the following types: `entity`, `entities`, `enumeration`, `id`, `idref`, `idrefs`, `nmtoken`, `nmtokens`, `notation`, or `string`. When the type "enumeration" is selected, the `dt:values` attribute should also be supplied, listing the allowed values. Later today you will learn more about XDR data types. |
| dt:values | When `dt:type` is set to "enumeration," this attribute lists the possible values. |

**TABLE 5.3**  continued

| Attribute | Description |
| --- | --- |
| name | Name of the attribute type. This attribute is required. References to this attribute type within an ElementType definition are made in the schema with the attribute element. The name supplied here corresponds to the type attribute of the attribute element. |
| required | Indicator of whether the attribute must be present on the element. |

In your XML instance, the attribute is on the message element. Therefore, the ElementType element for the note element will contain an AttributeType element and an attribute element to declare and define the new attribute. These always occur in pairs, just as the declarations and definitions were paired in the DTD syntax. You have seen the syntax for the AttributeType element. Now take a look at the attribute element.

The attribute element refers to a declared attribute type that appears within the scope of the named ElementType element. The syntax for this element is as follows:

```
<attribute
  default="default-value"
  type="attribute-type"
  [required="{yes | no}"]>
```

**Tip**

> The valid attributes of the attribute element are quite similar to those of the AttributeType element, as you can see by comparing Tables 5.3 and 5.4.

Table 5.4 summarizes the valid attributes of the attribute element in XDR.

**TABLE 5.4**  Attributes of the attribute Element in XDR

| Attribute | Description |
| --- | --- |
| default | Default value for the attribute. This specified default takes precedence over any default provided on the AttributeType element to which it refers. |
| type | Name of an AttributeType defined in this schema (or another schema indicated by the specified namespace). The supplied value must correspond to the name attribute on the AttributeType element. The type can include a namespace prefix. |

**TABLE 5.4**  continued

| Attribute | Description |
|---|---|
| required | Indicator of whether the attribute must be present on the element. Optional if the required attribute is present on the referenced `AttributeType`. |

Next, modify the `message03.xdr` schema to account for the removal of the empty element and the addition of the `number` attribute on the `message` element. Start by removing lines 7 and 10 (the declarations and definitions for the empty element.) The lines you are eliminating look like this:

```
7:              <element type="number"/>
...
10:      <ElementType name="number" model="closed" content="empty"/>
```

Now you will need to modify the `message ElementType` element. It was formerly empty, but now it will contain `AttributeType` and `attribute` elements to declare and define the new `number` attribute. It should look like this:

```
<ElementType name="message" model="closed" content="textOnly"
dt:type="string">
    <AttributeType name="number" dt:type="number" required="yes"/>
    <attribute type="number"/>
</ElementType>
```

Listing 5.8 shows the completed XDR schema to validate the `message04.xml` file.

**LISTING 5.8**  Declaring and Defining Attributes in XDR Schemata—`message04.xdr`

```
1: <?xml version="1.0" encoding="UTF-8"?>
2: <Schema
3:      name="Untitled-schema"
4:      xmlns="urn:schemas-microsoft-com:xml-data"
5:      xmlns:dt="urn:schemas-microsoft-com:datatypes">
6:      <ElementType name="note" model="closed" content="eltOnly">
7:              <element type="message"/>
8:      </ElementType>
9:      <ElementType name="message" model="closed" content="textOnly"
        dt:type="string">
10:             <AttributeType name="number" dt:type="number" required="yes"/>
11:             <attribute type="number"/>
12:      </ElementType>
13: </Schema>
```

5

**ANALYSIS** Lines 10–11 declare and define the attribute number on the message element. The AttributeType element, line 10, ensures that the value of the number attribute is of the data type "number", which specifies a number with no limit on the digits. Many other kinds of numbers can be specified, as you will learn today. The number attribute is also required, according to the value "yes" on the required attribute in line 10.

# Data Types in XDR

In an XDR schema, you can specify the data types of elements and attributes. Many possibilities exist for validated data types in XDR, which ideally suits it to use in a wide variety of data applications. Data types specify formatting of data and enable XML processors and applications to verify the data type as a function of constraint validation. For instance, ensuring a datum is a date value, integer, or text string can be done using data type constraints. For data types to be specified in an XDR schema, the Microsoft data type namespace

```
xmlns:dt="urn:schemas-microsoft-com:datatypes">
```

must be included in the declaration of the Schema root element.

By convention, the dt: prefix is assigned to this namespace and serves as a proxy throughout the XDR schema to identify data type components. Table 5.6 lists the data types validated by XDR schemata. This list of data types supported by XDR and additional information on data type validation can be found at http://msdn.microsoft.com/library/psdk/xmlsdk/xmlp11o3.htm.

**TABLE 5.5**   Data Types for XDR Schema

| Data Type | Description |
| --- | --- |
| bin.base64 | MIME-style Base64 encoded binary BLOB. |
| bin.hex | Hexadecimal digits representing octets. |
| boolean | 0 or 1, where 0 == "false" and 1 == "true". |
| char | String, one character long. |
| date | Date in a subset ISO 8601 format, without the time data, for example, "1994-11-05". The date is not validated. (For example, 2-31-99 will pass validation.) |
| dateTime | Date in a subset of ISO 8601 format, with optional time and no optional zone. Fractional seconds can be as precise as nanoseconds, for example, "1988-04-07T18:39:09". |
| dateTime.tz | Date in a subset ISO 8601 format, with optional time and optional zone. Fractional seconds can be as precise as nanoseconds, for example, "1988-04-07T18:39:09-08:00". |

**TABLE 5.5**  continued

| Data Type | Description |
| --- | --- |
| fixed.14.4 | Same as "number" but no more than 14 digits to the left of the decimal point, and no more than 4 to the right. |
| float | Real number with no limit on digits; can potentially have a leading sign, fractional digits, and, optionally, an exponent. Punctuation as in U.S. English. Values range from 1.7976931348623157E+308 to 2.2250738585072014E-308. |
| int | Number with optional sign, no fractions, and no exponent. |
| number | Number with no limit on digits; can potentially have a leading sign, fractional digits, and, optionally, an exponent. Punctuation as in U.S. English. (Values have the same range as the most significant number, R8, 1.7976931348623157E+308 to 2.2250738585072014E-308.) |
| time | Time in a subset ISO 8601 format, with no date and no time zone, for example, "08:15:27". |
| time.tz | Time in a subset ISO 8601 format, with no date but optional time zone, for example, "08:1527-05:00". |
| i1 | Integer represented in one byte. A number with optional sign, no fractions, no exponent, for example, "1, 127, -128". |
| i2 | Integer represented in one word. A number with optional sign, no fractions, no exponent, for example, "1, 703, -32768". |
| i4 | Integer represented in four bytes. A number with optional sign, no fractions, no exponent, for example, "1, 703, -32768, 148343, -1000000000". |
| i8 | Integer represented in eight bytes. A number with optional sign, no fractions, no exponent, and 19-digit precision. Range is from -9,223,372,036,854,775,808 to 9,223,372,036,854,775,807 |
| r4 | Real number with seven-digit precision; can potentially have a leading sign, fractional digits, and, optionally, an exponent. Punctuation as in U.S. English. Values range from 3.40282347E+38F to 1.17549435E-38F. |
| r8 | Same as "float." Real number with 15-digit precision; can potentially have a leading sign, fractional digits, and, optionally, an exponent. Punctuation as in U.S. English. Values range from 1.7976931348623157E+308 to 2.2250738585072014E-308. |
| ui1 | Unsigned integer. A number, unsigned, no fractions, no exponent, for example, "1, 255". |
| ui2 | Unsigned integer, two bytes. A number, unsigned, no fractions, no exponent, for example, "1, 255, 65535". |

5

**TABLE 5.5**  continued

| Data Type | Description |
| --- | --- |
| ui4 | Unsigned integer, four bytes. A number, unsigned, no fractions, no exponent, for example, "1, 703, 3000000000". |
| ui8 | Unsigned integer, eight bytes. A number, unsigned, no fractions, no exponent. Range is 0 to 18,446,744,073,709,551,615. |
| uri | Universal Resource Identifier (URI), for example, "urn:schemas-microsoft-com:Office9". |
| uuid | Hexadecimal digits representing octets, optional embedded hyphens that are ignored, for example, "333C7BC4-460F-11D0-BC04-0080C7055A83". |

## A Data Type Example

In the message instance, you placed an attribute on the message element called number. You encoded this attribute as a dt:type="number", which meant that any numeric value would satisfy the constraint. Suppose that you wanted to ensure that the value provided for this number were an integer? You would need to modify the data type attribute accordingly. Based on the information provided in Table 5.5, the new attribute would look like this:

```
dt:type="int"
```

In the next example, you'll make that change plus a few more to experience a variety of data type validation options available to XDR. To ensure that your own code validates in the same fashion as the example, be careful to format the attribute values in the message04.xml file exactly like those shown here.

Start by modifying your message03.xml document, adding a date and from attribute on the message element start tag. The date should be in the form CCYY-MM-DD, where CC=century, YY=year, MM=month and DD=day. The value for the from attribute should be a string. Here is one possibility for these changes:

```
<message number="10" date="2001-07-29" from="Kathy Shepherd">
```

You can choose different numbers, dates, and text strings, but ensure that they follow the syntax shown precisely so the data validation will work properly. When you have completed all of the changes to your own XML document, save it as message05.xml and then you can begin to modify the XDR document for purposes of validation. Listing 5.9 shows the complete XML document with the new attributes included.

**LISTING 5.9**  New Attributes—`message05.xml`

```
1: <?xml version="1.0"?>
2: <note xmlns="x-schema:message05.xdr">
3:     <message number="10" date="2001-07-29" from="Kathy Shepherd">
4:        Remember to buy milk on the way home from work
5:     </message>
6: </note>
```

The XDR schema will need to validate the `number` attribute value as an *integer*, the value for the `date` attribute as a *date*, and the value associated with the `from` attribute as a *string*. Don't forget to also declare a content type for the `message` element, which contains only text as a *string*. Assume that each of these attributes is required. You now have all of the information that you need to encode the declarations and definitions for the new attributes and ensure that they are validated against known data types. The declaration and definitions should look like this:

```
10:          <AttributeType name="number" dt:type="int" required="yes"/>
11:          <AttributeType name="date" dt:type="date" required="yes"/>
12:          <AttributeType name="from" dt:type="string" required="yes"/>
13:          <attribute type="number"/>
14:          <attribute type="date"/>
15:          <attribute type="from"/>
```

**ANALYSIS** Lines 13–14 will establish that these attributes will be on the element declared by the `ElementType` element that contains them. Lines 10–12 enforce data types. Because all of the attributes are required, according to the constraints shown, if one is missing in an XML document, that document will not be valid.

Listing 5.10 presents the complete XDR schema that validates the data types appropriately.

**LISTING 5.10**  XDR Schema to Validate Specified Data Types—`message05.xdr`

```
1: <?xml version="1.0"?>
2: <Schema
3:     name="message"
4:     xmlns="urn:schemas-microsoft-com:xml-data"
5:     xmlns:dt="urn:schemas-microsoft-com:datatypes">
6:     <ElementType name="note" model="closed" content="eltOnly">
7:          <element type="message"/>
8:     </ElementType>
9:     <ElementType name="message" model="closed" content="textOnly"
        dt:type="string">
10:          <AttributeType name="number" dt:type="int" required="yes"/>
```

---

**LISTING 5.10**  continued

```
11:            <AttributeType name="date" dt:type="date" required="yes"/>
12:            <AttributeType name="from" dt:type="string" required="yes"/>
13:            <attribute type="number"/>
14:            <attribute type="date"/>
15:            <attribute type="from"/>
16:       </ElementType>
17: </Schema>
```

---

**ANALYSIS**  Line 9 contains the declaration of the message element as a textOnly element that is expressed as a string. Note the data types of integer (int), date and string correspond to each of the number, date and from attributes on lines 10–12. In the listing shown, they are also coded as required attributes. Test the validity of your message05.xml document by parsing it with the validation script downloaded on Day 4. The expected results are depicted by Figure 5.2.

**FIGURE 5.2**

*A well-formed and valid XML document, conforming to defined data type constraints.*

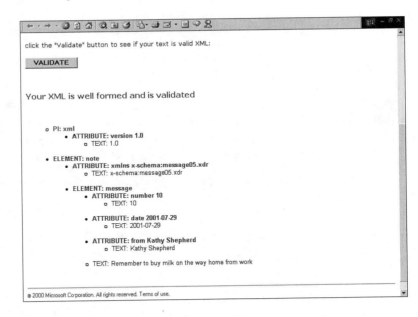

Suppose you modified the message05.xml document so it looked something like Listing 5.11.

**LISTING 5.11**   A Data Type Error—`message06.xml`

```
1: <?xml version="1.0"?>
2: <note xmlns="x-schema:message05.xdr">
3:     <message number="ten" date="2001-07-29" from="Kathy Shepherd">
4:         Remember to buy milk on the way home from work
5:     </message>
6: </note>
```

In line 3, the number is spelled out and not numeric. When you run this through the Microsoft validation script, you will receive an error similar to the one shown in Figure 5.3 because the integer data type does not allow alphabetic characters. The MSXML parser reports that it is unable to parse the value `"ten"` (see line 3) as an `int` (integer) data type.

**FIGURE 5.3**

*MSXML error message indicating that the XML instance does not satisfy all of the constraints defined by the associated XDR schema.*

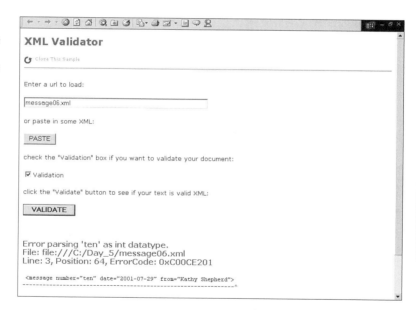

# Occurrence Indicators in XDR

The XDR schema requires a way to indicate multiple child elements. You can specify how many times a child element will appear within its parent element using the `minOccurs` and `maxOccurs` attributes of the `element` element. The full syntax of an `element` element is this

```
<element
  type="element-type"
```

```
[minOccurs="{0 | 1}"]
[maxOccurs="{1 | *}"] >
```

You have seen `element` elements that included the required `type` attribute. This attribute associates the declaration with the element in the XML instance document.

The `minOccurs` attribute might only have values of `"0"` or `"1"` as indicated. Stating that `minOccurs="1"` is the same as requiring at least one occurrence of a child element. An element with a `minOccurs="0"` attribute is really an optional child element.

The only possible values of the `maxOccurs` attribute are `"1"` and `"*"`. When `maxOccurs` has a value of `"*"`, an unrestricted number of child elements can be contained within the parent element.

The `minOccurs` and `maxOccurs` attributes have the default value "1." An element with neither attribute specified uses these default values and must appear only once in a content model.

In the next exercise, add `message` elements to your XML document to allow these constraints to be tested via an XDR schema. In Listing 5.12, you can see an example of this with the `note` element now containing multiple `message` elements. Add some to your own XML document and save the result as `message07.xml`. Your message elements might contain different text data and different values for the attributes, but be careful not to invalidate your instance by using, for example, an improper date format.

**LISTING 5.12**   A Message Instance with Multiple Child Elements— `message07.xml`

```
 1: <?xml version="1.0"?>
 2: <note xmlns="x-schema:message07.xdr">
 3:     <message number="10" date="2001-07-29" from="Kathy Shepherd">
 4:         Remember to buy milk on the way home from work
 5:     </message>
 6:     <message number="12" date="2001-07-30" from="Greg Shepherd">
 7:         I need some help with my homework
 8:     </message>
 9:     <message number="14" date="2001-07-31" from="Kristen Shepherd">
10:         Please play Scrabble with me tonight
11:     </message>
12: </note>
```

Now that you have an XML document with multiple `message` elements, you can modify the XDR schema to indicate, for instance, that a minimum of one `message` element is required, but any number after one is acceptable. Suppose, for instance, that this document is part of a system that keeps track of messages received throughout the day. It has the capability of storing multiple records, but it needs at least one record to maintain its data integrity. The schema you will create next can enforce those constraints through the use of the minOccurs and maxOccurs attributes.

The minOccurs and maxOccurs attributes are encoded on the element element that is contained by the ElementType element relating to the XML document element you are constraining. That might seem confusing, but all that it means is that the note element, in your XML document, contains a message element that has occurrence constraints imposed upon it. The occurrence constraint suggested by the scenario is that at least one valid message element must exist, but that many can be present as long as at least one exists. Therefore, the new constraint should look like this:

```
<element type="message" minOccurs="1" maxOccurs="*"/>
```

Add these constraints to your message06.xdr document and save the result as message07.xdr. Then test the validation constraints by loading the message07.xml document into the Microsoft XML Validation script. Listing 5.17 provides the complete XDR schema required to validate message07.xml.

**LISTING 5.13**   XDR Schema with minOccurs and maxOccurs Attributes—message07.xdr

```
 1: <?xml version="1.0" encoding="UTF-8"?>
 2: <Schema
 3:      name="message"
 4:      xmlns="urn:schemas-microsoft-com:xml-data"
 5:      xmlns:dt="urn:schemas-microsoft-com:datatypes">
 6:      <ElementType name="note" model="closed" content="eltOnly" order="seq">
 7:           <element type="message" minOccurs="1" maxOccurs="*"/>
 8:      </ElementType>
 9:      <ElementType name="message" model="closed" content="textOnly"
dt:type="string">
10:           <AttributeType name="number" dt:type="int" required="yes"/>
11:           <AttributeType name="date" dt:type="date" required="yes"/>
12:           <AttributeType name="from" dt:type="string" required="yes"/>
13:           <attribute type="number"/>
14:           <attribute type="date"/>
15:           <attribute type="from"/>
16:      </ElementType>
17: </Schema>
```

**ANALYSIS**   Line 7

```
<element type="message" minOccurs="1" maxOccurs="*"/>
```

indicates that the note element contains at least one (minOccurs="1")and can contain any number greater than one (maxOccurs="*") message child element.

Tip

> Although it might prove beneficial for some applications, setting the minOccurs or maxOccurs constraints to any value other than the ones defined is not possible at this time. Therefore, it is not possible, for instance, to enforce a predefined range of child element occurrences using these attributes.

## Additional Data Type Constraints in XDR

If you choose to use a string or number (or bin.hex, or bin.base64 types), you can set the minimum or maximum acceptable lengths for these attributes. The minLength and maxLength attributes belong to the Microsoft data type namespace and are enforced at the time or parsing or processing the associated XML document. These attributes are encoded on the AttributeType, using the following syntax:

```
<AttributeType name="idref"
        dt:type="(primitive-type, one of: string | number | bin.hex |
bin.base64)"
        required="(yes | no)"
        dt:minLength="positive integer"
        dt:maxLength="positive integer"/>
```

Suppose you want to limit the size of the from attribute value to meet the needs of a database field in an application that is ultimately going to use the information stored in your XML-based message system. Perhaps your program requires that the from field contains no fewer than 8 characters, but no more than 15. You could use the minOccurs or maxOccurs constraints to enforce this rule.

As an example of this, Listing 5.14 provides additional datatype constraints that are placed on the from attribute value, such that it must be a minimum of 8 characters and a maximum of 15 characters in length. Make these changes to your XDR schema and save it as message08.xdr. Modify your XML instance, message07.xml, to associate the new XDR document by changing the xmlns declaration in the note element of that XML instance.

**LISTING 5.14**  Length Constraints Placed on the from Attribute—message08.xdr

```
1: <?xml version="1.0" encoding="UTF-8"?>
2: <Schema
3:     name="message"
4:     xmlns="urn:schemas-microsoft-com:xml-data"
5:     xmlns:dt="urn:schemas-microsoft-com:datatypes">
6:     <ElementType name="note" model="closed" content="eltOnly" order="seq">
7:         <element type="message" minOccurs="1" maxOccurs="*"/>
```

**LISTING 5.14** continued

```
 8:      </ElementType>
 9:      <ElementType name="message" model="closed" content="textOnly"
         dt:type="string">
10:          <AttributeType name="number" dt:type="int" required="yes"/>
11:          <AttributeType name="date" dt:type="date" required="yes"/>
12:          <AttributeType name="from" dt:type="string" required="yes"
13:                                     dt:minLength="8"
14:                                     dt:maxLength="15"/>
15:          <attribute type="number"/>
16:          <attribute type="date"/>
17:          <attribute type="from"/>
18:      </ElementType>
19: </Schema>
```

**ANALYSIS**  Lines 12–15 establish the constraints to be placed on the `from` attribute in the message document instance. In particular, line 13 declares that the value for the `from` attribute must contain a minimum of 8 characters. Line 14 sets the maximum length of the `from` attribute value at 15 characters.

When you have made the changes to your documents, load the results into the validation script to catch any errors. The results should look like those depicted by Figure 5.4.

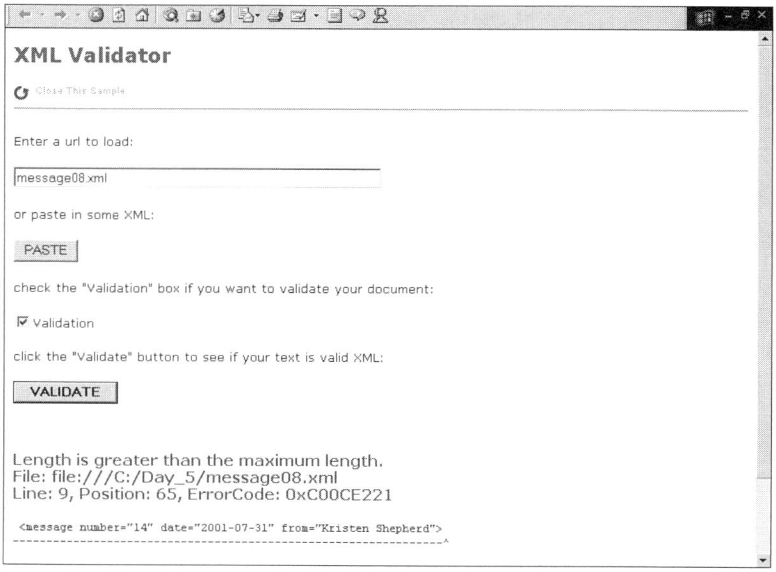

**FIGURE 5.4**

*MSXML error message indicating that the length of the* from *attribute value exceeds the maximum set by the XDR schema*

5

# Establishing Content Groups

Suppose that you need to be able to validate a number of optional elements in an XML instance using XDR. In your message application, for instance, you might like to have a choice between two elements, either `complete` or `incomplete`. For the purpose of the scenario, a `message` element that includes a `complete` element will mean that the message has been received in its entirety by the application. Perhaps a telecommunication error or some other obstruction periodically causes messages to be received that are deemed to be incomplete. In such a case, your imaginary application will place an `incomplete` element within the `message` element, rather than a `complete` element.

In fact, some real-world applications include similar functionality for e-commerce transaction systems. Rather than excluding an entire transaction, it is sometimes desirable to pass as much of the data as possible and note that it is incomplete so that a portion of the subsequent processing might still be initiated and an error routine instantiated to report the status to the originating application. (If you are interested in this form of processing, a good source of additional information can be found on the XML/EDI (Electronic Data Interchange) Web site at `http://www.xmledi-group.org/xmledigroup/guide.htm`.)

For the purpose of this example, assume that you only need to know whether the message is complete. Additionally, you want the application to validate the XML instance in a manner that requires either one or the other element to be included. Modify your XML instance to add this information. After each `message` element, add a new element called `receipt`. Within the new `receipt` element, place either a `complete` or `incomplete` empty element as a child element and save the result as `message09.xml`. It really doesn't matter which messages you follow with complete receipts and which you make incomplete, but ensure that you have only one of either the `complete` or `incomplete` elements within each new `receipt` element. Listing 5.15 shows the XML document with one possible combination of the new elements.

**LISTING 5.15**   A Valid Instance Using an Element Grouping—`message09.xml`

```
 1: <?xml version="1.0"?>
 2: <note xmlns="x-schema:message09.xdr">
 3:     <message number="10" date="2001-07-29" from="Kathy Shepherd">
 4:        Remember to buy milk on the way home from work
 5:        </message>
 6:
 7:     <receipt>
 8:          <complete/>
 9:     </receipt>
10:
11:     <message number="12" date="2001-07-30" from="Greg Shepherd">
```

**LISTING 5.15**   continued

```
12:          I need some help with my homework
13:          </message>
14:
15:      <receipt>
16:            <complete/>
17:       </receipt>
18:
19:
20:          <message number="14" date="2001-07-31" from="Kristen Shepherd">
21:          Please play Scrabble with me tonight
22:          </message>
23:
24:      <receipt>
25:            <incomplete/>
26:       </receipt>
27: </note>
```

**ANALYSIS**   Quite a few changes were made to the document instance for this example. After each message element, a new receipt element was added on lines 7, 15, and 24. Lines 8 and 16 include the new complete elements in this example; yours may vary. The incomplete element was added in the last receipt element, on line 25.

To validate this, you will create a content group in the XDR schema that includes both elements, complete and incomplete. You will also establish a constraint that enforces the inclusion of one or the other in a conforming XML message document. Such a content group is contained by an XDR group element. The group element enables you to establish strictures for a collection of child elements within a parent element. The XDR group element is contained within an ElementType element and typically has the following syntax:

```
<group order="(one | seq | many)" minOccurs="(0 | 1)" maxOccurs="(1 | *)">
     <element type="ElementType"/>
     <element type="ElementType"/>
     <element type="ElementType"/>
     <element type="ElementType"/>
     <element type="ElementType"/>
...
</group>
```

The group element permits the inclusion of order, minOccurs, and maxOccurs attributes. It might contain any number of child element elements. For the purpose of this example, choose to encode your group element with an order="one" attribute so that a compliant XML instance will include only one of the child element elements listed. Group elements contain child elements as a way of encoding the fact that the child elements belong to a set. Your group element will include two child elements that look like this:

**5**

```
<element type="complete"/>
<element type="incomplete"/>
```

Because these `element` elements declare new element types in your XML instance, you will need to include an `ElementType` element for each, in the XDR schema. Specifically, you will need to add the following `ElementType` elements:

```
<ElementType name="complete" model="closed" content="empty"/>
<ElementType name="incomplete" model="closed" content="empty"/>
```

In addition to the new grouping, you will need to account for the new `receipt` element that contains the choice of either the `complete` or `incomplete` element.

You will need to make quite a few additional changes to the XDR schema to test this example. For instance, you will need to

- Change the root element to include the new `receipt` container element and set the `order` attribute to many (`<ElementType name="note" model="closed" content="eltOnly" order="many">`).
- Add the `receipt` element to the content set for the root element (`<element type="receipt"/>`).
- Add an `ElementType` element for the `receipt` element that contains the new `group` element container with `element` elements for `complete` and `incomplete` as content elements.

The new `ElementType` element for the `receipt` element will look like this:

```
<ElementType name="receipt" model="closed" content="eltOnly">
    <group order="one">
        <element type="complete" />
        <element type="incomplete" />
    </group>
</ElementType>
```

This `ElementType` element is interpreted to mean that the `receipt` element contains only other elements that are exclusively defined within the current schema (`model="closed"`). The `group` element permits the choice of one of its child elements for inclusion as a child of the `receipt` element. The choices are either the `complete` or `incomplete` element.

The finished XDR schema is presented as Listing 5.16.

**LISTING 5.16**  A `group` Element with an `order="one"` Constraint—`message09.xdr`

```
1: <?xml version="1.0" encoding="UTF-8"?>
2: <Schema
3:     name="message"
4:     xmlns="urn:schemas-microsoft-com:xml-data"
```

**LISTING 5.16**  continued

```
 5:        xmlns:dt="urn:schemas-microsoft-com:datatypes">
 6:        <ElementType name="note" model="closed" content="eltOnly"
 7:                        order="many">
 8:             <element type="message" minOccurs="1" maxOccurs="*"/>
 9:             <element type="receipt"/>
10:        </ElementType>
11:        <ElementType name="complete" model="closed" content="empty" />
12:        <ElementType name="incomplete" model="closed" content="textOnly"
13:                        dt:type="string"/>
14:         <ElementType name="message" model="closed" content="mixed">
15:             <AttributeType name="number" dt:type="int" required="yes"/>
16:             <AttributeType name="date" dt:type="date" required="yes"/>
17:             <AttributeType name="from" dt:type="string" required="yes"/>
18:             <attribute type="number"/>
19:             <attribute type="date"/>
20:             <attribute type="from"/>
21:        </ElementType>
22:        <ElementType name="receipt" model="closed" content="eltOnly">
23:             <group order="one">
24:                   <element type="complete" />
25:                   <element type="incomplete" />
26:             </group>
27:        </ElementType>
28: </Schema>
```

**ANALYSIS**  Line 9 declares the new `receipt` element as content within the root element `note`.

Lines 11–12

```
11:        <ElementType name="complete" model="closed" content="empty" />
12:        <ElementType name="incomplete" model="closed" content="textOnly"
```

define new empty elements `complete` and `incomplete`.

Line 22 begins the definition of the new `receipt` element and lines 23–26 declare a `group` element with an `order="one"` attribute. This signifies that a conforming XML document instance needs only one of the elements `complete` or `incomplete` within the `message` parent element to be valid. Line 27 is the closing tag of the `receipt` `ElementType` definition.

# Additional Benefits of XDR

Today, you have studied the syntax of the XDR schema language. You have seen that an XDR schema is constructed from a vocabulary that uses XML syntax. In other words,

5

the schema language comprises elements and attributes in the same way that an XML document instance does. This vocabulary is contained within either the XML-Data namespace (`urn:schemas-microsoft-com:xml-data`) or the Microsoft data types namespace (`urn:schemas-microsoft-com:datatypes`). This offers you, the developer, an advantage. Because you already know the syntax rules for a well-formed XML instance, you can focus on the semantics of the XML-Data Reduced vocabulary, rather than the semantics of the markup. When you created DTDs, you were required to learn both. XDR does not, for instance, use an extensive set of symbols that have unique meaning. XDR schemata can be "checked" with a parser to ensure that they are well formed, thereby giving you tools to find dropped terminating slashes, missing angle brackets, or poorly formed tags. This can save you considerable time in the long run.

Several other characteristics of XDR are worth mentioning. In this section, a very brief overview of some of these will be presented for your consideration.

## Extensibility in XDR Schemata

XML-Data Reduced Schemata are extensible because they are built on open content models employing an XML syntax that is extensible by definition. This offers considerable advantages over the DTD approach you studied on Day 4. Document authors extend XDR schemata and can add custom elements and attributes to an XDR schema instance. If you choose to extend an XDR schema, then you must include a custom namespace declaration to differentiate extended elements and attributes from those that are predetermined by XDR. The standard vocabulary for XDR is defined by the data and data type namespaces, as mentioned earlier. When you extend the language, you define a new namespace to hold your custom elements and attributes.

XDR schemata are typically extended only in situations where the standard XDR vocabulary does not easily provide the required constraints to satisfy a particular application requirement. For instance, in keeping with the message-processing scenario you explored today and yesterday, suppose that the application was capable only of receiving and handling a finite number of messages in a given period of time. You might want to add an additional constraint to a declaration for a `limit` element. You might choose to declare the `limit` element and assign it an `int` data type with constraints that belong to the `mystuff` namespace. One approach to doing this might involve an `ElementType` declaration like this:

```
<ElementType name="limit" xmlns:mystuff="urn:mystuff-extensions:limits">
  <datatype dt:type="int" />
  <mystuff:max>100</mystuff:max>
</ElementType>
```

This snippet of code shows a new `mystuff:max` element that belongs to the `urn: mystuff-extensions:limits` namespace. Although validation will only check that the value of a particular `limit` element is an integer, your application could use the information provided by the custom elements in your own namespace to perform additional validation. You will learn more about creating your own namespace declarations on Day 8.

> **Tip**
>
> When you extend an XDR schema, the MSXML parser will not validate your extended vocabulary except on the basis of data types. However, a custom application that expects certain data not well documented by XDR is an approach that works to mark up those data in XML.

## Transformation of XDR Schemata

Using a programming technology called XSLT (Extensible Stylesheet Language Transformations), you can programmatically transform an XML instance document into another XML instance document, into HTML, or into some other form of markup. You will learn all about XSLT on Day 16.

Because XDR schemata are written in XML syntax, they too can be transformed into other markup dialects. One reason for doing this is to change an XDR instance into an XSD (XML Schema Definition language) instance. Microsoft has produced an XSLT program to do this for document authors who have learned XDR, but want to use XSD schemata instead. As mentioned earlier, you can also obtain a commercial application to this, such as XML-Spy from `http://www.xmlspy.com`). This type of transformation is not something that is possible with DTDs. To convert DTDs into XDR, XSD, or another schema language requires an application outside of XML technologies.

5

# Summary

Today, you learned about the XML-Data Reduced Schema Language (XDR). You saw many differences between XDR schemata and DTDs. In particular, XDR schemata are documents expressed in XML syntax that provide more sophisticated and powerful validity measures, including constraints for data types. Because XDR schemata are valid XML instances in their own rights, they can be manipulated, searched, and transformed into other markup dialects in the same way that XML document instances can.

# Q&A

**Q  Do XDR and other forms of XML-based schemata aim to replace DTDs?**

**A**  Schemata that are written using XML grammar have many advantages over DTDs. In time, it may follow that DTDs will diminish in popularity, but for now, there are many implementations that rely on the stability of proven DTDs.

**Q  What are some of the specific functions served by an XDR schema?**

**A**  A schema establishes the structure of an XML document by enforcing validation constraints. In so doing, the schema ensures the presence of required elements and attributes and checks the relationships among elements. An XDR schema offers sophisticated data type validation.

**Q  What is the role of MSXML in XDR?**

**A**  The Microsoft product MSXML is a validating parser that ships with the company's Internet Explorer browser tool suite. By instantiating the MSXML object, you can parse an XML document with or without an associated schema.

**Q  What is a URI?**

**A**  A Universal Resource Identifier is just a label that helps to distinguish one namespace from another. You will learn more about namespace declarations and syntax on Day 8.

The exercise is provided so that you can test your knowledge of what you learned today. The answers are in Appendix A, "Answers to the Questions."

# Exercise

On Day 4 you created a DTD for your Music Collection Markup Language (MCML). Create an XDR schema to validate MCML files.

# DAY **6**

# The XML Schema Definition (XSD) Language

In the past two days, you have created DTDs and XDR schemata to validate XML document instances. You have authored element constraint declarations and attribute definitions to enforce business rules. You have explored the differences between DTD and Schemata based on XML syntax. Today, you will learn

- The highlights of the XML Schema Definition (XSD) Language
- How to create and read XSD schemata for the encoding of element and attribute constraints
- Some of the issues that characterize a choice between schema vocabularies

# The World Wide Web Consortium Schema Approach

Yesterday, you learned some of the ways that XML-Data Reduced (XDR) schemata improve on Document Type Definitions (DTDs). You also learned about a number of alternative schema languages. The XDR approach is significant because it has been widely implemented in a variety of e-commerce solutions—such as BizTalk and related initiatives—by its creators at Microsoft. However, XDR requires the use of Microsoft's MSXML tool suite, which might prove to be a limitation with regard to implementation on some platforms or integration with certain legacy data models.

DTDs, of course, are widely supported and broadly implemented. The problems with DTDs start with the fact that they are not expressed using XML syntax, forcing developers to learn a new language, use non-XML tools, and so on. Additionally, DTDs do not provide for rich data type validation.

The W3C has formalized a recommendation for the XML Schema Definition Language (XSD) by coalescing the most popular schema languages into a single industry standard. The intent is to produce a standard that is so widely implemented that it can be considered truly *platform independent*. Time will tell if this is to be the case.

Now that the W3C specifications for Schema Languages are complete, it is expected that there will be growing support in the vendor community to implement the XML Schema Definition (XSD) Language in products that are currently optimized to validate other dialects. For instance, Microsoft has committed to support the XSD language in its browser as well as in the MSXML suite of tools. As of this writing, the current version of the MSXML parser toolset (version 4) and the Microsoft XML 4.0 Parser SDK offer support for XSD. IBM, SUN, and Apache are among the major players that have released parsers to support XSD. Others will follow. Nonetheless, it is anticipated that DTDs and XDR schemata will survive for some time until transition of supporting software is complete.

The XML Schema Definition Language, also referred to as just the XML Schema Language, is quite similar in many regards to the XDR language you have already learned. An XSD schema is meant to do the following:

- Enumerate the elements in an XML instance document and ensure that only those that are declared are included
- Declare and define any attributes that modify document elements
- Establish the parent-child relationships among elements

- Define states and content models for elements and attributes
- Enforce data types
- Establish default values
- Offer extensibility to the schema author
- Support the use of namespaces

## Status of XSD

Today's lessons will feature a useful subset of important concepts that help to character-ize the XSD language. The objective will be to provide you with some comparative information so that you can evaluate XSD relative to other approaches. Many analysts predict that XSD will gain in popularity now that it has been finalized as a standard, or recommendation of the W3C. Several distinct steps characterize the W3C road to stan-dardization. You can read about the other steps in the standards process undertaken by the W3C in the next section.

It is likely that material in today's lesson will change after publication. The latest update on the XSD specification can be obtained from http://www.w3.org/XML/Schema.

## The W3C Recommendation Track

Several of the technologies presented in this book, at least at the time of this writing, are not yet formal standards. On May 2, 2001, XSD became a W3C recommendation. The W3C (http://www.w3.org) is the body responsible for the creation, publishing, and maintenance of standards for Web technologies and related efforts. Formalization by the W3C requires satisfaction of all of the steps in an elaborate process of review. The process is referred to by the W3C as the "Recommendation Track," a systematic approach to building consensus around Web technology initiatives.

The W3C refers to a "standard" as a "Recommendation." This level of maturity for any technology is reached only after progression through several distinct phases. The next sections are quoted from material that is available on the W3C Web site at http://www.w3.org/Consortium/Process-20010208/tr.

Working Draft

A technical report on the Recommendation track begins as a Working Draft. A Working Draft is a chartered work item of a Working Group and generally represents

6

work in progress and a commitment by W3C to pursue work in a particular area. The label "Working Draft" does not imply that there is consensus within W3C about the technical report.

Last Call Working Draft

A Last Call Working Draft is a special instance of a Working Draft that is considered by the Working Group to fulfill the relevant requirements of its charter and any accompanying requirements documents. A Last Call Working Draft is a public technical report for which the Working Group seeks technical review from other W3C groups, W3C Members, and the public.

Candidate Recommendation

A Candidate Recommendation is believed to meet the relevant requirements of the Working Group's charter and any accompanying requirements documents, and has been published in order to gather implementation experience and feedback. Advancement of a technical report to Candidate Recommendation is an explicit call for implementation experience to those outside of the related Working Groups or the W3C itself.

Proposed Recommendation

A Proposed Recommendation is believed to meet the relevant requirements of the Working Group's charter and any accompanying requirements documents, to represent sufficient implementation experience, and to adequately address dependencies from the W3C technical community and comments from previous reviewers. A Proposed Recommendation is a technical report that the Director has sent to the Advisory Committee for review.

W3C Recommendation

A W3C Recommendation is a technical report that is the end result of extensive consensus-building inside and outside of W3C about a particular technology or policy. W3C considers that the ideas or technology specified by a Recommendation are appropriate for widespread deployment and promote W3C's mission.

# XSD Basics

As you learned on Days 4 and Day 5, schemas, regardless of the vocabulary or syntax used to express them, are written expressly to enforce business rules by adding constraints to XML documents. Schema languages based on XML syntax have an advantage over DTDs because the former comprise a set of markup tags that can be evaluated to ensure that a document is well-formed using a standard XML parser.

XML Schemas (XSD) divide the tags used in your XML document into two groups: complex types and simple types. Complex type elements can contain other elements and have attributes; simple types cannot. These are examples of simple elements:

```
<message>Remember to buy milk on the way home from work</message>
<delivery>email</delivery>
```

The following snippet comprises elements that are deemed complex because they have element content or attributes:

```
<message number="10" date="2001-07-29" from="Kathy Shepherd">
    Remember to buy milk on the way home from work
    <receipt>
        <complete/>
    </receipt>
</message>
```

The `message` element, a complex type element, is modified by `number`, `date`, and `from` attributes. The `message` element contains elements and data, such as mixed content. The `receipt` element, a child of the `message` element, contains an empty `complete` child element.

You will learn how to encode simple and complex element types today.

**Tip**

> On Days 4 (DTD) and 5 (XDR), you learned that schema rules applying to elements or attributes comprise two distinct steps. This is true of XSD as well. The two steps involve definition and declaration of types—either element types or attribute types.

## XSD Namespace Considerations

You will explore the concept of namespaces in depth on Day 8. For now, as you did with XDR schemata, you need to encode a standard namespace for all of your XSD instances. This namespace will identify the collection of elements and attributes that comprise the XSD vocabulary.

The root element of an XML Schema is the `Schema` element that contains all other elements in the schema document. On the root element for an XSD schema you will create a namespace using the `xmlns` attribute. That `xmlns` attribute provides the prefix that will be added to the Schema element type names in the XSD instance. The current XML schema definition can be found at `http://www.w3c.org/1999/XMLSchema`. The following

6

Schema tag, for instance, follows the convention of establishing "xsd" as the prefix and then using it to associate elements with the named collection:

```
<xsd:schema xmlns:xsd=http://www.w3c.org/1999/XMLSchema>
```

 **Tip**

> By convention, the prefix xsd (XML Schema Definition) is used as a proxy to the XML Schema namespace in the XSD document.

In the XML document instance that will be validated on your schema, you must also include a namespace declaration. The namespace is always placed on the root element of the XML document instance with an XMLNS attribute in the following format:

```
xmlns:xsi="http://www.w3.org/2000/10/XMLSchema-instance"
```

This namespace holds the XML Schema elements and attributes that might be included in the XML document instance. By convention, the prefix xsi is used as a proxy to this namespace and is also affixed to the beginning of all elements and attributes belonging to the namespace, separated by a colon.

 **Tip**

> By convention, the prefix xsi (XML Schema Instance) is used as a proxy to the XML Schema namespace in the XML document instance.

Two attributes belonging to the XML Schema namespace that are commonly used to associate the XML document instance with its schema are xsi:schemaLocation and xsi:noNamespaceSchemaLocation. The xsi:schemaLocation and xsi:noNamespaceSchemaLocation attributes allow you to tie a document to its W3C XML Schema. This link is not mandatory, and other indications can be given using application-dependent mechanisms—such as a parameter on a command line—but it does help W3C XML Schema-aware tools—such as parsers—to locate a schema.

In the event that the XSD document is linked without a namespace—typically a fully qualified Uniform Resource Locator (URL) or a local file—the noNamespaceSchemaLocation attribute is used and looks like this:

```
xsi:noNamespaceSchemaLocation="file_name.xsd">
```

On the other hand, a namespace can be declared along with a filename, in which case the URI for the namespace and the URI of the schema will be separated by a whitespace character as part of the same attribute value, such as this:

```
xsi:schemaLocation="http://example.org/ns/books/ file_name.xsd"
```

It might be difficult to see on the preceding line, but a single whitespace character resides between the namespace (`http://example.org/ns/books/`) and the schema document name (`file_name.xsd`).

# Simple Element Types

In XSD, unlike the other two validation languages you studied, there is a concept of *named type*. When you create, for instance, the definition for a `simpleType` to describe elements that are deemed to be simple elements, you can also *name* the definition so that it can be reused elsewhere in the XSD instance. Recall the example snippet of XML that included two simple elements:

```
<message>Remember to buy milk on the way home from work</message>
<delivery>email</delivery>
```

You could create a `simpleType` and call it anything you want, for instance `msg`. This can be referred to as a *named constraint*. The encoding for this simple type could provide constraints that might be shared by any other simple elements in the schema. For instance, in the last example, a `simpleType` element could be associated with the `message` and `delivery` elements to declare the content of those elements as strings. It might look like this:

```
1: <xsd:simpleType name="msg" base="xsd:string"/>
2: <xsd:element name="message" type="msg"/>
3: <xsd:element name="delivery" type="msg"/>
```

The first thing you will notice is that all XSD elements begin with the prefix `xsd:`, which provides a proxy to the XSD namespace declared in the root element of the XSD schema instance. On line 1, the simple type is defined by the `xsd:simpleType` element and given the reference name `msg` via the `name` attribute. The `base` attribute on that element is a data type constraint limiting the valid `msg` content to string data. Lines 2 and 3 define the elements `message` and `delivery`, respectively. The constraints enforced on these elements are defined by the `simpleType` `msg`.

6

**Note**

> When you create a *named constraint*, you determine the name—it does not exist in your XML document instance. The name provides a referential association or link to a separate XSD constraint definition.

In practice, many document authors prefer to fully qualify their simple types by placing the appropriate attributes in the `xsd:element` element, rather than in the separate `xsd:simpleType` element. This is particularly the case when the elements being defined need only one or two attributes for full qualification of their constraints. You might choose to use the xsd:simpleType element or exclude it and add required attributes to the xsd:element element; either approach is valid. If you take the latter approach, the previous example would look like this:

```
1: <xsd:element name="message" type="xsd:string"/>
2: <xsd:element name="delivery" type="xsd:string"/>
```

In this example, the type attributes no longer contain the name associated with an xsd:simpleType element, but rather a fully qualified data type declaration. Note that the value for the declaration includes the xsd: prefix, which is interpreted to mean that the string definition belongs to the xsd namespace. In this way, a data type declaration for string is not confused with a reference to a simpleType element called string. Namespaces are valuable because they prevent this type of confusion, or *naming collision*.

Listing 6.1 shows a version of the message.xml document that you created previously, modified to include the namespace declarations required for use by XSD schemata.

**LISTING 6.1**  An XML Instance Showing an XML Schema Namespace and Schema Document Location—message01.xml

```
1: <?xml version="1.0"?>
2: <note
3:     xmlns:xsi="http://www.w3.org/2000/10/XMLSchema-instance"
4:     xsi:noNamespaceSchemaLocation="message01.xsd">
5:     Remember to buy milk on the way home from work
6: </note>
```

**ANALYSIS**  The start tag of the note element is on lines 2–4. Line 3 includes the namespace for the reference to the XML Schema instance. Line 4 provides an association to the XSD file used to validate the instance.

As noted earlier, all elements in an XSD schema begin with the prefix xsd:. This prefix serves as a proxy to the XSD namespace through the declaration xmlns:xsd=http://www.w3.org/2000/10/XMLSchema. This namespace should appear within the start tag on the root element (xsd:schema) of the XSD schema document. As with all namespace proxies, the purpose of the prefix (or proxy) is to identify the elements that belong to the vocabulary of the XML Schema Definition language rather than the vocabulary of a schema author. You will learn more about namespaces on Day 8. In the meantime realize that although this namespace seems to include something that looks like a Website address, or URL, the processor does not resolve this location.

After you have created the `message01.xml` using a text editor, create an xsd file for it and save it as `message01.xsd`. An example schema is provided in Listing 6.2.

**LISTING 6.2**    A Simple XSD Schema for the Message Instance—`message01.xsd`

```
1: <?xml version="1.0"?>
2: <xsd:schema
3:     xmlns:xsd="http://www.w3.org/2000/10/XMLSchema">
4:     <xsd:element name="note" type="xsd:string"/>
5: </xsd:schema>
```

**ANALYSIS**    Line 3 is the XSD namespace declaration shown as an `xmlns` attribute on the `xsd:schema` root element. Line 4 declares and defines the `note` element with a `string` data type, originating from the `xsd:` namespace.

# XSD Data Types

The XSD language has a number of simple data types built in, just as XDR has. In addition to those data types that are built in, such as `string` and `decimal`, XSD includes functionality for the development of types that are derived from the built-in types. For instance, an inventory control attribute might have a custom inventory type derived from a numeric string. The schema author can create derived types and use them throughout the XSD document. A complete list of the simple data types that are included in XSD can be obtained at `http://www.w3.org/TR/xmlschema-0/`. Table 6.1 summarizes some of the common built-in types.

**TABLE 6.1**    XML Schema Simple Data Types

| Simple Type | Description |
| --- | --- |
| string | Alphanumeric string |
| normalizedString | stringwithwhitespacecharactersremoved |
| byte | -1, 126 |
| unsignedByte | 0, 126 |
| base64Binary | GpM7 |
| hexBinary | 0FB7 |
| integer | -126789, -1, 0, 1, 126789 |
| positiveInteger | 1, 126789 |
| negativeInteger | -126789, -1 |
| nonNegativeInteger | 0, 1, 126789 |
| nonPositiveInteger | -126789, -1, 0 |

6

**TABLE 6.1**  continued

| Simple Type | Description |
| --- | --- |
| int | -1, 126789675 |
| unsignedInt | 0, 1267896754 |
| long | -1, 12678967543233 |
| unsignedLong | 0, 12678967543233 |
| short | -1, 12678 |
| unsignedShort | 0, 12678 |
| decimal | -1.23, 0, 123.4, 1000.00 |
| float | -INF, -1E4, -0, 0, 12.78E-2, 12, INF, NaN |
| double | -INF, -1E4, -0, 0, 12.78E-2, 12, INF, NaN |
| boolean | true, false1, 0 |
| time | 13:20:00.000, 13:20:00.000-05:00 |
| dateTime | 1999-05-31T13:20:00.000-05:00 |
| duration | P1Y2M3DT10H30M12.3S |
| date | 1999-05-31 |
| gMonth | --05-- |
| gYear | 1999 |
| gYearMonth | 1999-02 |
| gDay | ---31 |
| gMonthDay | --05-31 |
| Name | shipTo |
| QName | po:USAddress |
| NCName | USAddress |
| anyURI | http://www.example.com/, http://www.example.com/doc.html#ID5 |

# Complex Element Type Definitions

The constructs of simple and complex element types are design characteristics unique to the XSD language. As noted earlier, complex element types are defined in XSD as those that allow other elements in their content and those that might include attributes.

In the next example, you will see a complex element type in the message document instance you have been manipulating over the past several days. Listing 6.3 shows the modified message instance in which the `note` element contains a `message` element. Because one element contains element content, a complex element type will be required in a validating XSD schema. Recall that the `simpleType` is reserved for elements holding only values and no elements or attributes.

**LISTING 6.3**  An XML Document with an Element That Has Element Content—
`message02.xml`

```
1: <?xml version="1.0"?>
2: <note
3:     xmlns:xsi="http://www.w3.org/2000/10/XMLSchema-instance"
4:     xsi:noNamespaceSchemaLocation="message02.xsd">
5:     <message>Remember to buy milk on the way home from work</message>
6: </note>
```

**ANALYSIS**  In this XML instance, the `note` root element (lines 2–6) is considered a complex element type because it contains a `message` child element on line 5. The root element includes the `xmlns` for the XML schema instance (`http://www.w3.org/2000/10/XMLSchema-instance`) associated with the prefix, `xsi` on line 3. The `xsi:noNamespaceSchemaLocation` attribute (line 4) on the `note` element has a value of `"message02.xsd"`, which associates the XSD file with the instance.

Based on the XSD concept of a complex element, the schema you create for this document instance must establish the relationship between `note` and `message`. In particular, the `message` element is a child of the `note` element. The shortest form of this construct looks something like this:

**LISTING 6.4**  XSD Snippet with a Complex Type

```
1: <xsd:element name="parent_element_name">
2:     <xsd:complexType>
3:         <xsd:element name="child_element_name" type="simple_type_ref"/>
4:     </xsd:complexType>
5: </xsd:element>
```

**ANALYSIS**  Line 1 begins the declaration of the parent element in a complex type. The `complexType` element spans lines 2 through 4 and contains child elements. In the example code snippet, only one child element is included on line 3. The name of the child element in the XML document instance is provided as the value of the `name` attribute on the `xsd:element` element. The `type` attribute refers, in this example, to the simple type declaration for the child element. If the child is a complex element type, then the `type` attribute will refer to the named `complexType` elsewhere in the XSD schema.

6

Listing 6.5 is an XSD schema for the message document instance. However, in this example, a few additional features have been added as compared with the short form sample provided earlier. For instance, the xsd:sequence element has been added. This element allows you to indicate the sequence of child elements in a set. The example shown here has only one child element, the xsd:element declaring the message element in the XML instance document. However, in a situation where note has several child elements, wrapping those child elements in xsd:sequence permits you to control the order of the child elements in the XML instance document.

**LISTING 6.5**  XSD Schema with an xsd:ComplexType Element—message02.xsd

```
 1: <?xml version="1.0"?>
 2: <xsd:schema
 3:     xmlns:xsd="http://www.w3.org/2000/10/XMLSchema">
 4:     <xsd:element name="message" type="xsd:string"/>
 5:     <xsd:element name="note">
 6:          <xsd:complexType>
 7:                  <xsd:sequence>
 8:                          <xsd:element ref="message"/>
 9:                  </xsd:sequence>
10:          </xsd:complexType>
11:     </xsd:element>
12: </xsd:schema>
```

**ANALYSIS** The complex type is defined in lines 6–10. Line 7 declares a sequence, although there is really only one child element, message, in this example. If more than one child element is included within a parent element, the sequence element can be used to establish the valid order constraints, if any, to apply to the child elements. In other words, a sequence element just indicates that the child elements must appear in the instance document in the order they are declared in the XSD document. Line 8 uses a ref attribute to provide a reference to the simple type definition for the message element, which is made on line 4. The ref attribute functions identically to the type attribute shown in earlier examples to allow the schema author to make definitions for elements only once, even if the elements are reused in multiple declarations.

# XSD Occurrence Constraints

Unlike other schema languages, XSD allows you to define the cardinality (that is, the number of possible occurrences) of an element with some precision. You may set the minimum number of occurrences of an element with the minOccurs attribute on the xsd:element element and the maximum number of occurrences with the maxOccurs attribute on the xsd:element element. The use of these attributes might seem reminiscent of the approach you took yesterday with XDR schemata, but the similarity ends there. In the case of XSD, there are fewer restrictions on the acceptable values available for use with these attributes. With XSD, the W3C has provided a means of encoding a defined range of occurrences if that is desirable. This is one of the distinguishing characteristics of XSD, relative to XDR, DTD, or other schema definition languages.

The minOccurs and maxOccurs attributes have default values of "1" if nothing else is declared. The maxOccurs attribute can also be set to "unbounded", which is the same as "*" in XDR or DTD.

Consider the XML instance in Listing 6.6. This document contains several nested child elements. The note root element contains two notes, each of which contains only one empty number element followed by any number of message elements.

**LISTING 6.6**    XML Message Instance with Complex Nesting—message04.xml

```
 1: <?xml version="1.0"?>
 2: <note
 3:     xmlns:xsi="http://www.w3.org/2000/10/XMLSchema-instance"
 4:     xsi:noNamespaceSchemaLocation="message04.xsd">
 5:     <notes>
 6:             <number/>
 7:             <message>Remember to buy milk on the way home from work</message>
 8:             <message>Skim Milk is preferred</message>
 9:     </notes>
10:     <notes>
11:             <number/>
12:             <message>Pick up shirts from the cleaners</message>
13:             <message>Got to the bank</message>
14:             <message>Cut the lawn</message>
15:     </notes>
16: </note>
```

Suppose you want to enforce constraints on this instance such that

- A maximum of two notes is all that are permitted.
- The occurrence of notes is optional.
- The number element must precede the message element.
- At least one message element exists.
- The number of message elements must exceed one.

6

To create an XSD schema to enforce these constraints, you will need to account for element cardinality, order, and whether elements are required or optional. To constrain cardinality, you will use the minOccurs and maxOccurs attributes on the appropriate xsd:element elements. In XSD, you can add requirement strictures by carefully encoding the same minOccurs and maxOccurs attributes. For instance, if you set a minOccurs attribute to zero for a particular element, then that element is considered optional. If you set minOccurs on a particular element to one or exclude minOccurs altogether because one is the default, then that element is considered a required element. (That is, at least one occurrence of the element is mandatory). You already know that an indeterminate value greater than one for maxOccurs is encoded with a value of "unbounded".

Listing 6.7 shows one possibility for an XSD schema that validates the message04.xml based on the description of the constraints noted earlier.

**LISTING 6.7**    minOccurs and maxOccurs in XSD—message04.xsd

```
 1: <?xml version="1.0"?>
 2: <xsd:schema xmlns:xsd="http://www.w3.org/2000/10/XMLSchema">
 3:     <xsd:element name="message" type="xsd:string"/>
 4:     <xsd:element name="number"/>
 5:     <xsd:element name="note">
 6:         <xsd:complexType>
 7:             <xsd:sequence>
 8:                 <xsd:element name="notes" minOccurs="0" maxOccurs="2"/>
 9:             </xsd:sequence>
10:         </xsd:complexType>
11:     </xsd:element>
12:     <xsd:complexType name="notesType">
13:         <xsd:sequence>
14:             <xsd:element ref="number"/>
15:             <xsd:element ref="message" maxOccurs="unbounded"/>
16:         </xsd:sequence>
17:     </xsd:complexType>
18: </xsd:schema>
```

**ANALYSIS**  Line 8 defines the occurrence constraints (minOccurs="0" maxOccurs="2") for the notes child element of the note root element. In particular, a conforming XML instance can contain from zero (minOccurs="0") to two notes child elements (maxOccurs="2"). Because zero is encoded, notes is actually an optional child element.

Line 15 indicates that at least one message element must follow the number element in the derived, complex sequence contained within each notes parent element. This is determined by the container element <xsd:sequence>. However, the value "unbounded" indicates that the number of permissible message elements is unlimited.

Line 12 declares the derived complex type, referred to as "notesType". This new complex type is not an element type, but rather an association between a name and constraints that govern the appearance of that named type in a document instance. In other words, notesType does not exist in the originating XML document; nonetheless, notes elements in the XML document must conform to constraints placed by the derived complex group. Therefore, notes elements must contain only one empty number element followed by any number of message elements. This complex sequence is named notesType for referential purposes only; you can name it anything that you want.

# Attributes in XSD Schemata

The declaration of attributes in XSD is quite similar to the declaration of elements, except attributes are declared with attribute declarations, rather than element declarations. As noted earlier, attribute declarations belong within the definitions of complex types in the schema. You have seen, with regard to element declarations, that the declarations are not *types*, but rather associations between a name and constraints that govern the appearance of the name in valid document instances. The same is true of attribute declarations.

By way of example, Listing 6.8 provides an XML instance document that contains elements as well as attributes. In particular, the message element, lines 5–7, comprises text content and a number attribute.

**LISTING 6.8**   Elements and Attributes—message05.xml

```
1: <?xml version="1.0"?>
2: <note
3:       xmlns:xsi="http://www.w3.org/2000/10/XMLSchema-instance"
4:       xsi:noNamespaceSchemaLocation="message05.xsd">
5:       <message number="10">
6:          Remember to buy milk on the way home from work
7:       </message>
8: </note>
```

6

This must be encoded in XSD as a complex type. An XSD schema to validate this document is provided in Listing 6.9. This listing provides several additional features, not yet discussed, that will be described in the analysis of the instance.

Data typing in XSD is a multi-stage process in most cases. You begin by restricting content of typed elements by a broad category and then narrow down the broad category with a more specific type. This might seem redundant, but it becomes useful in large schemata with many variable types defined. The first, more general, type is encoded using an `xsd:restriction` element with a `base` attribute declaring the broad category restriction. The broad base is typically a `string`. The child elements of the `xsd:restriction` elements provide specific detailed definition for data types. This is shown in detail in Listing 6.9.

**LISTING 6.9**  An XSD Schema with Attribute Validation—`message05.xsd`

```
 1: <?xml version="1.0"?>
 2: <xsd:schema xmlns:xsd="http://www.w3.org/2000/10/XMLSchema">
 3:     <xsd:complexType name="messageType">
 4:         <xsd:simpleContent>
 5:             <xsd:restriction base="xsd:string">
 6:                 <xsd:attribute name="number"
                                    type="xsd:integer"
                                    use="required"/>
 7:             </xsd:restriction>
 8:         </xsd:simpleContent>
 9:     </xsd:complexType>
10:     <xsd:element name="note">
11:         <xsd:complexType>
12:             <xsd:sequence>
13:                 <xsd:element name="message"
                                  type="messageType"/>
14:             </xsd:sequence>
15:         </xsd:complexType>
16:     </xsd:element>
17: </xsd:schema>
```

**ANALYSIS**  Lines 3–9 define a complex type, named `messageType`, which ensures that the `message` element contains a required attribute, `number`, with an integer data type.

Note that the `simpleContent` element (line 4) and the `complexType` element (line 11) do not include names. You might include a name if you plan to reuse the content definitions elsewhere in the schema. By comparison, the `complexType` element on line 3 is named `messageType`. The declaration for the `message` element (line 13) contains a reference (`type="messageType"`) to the complex type declaration (lines 3–9) containing the attribute declaration (line 6).

The `sequence` element (lines 12–14) is only included to provide you with the typical location and syntax employed for instances that contain multiple child elements, requiring sequence constraints.

Lines 5 and 7 establish the base for the data type, in this case a string that is further qualified as an integer value. The `restriction` element is used to indicate the existing (base) type and to identify the facets that constrain the range of values.

**Note**

> In XSD, the term *facet* is used to describe the variable constraint features available to modify each valid data type. For instance, a string might be constrained by its allowable length, minLength, maxLength, user-defined pattern, use of whitespace, or an enumerated list of valid values. By comparison, it is not logical to expect a Boolean—returning either true or false—to be constrained by, for instance, allowable length, minLength, maxLength, or enumeration. Therefore, a Boolean does not support facets for those constraints.
>
> XSD offers unrivaled support for numerous simple data types and applicable facets. You can access an exhaustive list of these at `http://www.w3.org/TR/xmlschema-0/#SimpleTypeFacets`.

The data types presented in Table 6.1 relative to elements are supported for attributes as well. The list of data types supported by XSD is much greater than those offered with XDR. The W3C has placed considerable importance on the richness of the XSD data type set.

The support for data types by XDR and XSD distinguishes these languages from DTDs that did not provide much in the way of support. The W3C has endeavored to ensure that XSD includes the richest and most complete set of data types. XSD provides for two types of data types: primitive and derived. *Primitive* data types are those that are not defined in terms of other data types; they exist on their own and form the basis for other types. *Derived* data types are those that are defined in terms of *primitive* data types or other derived data types. Consider, by way of example, the primitive type float and the derived type integer. Float is a well-defined mathematical concept that cannot be defined in terms of other data types, whereas an integer is a special case of the more general data type decimal. Integer is, in fact, said to derive from decimal.

In Listing 6.10, a slightly more complex collection of attributes is depicted along with different data types for each.

**LISTING 6.10**   Multiple Attributes—`message06.xml`

```
1: <?xml version="1.0"?>
2: <note
3:     xmlns:xsi="http://www.w3.org/2000/10/XMLSchema-instance"
4:     xsi:noNamespaceSchemaLocation="message06.xsd">
5:     <message number="10" date="2001-07-29" from="Kathy Shepherd">
6:         Remember to buy milk on the way home from work
7:     </message>
8: </note>
```

6

**ANALYSIS** On line 5, a numeric (xsd:integer), date (xsd:date), and string (xsd:string) attribute are depicted in the XML instance document. The declaration of these attributes will require explicit definition of data types to constrain their values. The xsd:attribute elements in each case will look like this:

```
<xsd:attribute name="number" type="xsd:integer" use="required"/>
<xsd:attribute name="date" type="xsd:date" use="required"/>
<xsd:attribute name="from" type="xsd:string" use="required"/>
```

Each attribute in this example is declared by name (corresponding to the element name in the XML instance document), type (declaring the data type in accordance with the constraints described earlier), and use (pertaining to whether the attribute is required or optional). If you declare that the attributes are required, rather than optional, then you would include the use="required" attribute value pair on each xsd:attribute element.

An XSD schema to validate this instance is shown in Listing 6.11.

**LISTING 6.11**  An XSD Schema to Validate an XML Instance with Multiple Attributes—message06.xsd

```
 1: <?xml version="1.0"?>
 2: <xsd:schema xmlns:xsd="http://www.w3.org/2000/10/XMLSchema">
 3:     <xsd:complexType name="messageType">
 4:         <xsd:simpleContent>
 5:             <xsd:restriction base="xsd:string">
 6:                 <xsd:attribute name="number"
                            type="xsd:integer" use="required"/>
 7:                 <xsd:attribute name="date"
                            type="xsd:date" use="required"/>
 8:                 <xsd:attribute name="from"
                            type="xsd:string" use="required"/>
 9:             </xsd:restriction>
10:         </xsd:simpleContent>
11:     </xsd:complexType>
12:     <xsd:element name="note">
13:         <xsd:complexType>
14:             <xsd:sequence>
15:                 <xsd:element name="message" type="messageType"/>
16:             </xsd:sequence>
17:         </xsd:complexType>
18:     </xsd:element>
19: </xsd:schema>
```

**ANALYSIS** Lines 5–9 define the string base for the attribute constraints using the <xsd:restriction base="xsd:string"> tag. Each attribute is a string (line 5) that is further constrained by a declaration on lines 6–8 for data type (integer, date, or string) and use. (Each attribute is required in a conforming XML document.)

# Three Approaches to Validity: DTD, XDR and XSD

For the past three days, you have learned three related, but distinct approaches to providing programmatically validated constraints to ensure conformance with data and document structural rules. DTDs have been around for a considerable length of time and have worked for a variety of applications. If you require concise encoding of constraints, then DTDs—the least verbose of the three languages presented—might be the answer. However, DTDs do not use the XML document syntax that is characteristic of other forms of schemata. Although expressing schemata in XML syntax does not necessarily improve the process, it does lead to ready extensibility and markup transformation options that do not exist for DTDs. Schemata based on XML vocabularies can include more expressive hierarchical markup and sophisticated content constraints.

Perhaps the most significant improvement associated with XML-based schemata is their ability to enforce comprehensive data type validation. As you learned yesterday and today, a rich set of data types is supported by XDR and XSD. XSD supports even more of these than XDR does.

XML-based schemata provide much better support for namespaces. You'll learn more about namespaces on Day 8, but important at this point is the fact that the namespace concept is key to the direction being promoted by the W3C.

XSD, a recent recommendation of the W3C, offers much promise for the future, with more comprehensive data types than XDR and a greater likelihood of being universally adopted as a platform-independent initiative. Visit the W3C Web site (http://www.w3.org) regularly to keep up on the exciting developments in this aspect of XML technology.

# Summary

Today, you learned some of the key implementation constructs for XSD, the approach that offers support for the richest set of data types. Your XML tool chest now includes the three most popular approaches to validating XML document instances. Watch for developments to unfold around the W3C with regard to XSD. You can remain current by visiting http://www.w3.org on a regular basis.

6

# Q&A

**Q** **Of the three schema languages introduced in this book (DTD, XDR, and XSD), which is being used the most?**

**A** A great deal of legacy code implements DTDs currently; however, the XDR approach is gaining rapid acceptance, primarily in the world of e-commerce, e-business, and supply chain management. Microsoft has improved development of solutions issuing core XML technologies with XDR validations. Nonetheless, the industry is expected to swing toward universal support of a single schema standard. Although it will likely take a long time for many legacy systems to adopt XSD, most vendors—even if they have a branded schema language—have already expressed an intent to fully support XSD.

**Q** **What is the difference between DTDs and XML-based schema languages in terms of data types?**

**A** DTDs do not provide for easy data type validation beyond simple text types. XML-based schemata support extensive data types in addition to standard document types. Validation of data types makes these languages more suited to use with data applications.

# Exercise

The exercise is provided so that you can test your knowledge of what you learned today. The answer is in Appendix A.

Yesterday you created an XDR schema for your Music Collection Markup Language (MCML). Based on the examples provided and the exercises completed today, create an XSD schema to validate MCML files.

# DAY 7

# XML Entities

Now that you have seen well-formed and valid XML, you'll have a chance to explore a special class of XML objects: XML Entities. In fact, the schemata that you authored were, in a sense, specialized external entities that were referenced by your XML document. Today, you will learn about

- Internal and external general entities in XML
- Syntax of entities and entity references
- Parameter entities and how they can be used to make DTD encoding modular

## Two Kinds of Entities

On Day 4, you saw some examples of entities in DTDs, but did not focus on the different types of entities that are supported by XML. Today, you will explore and compare different types of XML entities and see ways in which they can be used to solve particular encoding problems, offer shortcuts and savings, and provide modularity in coding.

In XML, two kinds of entities are available to encapsulate data. Predefined general entities are familiar to those who create HTML pages as a means of representing characters that might be confused with reserved markup characters. In an HTML document, when you need to render a <, >, or &, you must first encode the special character as an entity. The syntax for entities of this kind in HTML is

`&entity_name;`

When the browser resolves the HTML entity during interpretation of the page, a substitution takes place. The character that it represents replaces the entity phrase. In the case of XML, the same is true. A substitution takes place at the time that the document instance is processed. It is the parser that resolves the entity and places the referenced string in line with the surrounding content.

Parameter entities are defined and used only in external schemata, such as DTDs, although other schema languages have provisions for entity declaration. Parameter entities can reduce the amount of typing a developer does by placing commonly used phrases in small entity objects. Parameter entities also provide DTD authors with a means of developing DTD subsets and reusing external DTD logic in an almost modular fashion. You will read about both kinds of entities today and see how they are encoded in XML instances.

# General Entities

General Entities provide a means in HTML for encoding characters that are outside of the normal ASCII character set or that might interfere with markup. XML is less concerned about non-standard characters, such as those outside the normal ASCII character set range. This is because XML was designed to take advantage of the much more inclusive Unicode character set rather than ASCII. The 16-bit Unicode approach provides 65,536 possible characters, the 7-bit ASCII permits 128 characters, and the 8-bit set comprises 256 members. With the ASCII character set range, it doesn't take long to expend all of the available "spaces." Prior to Unicode, some languages needed to be represented graphically in HTML because the ASCII set had insufficient spaces to accommodate all of the characters required. Some European languages fill the 256 spaces of the ASCII set quite quickly. Asian languages typically comprise character and glyph sets in large numbers and combine to create tens of thousands of ideographs. The 16-bit Unicode standard is meant to accommodate these needs. Just in case it is stretched to its limits, however, XML also supports the 32-bit Unicode standard.

XML does include five built-in entities to aid the developer in avoiding any markup problems. These are shown in Table 7.1.

TABLE **7.1**    Five Predefined XML Entities

| Entity | Description |
|--------|-------------|
| &amp; | Ampersand (&) |
| &apos; | Apostrophe (') |
| &gt; | Greater-than (>) |
| &lt; | Less-than (<) |
| &quote; | Quotation Mark (") |

Beyond the predefined set of entities that XML provides, you can establish your own, just as you would declare an element. Entities can save you time and keystrokes. Repetitive and annoying tasks can be simplified by defining entities to substitute data during interpretation by an XML processor. The basic syntax for a general entity reference declaration in a DTD is

```
<!ENTITY entityname data_to_be_substituted>
```

The syntax for using the entity in an XML instance is

```
&entityname;
```

Entities cannot easily be declared in other schema languages. Today, you will use DTDs to establish entity declarations. Note that all of the entities presented so far have an ampersand, followed immediately by the name of the entity, and then a semi-colon. The entity provides a proxy to the entity definition in the schema. At the time of interpretation by an XML processor, the entire entity string is resolved by replacement with the entity reference.

Using this mechanism to create entities is particularly valuable for XML instances that contain repetitive data that is prone to change during the lifetime of the document. For instance, a legal contract could be marked up with entities used to designate the parties of the agreement. Entity substitution would ensure that the data describing the parties was resolved at runtime. Listing 7.1 depicts a snippet of a sales agreement marked up as a well-formed and valid XML document, using entities for the parties of the agreement. Using a text editor, create this document or something similar and save it as con-tract01.xml.

LISTING **7.1**    A Portion of a Contract in XML with Entities—contract01.xml

```
1: <?xml version="1.0"?>
2: <!-- listing 7.1 - contract01.xml -->
3:
4: <!DOCTYPE contract SYSTEM "contract01.dtd">
```

7

**LISTING 7.1** continued

```
 5: <contract>
 6:     <para1>&buyer; agrees to buy the property defined below
 7: on the terms and conditions set forth in this contract.</para1>
 8:     <para2 section="1">&buyer; will take title of the real property
 9: described below, for which consideration &buyer; agrees
10: to pay... </para2>
11: </contract>
```

**ANALYSIS** The contract root element (lines 2–11) contains a para1 (lines 6–7) and a para2 element (lines 8–10). The para2 element has a section attribute with a value of 1. Line 4 contains a DOCTYPE declaration that identifies the contract element as the root and declares a remote DTD at the URI contract01.dtd. On lines 6, 8, and 9, a &buyer; entity is included.

The DTD for this document will not only need to declare the structure of the element and attribute relationships, but also provide the entity reference that replaces the &buyer; entity after resolution by the XML processor. Suppose that the buyer referred to in this contract is Devan Shepherd. You could encode the entity reference in the DTD like this:

```
<!ENTITY buyer "Devan Shepherd">
```

This DTD snippet instructs the XML processor to substitute the string Devan Shepherd for each occurrence of the buyer entity in the XML instance. The processor will be able to locate each occurrence by recognizing the special syntax &buyer;. Listing 7.2 shows a complete DTD for the contract01.xml document instance. Create this example DTD and save it as contract01.dtd in the same directory as your contract01.xml file.

**LISTING 7.2** A DTD with an Entity Reference Declaration—contract01.dtd

```
 1: <?xml version="1.0" encoding="UTF-8"?>
 2: <!-- Listing 7.2 - contract01.dtd -->
 3:
 4: <!ELEMENT contract (para1, para2)>
 5: <!ELEMENT para1 (#PCDATA)>
 6: <!ELEMENT para2 (#PCDATA)>
 7: <!ATTLIST para2
 8:     section CDATA #REQUIRED
 9: >
10: <!ENTITY buyer "Devan Shepherd">
```

**ANALYSIS** Lines 4–9 declare the elemental and attribute structure of the XML document. These are interpreted to mean that the contract element contains element content, particularly the para1 and para2 child elements. The para1 element contains only text (#PCDATA) and para2 does likewise. The para2 element also has a required section attribute that contains only character data (CDATA). Line 10 defines the entity reference to indicate that Devan Shepherd references the buyer entity.

To see the results of the entity substitution, load your contract01.xml document into the Microsoft Internet Explorer browser. MSXML will resolve the entity and replace it with the referenced string obtained from the DTD. Figure 7.1 shows this result. Notice that the string Devan Shepherd now appears where the entity &buyer; was before parsing the document.

**FIGURE 7.1**

*The contract01.xml document with all entities resolved.*

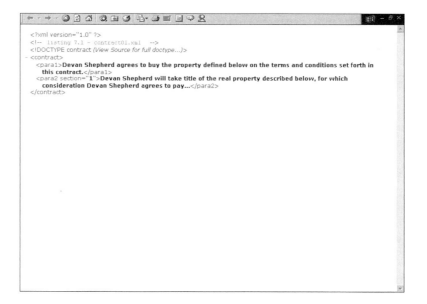

```
<?xml version="1.0" ?>
<!-- listing 7.1 - contract01.xml  -->
<!DOCTYPE contract (View Source for full doctype...)>
- <contract>
    <para1>Devan Shepherd agrees to buy the property defined below on the terms and conditions set forth in
      this contract.</para1>
    <para2 section="1">Devan Shepherd will take title of the real property described below, for which
      consideration Devan Shepherd agrees to pay...</para2>
  </contract>
```

Imagine that you had an entire multi-page document marked up in this fashion. For a real estate purchase contract, for instance, you might have the equivalent of a dozen legal-sized pages of text with, perhaps, three dozen &buyer; entities throughout various clauses of the agreement. The entity substitution would save you from having to ensure that each reference to the buyer was spelled correctly, properly capitalized, and in the precise spot required for the contract to be legal and binding. But even more importantly, the next time you require a purchase agreement, you would only need to change the entity reference once in the DTD to substitute a new buyer's name in every appropriate spot throughout the document.

7

This approach offers huge savings in terms of document reusability and data modularity. Carrying on from the simple legal example provided, you can see how entire collections of standard legal clauses—such asprecedents—and variables—such as parties of an agreement or action, temporal conditions, and so on—could be instantiated in a document instance through entity substitution.

The size of the reference to an entity is unlimited; therefore, entities offer a good means of substituting objects or text strings that are reused often, particularly if they are long.

# Parameter Entities

The `parameter entity` is encoded within the DTD to carry information for use in markup declarations. Typically, parameter entities are used to define a set of common attributes shared by several elements, or to provide a link to an external DTD. Those that target references entirely within the DTD are known as internal parameter entities, and those that reference data and objects outside the current DTD are known as external parameter entities.

Parameter entities are useful, but they can become quite difficult to read. Parameter entities are encoded in a DTD with a percent sign (%) in the reference and in the declaration. The percent sign is a flag that is used to designate a parameter entity as opposed to a general entity. The syntax of a parameter entity in a DTD is

```
<!ENTITY % entityname definition_of_entity>
```

The percent sign must be separated from the entity name by a space. The definition of the entity can be any valid DTD string. The string will be substituted at points where the entity is used in the DTD. In other words, an internal parameter entity functions like a general entity, except that the substitution takes place in the DTD, not the document instance.

Suppose you want to create a DTD for an invoice document, and that document contains a billing address, a shipping address, a vendor address, and a warehouse address. If the addresses were all quite similar in structure, then you could use a parameter entity to create the address structure once and reuse it as needed throughout the rest of the DTD. The address portion of the DTD might look something like this:

```
<!ENTITY % address
          "street         CDATA    #REQUIRED
           street2        CDATA    #IMPLIED
           city           CDATA    #REQUIRED
           state          CDATA    #REQUIRED
           zip            CDATA    #REQUIRED">
```

In this case, the `address` entity references a set of attribute declarations. A percent sign indicating that a parameter entity is being declared follows the `ENTITY` keyword. The parameter entity is called `address` and it references the string of attribute declarations contained by the double quotes (`"`).

With this established, you can use an `address` entity to substitute this pattern of attribute assignments on elements constrained by the DTD. For instance, to validate the billing address attributes on a `bill` element, you might include the following:

```
<!ELEMENT     bill      (#PCDATA)>
<!ATTLIST     bill      %address;>
```

The `bill` element contains parsed character data (`#PCDATA`) and has attributes. The attributes come from the `%address;` entity, declared elsewhere in the DTD. The percent sign is used here to begin the name of the entity, but no space is allowed between the percent sign and its associated name. This is how the parser knows that this is the entity. The entity reference declaration requires a space after the percent sign to set it apart from any entities.

When the XML parser resolves the entity in the DTD, the result will be effectively the same as a DTD written like this:

```
<!ELEMENT     bill                          (#PCDATA)>
<!ATTLIST     bill
              street          CDATA    #REQUIRED
              street2         CDATA    #IMPLIED
              city            CDATA    #REQUIRED
              state           CDATA    #REQUIRED
              zip             CDATA    #REQUIRED>
```

The entity will permit the substitution of the address attributes in pace of the `%address;` entity. Returning to the invoice scenario, a more complete DTD might look something like this:

```
<!ELEMENT     invoice        (bill, ship, vendor, warehouse)>
<!ELEMENT     bill           (#PCDATA)>
<!ATTLIST     bill           %address;>
<!ELEMENT     ship           (#PCDATA)>
<!ATTLIST     ship           %address;>
<!ELEMENT     vendor         (#PCDATA)>
<!ATTLIST     vendor         %address;>
<!ELEMENT     warehouse      (#PCDATA)>
<!ATTLIST     warehouse      %address;>
<!ENTITY   %  address
              "street   CDATA    #REQUIRED
              street2 CDATA    #IMPLIED
              city      CDATA    #REQUIRED
              state     CDATA    #REQUIRED
              zip       CDATA    #REQUIRED">
```

7

This saves effort that would otherwise be expended, including the full attribute list on each of the `bill`, `ship`, `vendor`, and `warehouse` elements.

External entities function in the same manner, except that the references are in a separate document. It is in this way that a DTD is really a specialized form of an external parameter entity.

# Entities in Other Schema Languages

You have looked at many entity examples today that all use DTD declarations. It is not as easy to declare entities in other schema languages. To declare entity substitution in XSD, for example, the easiest approach is to create a special element and then fix the element's content. In that way, you could use the element as the entity reference. You would need to further declare a unique namespace to accomplish this and ensure that the element you created was bound to that namespace.

Imagine, for instance, that you want to create the equivalent of a character entity, using the approach described, to represent a substitution string. Perhaps you want a short form for a long phrase, like the name of this book, Teach Yourself XML in 21 Days. In your XSD schema, you could establish an element and provide a fixed value for that element. The XSD declaration might look like this:

```
<xsd:element name="tyx21" fixed="Sams Teach Yourself XML in 21 Days, Second
Edition">
```

An XML instance document that made use of this element could include it as belonging to a specific namespace and then, when resolved by the parser, it could be expanded. Here is an example of a document snippet that uses the fixed content element:

```
<?xml version="1.0"?>
<message  xmlns="mystuff/message"
          xmlns:ent="mystuff/message/entities">

          ... other markup

          <Introduction>Welcome to <ent:tyx21>.  This book is about...
          </Introduction>

          ... other markup

</message>
```

When this is resolved by an XML processor, the `<ent:tyx21>` element will be substituted by the string Sams *Teach Yourself XML in 21 Days, Second Edition*.

# Summary

Today you have seen how entities can be used in XML as objects that serve the role of substituting referenced data at the point that the entity is resolved by the XML processor. In some cases, those substitutions help to avoid any markup problems. This is the case, for instance, when a special character, such as a less-than sign or an ampersand, is indicated by an entity that is later resolved by the parser. XML permits you to create your entities to reduce repetitive tasks, provide a means of substituting data that changes regularly, or make use of reusable modules of code.

# Q&A

**Q. What are the two kinds of entities in XML and how do they differ?**

A XML provides for general entities and parameter entities. General entities can be either internal or external and provide a means for substitution of data objects. Parameter entities exist only within a DTD rather than a document instance. Parameter entities provide a means of substitution or modularity of code.

**Q. In a DTD, how is a parser able to tell the difference between a parameter entity and a general entity?**

A A parameter entity reference is designated with an ampersand, followed by at least one space character and the entity name at the point of reference declaration.

# Exercise

The exercise is provided so that you can test your knowledge of what you learned today. The answer is in Appendix A, "Answers to the Questions."

Use the Music Collection Markup Language (MCML) instance from the challenge exercise on Day 4 and modify it to add a `style` child element in each `cd` element in your collection. Create a `&style;` entity with a text description something like this: "This CD is a compilation of the artist's top hits and is characteristic of the style we have come to enjoy." When you have finished, load your `cd.xml` document into a browser to ensure that the entities are resolved.

7

# PART II

# Processing XML

# DAY 8

# XML Namespaces

You have already used several XML Namespaces in your study of XDR and XSD schemata. You will recall that the XML processor uses namespaces during the validation process to help identify an XDR or XSD schema. Today, you will learn

- What namespaces are and why they are useful in XML programming
- XML namespace syntax
- The difference between URIs, URLs, and URNs
- How to declare explicit namespaces for elements and attributes in XML
- The meaning and declaration of the default namespace
- Selected standard namespaces used by various XML technologies

## Why Do You Need Namespaces?

The data model characterized by XML markup typically comprises a tree of elements. The tree structure helps to define the hierarchical nature of XML documents. You created and examined tree diagrams for simple XML documents on Day 2 when you learned the XML well-formed syntax in detail.

**Note** You will further explore the XML tree structure in detail on Day 12 when you learn to access XML documents using the Document Model Object (DOM) Application Program Interface (API). A DOM API provides you the programmatic means to access the *nodes*—such as elements, attributes, and comments—that comprise an XML document tree.

In XML markup, each element has an element type name, or tag name, and may or may not contain attributes. As you know, any attributes for a particular element are included in the start tag of the element that they serve to modify. Each attribute consists of a name and a corresponding value. The W3C calls the combination of element type names and attribute names the markup vocabulary (http://www.w3.org/TR/REC-xml-names/).

Applications that are created to use XML data typically make use of the markup vocabulary to determine how to process each element. Elements with different names are often handled differently, whereas those that share a name are processed in the same manner. For instance, message elements might be handled differently from response elements, but all message elements in a single document instance will, presumably, be handled in the same fashion.

Handling naming conventions in this manner works well if you, as the XML document author, ensure that all elements and attributes, which should be unique, are indeed uniquely named. However, self-authored names have the potential to cause difficulty in a distributed environment, like the Web, where it is common for data to be shared or XML documents to be merged. Many e-commerce business transactions, for instance, include the merging of data from multiple originating sources. Where this is the case, element or attribute names can be duplicated, making the processing more complicated or impossible. For example, if two business partners exchange XML data, each using the message element to represent different types (or classes) of data, then the processing application will not be able to differentiate the two. This results in message having two distinct meanings in a single document instance, a naming collision.

You've learned that XML allows you to place structured data into a text file, and that the nature of that structure includes intelligence about the data being marked up. If element type names representing different classes of data are included in the same document instance, then the intelligence and value of the data are compromised as a result.

## What Does a Naming Collision Look Like?

You have seen many examples of the rich markup available with XML that includes the ability for you to create your own tags. Of course, people with whom you share or merge

8

data can also create their own tags, as in the e-commerce example noted earlier. It is possible for each of you to create different elements that have the same name; in fact, there is a high likelihood that you may. When this happens, *naming collisions* result and the application is unable to tell the difference between the like-named elements.

Perhaps, by way of example, you are marking up a document about a committee structure that includes an element called chair that is used to identify a chairperson or leader of the committee. The document goes on to list the members by name. It may look something like the XML document instance shown as Listing 8.1.

**LISTING 8.1**  A Simple XML Document Depicting a Committee Structure—committee.xml

```
 1: <?xml version="1.0"?>
 2: <!-- Listing 8.1 - committee.xml -->
 3:
 4: <committee>
 5:     <chair>Kathy</chair>
 6:     <member>Merrenna</member>
 7:     <member>Doug</member>
 8:     <member>Greg</member>
 9:     <member>Kristen</member>
10: </committee>
```

Note that this XML document is merely a simple list of names, with one person designated as the *chair* of the committee. The rest of the members of the committee follow in member elements.

Later, this document will be merged with data provided by a meeting planner who will designate where individuals on the committee will sit around a conference table during an upcoming event. The planner's markup will also include an element called chair that identifies which seat each committee member will occupy around the meeting table. Listing 8.2 shows such a document.

**LISTING 8.2**  A Seating Plan XML Document Instance—seating.xml

```
 1: <?xml version="1.0"?>
 2: <!-- Listing 8.2 - seating.xml -->
 3:
 4: <seating>
 5:     <chair>head of table</chair>
 6:     <chair>first on the left</chair>
 7:     <chair>second on the left</chair>
 8:     <chair>first on the right</chair>
 9:     <chair>second on the right</chair>
10: </seating>
```

The result of merging the two documents into one will cause some confusion because the element `chair` is used in both original document instances to describe two different elements. Listing 8.3 presents the merged document.

**LISTING 8.3**    A Meeting Plan Document with Naming Collisions—`meeting.xml`

```
 1: <?xml version="1.0"?>
 2: <!-- Listing 8.3 - meeting.xml -->
 3:
 4: <meeting>
 5:     <chair>Kathy</chair>
 6:             <chair>head of table</chair>
 7:     <member>Merrenna</member>
 8:             <chair>first on the left</chair>
 9:     <member>Doug</member>
10:             <chair>second on the left</chair>
11:     <member>Greg</member>
12:             <chair>first on the right</chair>
13:     <member>Kristen</member>
14:             <chair>second on the right</chair>
15: </meeting>
```

The naming collision of the chair element in the resulting merged document provides a challenge to the application processing these data. The application cannot tell the difference between the `chair` element on line 5 that came from the committee markup and those originating from the seating plan that now reside on lines 6, 8, 10, 12, and 14 of the merged document instance. As far as an application is concerned, this document has a single class of data, and the `chair` element belongs to that class of data. For the most part, humans can readily determine the distinction, but an application will not be able to differentiate the two classes of `chair` elements without some additional information. Therefore, processing will be problematic until you inform the application about the two different types of `chair` elements to be considered.

Namespaces offer you a mechanism to uniquely identify like-named elements that belong to different classes of data. You will see soon how this mechanism works; but first, examine another sample of XML data that contains naming collisions.

Suppose that you have an XML document that describes a collection of items in an office. In the office are books and works of art that you want to itemize in the XML document. The XML document will, therefore, list two distinct classes of `item`: *books and art*.

Each `item` in the `collection` will have a `description` element, a `title` element, and an element to identify the creator of the item, such as an `author` for a book or an `artist` for a work of art. Listing 8.4 shows an example of the collection marked up in XML. Assuming that the `item` element is one example of a naming collision, can you identify others?

**LISTING 8.4**    An XML Document with Naming Collisions—`collection.xml`

```
 1: <?xml version="1.0"?>
 2: <!-- Listing 8.4 - collection.xml -->
 3:
 4: <collection>
 5:
 6:   <item>
 7:     <description>an XML book</description>
 8:     <title>Sams Teach Yourself XML in 21 Days, Second Edition</title>
 9:     <author>Devan Shepherd</author>
10:   </item>
11:
12:   <item>
13:     <description>a great painting</description>
14:     <title>Bermuda Longtails</title>
15:     <artist>E. Anthony</artist>
16:   </item>
17:
18: </collection>
```

The potential naming collisions in this example include `item`, which belongs to both the books and art classes of data. In other words, a book `item` means something different from an art `item`. The book `description` is different from an artwork `description`, both belonging to different classes of data. The element `title` in both types of items is another potential problem. These colliding element type names are problematic because the application that uses this data will not be able to differentiate the `item`, `description`, or `title` elements. You will see how to resolve this conflict through the declaration of namespaces.

## Preventing Naming Collisions with Namespace Declarations

An XML namespace is an identifier that uniquely references a collection of names that can be used as element type names or attribute names in an XML document. By establishing a namespace for a particular class of data, you inform the XML application that a particular element or attribute *belongs to* the specified namespace, or set of names characterizing that class of data.

The namespace effectively serves to qualify element type names and attribute names uniquely on the Web, or in any distributed system, to avoid naming collisions between elements with the same name. In the case of the meeting-planning example that you explored earlier, you could establish a *committee* namespace to include the chair element type pertaining to the *chairperson* of the committee, and a *seating* namespace to include the chair element type that identified the furniture around the conference table at which people were to sit. You will create those namespaces later today, but first, you will get a chance to see the syntax and learn the component parts of a namespace declaration.

## Syntax of an XML Namespace Declaration

You have seen several examples of XML namespace declarations on previous days. You can review those namespaces along with others that you will create based upon the standard syntax of an XML namespace declaration. The XML namespace begins with a reserved attribute keyword (xmlns) followed, optionally, by a colon and a prefix. The colon and prefix serve as a proxy later in the XML instance for the element type names and attribute names that are bound to the namespace that is qualified by the attribute value in the form of a URI image. The two typical forms of the XML namespace include a declarative simple form, such as

```
xlmns="URI"
```

The following is a sample of a simple declaration, using an imaginary URI:

```
xmlns="http://shepherdnamespace.com/XML"
```

If you want to associate several elements in an XML instance with a particular namespace, it makes sense to use a declaration that includes a prefix to serve as a proxy for that namespace, such as the following:

```
xmlns:prefix="URI"
```

## Error! Hyperlink reference not valid.

The following is a namespace declaration with a user-defined prefix included and an imaginary URI:

```
xmlns:committee="http://shepherdnamespace.com/XML/committee"
```

Namespaces can be declared as default namespaces, taking the first form xmlns="URI". A default namespace has a scope of an entire XML document instance. It declares a namespace to be used for all elements within its scope, and a prefix is not used. A default namespace covers all of the element types and attributes that are not included within the scope of an explicit namespace declaration.

With an explicit declaration, like the second example (`xmlns:prefix="URI"`), you define a shorthand, or prefix, to substitute for the full name of the namespace as a proxy designation later in the document instance. You use this prefix to qualify all of the element type names or attribute names belonging to that specific namespace, rather than to the default set.

At the outset today, you were reminded that XML documents constitute hierarchical tree structures comprising various nodes. Explicit declarations are useful when a particular document node contains element types or attributes from different namespaces.

The syntax for element types or attributes in the document instance that belong to an explicit namespace include the designated prefix followed by a colon and the element type or attribute name, as in

```
prefix:element
```

```
prefix:attribute
```

Sample:

```
<committee:chair>Kathy</committee:chair>
```

```
<filename committee:Listing="8.1">committee.xml</filename>
```

In the example shown, the element type `chair` and the attribute `listing` have a prefix of code indicating that they belong to the `http://shepherdnamespace.com /XML/committee` namespace. Don't forget that this URI, although it looks like a Web address, is just a label that identifies a particular collection of elements and attributes. The application does not attempt to make a connection to `shepherdnamespace.com`.

The prefix serves as a shortcut to save the document author from explicitly declaring the complete namespace for each element type and attribute that belongs to it. The fully qualified element and attribute resolved by the XML parser, as though expanded into complete namespace declarations would look like this:

```
<name xmlns="http://shepherdnamespace.com /XML/committee">
                        A Simple XML Document
                        Depicting a Committee Structure</name>
```

```
<filename code:Listing="8.1"
        xmlns:code="http://shepherdnamespace.com /XML/committee">
                        committee.xml</filename>
```

## Uniquely Identifying XML Namespaces

An XML namespace URI serves merely as *a unique label* for the collection of elements and attributes that it identifies. You should understand that this URI is nothing more than a series of characters used to differentiate names.

Tip

> A URI used in an XML namespace is nothing more than a label, or a string of characters, which uniquely identifies the namespace. It makes no difference what—if anything—a URI points to. A URI merely serves as a unique moniker for the collection of element type names and attribute names it characterizes.

Confusion results for some readers because of the familiar form of certain URI character streams used by various popular XML technologies. For instance, some URIs comprise URLs. You will recall from Day 6 that the URI used to identify an XML Schema Definition (XSD) Schema to an XML parser is declared in the root element of the schema and always takes the form:

```
xmlns:xsd="http://www.w3.org/2000/10/XMLSchema"
```

It certainly looks as though the `xmlns:xsd` attribute value is a URL. Try entering the URL portion of this string in a Web browser to see what you get. If you view this Web site with Microsoft Internet Explorer 5.0 or above, you will get a transformed view of the XML schema that is used to validate an XSD schema. In other words, the W3C has placed an XML document at this URL, knowing that people will try to resolve the URL that forms part of the namespace for XSD, perhaps out of curiosity.

Based on what you have learned so far, do you think that an XML parser resolves this URL when it performs a validation according to the constraints programmed in an XSD schema? In other words, does the XML parser download the schema that you saw at `http://www.w3.org/2000/10/XMLSchema` when it validates your XML document? The answer to both versions of the question is "no." Remember that a namespace is just a label. The URI is simply a unique label. If the URI includes a URL, the XML parser does not resolve that Web address when the namespace is declared.

Why, then, do you think that a URL might be used to identify a namespace? The fact is that a URL can be globally unique across the entire Internet. When you register a host or domain name, you make it yours in a current estimated universe of approximately 450 million current domain names, at the time of this writing (source: *Internic News*, Network Solutions, Inc., 2001). The Internic, a domain registry service, currently allows domain names to be registered with up to 22 characters before the "dot" in the URL. These characters include any combination of English alphanumeric characters and the minus sign or dash character, provided it is not the first character in the string. Therefore, for the mathematically inclined, the total possible unique choices for names before the "dot" in a URL address would be 37 characters permuted into 22 positions, which is equal to $3.17 \times 10$ raised to the power of 34, or 31,700,000,000,000,000,000,000,000,000,000,000 possibilities.

8

By appending information to your own unique domain address, you can be relatively certain to create a unique label for your namespace. This is precisely the rationale used by the W3C to establish a unique namespace for the XSD schema namespace that you declared in your work on Day 6.

A URI can also be created in the form of a *Uniform Resource Name* (URN) rather than a URL. On Day 5, you learned to create schemata using the Microsoft XML Data Reduced Language (XDR). You might recall that you declared two namespaces in the root element of each XDR schema you authored. These namespaces were URNs rather than URLs; they did not provide a Uniform Resource Locator that followed the syntax for a Web address. By definition, a URN is any URI that is not a URL. This seems like a somewhat oversimplified definition, but it does serve to differentiate URNs from URLs. In the case of XDR schemata the namespaces you coded included the following URNs:

```
xmlns="urn:schemas-microsoft-com:xml-data"
xmlns:dt="urn:schemas-microsoft-com:datatypes"
```

The first declaration established the namespace that pertained to the entire XDR document, known as the default namespace. You will learn all about default namespaces in the section titled "Putting Namespace Declaration Theory to Practice." You might recall that the second namespace identified a prefix that served as a proxy for the data type namespace used to identify data type attributes used as validation constraints in XDR. Later in the XDR document instance, you were able to include dt:type attributes that provided strictures for the valid data types of an element or attribute. For instance, in the example

```
<AttributeType name="purchase_date" dt:type="date" required="yes"/>
```

a required purchase_date attribute for a particular element is only valid if the value for that attribute is expressed as a date string that complies with the data type syntax prescribed. In the example, the only name that belongs to the data type namespace is the attribute type, encoded as dt:type. The AttributeType element and the name and required attributes belong to the default urn:schemas-microsoft-com:xml-data namespace.

**Note**

A group known as the Internet Engineering Task Force (IETF) is working on a predefined syntax for URNs, based on an initial note by R. Moats (AT&T), May 1997. This syntax will provide for the resolution using Internet Protocols of names, which have a greater persistence than that currently associated with Internet host names or domains that URLs use. If the IETF approach is successful, Uniform Resource Names may eventually be URI schemes that improve on URLs in reliability over time, including authenticity, replication, and availability.

The document author can use virtually any name for a namespace except the reserved namespace `xml`, which is the intellectual property of the W3C.

## How Are Namespaces Used by Applications?

In the examples discussed today, predefined namespaces for XSD and XDR offer important information to the XML applications that recognize them. The use of these prescribed namespaces is not merely convention; it is required by the applications that validate the XML document instances. Even though an XML parser does not resolve a URL during the process of validating the constraints of an XSD schema, it does require that particular namespace be included. In fact, when the parser encounters that exact namespace, it knows to employ the XSD rules for syntax that are built in to the application. This is true of other XML applications. The namespace is just a label, like a flag in other computer languages, which instructs the application to process the element types and attributes that belong to the collection named by that label in a particular manner. The rules for processing the element types and attributes are built in to the application before it parses the XML document.

# Putting Namespace Declaration Theory into Practice

Now that you know the syntax and theory behind namespace declarations, open a text editor and create explicit namespaces to resolve the naming collisions shown in the earlier sample listings.

Starting with the Committee Meeting Plan example, declare explicit namespaces for the element types that originated from the `committee.xml` markup and for those that came from the `seating.xml` source document. In the case of the committee element types, create a namespace that has a `cmte` prefix and use the following URI:

```
http://shepherdnamespace.com/XML/committee
```

Don't forget that although this URI looks like a valid URL, whether it points to an actual Web site is inconsequential. The URI is just a label used internally by an XML processor. For the seating element types, designate a namespace with a `seat` prefix that comprises a URN:

```
urn:XML_in_21_Days:seating
```

Save your completed work in a revised meeting file named `meeting02.xml`. You should obtain a result that looks like the code in Listing 8.5.

**LISTING 8.5**   An XML Meeting Document with Namespace Declarations—`meeting02.xml`

```
 1: <?xml version="1.0"?>
 2: <!-- Listing 8.5 - meeting02.xml -->
 3:
 4: <meeting xmlns:cmte="http://shepherdnamespace.com/XML/committee"
 5:          xmlns:seat="urn:XML_in_21_Days:seating">
 6:   <cmte:chair>Kathy</cmte:chair>
 7:       <seat:chair>head of table</seat:chair>
 8:   <cmte:member>Merrenna</cmte:member>
 9:       <seat:chair>first on the left</seat:chair>
10:   <cmte:member>Doug</cmte:member>
11:       <seat:chair>second on the left</seat:chair>
12:   <cmte:member>Greg</cmte:member>
13:       <seat:chair>first on the right</seat:chair>
14:   <cmte:member>Kristen</cmte:member>
15:       <seat:chair>second on the right</seat:chair>
16: </meeting>
```

**ANALYSIS**   The XML namespaces that you designated are declared as the values of `xmlns` attributes on the root element `meeting`. The committee namespace `http://shepherdnamespace.com/XML/committee` indicates a `cmte` prefix that is added to each of the element type names in the start and end tags of the elements that belong to that namespace. These are shown on lines 6, 8, 10, 12, and 14.

Line 5

```
5:          xmlns:seat="urn:XML_in_21_Days:seating">
```

includes the namespace declaration for the element types that originated from the `seating.xml` source document. The prefix `seat` is added to each of the `chair` elements that belong to the `seat` namespace. These elements are on lines 7, 9, 11, 13, and 15.

Next, follow the same process for the office collection XML document depicted by Listing 8.4. You will recall that it included element types from two data classes: one characterized as books and the other as works of art. Using a text editor, create a new document, `collection02.xml`, which incorporates a default namespace for the book elements with a URI of `http://www.devan.org/books` and an explicit namespace with an `art` prefix and a URI of `urn:mystuff:artwork`. When you have finished, compare your result with the example shown in Listing 8.6.

**LISTING 8.6**   A Collection Document with XML Namespace Declarations—`collection02.xml`

```
1: <?xml version="1.0"?>
2: <!-- Listing 8.6 - collection02.xml -->
```

**LISTING 8.6** continued

```
 3:
 4: <collection xmlns="http://www.devan.org/books"
 5:            xmlns:art="urn:mystuff:artwork">
 6:
 7:    <item number="1">
 8:        <description>an XML book</description>
 9:        <title>Sams Teach Yourself XML in 21 Days, Second Edition</title>
10:        <author>Devan Shepherd</author>
11:    </item>
12:
13:    <art:item number="1">
14:        <art:description>a great painting</art:description>
15:        <art:title>Bermuda Longtails</art:title>
16:        <art:artist>E. Anthony</art:artist>
17:    </art:item>
18:
19: </collection>
```

**ANALYSIS** Lines 4 and 5

```
 4: <collection xmlns="http://www.devan.org/books"
 5:            xmlns:art="urn:mystuff:artwork">
```

show the root element of the XML document with a default namespace (line 4) and an explicit namespace with a prefix (art) on line 5.

Because the first item element (lines 7–11) and its child elements belong to the default namespace, no prefix is provided in the element tags. By comparison, the second item element and its child elements belong to the urn:mystuff:artwork namespace; therefore, each element start and end tag includes an art prefix in the element type name.

# Selected Standard XML Namespace URIs

You have already seen the XDR and XSD namespaces along with several others. Table 8.1 provides a reference listing of several standard XML namespaces in common use. Some of these will be used on subsequent days.

**TABLE 8.1** Selected Standard XML Namespace URIs

| Application | Namespace URI |
| --- | --- |
| XDR schema | urn:schemas-microsoft-com:xml-data |
| XDR data types | urn:schemas-microsoft-com:xml-data |
| XSD schema | http://www.w3.org/2000/10/XMLSchema |

**TABLE 8.1**   continued

| Application | Namespace URI |
|---|---|
| XSL Formatting Vocabulary | `http://www.w3.org/1999/XSL/Format` |
| XSLT Transform Vocabulary | `http://www.w3.org/1999/XSL/Transform` |
| XHTML | `http://www.w3.org/1999/xhtml` |

8

# Summary

Today, you learned that naming collisions can occur when documents from various sources are merged. Document authors are free to create their own element type names and attribute names; therefore, like-named tags can result in merged mark-up vocabularies. Namespaces provide a means for developers to prevent naming collisions by designating unique identities for like-named elements that belong to different classes of data. Each class of data can be assigned to a specific namespace. In this way, the namespace becomes a collection of element type names and attribute names that characterize that particular class of data.

Namespaces are identified with URIs that can comprise URLs or URNs. Document authors use URIs to ensure, to the extent possible, that each namespace is globally unique. URIs that comprise URLs are not resolved by the XML application; rather, all URIs merely provide a label that instructs the application to process elements and attributes in a particular fashion on the basis of pre-existing logic.

A number of standard namespaces are identified with particular technologies. Use of these specific namespaces is required by some XML applications.

# Q&A

**Q  What is a naming collision?**

**A**  A naming collision occurs when two different element types or attributes relating to two classes of data have the same name in a mark-up document.

**Q  When can a naming collision occur?**

**A**  Naming collisions occur most often when XML data from multiple sources are merged into a single document instance. In such a case, it is possible for two like-named element types or attributes to refer to completely different types of data.

**Q  How can a naming collision be avoided?**

**A**  Namespaces provide the developer with a simple mechanism for uniquely identifying and differentiating like-named tags to avoid potential naming collisions.

**Q** How does the syntax of a default namespace differ from an explicitly defined namespace expressed in the same document instance?

**A** A default namespace does not provide a prefix to serve as a proxy throughout the remainder of the XML document instance. Element type names and attribute names that do not include a prefix belong to the default namespace. An explicit namespace will include a prefix that is attached to the element type and attribute names in the start and end tags of the elements belonging to the explicit namespace.

**Q** Why do you have to use a specific, standard namespace to identify XML elements that belong to an XSD schema?

**A** The specific namespace (`http://www.w3.org/2000/10/XMLSchema`) is recognized by all XML applications and parsers that have the syntax rules for XSD built in. In fact, the specific namespace is the only one that identifies the XML document elements and attributes as belonging to the XSD collection; therefore, nothing else will allow the parser to validate the XML instance document against the constraints you program via XSD.

# Exercise

The exercise is provided so that you can test your knowledge of what you learned today. The answers are in Appendix A.

During the first week, you created a well-formed XML instance document to mark up a collection of audio CDs. You later validated that document using DTDs, XDR, and XSD schemata and added some entities. Today you will add a new class of data to your Music Collection Markup Language (MCML). The new class of data will be used to mark up data records that are vinyl Long Playing (LP) records rather than CDs.

Follow these steps:

1.  Add a data record to the MCML for an LP called *King of Blue*, by *Miles Davis*. The LP contains *11* tracks.

2.  Encode the result such that the new class of data will belong to a namespace with the URI `urn:myoldies:LPs`.

3.  Declare a `vinyl` prefix and use it as appropriate in the MCML mark-up.

4.  Create a new element type for use in marking up LPs to avoid having the data stored within a `CD` container element.

# DAY 9

# XML Path Language (XPath)

You have learned that XML provides an efficient and effective means of describing highly structured data with self-describing tags. The value of the intelligence that is stored with the data as a result of these author-generated data descriptors adds value to the structure. However, XML on its own does not provide a means to locate specified subsets of the data stored in a document. The XML Path Language provides expression syntax for locating specified parts of the data stored in a document instance. Today, you will learn

- The importance of the XPath language for locating specific data components within an XML structure
- The basics of XPath syntax and usage
- How to locate the seven node types exposed by XPath
- The fundamentals of relative XPath navigation using location paths
- The use of selected XPath operators and functions

# What Is XPath?

The XML Path Language (XPath) provides you with a means of locating specific nodes in an XML document tree. Unlike XML, XPath is not a structural language. Rather, it is a string-based language of expressions that is used by other XML technologies to locate and navigate specified nodes of an XML structure. The W3C recommends XPath version 1.0.

XPath was designed to work with Extensible Stylesheet Language Transformations (XSLT), which transforms XML documents into other forms—such as other XML documents or HTML—and the XML Pointer Language (XPointer), which offers a method to "point" to particular information inside an XML document. In fact, partway through the development of XSLT, the W3C recognized significant overlap between the expression sequences being designed and those that were described for XPointer. The W3C brought members of each group together to develop a separate, but single, non-overlapping expression language for use by both technologies. XPath was published on November 16, 1999, the same day as XSLT. You will learn about the role of XPath in XSLT on Day 16, when you create your own XML to HTML transformations. XPointer is covered in detail on Day 11.

XPath acts as a sublanguage within XSLT and XPointer. An XPath expression can be used in string manipulation, numeric calculations, and in Boolean logic. However, the main use for XPath and the function that helps to give it its name is to address parts of an XML document using a path notation that is similar to those used to resolve URLs that must navigate through XML document hierarchies. XPath is formed of simple expressions, analogous to regular expressions in other languages, characterized by path symbols, node names, and reserved words in a compact string that is written in a non-XML syntax. XPath serves the function of locating component parts of an XML document, but it operates on the abstract logical structure of the instance rather than its syntax. You'll see what this means as you explore an XML document using XPath expressions later today.

# Exposing the Nodes of an XML Document Tree

As you know, data stored in an XML document can be represented as a hierarchical tree structure of nodes. Some of these nodes can contain other nodes. For instance, an element can contain other elements. Elements can also contain character data; however, if they do, the character data represents a separate child node. Accessing the data contained by an element requires that you traverse the structure to the text child node of the element node. You are familiar with element and attribute nodes and know that there are nodes for comments in an XML document instance as well. In fact, XPath is aware of seven node types. Using XPath results in the creation of a structured, searchable hierarchy of the nodes in a document instance.

To reiterate, the principal concept behind XPath is the traversal of an XML document to arrive at a prescribed node. The traversal is accomplished through the use of expressions that are constructed following XPath syntax rules. When XPath expressions are evaluated, they result in a data object that can be characterized as one of the following:

- **Node**—A single selected node is located.
- **Node set**—Several nodes that share specified relationship characteristics are selected.
- **Boolean**—The expression produces either a true or false result.
- **String**—A resolution of the expression produces a string based on the content of a node or nodes in path traversed.
- **Number**—A calculation performed during evaluation of the XPath expression might produce a floating-point numeric result.

## The Seven Document Nodes of XPath

The node tree produced by XPath is similar to the tree structure that comprises the Document Object Model (DOM). The DOM provides you with an Application Program Interface (API) so that you can access, interrogate, modify, or add exposed nodes in a document tree under program control. You will learn all about the DOM on Day 12.

XPath has the following seven node types: root, element, attribute, comment, text, processing instruction, and namespace. The XPath tree has only one root node that contains all other nodes in the tree. Do not confuse the root node with the root element of an XML document. The root node contains all other nodes, including the root element, all other elements, any processing instructions, namespaces, comments, or text in the entire document instance.

| Tip | The root node in an XPath tree is not the same as the root element in an XML document instance. The root node contains the root element and all other element nodes, attribute nodes, comment nodes, text, processing instruction nodes, and namespace nodes. |

## Node Relationships

As noted earlier, the root node serves as a container for all other nodal content in the XML document instance. The root node and the element nodes contain ordered lists of child nodes. Each node except the root node has a parent node. Parent nodes can contain zero to many child and descendent (that is, grandchild) nodes. Interestingly, the only nodes that can be child nodes are element, comment, processing instruction, and text nodes. You will recall that an attribute is analogous to an adjective; an attribute modifies an element, which is like a noun in spoken languages. An attribute is not a child of an element; it simply provides additional information about the element. An attribute is attached to an element, but is not a child construct of the element. Although it might seem confusing, the fact is that an attribute can have a parent, but it is not a child of that parent. A parent contains its child elements. As you discovered on Day 2, even an empty element that has no content can have associated attributes. An attribute is not considered content of an element. Using similar logic, a namespace node can have a parent, but it is not the child of its parent. A namespace merely provides additional information about the parent; it describes the namespace to which its parent is bound. In fact, the namespace node is really a specialized instance of the attribute node.

**Tip**

> Attribute and namespace nodes have parent nodes, but do not constitute child nodes of those parent nodes in XPath. Attribute and namespace nodes provide information or modify their parent nodes, but they are not content of their parent nodes. A child node must be contained by a parent node.

# Examining the Nodes of an XML Document Instance

To better understand the component parts of an XPath node tree, an XML document will be presented along with a diagram of the XPath nodes that correspond to the document. You will see a version of the document that you manipulated on earlier days first in its XML version and then as a nodal tree that can be searched using XPath expressions. Listing 9.1 depicts the XML message document, `message01.xml`, which you used previously. To represent all seven XPath nodes, the document now includes a processing instruction and comments.

**LISTING 9.1**   An XML Document That Includes All Seven XPath Nodes—`message01.xml`

```
 1: <?xml version="1.0"?>
 2: <!-- Listing 9.1 - message01.xml -->
 3:
 4: <note xmlns="urn:STY_XML_in_21Days:XPath">
 5:
 6:     <?MessageProcessor command = "AcceptMessage" ?>
 7:     <!-- This is an example of a processing instruction -->
 8:
 9:     <message type="phone message">
10:         Remember to buy milk on the way home from work
11:         <status>urgent</status>
12:     </message>
13: </note>
```

**ANALYSIS**   This relatively simple document instance has a `note` root element starting on line 4 that includes a namespace with the URI `urn:STY_XML_in_21Days:XPath`. Line 6

```
6:     <?MessageProcessor command = "AcceptMessage" ?>
```

constitutes a processing instruction. On Day 14, you will use processing instructions to link XML document instances to cascading stylesheets (CSS) to style the output for client-side rendering. On Day 15, you will use similar processing instructions to associate an Extensible Stylesheet Language (XSL) Stylesheet with XML documents for the same purpose. Processing instructions provide special instructions to the application parsing the XML document. The example on line 6 might instantiate a `MessageProcessor` that acts on the message data provided by this XML document instance.

Lines 2 and 7 are comments. Note that the comment in line 2 occurs before the root element of the XML instance and the one on line 7 is within the `note` element. Because the root node is outside the root element, XPath can locate the comment on line 2 as easily as the comment on line 7.

The XML declaration on line 1 is not contained in a document node. You might have assumed that it was a processing instruction, but technically it is not, and XPath does not have an expression to locate this information.

The rest of the nodes in this document comprise element and attribute nodes that XPath can readily locate.

To better illustrate the node tree that results from XPath, see Figure 9.1. Such a tree shows each of the node types along with the content of the nodes. The boxes represent each node type known to XPath along with the content of the nodes. The lines between each box depict the relationships amongst nodes. You should be able to map the nodal boxes in Figure 9.1 back to the actual nodes they represent in Listing 9.1. Step through the diagram one node at a time as you read along with description provided.

FIGURE 9.1

*An XPath tree for Listing 9.1—* `message01.xml`.

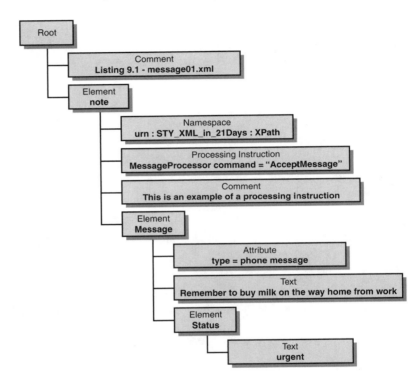

The Root node is shown to contain all other nodes in the XPath tree. The XML declaration on line 1 of Listing 9.1 is not included in the diagram because it has no representation in the XPath result tree. The first child of the Root node is the comment node that occurs in the document instance prior to the `note` root element. The element node for the `note` element is next.

The lines originating from the `note` element box terminate on the namespace node, the processing instruction node, the comment node, and the `message` element node. XPath considers each of these related to that element node. The `urn:STY_XML_in_21Days:XPath` namespace node is not the child of the `note` element node, even though this node is the namespace's parent node. The `MessageProcessor command = "AcceptMessage"` processing instruction node, comment node, and `message` element node are considered child nodes of the `note` element node.

The message node is the parent of a type attribute node even though the attribute node is not a child of that parent. The message node contains a text node and a status element node as child elements. The status element node contains a text node.

## Complex Nodal Relationships

You have seen the simple relationships among nodes for the message01.xml document instance. However, some relationships may, at first, seem less obvious. You have walked through parent and child relationships. Next you will be able to consider ancestor and descendent relationships known to XPath.

9

**Tip**

The order of nodes in an XPath tree is determined by the order in which they are encountered in the original XML instance document. This order is referred to as *document order*. It begins with the root node and progresses down the XPath tree in a parallel fashion to the order of elements, comments, processing instructions, text, attributes, and namespaces in the document tree.

Each node in an XPath tree comprises a string representation referred to as a *string-value* that XPath utilizes to make node comparisons. The string-value of an element is the complete text content of that element, plus the text of its descendents. Line 11 of Listing 9.1

```
11:        <status>urgent</status>
```

includes the markup and content for the status element. Now consider the text node of the status element, which has a string-value of urgent. The status element node has only its associated text node as a descendent, so that is all that is included in the string-value for this node. The status element node and its child text node have the same string-values.

**Tip**

The string-value of any element node is determined by concatenating the string-values of all of its descendent text nodes.

The string-value of the message element from Figure 9.1 is more involved. It contains the text content of the message element node, which in turn includes the text nodes of its descendent nodes (status)—all the nodes that follow—in document order. Therefore, the string-value of the message element node is Remember to buy milk on the way home from work urgent. This is the result string formed by concatenating the string-values of the text node and all of its descendent text nodes. The string-value of the immediate child node of the message element node is still just Remember to buy milk on the way home from work and the string value of the status element remains urgent. However, the string-value of the message element node is the concatenation of the other two, descendent string-values.

**Tip**

Descendent nodes are all of those that follow the node in document order.

Based on what you have learned, can you determine the string-value of the root node of the document in Listing 9.1? It must be determined by concatenating the string-values of its text node descendents. Therefore, it is Remember to buy milk on the way home from work urgent, just like the message element node because there are no other descendent text nodes in this document instance.

The string-value of attribute nodes contains the value of the attribute only. Therefore, the string-value of the type attribute node is phone message. String-values for comment nodes are the text of the comment, or Listing 9.1 - message01.xml for the comment node belonging to the comment on line 2 of Listing 9.1.

Processing instructions have string-values that comprise the instruction after the first argument. Line 6 of message01.xml

```
6:      <?MessageProcessor command = "AcceptMessage" ?>
```

provides the markup for a processing instruction. The first argument of that instruction is MessageProcessor, so the string-value of the processing instruction node will be command = "AcceptMessage". This is valuable for processing instructions that include URLs, as in the case of linked stylesheets. You will learn about stylesheets on Days 14 and 15.

Namespace nodes have their URIs as string-values. The string-value of the namespace associated with the note element is urn:STY_XML_in_21Days:XPath.

Table 9.1 serves to summarize what you have discovered about the seven XPath node types.

**TABLE 9.1** The Seven XPath Node Types

| Node Type | Description | String-value |
|---|---|---|
| Root | There is only one root node that contains all other document nodes. This is always the first node encountered in document order. | Concatenated string-values of all descendent text nodes in document order. |
| Element | Element nodes correspond to elements in XML documents and can contain other nodes. | Concatenated string-values of all descendent text nodes in document order. |
| Attribute | Attribute nodes represent XML attributes and have element node parents, but are not child elements of their parent node. | The value of the attribute. |
| Namespace | Namespace nodes represent XML namespaces and have parents, but are not child elements of their parent node. | The URI of the namespace. |
| Processing instruction | Processing instruction nodes represent XML processing instructions. | The value following the initial argument of the instruction. |
| Text | Text nodes contain text or character data content of elements. | The text data contained in the text node. |
| Comment | Comment nodes contain the text of comments. | The text of the comment. |

# Naming XPath Relationships—Eleven Types of Axes

You have read about child and parent nodes and know that some nodes have parent nodes, but do not constitute child nodes of those parents in XPath. Attribute and namespace nodes, for instance, provide information, or modify their parent nodes, but are not content of their parent nodes. A child node must be contained by a parent node. You have considered the concept of parent and child relationships as they apply to XPath expressions.

Xpath recognizes eleven primary named node relationships in an XML document. When you create XPath expressions, you provide an address and a location path to that address. This is known as an *axis* that can be traversed in a relative fashion. For the process to get from where you are to the node or nodes you are trying to locate requires, in part, that the location path be traversed on the basis of these axis relationships.

So that you might better understand these relationships, you'll have an opportunity to examine each of these one at a time in the section that follows. You will be provided a text description along with a figure depicting the selected nodes based on the relationship presented. The selected nodes will be those that are characterized by the result of resolving a relationship descriptor, or the result after having traversed a specified location path. A context node is indicated in the figures to show a starting point for the relationship. From your current point of reference in the context node, you instruct the process to traverse the relative location path to select target nodes that satisfy the relationship characterized by the XPath expression. This means that the same relative location path traversed from two different originating context nodes might terminate at different selected nodes. You will see a variety of combinations of this concept as you follow along with the examples provided. First, however, it is important to clarify what is meant by context node and selected nodes. Examine the simple XML document instance depicted by Listing 9.2 closely.

**LISTING 9.2**    An XML Document Instance with Nested Element Types—driveway.xml

```
 1: <?xml version="1.0"?>
 2: <!-- Listing 9.2 - driveway.xml -->
 3:
 4: <driveway>
 5:         <car>
 6:             <mfgr>Ford</mfgr>
 7:             <model>Mustang</model>
 8:             <color>green</color>
 9:         </car>
10: </driveway>
```

Suppose that the context node for an XPath expression applied to this document instance is the car element node and you want to locate its parent node. The selected node, in this case the parent, will be the driveway element node. Likewise, if you assume the same context node (car element node), then selecting its child nodes will result in location of the mfgr, model, and color element nodes. In each case, the selected nodes are determined on the basis of their relative association with the context node. Naturally, because of the relative nature of XPath, it is important to keep track of the context node when you are authoring location path expressions.

## The Concept of Self

In an XPath expression, the context node might, in fact, be the node you are trying to locate. If this is the case, then the context node and the selected node are the same node. Figure 9.2 shows a tree that represents the nodes of an XML document. This is much like many other tree structures that you have already explored in earlier reading. The names of the nodes are not required for the purpose of this discussion; therefore, they have been omitted. You can see, nonetheless, that lines joining them depict relationships among the nodes. Clearly, some are subordinate to others if they appear lower on the tree structure. Additionally, those that are situated next to one another horizontally are siblings and have the same number of parent nodes occurring at higher levels in the tree. Some parent nodes have more than one child.

**FIGURE 9.2**

*An XPath node tree selecting only the context node.*

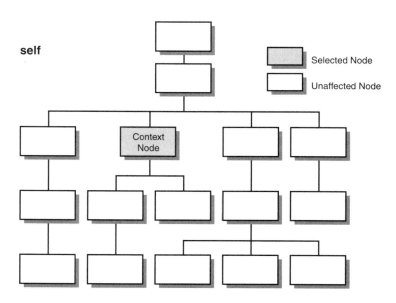

You can see the context node on the second branch of the node tree. According to the legend in the upper-right corner, the selected node is shown in gray. In this case, the context node and the selected node are the same. In other words, the evaluation of an XPath expression that locates self returns the context node. The concept of self is important in XPath as it may be combined with certain other named relationships so that the context node is purposefully included in the resulting node set along with the other selected nodes. You will see several examples of that later today.

## The Parent Node

You have seen parent nodes before. You know that they typically contain child nodes—with the exception of the attribute and namespace exceptions noted earlier. Parent nodes occupy a superior place on the node tree relative to their respective child nodes. With regard to a context node, a parent node is one generation, or level, superior to the context node on the XPath tree; therefore, a selected node that results from an evaluated XPath expression to locate a parent node should produce a single superior node result. Figure 9.3 depicts this relationship.

**FIGURE 9.3**

*An XPath node tree depicting a parent relationship.*

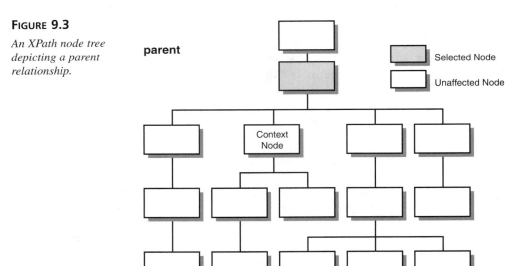

Note that the correct selection resulting from a parent relationship is a single node. In subsequent relationships, you might see multiple nodes, or node sets, selected as the result of an evaluated XPath expression.

 **Tip**

With XPath, a location path expression can return a collection of nodes that share specified relationship characteristics. Such a collection is referred to as a *node set*.

## Child Relationships

As described earlier, a child node is contained within a parent node. An XPath expression in search of child nodes will locate only those that are subordinate to the context node. A context node can have any number of child nodes, but the child nodes will only reside at one level below the context node. You can see a case of selected child nodes in Figure 9.4.

**FIGURE 9.4**

*Two child nodes of the context node are selected.*

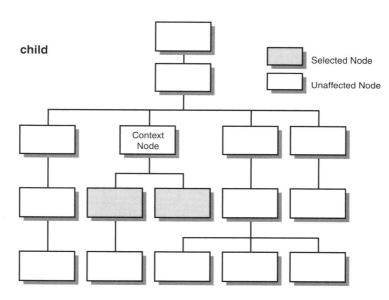

Did you notice that one of the child nodes has a child node? This lower descendent is not selected by an XPath expression requesting only child nodes because it resides more than one level removed from the context node. You will see how to refer to node sets that include all descendents shortly.

## Parents and Grandparents

Ancestor nodes include the parent node as well as the parent's parent node and so on up the XPath tree—in reverse document order—right back to the root node. In Figure 9.5, the selected nodes show this ancestor relationship.

You have learned that the XPath expression to locate a parent node results in only a single node response, whereas an ancestor expression selects all of the superior nodes that directly precede the context node. Only the number of ancestor nodes that exist between the context node and the root node limits this lineage. The root node is the ultimate ancestor of all other nodes in the tree.

**FIGURE 9.5**

*An XPath node tree depicting an ancestor relationship.*

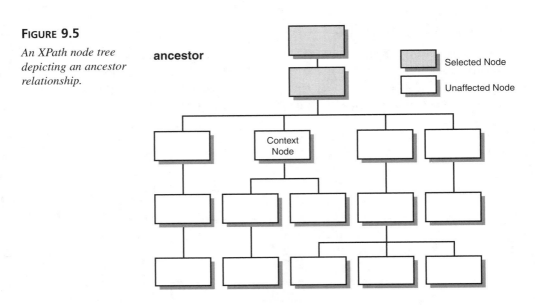

**FIGURE 9.5**

*An XPath node tree depicting an ancestor relationship.*

## Ancestor-or-Self

The ancestor-or-self relationship includes all of the nodes located by an ancestor expression, plus the context node of self. In the case of the sample XPath tree, ancestor-or-self will select for three nodes, as shown in Figure 9.6.

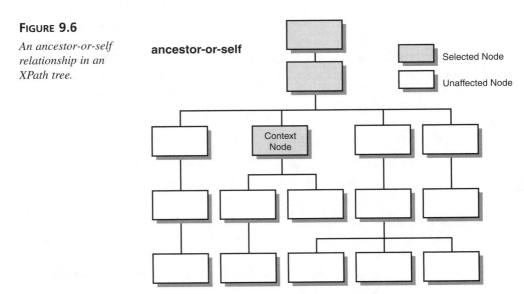

**FIGURE 9.6**

*An ancestor-or-self relationship in an XPath tree.*

# Descendent

To select the child elements and all of the grandchild elements, great grandchild elements, and so on requires the use of the descendent relationship. Figure 9.7 shows three nodes selected as a result of this relationship. Each of these nodes is subordinate to, or nested within, the context node.

**FIGURE 9.7**

*An XPath node tree depicting a descendent relationship.*

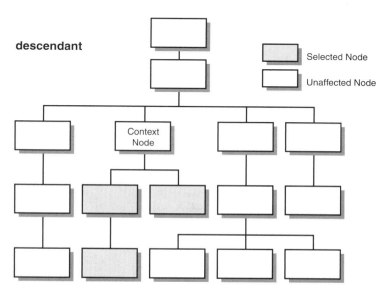

A *descendent* relationship can contain any number of nodes. The node-set begins with the context node and continues until it reaches the end of the lineage that is subordinate to the context node.

# Descendent-or-Self

Just as in the case of an ancestor-or-self relationship, it is possible to select a node-set that incorporates the descendents in addition to the context node. Such a relationship is termed a descendent-or-self relationship. This relationship is depicted by Figure 9.8, showing four selected nodes on the example XPath tree.

The descendent-or-self relationship contains the context node, plus all nodes that are nested within the context node until the end of the lineage is reached.

**FIGURE 9.8**

*An XPath node tree depicting a descendent-or-self relationship.*

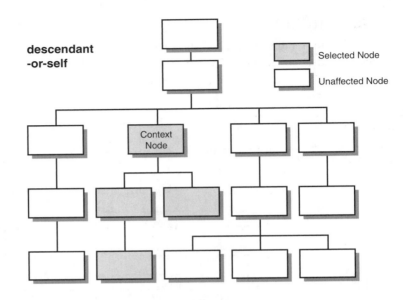

## Selecting Nodes Following the Context Node

You have learned that XPath traverses a node tree in either document order or reverse document order. The concept of *following* nodes selects all the nodes that exist beyond the context node. The *following* nodes begin with the peers of the context node and include all of the descendents of those peers. Which nodes are considered following is evaluated on the basis of the document order of the nodes in the tree. Any nodes that are traversed prior to reaching the context node are excluded from the following relationship. Figure 9.9 shows a following relationship that selects seven nodes.

Did you notice that the following relationship does not include the child or descendent nodes of the context node? It includes only those nodes that follow at a peer level, plus the descendents of those peers.

## Selecting Subsequent Peers

The following-sibling relationship selects nodes that are subsequent peers as discovered by traversing the XPath tree in document order. Only those nodes that are at the same level as the context node will be selected. Descendents of the siblings are excluded from the selected node set. Figure 9.10 depicts this relationship.

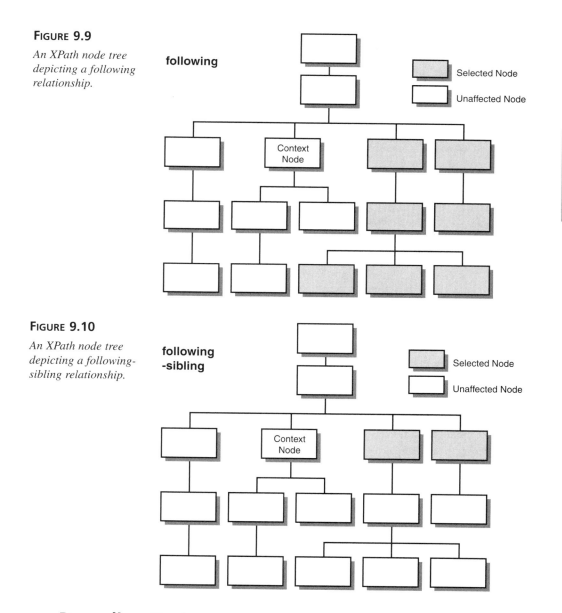

**FIGURE 9.9**

*An XPath node tree depicting a following relationship.*

**FIGURE 9.10**

*An XPath node tree depicting a following-sibling relationship.*

## Preceding Nodes

Selection of preceding nodes is resolved in a manner that is similar to following, except that the peers and descendents of peers are those that occur before the context node as encountered in document order. This relationship is shown by Figure 9.11.

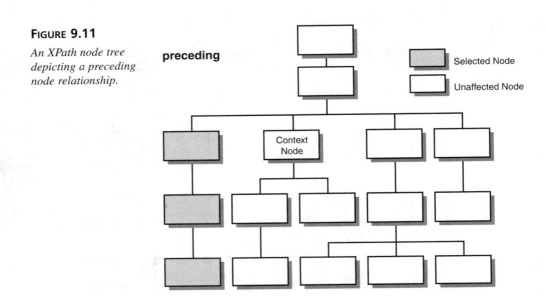

**FIGURE 9.11**

*An XPath node tree depicting a preceding node relationship.*

Note that preceding elements are only those that reside at the same horizontal level or a level lower than the context node, but occurring prior to the context node in a document. Nodes that are at a higher level, such as parent or ancestor nodes, are not considered preceding.

## Preceding-Sibling Nodes

Not surprisingly, a preceding-sibling relationship exists that selects only those nodes that are peers of the context node, traversed prior to the context node in document order. Figure 9.12 depicts this relationship.

In this section, you learned about the standard relationship types that are possible in XPath. You saw that the nodes selected were those that were around the context node in various relative directions. Accessing this relative positioning might prove useful for traversing a large and complex document. Suppose, for instance, that you have a large financial reference document, encoded in XML, that includes all of the various sales taxes for each state. Perhaps each state has child elements that include a variety of taxes for gasoline, alcohol, and so on. You might use a relationship-based location path to locate all of the child taxes for a particular state to use in further processing.

You saw that the XPath tree is traversed in document order, which has an impact on the nodes that are considered to be preceding or following the context node. In the next section, you will learn to write XPath expressions combining these relationships with node names. This will provide you more certain control over the selection process and allow you to locate specific nodes.

**FIGURE 9.12**

*An XPath node tree depicting a preceding-sibling relationship.*

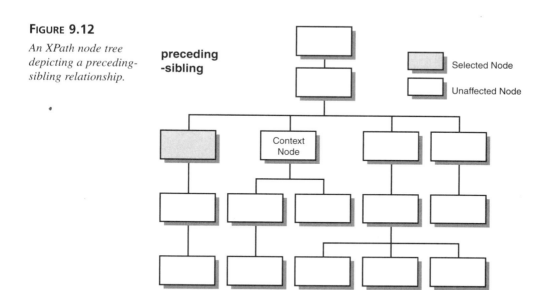

# Formulating and Testing XPath Expressions

You have seen the relative nature of XPath, as expressed through named relationships, and the manner in which these axes are traversed to select nodes. In this section, you will learn to create absolute path expressions that select particular elements, attributes, or other nodes. Later, you will see how to combine these with some of the relationship axes discovered earlier today. The learning objective for this section is to experience some of the syntax and a selected subset of popular options available with XPath rather than learn an exhaustive list of all the possible expression combinations.

To select particular nodes, you'll work with an actual XML document that has several nested elements and traverse the nodes using XPath expressions that you write. Start by creating a simple XML document. Imagine that you open your desk drawer and discover a number of pens and pencils of various types. In this case, imagine that some of the pencils are marked "H" and others are marked "HB." You also find a few boxes just large enough to hold several pencils. One of the boxes is sitting in a tray. These relationships will form the hierarchy of the XML document with child, parent, ancestor, and descendent nodes. To work along with the examples provided, it is recommended that you create a document that looks just like the one in Listing 9.3 and save it as drawer.xml.

**LISTING 9.3**    The Contents of a Desk Drawer as an XML Document—drawer.xml

```
 1: <?xml version="1.0"?>
 2: <!-- Listing 9.3 -drawer01.xml -->
 3:
 4: <drawer>
 5:        <pencil type="HB"/>
 6:        <pen/>
 7:        <pencil type="H"/>
 8:        <pencil type="HB"/>
 9:        <pencil type=" HB "/>
10:        <box>
11:              <pencil type="HB"/>
12:        </box>
13:        <tray>
14:              <box>
15:                    <pencil type="H"/>
16:                    <pencil type="HB"/>
17:              </box>
18:        </tray>
19:        <pen/>
20: </drawer>
```

In keeping with the scenario, the drawer element type, beginning on line 4, contains a number of pencil element types, pen element types, box element types, and a tray element type. In some cases, a pencil element is contained within a box element. One box element is contained within a tray element. The pencils have type attributes with a value of either H or HB.

To test the XPath expressions that you write, you'll download an XPath testing tool from the Web. According to the Web site description, the XPath Visualizer Version 1.3 "is a full blown Visual XPath Interpreter for the evaluation of any XPath expression and visual presentation of the resulting node set or scalar value." To follow along with the exercises in this section, you need to download a copy of the XPath Visualizer, version 1.3 from http://www.vbxml.com/xpathvisualizer/default.asp. You can use this application to test all of the examples that are provided in the remainder of this section. The XPath Visualizer was designed as a learning tool for XPath; however, it is also a good tool to use when you are creating complex XPath expressions for use in XSLT or XPointer.

The Visualizer is written as a collection of simple HTML pages with some JavaScript used to manipulate the nodes located by XPath. A cascading stylesheet and XML stylesheet are also included to provide a color scheme to indicate selected nodes. Microsoft Internet Explorer version 5 or higher must be installed on your system because the XPath Visualizer instantiates the MSXML object that comes bundled with that browser distribution. You learned a bit about the MSXML parsers on Day 3. As of the date of this writing, the latest release of MSXML is version 4.0, which is available in a preview form at http://msdn.microsoft.com/downloads/. Version 2.0 is all that is required to run the XPath Visualizer, so if you have Microsoft Internet Explorer 5.0 or higher loaded on your computer, you do not need to download MSXML 4.0.

After the XPath Visualizer files are downloaded, place all of the XPath Visualizer files included in the download in their own subdirectory on your computer. To launch the application, point your Microsoft Internet Explorer browser at the XPathMain.htm file in your XPath Visualizer subdirectory. When the page loads, click the Browse button and locate your drawer.xml file. The file path will be displayed in the form field to the left of the button. Click the Process File button. This should result in a refresh of the browser window display that includes a listing of the drawer.xml document with each of the element nodes highlighted in yellow on the page. You will see that aside from the color highlights added by the XPath Visualizer, the XML document looks like it might normally when Internet Explorer transforms it with XSLT for display. The same transformation takes place in this case with the addition of the extra styling required to highlight XPath selected nodes. You will learn more about transformations when you study XSLT on Day 16.

When you click the Process File button on the XPath Visualizer window for the first time, it enters the //* expression automatically for you in the field below the file name. This field is called the XPath expression field. This particular XPath expression is used to select all element nodes in the tree. You'll read more about the use of the asterisk wildcard and the slash notation later in this section. When the application evaluates this XPath instruction, it highlights all of the element nodes in the display. You will be able to add any of the expressions discussed throughout the remainder of this section directly into that field to select particular nodes in your XML document. Figure 9.13 depicts a Microsoft Internet Explorer browser window with the XSLT Visualizer loaded and all of the element nodes in the drawer.xml document highlighted in yellow.

## Selecting Nodes by Name with Single Slash Syntax

In the sections that follow, you'll learn the syntax of popular XPath expressions. In each case, you can enter the string described in the XPath expression field of the Visualizer application to observe the selected nodes.

The slash (/) is used by XPath to refer to the root node in the XPath tree. When you start to create XSLT patterns with XPath expressions on Day 16, you'll make use of the single slash in many of your programs. Today you will use it to reference the root node and work down the tree to locate the desired nodes.

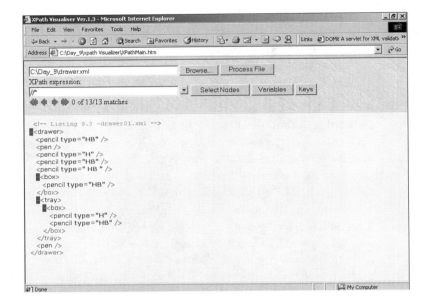

FIGURE **9.13**

*XPath Visualizer displaying all of the element nodes in the* drawer.xml *file.*

## Select the Root Element

The basic syntax of an XPath expression is quite similar to the addressing system used by various file systems. In this example, you enter /drawer in the XPath expression field of the Visualizer application to select the drawer root element. After you have entered the string, activate the Select Nodes button of the application and only the drawer element will be highlighted in yellow. The application will also report the number of matches it has located based on the expression you enter. In this case, it tells you that there is only one match for a root element node in the XML document instance. This makes sense because an XML document can only have one root element.

In a literal sense, the expression is interpreted to mean that you are selecting the drawer element child of the root node. This works to select the known root element by name.

As a test, try entering /pen in the XPath expression field and activating the Select Nodes button. When the XPath expression is evaluated, no matches will be found; the indicator will tell you that there are zero matches and none of the nodes will be highlighted. In the next example, you will see the syntax required to locate the pen nodes in this XML instance.

## Select a Child of the Root Element

Because XPath needs to be given a specific relationship or axis to follow to locate a node, you will have to create an expression that includes the root node, followed by the

9

root element, followed by the target element. In other words, you should enter /drawer/ pen if you are trying to locate pen elements. Try this and view the results. You should see the two pen elements highlighted and the counter on the display should tell you that two matching nodes were selected. The expression is interpreted to mean "Select all pen elements that are children of the drawer root element."

Try to select all of the pencil elements in the document instance using the same syntax. Write an XPath expression that looks like /drawer/pencil. When you evaluate this expression, the application indicates that it found four matches and highlights the first four pencil elements. The other two pencil elements in the document instance were not selected because they are not child elements of the root element. The expression you build will only select child elements of the root and not the descendents of that root element. You will learn how to encode an expression to return descendents shortly.

## Selecting an Element Based on a Known Lineage

Following the same logic that you applied earlier, you should be able to select all of the pencil elements that are child elements of the particular box element that is a child of tray in the document instance. To do so, build an XPath expression that traverses the precise path in document order required to reach the desired element. Specifically, enter /drawer/tray/box/pencil and activate the Select Nodes button.

The result will be a selection of two pencil elements that are child elements of the particular box element contained within the tray element.

## Selecting All Elements by Name

Suppose that you really needed to select all of the pencil elements regardless of their lineage. XPath provides the double slash (//) as a means of accomplishing this. The double slash can be interpreted literally as "select all elements that satisfy some criterion you provide." To select all pencil elements, enter the expression //pencil and evaluate the result. XPath will locate seven pencil element nodes regardless of the ancestry.

## Selecting All Elements by Ancestry

You can use the double slash operator with a parent/child relationship to select all of the child elements of a specified parent. In this case, the order of the elements is critical and the parent must precede the child in the expression. Try this syntax by creating an expression that will be interpreted as "Select all of the pencil elements that are child elements of box elements." If you look at the XML document instance, you will see that there are three such pencil elements. The first is on line 11 of Listing 9.3; the other two are on lines 15 and 16 respectively.

The XPath expression to select these elements will look like //box/pencil. As described previously, this means "Select all pencil elements that are child elements of box elements."

## Using Wildcard Notation

The wild card notation in XPath is encoded with an asterisk. The asterisk works very much as it does in file system notations as an all-inclusive operand. To understand how the wildcard can be combined with other expressions, Table 9.2 provides several examples based on the drawer.xml document and the expected evaluation of each. Try these examples in the XPath Visualizer and then experiment by creating a few combinations of your own.

**TABLE 9.2**  Wildcard Examples

| Sample XPath Expression | Interpretation | Evaluated Response |
| --- | --- | --- |
| /drawer/* | Select all elements that are child elements (or are enclosed by) the drawer element. | Returns all child elements of drawer, eight in total. |
| /*/*/*/pencil | Select all third-generation pencil elements regardless of their ancestry. | Returns the two pencil elements that are contained by box, within tray, within the root element. |
| //* | Select all elements that descend from the root node. | Returns all elements in the document instance. |
| /* | Select all child elements of the root node. | Returns only the root element. |

## Choosing Specific Elements from a Collected Node Set

Square brackets are used in XPath to include a calculation or function evaluation integral to the expression. For instance, suppose you wanted to locate the third pencil element that was a child of the root element. You could use the square bracket notation to count to the third such element traversed in document order. The syntax for this expression is

```
Path[calculation or function]
```

To find the third pencil child element of the root, the XPath expression would look like this:

```
/drawer/pencil[3]
```

Try this and then experiment by placing different numeric values in the square brackets and changing the path before the brackets.

The function `last()` can be used in the expression in place of the numeric counter to select the last qualified node according to the axis encoded. Therefore, to choose the last pen element contained by the root element, you can use `/drawer/pen[last()]`.

Given that pencil has multiple occurrences, how might you select the last pencil from each parent that contains pencil elements? To solve this, you need to combine several of the axis declarations you have learned so far. First, you will need to use an axis that will select elements regardless of their ancestry. The double slash accomplishes this. Then you will need to specify the elements in which you are interested, which is `pencil` in this case. Finally, you'll need to select just the last of each set using the `last()` function. When you string all these together, the expression will look like this:

```
//pencil[last()]
```

the result of which will be the selection of the last `pencil` element contained by each parent element. There are three of these, and they occur on lines 9, 11, and 16 of Listing 9.3. Try this for yourself.

## Selecting For Attributes

In the `drawer.xml` document, the `pencil` elements have `type` attributes. You can use a variety of approaches in XPath to select attributes and attribute values and to combine functions and the syntax you have explored with attribute evaluations to narrow the selection specification. The attribute symbol (@) is used to indicate the inclusion of attribute selection logic in the XPath expression.

To select all attributes in the instance, you can combine the double slash with the attribute symbol and a wildcard, such as `//@*`). Try this in the XPath Visualizer; it should return all seven attributes in the XML document. You can select only those attributes of a given name by specifying that name. For instance, to select all `type` attributes, type `//@type` in the XPath expression field. Of course, because the `drawer.xml` includes only `type` attributes, you will consequently get seven matches, as you did when you selected all attributes.

Another function in XPath is `not()`, which permits selected exclusion of nodes. If you need, for instance, to select all of the elements in the `drawer.xml` document that do not have an attribute, you can write an XPath expression like this:

```
//*[not(@*)]
```

This expression is interpreted as "Select all elements that descend from the root node that do not include attributes." In the `drawer.xml` document, this will include the `drawer` root element, as well as `pen`, `tray`, and `box` elements.

XPath provides a means of using the values of attributes as selection criteria in expressions, similar to the encoding of an SQL WHERE statement. For instance, to select all pencil elements that have a type attribute that has an "HB" value, type //pencil[@type="HB"]. This expression returns four matches if you created your drawer.xml document exactly like the example in Listing 9.3. Look very closely at lines 8 and 9 of the listing:

```
8:       <pencil type="HB"/>
9:       <pencil type=" HB "/>
```

You will note that the lines differ. The attribute value in line 9 has white space characters between the quotes and the value. Therefore, the XPath expression returns only four matches because the attribute on line 9 does not match the selection criterion. Because XPath is such a powerful language, it provides you with a means to normalize extraneous white space characters in attribute values. The expression //pencil[normalize-space(@type)="HB"] returns five nodes that contain attributes because the normalization process makes " HB " equivalent to "HB".

## Additional XPath Functions

Table 9.3 lists examples of several additional functions that can be used in XPath expressions. In each case an example is shown, but you can substitute the name of the element, number, or letter as appropriate to create your own expressions.

**TABLE 9.3**  Additional Functions for Use with XPath Expressions

| Sample XPath Expression | Interpretation | Evaluated Response |
|---|---|---|
| //*[count(pencil)=2] | Select all elements that have exactly two pencil child elements. | Returns the second box element in drawer.xml. count() enumerates the argument. |
| //*[count(*)=1] | Select all elements that have only one unspecified child element. | Returns the box and tray elements. |
| //*[name()="pen"] | Select all elements named pen. | Returns two pen elements. This is equivalent to //pen. |
| //*[starts-with(name(),"p")] | Select all element names that start with the letter p. | Returns all pencil and pen elements, nine in total. |

**TABLE 9.3**   continued

| Sample XPath Expression | Interpretation | Evaluated Response |
|---|---|---|
| `//*[contains(name(),"x")]` | Select all element names that contain the letter x in their names. | Returns two instances of the box element. |
| `//*[string-length(name())=3]` | Select all element names that contain exactly three characters in their element names. | Returns all pen and box elements, four in total. |
| `//*[string-length(name())>3]` | Select all element names that contain more than three characters in their element names. | Returns nine elements with names of four or more characters. |

## Combining XPath Axes

You can combine multiple XPath expressions by stringing them together with a pipe or vertical bar character (|) separating them. If, for instance, you want to select all box elements and all pen elements, you can create an XPath expression that looks like `//box|//pen`. The number of combinations you choose to string together is unlimited; just remember that the effect is cumulative.

## Explicit Declarations of Relational Axes

You have learned that you can select the root element by selecting the child element of the root node. The syntax you have used to do this is

`/element_name`

In reality, this is a short form for a fully qualified version of the same expression, which looks like this:

`/child::element_name`

Therefore, the fully qualified expression required to return the root element of the drawer.xml file is `/child::drawer`. The child axis is the default axis in an XPath expression and can be safely omitted; this omission produces the short-form version. The fully qualified and short form can be mixed in the same XPath expression if desired. Thus, `/child::drawer/pencil` returns all of the pencil child elements of the drawer element, which, in turn, is a child of the root node.

The other named relationships that you learned earlier today might also be included in an XPath expression by including their axes, followed by two colons. For instance, to select all of the descendents of the `tray` element, you can encode an expression that looks like this:

```
/drawer/tray/descendent::*
```

This expression is interpreted as all of the descendents of the `tray` element, which is a child of the `drawer` element, itself being a child of the root node.

Suppose you want to locate only those `pencil` elements that have a `tray` element somewhere among their ancestors. You can use an expression such as `//tray/descendent::pencil` to locate all of the descendents of `tray`, which are called `pencil`.

If the context node has a parent, it resides in the parent axis. The expression `//box/parent::*` locates the parent nodes of all `box` elements.

You will recall that the following-sibling returned peers of the context node. Therefore, `//box/following-sibling::*` will locate the `tray` element and the next `pen` element in document order; these are the next peers of the `box` in document order. Compare this expression with `//box/following::*`, which returns all of the nodes after the context node (`box`) in document order.

Expressions have many other possibilities, some of which become quite complex. For instance, the expression `//pencil[position()=floor(last()div 2 + 0.5) or position()=ceiling(last() div 2 + 0.5)]` locates only the middle pencil elements in the document instance. These are beyond the scope of today's study, but you will cover some of this in more detail in the days to come.

## Summary

This chapter has introduced you to some of the basic concepts in the XML Path Language. XPath is an expression-based language rather than a dialect of XML, which has been designed to be concise and efficient. It is used to address parts of an XML document, referred to as *nodes*. You will learn more about XPath when you explore the technologies it was designed to facilitate, namely XPointer and XSLT. You will learn more about XPointer on Day 11 and XSLT on Day 16. Today you discovered the seven nodes that form an XPath tree: root, element, attribute, namespace, processing instruction, text, and comment. You saw how all of the nodes are subordinate to the root node and learned that the root node is different from the root element in an XML document instance. You learned about 11 named nodal relationships that are used to select nodes and node sets in XPath. Then you built and tested XPath expressions that selected elements and attributes in various combinations and used functions and evaluative patterns.

## Q&A

**Q What is the nature of the data object resulting from XPath expressions?**

**A** When XPath expressions are evaluated, they result in a data object that can be characterized as one of the following:

- **Node**—A single selected node is located.
- **Node set**—Several nodes that share specified relationship characteristics are selected.
- **Boolean**—The expression produces either a true or false result.
- **String**—The resolution of the expression produces a string based on the content of a node or nodes in a path traversed.
- **Number**—A calculation performed during evaluation of the XPath expression might produce a floating-point numeric result.

**Q What are the node types that can be located using XPath?**

**A** XPath has the following seven node types: root, element, attribute, comment, text, processing instruction, and namespace.

**Q How is the concept of document order related to XPath?**

**A** XPath expressions cause a processor to traverse the node tree in the order in which the nodes exist in a document. Therefore, relationship axes such as preceding and following have meaning in XPath as they relate to the context node, or starting point, of the traversal defined by the XPath expression. Preceding nodes are those that occur before the context node in the order prescribed by the document structure. Following nodes consequently come after the context node in document order.

## Exercise

The exercise is provided so that you can test your knowledge of what you learned today. The answers are in Appendix A.

Process your `cd.xml` file in the XPath Visualizer and create expressions to select the following node results:

- Select all elements subordinate to the root node.
- Select all track elements that have a `total` attribute with a value of 16.
- Select all elements that contain the letter "i" in their names.
- Select any elements that have names with greater than 11 characters.
- Select all of the peers of the first `cd` element.

# DAY **10**

# The XML Link Language (XLink)

The Web has been successful, in part, due to its widespread support of hyper-linking as implemented by the anchor (<A>) tag in HTML. Hyperlinks effec-tively connect one Web page with another. However, the unidirectional, simple linking functionality that characterizes the Web today is not enough for the growing needs of an XML world. The W3C recommendation for linking in XML is called the XML Link Language (XLink), which became a W3C recommendation on June 27, 2001. Today, you will learn

- Why resource linking in XML using XLink is so important
- The differences between XLink and HTML linking
- About linking elements, link behaviors, and remote resource descriptions
- The meaning and syntax of extended links
- About arcs and out-of-line links

# Hypertext Linking

*Hypertext* is a term that was coined in the early 1960s by Ted Nelson. who at the time was a graduate student at Harvard University working on a term project, later called *Project Xanadu*. Earlier references to this concept of a machine-readable text structure that is not sequential, but is organized so that the related items of information can be connected dates back to an article by Vannevar Bush called "As We May Think," published in 1945 (`http://www.theatlantic.com/unbound/flashbks/computer/bushf.htm`). Bush called his system Memex, which was based on microfilm indexing. Nelson described the first computer-based hypertext along with an algorithm known as "zippered lists" at a national conference of the Association for Computing Machinery in 1965.

The fundamental idea behind hypertext was that documents stored in an electronic form could comprise a collection of instances, or *nodes*. The nodes would, in turn, contain cross-references, or *links,* that, with the aid of an interactive browser program, would allow the reader to move easily from one document to another. This is precisely what hypertext on the Web has come to mean. According to the W3C (`http://www.w3.org/Terms.html`), some call the extension of hypertext to include other media such as sound, video, and graphics *hypermedia*, but most often, the media extension is called hypertext as well.

In fact, from its earliest conception, the Web was never expected to comprise pages of information in isolation. Rather, mechanisms were provided to indicate the relationships among pages and permit a link to be activated. The most obvious example in HTML is the anchor tag, which offers a means for a programmer to establish a link that is activated by a mouse click in a browser window. You will read today about some of the inherent limitations of HTML anchor links and how the XML Link Language (XLink) aims to improve the older approach.

XLink is a standardized XML vocabulary that can be added to elements in an XML instance document to describe simple or very elaborate extended links among Web-based resources. The objective for delivery of XLink was to provide a means to widen the extremely narrow concepts of links that were previously limited to either the unidirectional anchor links in HTML or the ID/IDREF concept of internal element linking in XML. You are probably familiar with HTML links, but even if you are not, a short review is offered in the next section. You learned several approaches to enforce ID/IDREF links in XML on Days 4, 5, and 6.

## HTML Links

Using the anchor (<A>) tag, HTML makes it possible to embed hypertext links in Web documents. When it's activated, the anchor tag associated with an externally referenced document, for instance, downloads the content of another HTML page in place of the page on which the link originated. The HTML link facility is a unidirectional function because no provision exists in the linking syntax to provide, for instance, a link back to the originating document. Many browser implementations provide a Back button that effectively serves this purpose if the link is activated inside a browser window. The target of an HTML link is expressed as the value of an HREF attribute on the HTML <A> tag. The HTML <A> tag wraps text or another object that serves as a button on the page. The link is typically activated when a user, browsing the page, moves the mouse cursor over the link object and clicks the mouse button. The simplest form of an HTML anchor tag takes the following form:

```
<A HREF="[URL]">[text | other HTML element]</A>
```

The <A> tag in HTML will accept any URL as the value of the HREF attribute. The content of an anchor tag can be text or another element. Anything that is appropriately contained by the anchor element will become a link activator. In most browser implementations, a link activator will provide a means for a user's clicks to initiate the link function. All text characters or other objects until the closing tag is reached will serve as the link activator. Listing 10.1 shows an HTML page with an embedded HTML link.

**10**

**LISTING 10.1** HTML Page with an Embedded Hyperlink—HTMLlink01.html

```
 1: <!DOCTYPE XHTML PUBLIC "-//W3C//DTD HTML 4.01 Transitional//EN"
 2:  "http://www.w3.org/TR/html4/loose.dtd">
 3:
 4: <!-- Listing 10.1 - HTMLlink01.html -->
 5:
 6: <HTML>
 7:
 8:   <HEAD>
 9:     <TITLE>HTML Link Document</TITLE>
10:   </HEAD>
11:
12:   <BODY>
13:     <P>This is a simple HTML page with an embedded link to the
14:     <A HREF="http://architag.com">Architag</a> Web site.</P>
15:   </BODY>
16:
17: </HTML>
```

**ANALYSIS** Lines 1 and 2 declare this HTML page to be HTML version 4.01, transitional. Line 6 shows the root element of the HTML page, which is always HTML. Lines 8–10 are the HEAD element containing an HTML TITLE element and text content. Lines

12–15 hold the BODY element. A <P> child element (line 13 and 14) exists within the BODY element. The <P> element in HTML corresponds to a paragraph. On line 14

```
14:      <A HREF="http://architag.com">Architag</a> Web site.</P>
```

you will see the link that has been embedded into the string of text as an <A> child element of the P element. A user viewing this page in a compatible Web browser will be able to activate a hyperlink that downloads the page located at http://architag.com by placing his mouse over the word Architag and clicking the mouse.

Figure 10.1 depicts the typical HTML anchor tag link relationship between two Web pages. The source document contains an <A> element with a valid URL provided as the value of an HREF attribute on the <A> element. When the link is activated, typically by a mouse click, the content of the page located at the URL is downloaded.

**FIGURE 10.1**

*An HTML link established via an embedded <A> tag.*

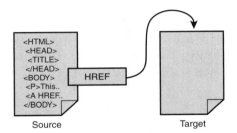

Source                          Target

As you have seen, HTML links are relatively simple, unidirectional mechanisms. Nonetheless, their impact on information delivery over the Internet is in part what revolutionized and popularized the World Wide Web. A simple HTML anchor tag can be used to insert images, permit a user to seemingly leap from inside one Web document to another document (as shown in the example in this section), or jump to another part of the same document.

Several special attributes for the anchor tag provide some limited link reference control. The rel attribute, for instance, is used to name the relationship that exists between a source document and a target document. The following code provides an example.

```
<A HREF="http://architag.com" rel="goto_Architag">Architag</a> Web site.</P>
```

The rel attribute names the link for use by the programmer, perhaps as a means of improving documentation, but it serves little purpose beyond that. It is effectively just a label. The rev attribute is meant to describe a reverse link, giving the relationship from the target document back to the source document. Again, the link reference is just a label that looks like the following code:

```
<A HREF="http://architag.com" rel="goto_Architag" rev"example_doc">
        Architag</a> Web site.</P>
```

The `rev` attribute provides a label for the reverse link relationship that symbolizes the path to be followed to return to the originating document, but there is no functionality to implement this in current browsers.

Another linking element in HTML is implemented with the `<LINK>` tag. `<LINK>` describes the position of a document in a hierarchy, but the link specified is not rendered—only an anchor tag affects rendered links. This kind of link associates another document for use by a specified process or user agent. For instance, the `LINK` element is used to associate a cascading style sheet with an HTML page for processors that are able to render on that basis.

HTML linking does suffer some limitations. For instance, URLs are capable of pointing to only a single document. To point to a section within a target document requires that a named anchor be placed manually in that document prior to the link being activated. If you need a link to the fourth sentence of the eighth paragraph of the third section of the desired document, a named anchor must already exist at that location in the document. If you then need to link to the fifteenth sentence, three paragraphs earlier, a named anchor must be present there as well. In other words, this method will neither work for documents that are not saved on the server with specific named anchors in advance, nor will it work for documents to which you have read-only access.

Even though the Back button and history feature built in to most browsers will permit you to trace back along a browser path followed to get to a target page, this approach is not entirely reliable. Nothing in the HTML page retains that history. The link to another page is just a one-way traversal. The source document has information about the target document, but not vice versa.

It is possible for you to encode HTML links in your XML documents. You can do this using XSLT to transform an XML instance into HTML for rendering in a browser. This approach offers simple linking; however, XLink promises more powerful linking.

# How Does XLink Improve on HTML Links?

XLink is a W3C recommendation for powerful links between documents. XLink was designed to work with XML to achieve everything that is possible using HTML links, but also provide a means of supporting multidirectional links. This means that links can travel in more than one direction among documents. Using XLink, you can encode for two unidirectional links between documents: a multidirectional link or multiple multidirectional links. You will learn today how to create XLinks to implement a variety of relational connections among documents.

10

XLink is implemented in the form of attributes on elements. Therefore, any element can function as a link in an XML instance, unlike HTML in which only the <A> element can carry a hypertext link. Links can be stored within an XML instance or in a separate, related file of links.

When XLink is combined with XPointer, the options become even more substantial. XPointer permits you to establish links to arbitrary positions in an XML document, eliminating the requirement for pre-established named anchors in target documents. You will learn more about XPointer tomorrow.

XLink can be used to link more than just documents. XLink can establish links among database records, video, audio, and any other object, which may collectively be referred to as *resources*. Suppose, for instance, that you work in an advertising firm. You might want advertising copy to be linked to all of the press releases, brochures, and so on that were created using the copy. Then perhaps you might want to link the copy to an audio track distributed via the Web. Perhaps you might then link the copy and the audio to a video to create a full multimedia presentation. Next, assume that this package of advertising is intended for an international audience and that the video must be linked to copy and audio in several other languages. You begin to see how these otherwise disparate resources can be unified into a collection through associations expressed as links. XLink provides the means to express such a collection of related resources.

XLink-aware applications are able to traverse the links to process resources, whether they are locally or remotely linked. This means that you can reach resources regardless of where they reside on the Internet. Those resources can, in turn, be linked to others, and so on. This offers incredible flexibility.

## Limitations of XLink

The biggest single limitation of XLink is that it is not widely supported by browser vendors. This lack of support is due, in part, to the fact that XLinks transcend the functionality implemented by browsers. In time, new device classes and user agents will be developed that are capable of utilizing complex multi-directional links. In the meantime, Internet Explorer and the Opera browser support no form of XLink. Netscape version 6.0 and the Mozilla browser engine offer limited support for XLink, but this support is incomplete.

# Linking Elements

In XML, an element that uses XLink attributes to exert the existence of a link and describe the nature of that link is considered to be a *linking element*. Unlike the case of

HTML where a link is established with a LINK or <A> tag, an XLink linking element can be *any* XML element. An XML element can qualify as a linking element if two requirements are met:

- The element must include attributes from the XLink dialect that begin with a unique prefix. By convention, the prefix is typically XLink:.
- The prefix must be bound to the XLink namespace URI http://www.w3.org/1999/xlink.

**Tip** | Even though you can choose any prefix to bind XLink attributes to the XLink namespace, it is good programming practice to use <u>XLink:</u> in accordance with convention.

**10**

The XLink attributes serve a particular role in the description of a link.

XLink defines eight attributes to describe a linking element. These attributes, belonging to the XLink namespace (http://www.w3.org/1999/xlink), are added on elements in your XML document. Table 10.1 summarizes the attributes that comprise the XML Linking Language.

**TABLE 10.1**   Valid Attributes Comprising the XLink Vocabulary

| Attribute | Description |
| --- | --- |
| type | A string that determines the link type |
| href | Any valid URL that determines the location of a target resource |
| from | A string declaring the resource that is the source in an arc relationship |
| to | A string declaring the target in an arc relationship |
| show | A string declaring how a resource will be revealed |
| actuate | A string that declares how a link will be initiated |
| role | An application-specific string that is used to describe the function of a link's content |
| title | A label for a link |

You will see examples of most of these attributes and some of the valid values of those attributes shortly.

XML linking elements contain an xlink:type attribute, which describes the nature of the link being encoded. Linking elements are either simple or extended. A *simple link* (xlink"type="simple") is one that links one resource to another in much the same way that an HTML link does. *Extended links* (xlink:type="extended") exist to provide a means of linking multiple combinations of local and remote resources. You will see examples of both types of links today. The xlink:type attribute has several other valid values, including locator, arc, resource, title, and none. These values will be discussed briefly in the sections that follow.

The xlink:href attribute on a linking element has a value that is the URL of the resource being linked to. This can be a local resource or a remote resource, and any valid URL is acceptable as the value of this attribute.

## A Basic XLink Example

You now know enough XLink syntax to create a basic XML linking element for the message processing markup language used during previous days. To recall the scenario, you have created several different XML documents during the past nine days that mark up messages. The data are presumably recorded by an application that receives messages while the recipient is unavailable. Suppose that you want to establish a link between a message received and a remote resource that contains information about the sender of the message. You might, for instance, access a remote resource that contains identifying information, such as name, email address, or phone number.

Assume that you are establishing a link from a message element—that is, the local resource—in the message markup language. Assume also that this is a simple link to a remote resource that is located at http://www.architag.com/devan/ks.html. You will need to use the two attributes you read about earlier in the following way:

```
xlink:type="simple"
xlink:href="http://www.architag.com/devan/ks.html"
```

The first attribute (xlink:type="simple") establishes the fact that the type attribute belongs to the xlink namespace, declared elsewhere in the element markup or that of one of its ancestors. The value simple describes a simple relationship between two resources. The xlink:href attribute provides the address of the target resource.

These attributes would be placed on the linking element, and the xlink: namespace would be declared in the instance. Listing 10.2 shows a complete XML instance with the simple linking element encoded via XLink.

**LISTING 10.2**   An Example of a Simple Linking Element in XML—message01.xml

```
1: <?xml version="1.0"?>
2: <!-- Listing 10.2 - message01.xml -->
3:
4: <note xmlns:xlink="http://www.w3.org/1999/xlink">
```

**LISTING 10.2**   continued

```
5:      <message xlink:type="simple"
6:              xlink:href="http://www.architag.com/devan/ks.html">
7:        Remember to buy milk on the way home from work
8:      </message>
9: </note>
```

**ANALYSIS**   The XML namespace for XLink (http://www.w3.org/1999/xlink) is declared
on line 4 and given a prefix of xlink:. The type and href attributes are encoded
on the local resource (message element) to establish a simple link to a remote resource
located at http://www.architag.com/devan/ks.html.

Did you notice that the message element retains the semantic name (message) that
describes its content and not the link that is encoded on it? In HTML, a link element
describes function rather than content.

## Validity Concerns

Because these attributes are encoded on an XML element, you will need to account for
them in a schema if your document requires validation. If you are using a DTD to validate your XML instance, you can take advantage of the #FIXED attribute operand to set
the required value of attributes that must conform precisely with a known value. For
instance, there is only one valid namespace that can be used for XLink, so that can be
fixed in the DTD. You can fix other attribute values. Listing 10.3 shows a DTD that can
be used to validate the XML instance in Listing 10.2 if it is properly associated with that
instance. After you create this association, you will be able to parse the document with
Microsoft Internet Explorer, provided you have version 5 or greater loaded on your
system.

**LISTING 10.3**   A DTD to Validate the Message Instance—message01.dtd

```
 1: <!-- Listing 10.3 - message01.dtd -->
 2:
 3: <!ELEMENT note (message)>
 4: <!ATTLIST note
 5:     xmlns:xlink CDATA #FIXED "http://www.w3.org/1999/xlink"
 6: >
 7: <!ELEMENT message (#PCDATA)>
 8: <!ATTLIST message
 9:     xlink:type CDATA #FIXED "simple"
10:     xlink:href CDATA #REQUIRED
11: >
```

**ANALYSIS** The note element contains a message element and has an xmlns:xlink attribute, for which the only valid value is "http://www.w3.org/1999/xlink". The message element contains text data and has two attributes: xlink:type and xlink:href. The type attribute allows only the value "simple", whereas the href attribute can have any character data string as a value.

Currently, DTDs are most often used with XLink for validation; however, you can accomplish the same validation using another schema language, such as XDR or XSD. For comparison purposes, Listing 10.4 provides an XML Schema Language (XSD) schema for validation of the instance.

**LISTING 10.4**   XML Schema to Validate the Message Instance—message01.xsd

```
1: <?xml version="1.0" encoding="UTF-8"?>
   <!-- Listing 10.4 - message01.xsd -->
2: <xsd:schema xmlns:xsd="http://www.w3.org/2000/10/XMLSchema">
3:     <xsd:element name="note">
4:          <xsd:complexType>
5:              <xsd:sequence>
6:                  <xsd:element name="message" type="messageType"/>
7:              </xsd:sequence>
8:              <xsd:attribute name="xmlns:xlink" type="xsd:string"
                   use="fixed" value="http://www.w3.org/1999/xlink"/>
9:          </xsd:complexType>
10:    </xsd:element>
11:    <xsd:complexType name="messageType">
12:         <xsd:simpleContent>
13:             <xsd:restriction base="xsd:string">
14:                 <xsd:attribute name="xlink:type"
                       type="xsd:string" use="fixed" value="simple"/>
15:                 <xsd:attribute name="xlink:href"
                       type="xsd:string" use="required"/>
16:             </xsd:restriction>
17:         </xsd:simpleContent>
18:    </xsd:complexType>
19: </xsd:schema>
```

**ANALYSIS** Line 2 assigns the standard namespace ("http://www.w3.org/2000/10/XMLSchema") for an XSD instance document. The declarations for the note element are contained on lines 3–10. The note element contains the message element, as declared on line 6, and has an xmlns:xlink attribute for which the only valid value (use="fixed") is "http://www.w3.org/1999/xlink". According to the message element declaration on line 6, its content is defined by a complexType called "messageType", which is shown on lines 11–18. The xlink:type attribute on the `message` element is defined as `fixed xsd:string` with a value of `simple`. The `xlink:href` attribute is permitted to have any `xsd:string` as content. Both of these attributes are required to be present in a conforming XML instance document.

## Descriptive XLink Attributes

The `xlink:title` and `xlink:role` attributes introduced in Table 10.1 help to describe the link. The `title` attribute is a descriptive title assigned to the link. The `role` attribute is an application-specific string (URI) that is used to describe the function of a link's content. Listing 10.5 repeats the message document with the `xlink:title` and `xlink:role` attributes assigned.

**LISTING 10.5**   Simple XLink Example—`message02.xml`

```
 1: <?xml version="1.0"?>
 2: <!-- Listing 10.5 - message02.xml -->
 3:
 4: <note xmlns:xlink="http://www.w3.org/1999/xlink">
 5:     <message
 6:         xlink:type="simple"
 7:         xlink:href="http://www.architag.com/devan/ks.html"
 8:         xlink:role="message"
 9:         xlink:title="message processing example">
10:             Remember to buy milk on the way home from work
11:     </message>
12: </note>
```

**ANALYSIS**   Lines 8 and 9 show the addition of `xlink:role` and the `xlink:title` attributes.

# Simple Link Behavior

The links that you have explored so far are simple links that merely establish connectivity. By including link behavior attributes, you can control the impact of traversing this link by an XLink-compliant application. In this way, you can instruct the application to associate the remote resources with the local resource in a variety of predefined ways.

## Presentation

The `xlink:show` attribute is used to determine the desired presentation of the remote resource by an XLink-compliant processor. Consider the function of a replacement-style HTML anchor link. When the user initiates a link with a mouse click at the correct place in the browser window, the content of the current page is often replaced by the content at the target URL. XLink has a `show` value called `replace` that does the same thing in an

XLink-compliant browser. In other words, the local resource will be replaced by the remote resource when an `xlink:show="replace"` XLink is activated.

Table 10.2 summarizes the possible values for this attribute.

**TABLE 10.2**  Possible Values for the `xlink:show` Attribute

| Value | Description |
| --- | --- |
| replace | Load the remote resource in the same window as the local resource by replacing the visible content. |
| new | Spawn a new application window in which to present the content of the remote resource. |
| embed | Embed the remote resource within the current resource. For example, a graphic or sound file could be embedded in a document instance. |
| other | Refers to an application-specific call. For example, this is unrestricted by the XLink specification, but is provided for use by an application. |
| none | Unrestricted. |

## Actuation

Another behavior attribute is the `xlink:actuate` attribute that is used to determine the timing of traversal to the remote resource. Again drawing on HTML as an example, consider the activation sequence for an anchor link. Without additional scripting, an anchor link is activated when the user clicks on a designated region of the display, such as at the point where the anchor tag is encoded on the rendered screen. XLink includes an `onRequest` actuation value that effectively accomplishes the same thing. There are several other options for the `xlink:actuate` attribute, as summarized by Table 10.3.

**TABLE 10.3**  Possible Values for the `xlink:actuate` Attribute

| Value | Description |
| --- | --- |
| onRequest | Similar to an HTML anchor link, a user initiates a control on the processing application, such as a mouse click, which starts the traversal of the link. |
| onLoad | This loads the remote resource as soon as the local resource has been read into memory by the processing application. An XLink compliant browser locates the remote resource as soon as the page with the link is loaded. |
| other | Application-specific call. This is unrestricted by the XLink specification, but is provided for use by an application. |
| none | Unrestricted. This is also unrestricted by the XLink specification, and is not implemented by an application. |

## XLink Behavior Exercises

At the time of this writing, not many browsers or generic applications support XLink. However, one that provides at least partial support, Netscape version 6.0 (`http://home.netscape.com/browsers/index.html?cp=hop06d16`), can be used to test the next few examples. You will not be able to execute the XLink code in Internet Explorer.

Modify your `message02.xml` document to include an `xlink:actuate` attribute with an `onRequest` value and an `xlink:show` attribute with a `replace` value encoded. The new attributes should look like this:

```
xlink:actuate="onRequest"
xlink:show="replace"
```

Save your modified XML document as `message03.xml`. Listing 10.6 shows the complete document.

**LISTING 10.6**    A Message Instance Including XLink Behavior Attributes—`message03.xml`

```
 1: <?xml version="1.0"?>
 2: <!-- Listing 10.6 - message03.xml -->
 3:
 4: <note xmlns:xlink="http://www.w3.org/1999/xlink">
 5:     <message
 6:         xlink:type="simple"
 7:         xlink:href="http://www.architag.com/devan/ks.html"
 8:         xlink:role="message"
 9:         xlink:title="message processing example"
10:         xlink:actuate="onRequest"
11:         xlink:show="replace">
12:             Remember to buy milk on the way home from work
13:     </message>
14: </note>
```

**ANALYSIS**    Lines 10 and 11 include the `xlink:actuate` and `xlink:show` attributes. The actuation for this link is set to `onRequest`, meaning that a user will need to initiate an application command—such as a mouse click on a hypertext link in a browser window—to cause the processor to traverse the link. When the link is followed, the content of the local resource will be replaced by the content of the remote resource.

When you load the completed code into Netscape 6, you should see the text content of the `message03.xml` document only. However, it will be underlined, just like the content of an HTML <A> element. This happens because the XLink processor has been programmed to present a hypertext link in this fashion. Keep in mind that another processor

10

might handle the link in a different manner. When you click on the link, the content of the local page (shown in Figure 10.2) should be replaced with the content of the page stored at the remote Web address `http://www.architag.com/devan/ks.html` (depicted by Figure 10.3).

**FIGURE 10.2**

*The* `message03.xml` *document viewed in Netscape 6.*

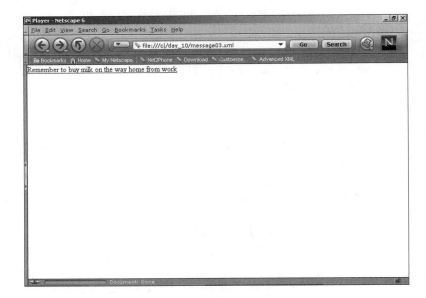

**FIGURE 10.3**

*The result of activating the XLink.*

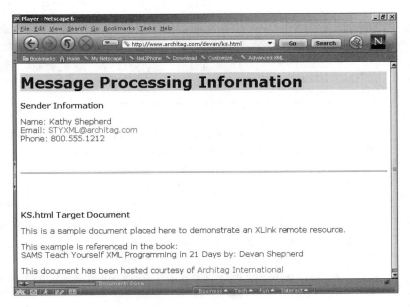

Edit your message03.xml document and try changing the value of your xlink:show attribute in line 11 to new. Save your changes as message04.xml and execute the link in Netscape 6. The browser will spawn a new window to render the result of downloading the content from the remote link. You might also try changing the xlink:actuate attribute in line 10 to onLoad. The resulting link might actuate too quickly for you to notice that it was traversed at the time that the local document was loaded. Netscape 6 does not currently support most of the other values for these attributes.

# Extended Links

As described earlier , the capabilities of XLink go far beyond simple links. *Extended links* provide multiple combinations of local and remote resources in multiple directions. Extended links comprise a set of resources and a set of connections among those resources. The resources might be local or remote. Local resources are part of the linking element, whereas remote resources are outside of the linking element. Remote resources are typically in another document, but they do not need to be to be considered remote, relative to the linking element. Each resource can be either a target or a source of link, or it can be both. If a link does not contain local resources, then it is termed an *out-of-line* link.

An extended link is encoded with a value of extended for the xlink:type attribute. Extended links generally point to multiple remote resources. They might also originate from more than one source. The concept of local and remote becomes confusing because it is highly referential. One resource might be a local resource in the context of one XLink, but it might also be a remote resource when a different XLink is traversed. Currently not enough software products or devices adequately support complex extended linking. When these tools are available, extended links promise powerful options that might not be practical today.

## Locators

As noted earlier, remote resources are those that are outside of the extended link element. XLink provides the concept of *locator* elements to help ascertain where the remote resources are. Locator elements are child elements contained by the extended link element. Locator elements can be given any name, but they must have an xlink:type attribute with a "locator" value. The xlink:href attribute is required on a locator element and serves to point to the remote resource. Related to locator elements are resource elements, which are formed the same way, but serve to locate local resources rather than remote resources.

Suppose that your message processing system, the system you used for exploring examples earlier today, not only tracked messages and the people that sent those messages, but also the actions that were associated with the messages. You have likely seen preprinted telephone message pads with fields for caller information and actions. Imagine, for instance, that your automated system tracked the sorts of actions that are typically included on a handwritten telephone message pad. Some of the actions associated with a message might indicate that the sender of the message

- Telephoned
- Wants to see you
- Returned your call
- Wants you to return the call
- Wants you to process the message
- Will call back

Following this scenario a bit further, a message might have multiple actions associated with it. XLink extended links provide a means of encoding one-to-many, and indeed many-to-many, link relationships. Assume that a single message element is linked with several of the action items listed. You might encode such an extended link relationship like the example provided in Listing 10.7. However, browsers do not, as of this writing, support extended links; therefore the remaining examples will not function in Netscape 6.

**LISTING 10.7**   Extended XLink with Locators—`message05.xml`

```
 1: <?xml version="1.0"?>
 2: <!-- Listing 10.7 - message05.xml -->
 3:
 4: <note xmlns:xlink="http://www.w3.org/1999/xlink"
 5:            xlink:type="extended">
 6:      <message xlink:type="resource">
 7:              Remember to buy milk on the way home from work
 8:      </message>
 9:
10:      <action xlink:type="locator"
11:                    xlink:href="phoned.xml"/>
12:
13:      <action xlink:type="locator"
14:                    xlink:href="see_you.xml"/>
15:
16:      <action xlink:type="locator"
17:                    xlink:href="Will_call_back.xml"/>
18:
19: </note>
```

**ANALYSIS** The `note` element describes an extended link (line 5) with four resources. The first resource is the local `message` resource (lines 6–8). The three `action` locators are remote resources (lines 10, 13, and 16). Notice that all four resources are child elements of the `note` extended link container element (lines 4–19). Because the `message` element is a local resource, it has the `resource xlink:type` value (line 6) in place of the `locator` value assigned to remote resources. Each of the remote `action` locators includes a URL (lines 11, 14, and 17) declaring the address of the remote resource.

## Arcs

When you created simple links earlier today, you were able to use the `xlink:show` and `xlink:actuate` attributes to define how and when the links were traversed. In the case of extended links, the situation becomes a lot more complex due to the number of possible links that can be activated at any point in time. Consider, for instance, the sixteen possible links among the resources encoded in message05.xml (Listing 10.7).

Each of the different links between resources might have different rules regarding behavior, such as actuation and show instructions. Each relationship is called an *arc* in XLink and is encoded with an `xlink:type` attribute given the value `arc`. The behavior rules go along with each arc declaration to describe how and when the links will be traversed. Additionally, `arc` elements have `xlink:from` and `xlink:to` attributes describing, explicitly, which resources the arcs go to or come from. The success of this process requires that the resources have `xlink:label` attributes that serve as referential labels for the `from` and `to` pointers. Figure 10.4 represents an extended XLink model.

**FIGURE 10.4**

*Extended XLink model with local resources, remote resources, and arcs.*

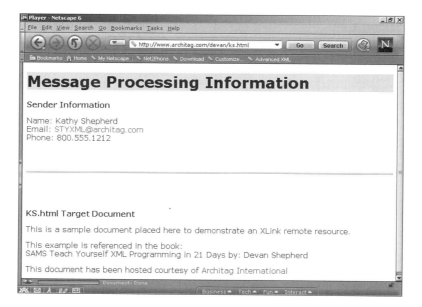

## A Complex Extended Link Example

Suppose that your message processing system is capable of tracking messages with links to multiple actions, as described earlier, and also to external resources associated with multiple senders. Perhaps the external sender resources provide names and contact information for each of the senders. A complex extended link listing can be used to express these relationships. Listing 10.8 adds two senders and two arcs to Listing 10.7. Each sender is actually a locator element used to address a remote resource. The arc elements indicate the traversal to and from various named resources.

LISTING **10.8**   Complex Extended Link Example—message06.xml

```
 1: <?xml version="1.0"?>
 2: <!-- Listing 10.8 - message06.xml -->
 3:
 4: <note xmlns:xlink="http://www.w3.org/1999/xlink"
 5:            xlink:type="extended">
 6:
 7:     <message xlink:type="resource"
 8:              xlink:role="message"
 9:              xlink:href="msg.xml"/>
10:
11:     <sender xlink:type="locator"
12:             xlink:href="ks.xml"
13:             xlink:role="sender"/>
14:
15:     <sender xlink:type="locator"
16:             xlink:href="gs.xml"
17:             xlink:role="sender"/>
18:
19:     <action xlink:type="locator"
20:             xlink:href="phoned.xml"
21:             xlink:role="action"/>
22:
23:     <action xlink:type="locator"
24:             xlink:href="see_you.xml"
25:             xlink:role="action"/>
26:
27:     <action xlink:type="locator"
28:             xlink:href="Will_call_back.xml"
29:             xlink:role="action"/>
30:
31:     <relate xlink:type="arc"
32:             xlink:from="message"
33:             xlink:to="sender"/>
34:
35:     <relate xlink:type="arc"
36:             xlink:from="message"
```

**LISTING 10.8**   continued

```
37:                          xlink:to="action"/>
38:
39:      <relate xlink:type="arc"
40:                     xlink:from="sender"
41:                     xlink:to="action"/>
42:
43: </note>
```

**ANALYSIS**   Lines 7–9 hold the message element with a role attribute, whose value is
message. Each of the locator elements is either a sender or an action, as
indicated by the value of their respective xlink:role attributes. The three relate elements include xlink:to and xlink:from attributes that define arcs between various
resources on the basis of their role names. For instance, an arc is defined between the
message resource element and each sender locator resource element.

You have read about some exciting theoretical constructs that are not, as of this writing,
fully supported by tools. However, when this technology becomes a reality, it will offer
you new ways to associate data from multiple sources, regardless of their origin on the
Internet.

# Summary

The XML Link Language (XLink) provides XML with a much more powerful linking
facility than is provided by the linking capabilities of HTML. XLink facilitates simple
and extended links designed to locate local and remote resources, not just documents.
XLink offers rich functionality for actuation and display of resources through the encoding of linking elements. The markup that specifies how to traverse a link is called an arc.
The arc identifies a start and end point for a link along with behavior attributes. XLink is
not widely supported by browsers or processors, although it is likely that browsers will
continue to evolve and include support for XLink. It is also anticipated that new and
unique devices and user agents will be developed to exploit the power of this technology
in the future.

# Q&A

**Q  What is the difference between the two fundamental types of XLink?**

**A  A simple link is a unidirectional link, similar to HTML links, but with more func-
tionality. An extended link provides for multiple multidirectional links to various
resources.**

**Q  Do XLink attributes require validation?**

**A**  Because XLink attributes are merely additional attributes on an element in an XML instance, they require validation if the instance has an associated DTD or other form of schema.

**Q  What is the role of a locator in XLink?**

**A**  The locator provides the address, typically a URL, of a remote resource. The URL characterizes the end-point on the arc traversed by execution of the XLink.

# Exercise

The exercise is provided so that you can test your knowledge of what you learned today. The answer is in Appendix A.

Over the course of the past week and a half, you have continued to manipulate your music collection markup language (MCML) with new features. Today, add a simple link to one of the CD elements that is actuated by a mouse click and results in the current browser window being replaced by new content from a document called `shelf.xml`. You will need to create `shelf.xml` and have it contain a description of where the CD can be found. Prove your solution by using Netscape 6 to execute your link.

# DAY **11**

# XML Pointer Language (XPointer)

The XML Pointer Language (XPointer) provides you with a means of addressing and locating information that is inside another XML document. XPointer makes use of, and extends, the XML Path Language (XPath) that you studied on Day 9. XPointer combines XPath expressions with URIs. You have already explored both of these technologies in detail, so today you will focus on how the two can be incorporated into an XPointer expression. Today, you will learn

- How XPointer improves on the named anchor approach to fragment identification in HTML
- The syntax of XPointer expressions
- Several special-purpose XPointer operands
- How to use XPath relationship expressions in XPointer
- Several special characteristics of XPointer

# HTML "Pointing" Using Named Targets and Hypertext Links

The XPointer specification, a working draft of the W3C dated July 9, 1999, describes a string-based expression that supports addressing directly into the internal structures of XML documents. XPointer strings provide for specific reference to elements, character strings, and other parts of XML documents because they are based on the expressive and selective XPath language. This is one distinguishing feature of XPointer that sets it apart from the HTML anchor link locator.

 **Note**

It is recommended that you read the material about XPath (Day 9) and XLink (Day 10) before reading today's material. The material covered today offers a review and extends some of the features of those technologies, but is not meant to be read in isolation of those chapters.

As a point of reference, review how basic pointing is accomplished in HTML. To locate a subset, such as a fragment, of an HTML page requires that a name be established at a specific location prior to interrogation and that the calling document address that named link specifically. This works in HTML to locate named fragments within the same document or those in a different document. The syntax of the named target label is as follows:

```
<a name="target_name">Target text or object</a>
```

This establishes a flag at the point where the anchor resides on an HTML page. The flag could be at the top or anywhere within the markup on the page. The value of the name attribute is associated with this flagged fragment of the HTML page and provides an address. A separate anchor tag referring explicitly to the named value of the attribute can resolve the address. The syntax of the calling anchor tag is as follows:

```
<a href="URI#target_name">Link text or object</a>
```

The hypertext link created by this anchor tag points to the named fragment on the page at the URI indicated. When the user activates the link by performing a mouse click over the link text or object displayed on a browser window, the browser downloads the content fragment at the named target and renders it in place of the current page. Figure 11.1 depicts this function in HTML.

**FIGURE 11.1**

*An HTML hypertext link from one document to a named target in a different document.*

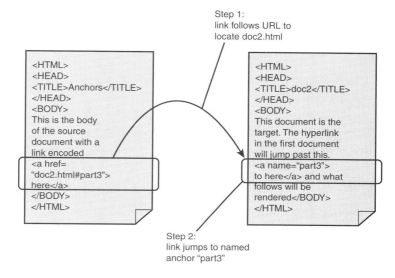

Step 1:
link follows URL to
locate doc2.html

```
<HTML>
<HEAD>
<TITLE>Anchors</TITLE>
</HEAD>
<BODY>
This is the body
of the source
document with a
link encoded
<a href=
"doc2.html#part3">
here</a>
</BODY>
</HTML>
```

```
<HTML>
<HEAD>
<TITLE>doc2</TITLE>
</HEAD>
<BODY>
This document is the
target. The hyperlink
in the first document
will jump past this.
<a name="part3">
to here</a> and what
follows will be
rendered</BODY>
</HTML>
```

Step 2:
link jumps to named
anchor "part3"

## Limitations of HTML Anchors

There are some limitations to the HTML approach described. First, you need to know the names of all targets available to you. If you have authored the page yourself, then this might be relatively simple. However, if you are accessing a remote page that you did not create, then the problem of knowing the target names can be significant. Of course, for this approach to work, the targets must exist in the first place. If they are not present, then you cannot reference a named anchor to locate a page fragment. This means that an HTML developer must have the forethought to place useful named anchors on the page in advance.

Another issue is one of security. Suppose you want to access fragments of an HTML page that are not already named. If you wish to create the appropriate named anchors, you will need full rights and privileges to access and modify the page on the server that serves as its host. Static Web pages are read-only documents; without host access rights, you cannot modify those pages. You can typically view the source of a read-only Web page and determine whether named anchors are already in existence, but without proper access authorities, you can't modify the read-only HTML page. XPointer, provides XML authors a means of accessing fragments in read-only XML documents.

# XPointer Expressions

XPointer uses the common expression language, XPath, which you learned on Day 9, and extends it considerably. XPointer is effectively XPath expressions placed in combination with qualified URIs, permitting you to

- Address ranges as well as nodes in a target document
- Locate information in a target resource by matching strings
- Utilize addressing expressions in URIs as fragment identifiers

The rich XPointer expression language permits you to locate information by navigating through a document's structure. In this way, you can select fragments based on properties such as element types, attribute values, character content, relative position, and order. This offers you a very powerful location capability with much finer granularity than is available with XPath alone. XPath can locate nodes in a document, whereas XPointer can locate nodes and patterns in element content, and can even provide an address to an individual character in a document.

## XPointer Syntax

XPointer uses a URI augmented addressing scheme not unlike the one used by HTML anchor tags. The syntax of an XPointer expression is

```
URI#scheme(expression)
```

When creating XPointers, you follow the URI immediately by a hash mark or pound sign (#) and an XPointer *fragment part*, which comprises a *scheme* and an *expression*. The URI in this string is separated from the fragment part (that is, scheme plus expression) by the hash mark. The URI is responsible for locating a resource—most typically a document—and the XPointer expression provides an address to a specific fragment within the located document.

You can have more than one fragment part in an XPointer expression, in which case the syntax is

```
URI#scheme(expression)scheme(expression)scheme(expression)...
```

The only scheme that is currently defined is xpointer, which informs the processor that the XPath language is being used as the expression addressing language. Perhaps in the future, there will be other expression languages available to extend this syntax beyond XPointer, in which case the scheme might be encoded in some other fashion.

You will typically string multiple fragment parts together only when the structure, validity, or nature of the target document is questionable. This is because although XPointer is resolved by reading from left to right through the expression string, the processor will stop reading the string as soon as a fragment path expression is satisfied. This is different from XPath, in which an entire expression is interpreted regardless. Using XPointer, you can include a fragment part and provide an alternate expression if the first fails.

Because XPointer is the only scheme currently described by the specification, a short-form version of the syntax is acceptable, which looks like this:

```
URI#expression
```

# XPointer ID References

One way to use XPointer is to place an `id` attribute on the element on which you intend to point. This is analogous to the HTML named target approach; it assumes that you are able to preplan your XPointers. A simple string after the hash mark with no other qualifiers is assumed to refer to an element with that ID. For instance, based on the message processing system you have used on several previous days, suppose you want to find a specific message that is marked up with a particular ID number. Assume that three messages are currently in the XML document and you want to use an XPointer expression to locate the first of those messages, identified by an `ID` attribute on the `message` element with a value of `m1`. Listing 11.1 is the XML instance document.

**LISTING 11.1**   XML Instance with ID Attributes on Message Elements—`message01.xml`

```
 1: <?xml version = "1.0"?>
 2: <!-- listing 11.1 - message01.xml -->
 3:
 4: <note>
 5:     <message id="m1" from="Kathy Shepherd">
 6:         Remember to buy milk on the way home from work
 7:     </message>
 8:     <message id="m2" from="Greg Shepherd">
 9:         I need some help with my homework
10:     </message>
11:     <message id="m3" from="Kristen Shepherd">
12:         Please play Scrabble with me tonight
13:     </message>
14: </note>
```

On lines 5, 8, and 11, `id` attributes have been added on the `message` elements.

To locate the `message` element that has an `id="m1"` attribute, you can use the short-form of the XPointer expression:

```
message01.xml#m1
```

This expression will locate the message element on line 5 of Listing 11.1. The more verbose version of this expression is

```
message01.xml#ID(m1)
```

The two forms of the XPointer expression function in identical ways. You can see or write either form. The verbose version is more in keeping with the syntax of other XPointer expressions, which typically involve a keyword of some kind followed by parentheses containing a value or argument.

## Absolute Addressing

In the previous example, the location term `id()` is able to locate a specific element without other addressing assistance. This is an example of an *absolute location term*. Four of these special terms are in the XPointer expression language. They follow the hash mark in an expression string, but cannot be combined. In other words, only one of the special terms is permitted in each expression phrase. Table 11.1 summarizes these terms.

**TABLE 11.1**  XPointer Absolute Location Terms

| Term | Description |
| --- | --- |
| `id()` | Locates any element with an `id` attribute that resolves the value specified by the expression |
| `root()` | Locates the root element of the document specified by a URI |
| `html()` | Locates the <A> attribute on an HTML page that is also well-formed XML (that is, XHTML), if the value of that attribute resolves the specification of the expression |
| `origin()` | Locates a document root element that is similar to `root()`), but only from a relative reference |

# Relationship Expressions

Relationship expressions or *relative location terms* address the location of an element on the basis of a context node. In other words, the expression might result in a different result depending on where the traversal begins. You learned all about relationships and XPath axes on Day 9. Using them in combination with a URI separated by a hash mark constitutes a relative XPointer expression. Relationship expressions function the same in the case of XPointer as they do in XPath, but please refer back to the explanations of these expressions on Day 9 for a refresher. You will recall that a variety of relationship axes exist; however, not all have value in XPointer. The ones that are relevant include

- Child
- Ancestor
- descendentDescendent

- Following
- Preceding
- Psibling—corresponding to preceding-sibling
- Fsibling—corresponding to following-sibling

You might be wondering why some of the XPath axes are not included in the preceding list, such as parent and descendent-or-self. This is because XPointer allows you to append arguments to the relative location terms in the preceding list, which effectively provides you a means of selecting any of the XPath standard axes. If, for instance, you choose the first ancestor relative to the point of context, you are effectively choosing the parent of that context.

Each of the relative location terms will accept up to four arguments to further define the expression. These arguments permit you to increase the sensitivity of the XPointer expression. The arguments have the same effect on the specificity of each of the relationships and are characterized by their absolute position between the parentheses appended to the relationship expression. The arguments are described briefly in the next sections. These are XPath expressions that are typical of XPointer usage; therefore, you should see some similarity between these examples and the types of expressions you created on Day 9. Nonetheless, different styles of examples are provided to reinforce the logic shared by XPath and XPointer and to provide you with more experience reading and thinking about expressions.

## Numeric Selection

The first argument provides the number of the desired selection from a set of eligible relationships. The argument can be a positive integer, negative integer, or the word `all`. The `all` argument selects all of the qualified members of a relationship set. A number selects the indicated member, counted in document order if the integer is positive, or reverse document order if a negative number is indicated. For instance, suppose you want to select all of the message elements in Listing 11.1 and you are currently residing in the context of the `note` element. In relationship terms, you want to choose all of the child elements relative to the context node. You could do that with an expression like this:

```
child(all,message)
```

This expression selects all `message` child element nodes contained by the current element. In Listing 11.1, this would result in selection of all the `message` elements, provided that the expression was resolved relative to the `note` element. If the context were elsewhere in the document, then this expression would not return the desired result. In fact, in the case of `message01.xml` (Listing 11.1), this expression would fail at every context other than that of the `note` element.

Presuming that the context is indeed the `note` element, how might you select the third message child element in an XPointer expression? The correct expression would be

```
child(3,message)
```

The numeric value (3) selects a particular element when this expression is resolved. In this case, parent element is chosen, which is the third `message` child element of the `note` context.

## Node Type

The second argument provides the type of node being traversed by the XPointer. Most of the time this is an element type name. You saw an example of this second argument in the last section. Here they are again:

```
child(all,message)
```

```
child(3,message)
```

In both sample XPointer expressions, the node type indicated is the `message` element type. The first example selects all `message` child elements, and the second chooses only the third child in the eligible set.

The node type argument provides a wildcard option for broadening the selection beyond a specified type. This is the `#element` argument value. To find all child elements relative to the context element regardless of their respective element types, you can encode the following XPointer:

```
child(all,#element)
```

This expression selects all child elements, regardless of their names.

## Attribute and Attribute Value Filters

The third and fourth arguments are attribute value pairs that can be used to filter the selection of elements on the basis of specified attributes on those elements. Suppose that you need to interrogate the `message01.xml` document (Listing 11.1) to locate the `message` element that had a value of `Kathy Shepherd` for the `from` attribute. You could write this expression in several ways, but one straightforward approach is characterized by

```
Child(all,#element,from,"Kathy Shepherd")
```

This expression selects all elements, regardless of their element type names, provided that they have a `from` attribute with a value of `"Kathy Shepherd"`.

In place of the attribute name in the third position of the argument string, you can use an asterisk (*). That means that any attribute with the designated value will satisfy the selection.

With regard to the fourth position in the argument string, you can use either an asterisk (*) as a wildcard for any value or #IMPLIED. #IMPLIED, which is borrowed from DTD logic, indicates that no value for the attribute was provided. If a value is provided for an attribute, that instance is not eligible given a #IMPLIED argument.

# Summary

XPointer is a technology that combines URIs with XPath expressions to fine-tune selections of nodes or points within a target document. XPointer extends XPath through the provision of some features that are unique to the former. As a consequence, XPointer provides you with a greater degree of granularity when that is important, resulting in a feature-rich technology that is not only powerful, but also selective.

# Q&A

**Q  Why can't you use HTML anchor tags to access fragments within a read-only document structure?**

**A**  In some cases, you can; however, you must the names of anchors that already exist in the HTML document at the beginning of predetermined fragments. If you need to access fragments that do not have associated and known named anchor tags, then the HTML approach will not help you. XPointer allows you to select on the basis of criteria that are not restricted by known names, such as patterns, element and attribute ordinals, and other products of XPath expressions.

**Q.  What is the relationship between XPointer and XPath?**

**A**  XPointer is the product of XPath, combined with URIs. XPath is used to make selections on document fragments after the document is located on the basis of the resolved URI.

**Q  Why does XPointer syntax provide multiple fragment parts?**

**A**  A fragment part comprises a scheme and an expression. Currently, XPointer is the only scheme. Multiple fragment parts can be strung together so that selection tests can be conducted on XML document instances. When the XPointer expression is traversed, it effectively tests the first fragment part. If that fragment part is resolved, the process stops. However, if the fragment part is not or cannot be resolved, then the process continues to the next fragment part if one exists. In this fashion, programmers can select alternative patterns.

11

# DAY 12

# The XML Document Object Model (DOM)

The Document Object Model (DOM) for XML offers a common application-programming interface (API) specification from the W3C. The XML DOM provides a standardized way to access and manipulate the information stored in XML documents by describing standard properties, events, and methods for connecting application code and XML documents. Today, you will learn

- About how to expose and manipulate DOM nodes
- About Object Models
- About primary API types
- About selected DOM objects, properties, methods, and events
- About how to write simple DOM scripts using JavaScript

## A DOM for XML

The XML DOM is an object model that exposes the contents of an XML document. Exposure implies that the contents can then be interrogated and, to some degree, manipulated. The W3C's Document Object Model (DOM) specification currently defines what a DOM should expose as properties, methods, and events. The W3C specification can be found at http://www.w3.org/DOM/.

 **Note**

> An excerpt from http://www.w3.org/DOM/ states this about the DOM: "The Document Object Model is a platform- and language-neutral interface that will allow programs and scripts to dynamically access and update the content, structure, and style of documents. The document can be further processed and the results of that processing can be incorporated back into the presented page."

This chapter will provide you with an opportunity to create scripts that use the DOM, although the intent is not to teach you JavaScript. If you would like more information about the JavaScript language, refer to *Sams Teach Yourself JavaScript in 24 Hours* (ISBN: 0-672-32025-8).

An XML document's structure is often compared to a tree with several nodes. Both structures comprise a variety of shapes for which any suitably chosen part is similar to a given larger or smaller part when compared as a whole. In other words, the constructs of the structural components and relationships are repeatable. In botany, a tree's nodes correspond to individual branches, a root, and a trunk, and the termination of these is a leaf, fruit, or nut. The termination nodes do not have children nodes. On the other hand, branches can have child branches that in turn can have child branches of their own in a continuously repeatable fashion. You know from your reading on previous days that this model offers a useful parallel to XML document structure, which is characterized by element, attribute, text, comment, and processing instruction nodes. Think of the leaf, nut, and fruit terminators on a tree, each incapable of having child nodes, as parallel constructs for attribute nodes and text-data nodes in an XML document, which are also void of child nodes. By establishing a reference to the child or parent of any node, you can recursively climb the tree and reach any part of the document. The DOM extends this relative structure and exposes each type of node as an object with its own set of properties and methods. The DOM defines an object hierarchy. Each node of the document tree can have any number of child nodes, and all nodes, except the root node, will have a parent node. Each node is numbered sequentially and can be named. The DOM spec provides the developer with a number of ways to use this generic document tree.

The node, therefore, is the smallest unit in the XML hierarchical document structure. The Node object is a single node on the document tree, and the Document Object is the root node of the document tree.

Table 12.1 summarizes the list of nodes accessible to the XML DOM.

**TABLE 12.1**    Nodes in XML DOM

| Node Name | Description |
|---|---|
| Node | A reference to a document component, such as an element, attribute, comment, or text string |
| Document | An object to represent an entire document, comprising all nodes |
| Element | An object representing a document element |
| Attribute | An object representing an attribute on an element as a name/value pair |
| Processing | The instructions used by an XML processor or parser, encoded in the document |
| Instruction | The programmer's comments that are ignored by the Comment parser |
| Text | An object containing text content of an element |
| CDATA Section | The text content that does not include markup characters |
| Document Fragment | A designated portion of an XML document |
| Entity | A token to be resolved by a parser into a replacement string |
| Entity Reference | A referential proxy to an entity, designated by an ampersand (&) immediately before the entity label and a semi-colon (;) immediately following the label |
| Document Type | A grammar that defines the elements and attributes |

The W3C designed the DOM at several levels. The first level is focused on the primary, or core, document models for HTML and XML encoding of documents. At this level, you will find sufficient functionality for document navigation and manipulation. Today you will use the Level 1 DOM almost exclusively.

Level 2 of the DOM includes a style sheet object model. By attaching style information to a document, you can manipulate the presentation information associated with a document. Level 2 provides a means of traversing the document via an event model and provides support for XML namespaces. You will explore the Simple API for XML as an event model for document traversal tomorrow.

The W3C anticipates a third level of the DOM to address loading and saving of documents with associated content model information, such as DTDs and other schemata. Level 3, which is not yet completed, is intended to provide validation support along with document formatting, key events, and event groups. For more information, refer to the public working draft at http://www.w3.org/DOM/.

Beyond level 3, it is anticipated that the DOM will include generic window system calls for Microsoft, Unix, and Macintosh operating systems. In addition, further functionality is being discussed that might include methods to

- Prompt users
- Interface query languages
- Address multithreading
- Implement synchronize
- Enhance security
- Provide repository functions

Other DOMs are becoming more popular that focus on particular markup languages or dialects. For instance, the Scalable Vector Language (SVG), used to describe two-dimensional, mathematically generated vector line graphics in an XML vocabulary has an SVG DOM available for programmers to use. The W3C introduced SVG as a markup language that allows for three types of graphics objects: vector graphics shapes (paths consisting of straight lines and curves), images, and text. Graphical objects can be grouped, styled, and transformed and composited into previously rendered objects.

SVG is currently a Candidate Recommendation of the W3C.

## Object Models

The DOM provides developers with a means of interfacing and interacting with a body of information that is stored as text. This has significant value in Web development, where formerly static documents become applications. In this way, the document becomes an interface to user information, not unlike a newspaper or magazine, but with the added potential to modify and customize the delivery of data. HTML in its most basic format is just a means of representing static information in a browser window. The functionality and presentation interface design is built into the browser application and leaves little control for the developer. Dynamic HTML (DHTML) provides a means for developers to control presentation and delivery of data over the Web, typically under the control of scripting languages, such as JavaScript or VBScript along with Cascading Style Sheets (CSS). Think of DHTML as implementing Web content with scripting in addition to style sheets.

An object model, generally speaking, provides a superstructure to support dynamic behaviors by exposing methods to objects represented by the model. If you are familiar with JavaScript or VBScript, then you likely already know about methods, events, and objects. Until the 4.0-generation of browsers introduced Dynamic HTML, JavaScript could not address and manipulate the contents of a document—at least not in a general sense. Netscape and Microsoft each introduced their own Document Object Models with the release of their 4.0 version browsers. Unfortunately, each company's implementation was not identical. The spirit behind the development of the Level 1 specification by the W3C was that the DOM API would be platform independent, as implemented by a common object suite. As browser technology evolves, this happens more naturally, but you should know that differences still exist between the Netscape and Microsoft implementations of DOMs. Microsoft, for instance, extends the W3C standard DOM with methods that are not available to Netscape browsers.

# Scripting DOM Structures

The DOM provides and exposes an organized structure of objects and scripts that can be used to access the nodes of that structure and manipulate them. A script might reference a node by an absolute or relative position, such as the first node in a document structure. A script might also insert or remove a node. In so doing, the content that is represented by each node can be revealed or updated as part of an application. In this way, DOM objects are structured, uniquely identified containers. The behaviors, therefore, that are enforced by scripts provide you with a means of manipulating these container objects as well as their content.

The *Document Object* is the root node container for all other objects defined in the XML document. The Document Object provides access to the Document Type definition (DTD) and exposes the child elements within the document structure. At the root level of the document is the *Root Element Node*, which is different from the true root node of the document. The document tree is an ordered and addressable collection of nodes, as you learned on Days 9, 10, and 11. Because the objects on the tree are identifiable, you can reference them and their contents. For instance, JavaScript allows you to reference the text contained by the first child node of the document in the following manner:

```
mystuff.documentElement.childNodes.item(0).text
```

This might seem a bit complex at first, but it is actually quite logical. The document known as `mystuff` contains a `documentElement` with `childNodes`. This line references the first of those child nodes (item(0)), and the text contained by that node is the target of any subsequent script action or behavior. You will note that the item number begins counting from zero; this is a script language characteristic.

As you know, one of the strengths of XML is that you can create your own set of elements. In this way, you can create objects based on the semantics of an application and then access those objects via scripts. Typically, you will want to know more than the numeric ordering of the object or the object's name; you will likely want to know the

12

context of the object in a document. It is for this reason that a script might look at the relationships of objects to ascertain the context of the object in the document.

## DOM Relationships

With the DOM, it is possible for you to traverse the object hierarchy. In other words, given an object as a starting point, you can determine the following:

- The location in the document tree
- The child nodes of the object
- The parent nodes of the object
- The siblings and ancestors of the object

## The DOM as a Universal API

As you have seen, the objective for the DOM specification is to provide a common interface (API) for developers to use during manipulation of document objects. The API provides the handles that a developer can use to reference objects and methods. Major application software development companies have provided implementations of the DOM for particular languages. The concept is that the DOM API is meant to reside independently of the particular language that implements it. That means that the implementations in Java, C, C++, C#, JavaScript, Visual Basic, VBScript, Perl, and so on should be highly similar.

For this platform-agnostic approach to be a reality requires that the DOM be specified in a relatively generic description language. The W3C DOM specification uses a language known as the Interface Definition Language (IDL) to describe the nature of interfaces expected of every DOM implementation. IDL is a standard (ISO standard 14750) developed by a collaborative known as the Object Management Group. More information about IDL can be found at http://www.omg.org/.

## Primary API Types

You read earlier about all the nodes that are exposed by the DOM; however, most programmers will use three primary API types to begin. These primary API are the *Node* node, the *Document* node, and the *Element* node. Because these nodes are the most readily encountered, you will be able to accomplish most DOM programming tasks using these three API types. You will recall that the *Node* node is the base type of most objects in the DOM. It might have any number of child nodes and might have a parent node. In fact, it will typically have a parent node except in the case where it describes the root node in a document hierarchy, which does not have a parent.

The *Element* node object is used to represent elements in the XML document. As you know, elements might have text content (for example, the string of characters between a start and end tag for the element), other element content, and attributes as modifiers on the element. Element objects have a list of attribute objects that represent the combination of those attributes that are expressed in the document instance and those that are defined by an associated schema to have default values, whether or not they are encoded by the XML instance.

The *Document* object represents the root node of a document. As such, it has no parent. Therefore a scripted method call (for example, `getParentNode()`) executed via the API to get the parent node of a document node will return a null value.

## Instantiating the DOM

The DOM can be instantiated in a variety of ways via parsers that support DOM processing. For the purpose of the exercises you will complete today, the MSXML parser will be used along with a JavaScript. The examples shown today use an approach that is limited to implementation with Microsoft Internet Explorer. Although Internet Explorer is available for a number of platforms and operating systems, not all visitors to a Web site will have this software. Therefore, some of the techniques you learn today should be considered as instructive with regard to accessing the DOM, although not necessarily practical for Web implementation. Microsoft Internet Explorer can be downloaded for Unix, DOS, Macintosh, and Windows operating systems free of charge from `http://www.microsoft.com`. The principles that you will learn today apply for other implementations of the DOM.

To address this shortfall, the DOM has many different implementations with a variety of processors and scripting methods available. If you are familiar with another scripting or application development language, you can find methods for accessing DOM objects via the Web or a link from the W3C DOM information page (`http://www.w3.org/DOM/`). You will find links to DOM implementations in PERL, Java, Python, and several other popular languages, with support for a variety of platforms.

Most of the implementations of the DOM share common functional characteristics. The DOM provides you with an interface for loading, accessing, and manipulating XML documents. Tomorrow, you will read about the Simple API for XML (SAX), which is an event-driven model. The major difference between these two approaches is that the DOM loads an entire document instance into memory at once, whereas the SAX processes a single event, such as a node, at a time and then moves on to process the next event in document order.

**12**

After a DOM-compliant processor parses the document, a tree structure will be built and exposed for read and write access by scripts or application languages. After the object tree is created, the parser manages it, thereby allowing programmers to use methods built in to the parser rather than creating unique logic. With the entire document tree in memory at once, random access to the content of all nodes is possible. Figure 12.1 shows the relationship between the XML document, the XML parser, the DOM tree created by the parser, and the application or script with read and write access on the exposed objects. When the parser loads an XML document into a DOM, the parser reads it in its entirety and generates a node tree that is then available in whole or in part to methods implemented by various application development languages and scripting languages. The document is considered a single node that contains all other nodes and their respective content.

**FIGURE 12.1**

*The DOM implemented by an XML parser exposes object nodes to a script or application.*

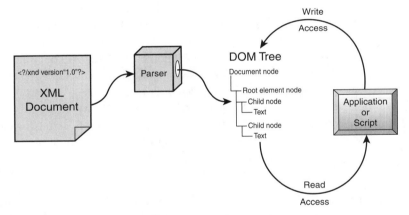

To begin scripting against the DOM tree, you will first have to create the document object. Doing so using JavaScript and the MSXML DOM parser involves creating a new `ActiveXObject` that instantiated the *Component Object Model* (COM) component that comes as part of the distribution library installed with Microsoft Internet Explorer 5.0 or above. The `ActiveXObject` is `XMLDOM` in the COM library. The JavaScript code will look like this:

```
Var oMystuff = New ActiveXObject("Microsoft.XMLDOM")
```

This script creates a new `ActiveXObject` for the document based on the Microsoft `XMLDOM` COM component available as part of the MSXML parser suite. The document object is placed in a variable called `oMystuff`. By convention, the lowercase *o* is being used to indicate a variable that represents an object.

As you may know, particularly if you are a Visual Basic, Java or Visual C++ developer, the *Component Object Model* (COM) enables the creation of integrated software components that are programming-language independent and location-transparent. This means that you can access the MSXML parser with any language that is capable of instantiating the COM component. Although you will use JavaScript today for most of the DOM scripting exercises, you could rewrite these to use VBScript by instantiating the DOM and creating the document object with the VBScript `CreateObject` method, like this:

```
Set oMystuff = CreateObject("Microsoft.XMLDOM")
```

This VBScript code is functionally equivalent to the JavaScript code, in that it creates a document object based on the same COM component in the MSXML parser distribution. The document object is placed in a variable called `oMystuff`.

Both of the examples shown create objects that are used for client-side scripting. In fact, most of the exercises you will work through today will be client-side DOM scripting; however, you can create an object in an Active Server Page (ASP) for server-side scripting using the same approach. The VBScript in an ASP page to create the document object for server-side scripting would look like this:

```
Set oMystuff = Server.CreateObject("Microsoft.XMLDOM")
```

This VBScript code works in the same way as the previous examples. It creates a server-side ASP (`Server.CreateObject`) document object based on the COM component in the MSXML parser distribution. The document object is placed in a variable called `oMystuff`.

# DOM Object Properties, Methods, and Events

The Microsoft XML DOM consists of four principal objects: `XMLDOMDocument`, `XMLDOMNode`, `XMLDOMNodeList`, and `XMLDOMNameNodeMap`. Other implementations of the XML DOM beyond the scope of today's discussion will use different objects depending on the language that implements them. Each object has its own properties, methods, and events. If you are unfamiliar with the basics of object-oriented programming (OOP) models or find the distinctions between properties, methods, and events confusing, refer to the online tutorial available from Sun Microcomputers at `http://java.sun.com/docs/books/tutorial/java/concepts/object.html`.

The `XMLDOMDocument` object will be used today. Some of the commonly used properties, methods, and events on this object are summarized in Tables 12.2–12.4. This set is made

12

available by the Microsoft implementation of the DOM Object. Other implementations might include others not listed here or might exclude some of those that Microsoft has provided as an extension of the DOM.

**TABLE 12.2**    Commonly Used Properties of XMLDOMDocument

| Property | Description |
| --- | --- |
| async | Indicates whether asynchronous download is permitted. When a document is being loaded and the async property is set to "false", async causes the parser to halt execution until the entire document is loaded into memory. |
| attributes | Contains a list of attributes for this node |
| childNodes | Contains a list of child nodes for those nodes that may have child nodes |
| dataType | Specifies the datatype for this node |
| docType | Contains the document type node that specifies the validating DTD for the document |
| documentElement | Returns the XML document's root node and contains the root element of the document |
| firstChild | Contains the first child of this node |
| lastChild | Contains the last child node of this node |
| namespaceURI | Returns the URI for the namespace node |
| nodeName | Contains the name of the element, attribute, or entity reference for the node |
| nodeType | Specifies the XML DOM node type, which determines valid values and whether the node may have child nodes |
| nodeValue | Contains the text associated with the node |
| parseError | Returns the IXMLDOMParseError object that contains information about the last parsing error |
| preserveWhiteSpace | Indicates whether to display whitespace in the XML document |
| readyState | Indicates the current state of the XML document |

**TABLE 12.2**　Continued

| Property | Description |
|---|---|
| resolveExternals | Resolves namespaces, DTDs, and external entity references when the document is processed |
| validateOnParse | Indicates whether the parser should validate this document |
| xml | Contains the XML representation of the node and all its descendants |

**TABLE 12.3**　Methods of XMLDOMDocument

| Method | Description |
|---|---|
| Clonenode() | Creates a new node that is an exact copy of the current node |
| CreateAttribute() | Creates a new attribute |
| CreateCDATASection() | Creates a CDATA section node |
| CreateComment() | Creates a comment node |
| CreateElement() | Creates an element node using the specified name |
| CreateEntityReference() | Creates an entity reference object |
| CreateNode() | Creates a node |
| CreateTextNode() | Creates a text node |
| GetElementsByTagName() | Returns a collection of elements that have the specified name |
| HasChildNodes() | Returns true if this node has child nodes |
| Load() | Loads an existing XML document from a specified location |
| LoadXML() | Loads an XML document from a supplied string rather than from a URL |
| NodeFromId() | Returns the node whose ID attribute matches the supplied value |
| RemoveChild() | Removes the specified child node from the list of child nodes and returns it |
| ReplaceChild() | Replaces the specified old child node with the supplied new child node in the set of child nodes |
| Save() | Saves the XML document |

**12**

**TABLE 12.4**　Events of XMLDOMDocument

| Event | Description |
|---|---|
| ondataavailable | Indicates that XML document data is available |
| onreadystatechange | Indicates when the readyState property changes |

# Loading an XML File from a URL

From Table 12.2, you know that the load() method can be used to load an XML document into a DOM Document Object, thereby exposing the nodes of the XML document to scripting. The JavaScript method encoding will have the following syntax:

```
oMystuff.load('filname.xml')
```

The object, oMystuff, which was created in a previous step, is now being loaded with the contents of filename.xml.

You will typically want to ensure that the parser is halted during the loading of the document into the object by the DOM parser. To do this, you will encode an async property with a value of false on the object being created. The JavaScript syntax for this property is

```
oMystuff.async = "false"
```

The async property is set to false to prohibit asynchronous download, thereby halting the processor until the entire instance is loaded into memory.

Now you know enough to string together the appropriate object creation, methods, and properties to load an XML document into the DOM. Using JavaScript, you will need to create the ActiveXObject for the document node and assign the async property a value of false, and then load the document from a URL. The syntax of this encoding will be:

```
1: var oMystuff = new ActiveXObject("Microsoft.XMLDOM")
2: oMystuff.async="false"
3: oMystuff.load("message01.xml")
```

**ANALYSIS** The new object is created in Line 1 as an instance of the Microsoft XML parser and named oMystuff. Line 2 assures that the parser will halt execution until the entire XML document is loaded into memory on the object. Line 3 provides the load method with a valid URL for the document to be loaded.

To test this scripting, you will start by creating a simple XML instance. You can reuse the message01.xml document from yesterday for this exercise. Listing 12.1 shows this document, saved as message01.xml, which you can copy if you no longer have the document from the previous day available to you. The only difference between this listing and the listing on Day 11 is the comment on line 2, which indicates that this listing is shown on Day 12 as Listing 12.1.

**LISTING 12.1**    A Simple XML Document—message01.xml

```
1: <?xml version = "1.0"?>
2: <!-- listing 12.1 - message01.xml -->
```

---

**LISTING 12.1**    continued

```
 3:
 4: <note>
 5:    <message ID="m1" from="Kathy Shepherd">
 6:       Remember to buy milk on the way home from work
 7:    </message>
 8:    <message ID="m2" from="Greg Shepherd">
 9:       I need some help with my homework
10:    </message>
11:    <message ID="m3" from="Kristen Shepherd">
12:       Please play Scrabble with me tonight
13:    </message>
14: </note>
```

The note element contains several message child elements with text content only. Each message element has ID and from attributes.

Next place the scripts described earlier in an HTML document structure to load the message01.xml file into a DOM Object for further processing. One approach to this is to create a script in the <head> section of an HTML document that performs the load. In the case of your message01.xml file, the might look like this:

```
1: </head>
2: <script language="javascript">
3: <!-- hide script from older browsers
4: var oMystuff = new ActiveXObject("Microsoft.XMLDOM")
5: oMystuff.async="false"
6: oMystuff.load("message01.xml")
7: -->
8: </script>
9: </head>
```

**ANALYSIS**   This code snippet includes a script, beginning on line 2, contained within the <head> section (lines 1–9) of an HTML page. Line 2 declares the script language (language="javascript") with a language attribute on the script element. Line 3 begins a comment that effectively hides the entire script from early browsers that are not JavaScript aware. Lines 4–6 are the document object creation and XML load steps discussed in detail earlier. Lines 7, 8, and 9 terminate the comment, script, and head section respectively.

This alone will only load the document and expose the nodes to further processing. Suppose you would like to return the text content of the XML document to the screen using a JavaScript alert. Quite simply, adding an alert to the script section of the document could do this. To ensure that the body section of your HTML page is not completely empty, you'll add some text at this time as well. Listing 12.2 shows a completed

**12**

HTML page that performs as described when loaded into the Microsoft Internet Explorer (IE) browser version 5.0 or above. Create this page and save it as DOM01.html; then load it into IE.

**LISTING 12.2** DOM Scripting Example—DOM01.html

```
 1: <!DOCTYPE HTML PUBLIC "-//W3C//DTD HTML 4.01 Transitional//EN">
 2: <!-- listing 12.2 - DOM01.html -->
 3:
 4: <html>
 5: <head>
 6: <title>DOM Scripting</title>
 7: </head>
 8: <script language="javascript">
 9: <!-- hide script from older browsers
10: var oMystuff = new ActiveXObject("Microsoft.XMLDOM")
11: oMystuff.async="false"
12: oMystuff.load("message01.xml")
13: alert(oMystuff.text);
14: -->
15: </script>
16: </head>
17: <body>
18:      Done!
19: </body>
20: </html>
```

**ANALYSIS** You have seen most of the component parts of this listing already. Lines 8–15 include the script that creates the DOM object (line 10) and loads the XML document (line 12). Line 13 includes a JavaScript alert. When executed, the alert will halt the parsing of the HTML page and produce a message on the screen that contains all of the text content of the oMystuff object. The object in this case includes the entire document instance, so all of the text content of the document node and all of its child nodes (for example, subtrees) are included. Line 18 includes the text Done!, which will be displayed when the script has completed and the user has cleared the alert message.

When you test this HTML page in IE, it should produce an alert message that looks like the one in Figure 12.2. This message lists the text content of the XML document, which corresponds to lines 6, 9, and 12 of Listing 12.1.

**FIGURE 12.2**

*A JavaScript* alert *message returning the text content of an XML document.*

## Returning Results to the Screen

Suppose you would like to return the results to the HTML page rather than present a JavaScript alert message. You can accomplish this in many ways. You could, for instance, remove the alert and reference the object in the body of the HTML page using a JavaScript `document.write` method in a separate script. Using this method, you might create a second script, within the body of the HTML page, which called the `oMystuff` object and returned the text content of the document node and all of its subtree nodes. Listing 12.3 demonstrates one means of accomplishing this. This approach works, but as you will see, it is not entirely efficient or practical. Modify the HTML page you created earlier and save it as `DOM02.html` so that it looks like the listing.

**LISTING 12.3**    Returning the Text Content of an XML Document to an HTML Page—
`DOM02.html`

```
 1: <!DOCTYPE HTML PUBLIC "-//W3C//DTD HTML 4.01 Transitional//EN">
 2: <!-- listing 12.3 - DOM02.html -->
 3:
 4: <html>
 5: <head>
 6: <title>DOM Scripting</title>
 7: <script language="javascript">
 8: <!-- hide script from older browsers
 9: var oMystuff = new ActiveXObject("Microsoft.XMLDOM")
10: oMystuff.async="false"
11: oMystuff.load("message01.xml")
12: -->
13: </script>
14: </head>
15: <body>
16: <script language="javascript">
17: <!-- hide script from older browsers
18:     document.write
19:     ("<h2>The text content of the XML file contains:</h2>")
20:
21:     document.write
22:     (oMystuff.text)
23:
24:     document.write
25:     ("<hr />")
```

12

LISTING 12.3    continued

```
26: -->
27: </script>
28: </body>
29: </html>
```

ANALYSIS    The first script in this listing (lines 7–13) is similar to the one in Listing 12.2, except the JavaScript `alert` has been omitted. A second script is created in the body of the HTML page on lines 16–27. Lines 18–19 write the string `<h2>The text content of the XML file contains:</h2>` to the page. Because the string contains HTML markup (`H2`), the string will be rendered accordingly, such as a Heading Level 2 string. Lines 21–22 write the results of issuing the `text` property on the `oMystuff` object (for example, all of the text content of the document node and its respective subtree nodes). Lines 24–25 simply produce a horizontal line the width of the browser window on the browser display. Line 27 closes the second script.

## Selecting a Node by Its Ordinal Position

The last exercise returned a continuous string comprising all of the text content for the entire document. Suppose you want to present only the text content of the second child node of the document. A quick review of the XML document (Listing 12.1) reveals that the second node containing text is the second message element. The second message element has the content `I need some help with my homework`. To selectively identify a node by an ordinal value, you will need to use properties that accept numeric sub-properties. In this exercise, you really want to return the text contained by the second child element node of the document element parent. This can be done in JavaScript by the following expression:

```
oMystuff.documentElement.childNodes.item(1).text
```

Notice that to select the second child node, you encode the item property with the value 1. This is because enumeration in JavaScript property values always begins with zero as the first counted instance, followed by one, two, and so on. Therefore, selecting the second child node requires that you set the `item` property to a value of 1.

In this example, you will also improve on the programming by combining the two previous scripts into one. For ease of implementation, place the combined script in the body

section of the HTML page. Listing 12.4 shows the completed HTML page, saved as
`DOM03.html`.

**LISTING 12.4**    Selecting the Text Content of a Node by Its Ordinal Position—`DOM03.html`

```
 1: <!DOCTYPE HTML PUBLIC "-//W3C//DTD HTML 4.01 Transitional//EN">
 2: <!-- listing 12.4 - DOM03.html -->
 3:
 4: <html>
 5: <head>
 6: <title>DOM Scripting</title>
 7: </head>
 8: <body>
 9: <script language="javascript">
10: <!--
11:
12:     var oMystuff = new ActiveXObject("Microsoft.XMLDOM")
13:     oMystuff.async="false"
14:     oMystuff.load("message01.xml")
15:
16:     document.write
17:     ("<h2>The selected XML element in the file contains:</h2>")
18:
19:     document.write
20:     (oMystuff.documentElement.childNodes.item(1).text)
21:
22:     document.write
23:     ("<hr />")
24:
25: -->
26: </script>
27:
28: </body>
29: </html>
```

**12**

**ANALYSIS**    The single script used to load and process the XML document is on lines 9–26 of this listing. Lines 12–14 include the object instantiation and the XML document load. Lines 19–20 include the selection of the text content of the second child node of the document element.

## Selecting XML Elements by Name

Suppose that you know something about the structure of the XML document you are exposing via the DOM and you want to select the text content of a particular element. This text might be the second `message` element in your `message01.xml` document, which, coincidentally, will return the same result as the exercises completed earlier. You could accomplish this by using the getElementsByTagName method. For the scenario described, it would be encoded like this:

```
oMystuff.getElementsByTagName("message").item(1).text
```

This expression returns the text content of the second (item(1)) message element contained in the oMystuff object.

Using the document.write method, add this to your HTML page and save the result as DOM04.html. Listing 12.5 shows a working solution.

**LISTING 12.5**    Selecting an XML Element by Name—DOM04.html

```
 1: <!DOCTYPE HTML PUBLIC "-//W3C//DTD HTML 4.01 Transitional//EN">
 2: <!-- listing 12.5 - DOM04.html -->
 3:
 4: <html>
 5: <head>
 6: <title>DOM Scripting</title>
 7: </head>
 8: <body>
 9: <script language="javascript">
10: <!--
11:
12:     var oMystuff = new ActiveXObject("Microsoft.XMLDOM")
13:     oMystuff.async="false"
14:     oMystuff.load("message01.xml")
15:
16:     document.write
17:     ("<h2>The selected XML element in the file contains:</h2>")
18:
19:     document.write
20:     (oMystuff.documentElement.childNodes.item(1).text)
21:
22:     document.write
23:     ("<br/><br/> Result by Tag Name:<br/>")
24:
25:     document.write
26:     (oMystuff.getElementsByTagName("message").item(1).text)
27:
28:     document.write
29:     ("<hr />")
30:
31: -->
32: </script>
33:
34: </body>
35: </html>
```

**ANALYSIS**  Lines 25–26 add the new method to the script. The code returns the text contained by the second message element on the document object. Lines 22–23 were added just to separate the results and identify the second return as the Result by Tag Name.

## Returning DOM Error Messages

A special property in the DOM (parseError) contains and returns an object that holds the details of the last parsing error encountered at the time of processing. By writing selected properties from this object, you can create an efficient error routine to test XML documents with DOM scripts. Table 12.5 lists the properties of the XMLDOMParseError object that is contained by the parseError property of the XMLDOMDocument object.

**TABLE 12.5**    Properties of the XMLDOMParseError Object

| Property | Description |
| --- | --- |
| E | |
| errorCode | Contains the error code of the last parse error |
| F | |
| filePos | Contains an absolute file position where an error occurred |
| line | Reports the line number where an error has occurred |
| linePos | Contains the position of the first offending character in an error on a line |
| reason | Provides a description of the error |
| srcText | Holds the full text of the line containing the error |
| url | Reports the URL of the XML document containing an error |

**12**

Suppose you would like to write a JavaScript routine to test an XML document. After finding an error, return the reason code, the offending line number, an English description of the error encountered, and the URL of the document in error. Using JavaScript, you can encode the parseError property on your document object and append the appropriate XMLDOMParseError properties. The code might look something like this:

```
1:  document.write
2:  ("<br>Error Reason Code: ")
3:  document.write
4:  (oMystuff.parseError.errorCode)
5:
6:  document.write
7:  ("<br>Error Line Number: ")
8:  document.write
```

```
 9:      (oMystuff.parseError.line)
10:
11:      document.write
12:      ("<br>Error Reason Description: ")
13:      document.write
14:      (oMystuff.parseError.reason)
15:
16:      document.write
17:      ("<br>URL of File with Error: ")
18:      document.write
19:      (oMystuff.parseError.url)
```

**ANALYSIS**  Lines 3–4 return the errorCode if a parsing error occurs when the XML document is loaded into memory. Lines 8–9 return a line number; lines 13–14 return a reason description, lines 18–19 return the URL of the offending XML document.

The next exercise involves adding these properties to a script to test for parsing errors. To force an error to occur, change the document load method in your script to search for a non-existent XML file. When the script is executed, it will search for the file and report an error when it is not located and parsed.

Listing 12.6 shows an HTML page with the complete script included. Create your script according to the sample provided and save it as DOMerror01.html.

**LISTING 12.6**    Error Script—DOMerror01.html

```
 1: <!DOCTYPE HTML PUBLIC "-//W3C//DTD HTML 4.01 Transitional//EN">
 2: <!-- listing 12.6 - DOMerror01.html -->
 3:
 4: <html>
 5: <head>
 6: <title>DOM Scripting</title>
 7: </head>
 8: <body>
 9: <script language="javascript">
10: <!--
11:
12:     var oMystuff = new ActiveXObject("Microsoft.XMLDOM")
13:     oMystuff.async="false"
14:     oMystuff.load("wrong_filename.xml")
15:
16:     document.write
17:       ("<br>Error Reason Code: ")
18:     document.write
19:       (oMystuff.parseError.errorCode)
20:
21:     document.write
22:       ("<br>Error Line Number: ")
```

**LISTING 12.6**   continued

```
23:    document.write
24:      (oMystuff.parseError.line)
25:
26:    document.write
27:      ("<br>Error Reason Description: ")
28:    document.write
29:      (oMystuff.parseError.reason)
30:
31:    document.write
32:      ("<br>URL of File with Error: ")
33:    document.write
34:      (oMystuff.parseError.url)
35:
36:  -->
37:  </script>
38:  </body>
39:  </html>
```

**ANALYSIS**   The error routine was described in detail earlier; in this listing it resides on lines 16–34. Line 14 (`oMystuff.load("wrong_filename.xml")`) attempts to load an XML document that does not exist. This will result in a parse error and will return the following information to the browser window:

```
Error Reason Code: -2146697210
Error Line Number: 0
Error Reason Description: The system cannot locate the object specified.
URL of File with Error: wrong_filename.xml
```

Parse error messages from the `XMLDOMParseError` object are typically quite informative. To see another report, modify your `message01.xml` document by mixing the case of one of the `message` element tags and saving the document as `message_bad.xml`. Listing 12.7 shows a poorly formed XML instance with mixed case tags on a `message` element.

**12**

**LISTING 12.7**   Poorly Formed XML Instance—`message_bad.xml`

```
 1: <?xml version = "1.0"?>
 2: <!-- listing 12.7 - message_bad.xml -->
 3:
 4: <note>
 5:    <message ID="m1" from="Kathy Shepherd">
 6:       Remember to buy milk on the way home from work
 7:    </message>
 8:    <message ID="m2" from="Greg Shepherd">
 9:       I need some help with my homework
10:    </message>
```

LISTING 12.7    continued

```
11:       <Message ID="m3" from="Kristen Shepherd">
12:           Please play Scrabble with me tonight
13:       </message>
14: </note>
```

**ANALYSIS**    The third message element (lines 11–13) has a start tag with a capital "M" and an end tag with a lowercase "m". This will result in a parse error when the document is loaded into the DOM document object.

To see the results of parsing an error like the one shown in Listing 12.7, change line 14 of your DOMerror01.html document to load message_bad.xml. To do so, the line will look something like this:

```
14:       oMystuff.load("message_bad.xml")
```

When the script is executed, you should receive an error report in the browser window that looks something like this:

```
Error Reason Code: -1072896659
Error Line Number: 13
Error Reason Description: End tag 'message' does not match
  the start tag 'Message'.
URL of File with Error: message_bad.xml
```

Based on this error report, you now know how to correct the XML document to make it well formed again. This kind of error checking can be built into almost any XML processing application with relative ease.

# Summary

Today you explored the Document Object Model (DOM) for XML. You learned how it provides you with a common API that can be used by a variety of scripting and application development languages. You saw how the DOM exposes the contents of an XML document as a hierarchical structure of related nodes. Finally, you wrote several scripts that used various document object properties and methods to locate nodes in an XML document and report on parser errors. Tomorrow you will read about an alternative to the DOM called the Simple API for XML (SAX), which is an event-driven model for XML processing.

# Q&A

**Q  What is an Object Model?**

**A**  In computer programming, an object model, such as the DOM, is a group of related objects that work in concert to complete a set of related tasks. By associating known methods, properties, and events with the objects, interfaces can be developed, called Application Programming Interfaces (APIs). The Document Object Model (DOM) offers an API that is independent of platforms and languages that implement it.

**Q  How does a programmer use the DOM?**

**A**  You create an instance of an XML parser by instantiating a DOM object. The Microsoft approach used to complete the exercises in this chapter exposed the XML DOM via a set of standard COM components in the MSXML parser suite that ships with Internet Explorer version 5 or greater.

**Q  How do you decide when to do client-side and when to do server-side scripting of the DOM?**

**A**  Client-side DOM applications are particularly useful for testing and validation purposes. There are, however, several opportunities for upstream DOM implementations. Server-side DOM parsing is particularly appropriate for situations that involve unattended or server-to-server application execution.  Sever-side DOM programs can also be executed under the control of a script. Therefore, you could construct a Web site that used server-side DOM programming to manipulate XML document instances.

12

# Exercise

The exercise is provided so that you can test your knowledge of what you learned today. The answers are in Appendix A.

Write a script to instantiate the DOM. Load your cd.xml document into the object and write the content of the `title` and `artist` elements for the first CD in your collection to the browser window.

Use the `getElementsByTagName()` method and append the appropriate `item()` method and `text` property to return the desired values.

## Exercise–Part 2

Modify your code to return the content of the `title` and `artist` elements for the second CD in your collection.0

DAY **13**

# The Simple API for XML (SAX)

The Simple API for XML (SAX) is a publicly developed standard for the events-based parsing of XML documents. Unlike the Document Object Model (DOM) approach that you studied on Day 12, which creates a tree-based representation for the information in your XML documents, SAX does not have a default object model. SAX defines an abstract programmatic interface that models the XML document instance through a linear sequence of method calls. Today, you will learn

- The differences between the DOM and SAX APIs and when you might choose one over the other
- How an event-based API works with hierarchical XML data
- How to write a simple JAVA program to instantiate the Sun Microsystems JAXP SAX-based parser

# A Simple API for XML

SAX 1.0 (the Simple API for XML) was released on May 11, 1998. SAX is a common, event-based API for parsing XML documents. It was developed as a collaborative project of the members of the XML-DEV Internet discussion group. SAX 2.0 is a newer version that incorporates support for namespaces and more complex query strings. Today, you will work with SAX 1.0 and use it to parse XML documents. For further details and the history of the project, refer to `http://www.megginson.com/SAX/`).

Like the DOM, the SAX provides a standard set of methods that can be implemented to programmatically manipulate the data and structural content in XML document instances. The SAX is an alternative method for parsing and accessing the parts of XML documents. As the document is processed, each part is identified and a corresponding event is raised. This distinguishes SAX from the DOM API. As you learned yesterday, the DOM reads an entire document instance into memory at once. SAX handles each markup component encountered as a separate event without requiring the entire document to be loaded into memory at the same time. This is not the only difference between SAX and the DOM API. For instance, DOM has the capability of adding and deleting nodes. In fact, with DOM you can create an entire XML instance from scratch. You cannot do this with SAX. You will read about other differences between the two today.

## SAX Parsers

SAX parsers are available in a number of different programming languages, such as Java, Python, PERL and Visual Basic, each of which provides a means of implementing the common methods that characterize the API. You will learn more about these methods shortly. The original work on SAX was done entirely in Java, and a majority of solutions are implemented as Java API distributions. Some of the popular parsers for SAX include those summarized by Table 13.1.

**TABLE 13.1**   Popular SAX Parsers

| Parser | Description |
| --- | --- |
| MSXML 3.0 | Microsoft's MSXML parser supports DOM and SAX, as well as a variety of other XML technologies. MSXML 3.0 is available at `http://msdn.microsoft.com/xml`. |
| MSXML 4.0 | Version 4 of the MSXML parser is significantly enhanced with improved support for XML technologies, including a sophisticated integration of the SAX and DOM so that you can *trigger* SAX events from a `DOMdocument` object and create SAX objects from DOM nodes. MSXML 4.0 is available at `http://msdn.microsoft.com/xml`. |

**TABLE 13.1**   continued

| Parser | Description |
| --- | --- |
| Xerces | Xerces, a product of Apache Software Foundation, is an efficient parser that supports DOM and SAX.  Xerces is available at `http://www.apache.org`. Xerces is platform neutral because it is written in Java and it is based on an open-source approach to coding. |
| JAXP | Sun Microsystems' SAX parser, known as JAXP, supports DOM and SAX. JAXP is available at `http://java.sun.com/xml`. JAXP is written in Java, thereby making it platform independent. |

# SAX and DOM Compared

You will recall that the DOM API approach creates a tree-based model that stores all of an XML documents data in a hierarchy of nodes. The entire document instance is loaded in memory at the same time and this offers an efficient means of providing you with a random access capability to expose every node in the document tree. The DOM has facilities for adding or removing nodes so that you can modify the document under program control.

Typically, when you create an events-based application, you build functions that are triggered by user-generated events or transactions. For instance, a script might await an `OnClick` event to fulfill a particular sub-routine. Writing an application to instantiate an events-based SAX parser involves a similar approach; however, it is the parser and not a user that generates the events. SAX parsers invoke methods when markup events are encountered during the parsing of a document. Parts of your XML document, such as the beginning or end of the document instance, start tags, end tags, attributes, and character data trigger events that are recognized during the processing of the document by a SAX parser.

The parser is designed to read and recognize the unique markup characters as they are encountered in the stream of data that comprises an XML document. Consider the simple XML document depicted by listing 13.1 as a source being presented to a SAX parser.

**13**

**LISTING 13.1**   A Simple XML Document—`message01.xml`

```
1: <?xml version = "1.0"?>
2: <!-- listing 13.1 - message01.xml -->
3: <note>
4:     <message from="Kathy Shepherd">
5:         Remember to buy milk on the way home from work
6:     </message>
7: </note>
```

Some of the events that could be objectified by the SAX include the following:

```
1: Start of Document
2: Start of Element ( note )
3: Start of Element ( message )
4: Attribute Name Value Pair ( from="Kathy Shepherd" )
5: Character Data ( Remember to buy milk on the way home from work )
6: End of Element ( message )
7: End of Element ( note )
8: End of Document
```

**ANALYSIS**     Line 1 is an event corresponding to the start of the document instance that is generated as the SAX parser processes this document. Line 2 represents the event that marks the start of the note element. The note element end tag generates the ending element event indicated on line 7. Lines 3 and 6 correspond to the start and end of the message element. Line 4 depicts the event corresponding to the from event on the message element. The event associated with the parsed character data content of the message element is shown on line 5.

In fact, several other potential events are associated with the sample instance shown in Listing 13.1 that have not been identified. For one thing, SAX deals with whitespace characters in an XML document differently from DOM. You will learn more about that today.

The SAX and DOM approaches obviously differ in how they reflect the XML instance document on programmatic types. With the event-based model projected by SAX, no tree structure is created in memory for an XML instance. Rather, data is passed to the application a character at a time in document-forward order. Because SAX does not demand resources for an in-memory representation of the document, it is a good alternative to the Document Object Model (DOM) in particular circumstances. With SAX, for instance, it is possible to systematically search large document instances to extract small portions of information. Additionally, the SAX allows you to halt processing after the exposure of desired information, rather than requiring that an entire document be loaded into memory for document processing. SAX can be used to build DOM trees. This, in part, is how many DOM parsers are constructed at an internal level. Conversely, you can traverse DOM trees and emit SAX streams; however, these complex operations are beyond the scope of today's study.

Because data is passed to a SAX application from the XML document instance as it is found, you can expect greater performance and less memory utilization or overhead as a consequence. However, the performance benefits of this approach are offset by more complex processing structures. Advanced queries performed on documents with many levels of nested child elements and complex intra-element relationships can become burdensome due to the inherent complexities of maintaining event context during processing. As a consequence, most developers prefer to use the DOM approach for documents that require modification or manipulation and choose a SAX parser to read excessively long XML documents that will not be changed. A growing trend in the XML programming community involves the combination of DOM and SAX solutions to meet particular needs.

# Choosing SAX Over DOM

Because an events-based parser processes documents in a serial manner, sometimes the Simple API for XML (SAX) presents an excellent alternative to the Document Object Model (DOM).

## Processing Large Documents

One of the most significant advantages of the SAX approach is that it requires significantly less memory to process an XML document than does a DOM parser. With SAX, memory consumption does not increase with the size of the file. For example, a 100 kilobyte (KB) document can occupy up to 1 megabyte (MB) of memory using a DOM processor; the same document requires significantly less memory when parsed by a SAX event-driven processor. If you need to process large documents, SAX might be the better alternative, particularly if you do not need to change the content of the document.

## Halting Processing Under Program Control

Because SAX allows you to halt processing at any time, you can use it to create applications that locate and retrieve particular data. For example, you can create an application that searches for an item in a catalogue or inventory system. When the application finds the desired item, it might return data related to it, such as the inventory number and availability, and then stop processing without interrogating the remainder of the document.

## Retrieving Small Amounts of Information

For many XML-based solutions, it is not necessary to read the entire document to achieve the desired results. You might, for example, imagine an online news application that could scan data on a newswire for relevant stories about a particular topic; it's inefficient to read all of the unnecessary data into memory. With SAX, your application might scan the data for news articles related only to the topic you indicate, and then create a subset document structure to pass along to your news reader application, browser, or perhaps to a wireless device. Scanning only a small percentage of the document significantly saves system resources.

13

## Choosing DOM Over SAX

Sometimes the DOM approach will provide a better solution to meet your needs.

### Random Access to a Document

SAX does not provide a means to load the entire document into memory at once. You must handle data in the order in which it is processed. When you require random access to nodes that have complex interrelationships, the DOM provides a better choice. SAX can be difficult to use when the document contains many internal cross-references, such as ID and IDREF attributes.

### Complex XPath Filters

Use the DOM if you must perform complex XML Path Language (XPath) filtering and retain complex data structures that hold context information. The tree structure of the DOM retains context information automatically. With SAX, you must retain the context information yourself.

### Modification and Creation of XML

As noted earlier, SAX does not have the capability to create a new XML document instance in the way that the DOM API can. The DOM is capable of creating XML documents. SAX can interrogate and report on events, but it can't be used to build an XML document instance for further processing, storage, or transmission. The DOM also allows you to modify a document in memory, as well as read a document from an XML source file. SAX is designed for reading, not writing, XML documents. The DOM is the better choice for modifying an XML document and saving the changed document to memory.

# Methods Invoked During the Processing of SAX Events

Although certain common methods belong to the SAX processing approach, various implementations might invoke additional methods on events. A summary of a popular minimal set of methods is presented in Table 13.2. These methods are implemented as part of the DocumentHandler interface that characterizes the API.

**TABLE 13.2**   Selected SAX Parser Methods

| Method | Description |
| --- | --- |
| documentLocator | Method that returns the filename, path, or URL of an XML document being processed |
| startDocument | Method invoked when the processor encounters the start of an XMLdocument |

**TABLE 13.2**   continued

| Method | Description |
| --- | --- |
| endDocument | Method called upon reaching the end of a document |
| startElement | Method called upon parsing an element start tag |
| endElement | Method called upon parsing an element end tag |
| characters | Method called when text characters or white-space characters are encountered |
| processingInstruction | Method called upon parsing a processing instruction |

# The SAX and Java

In December 1997, Peter Murray-Rust originally implemented in Java the first version of what later became the SAX. Murray-Rust is the author of the free Java-based XML browser JUMBO. Murray-Rust began by trying to support three different XML parsers with their own proprietary APIs in the JUMBO browser. After determining that this was an unnecessary complication, he insisted the originally implemented parser writers should support a common Java event-based API, which he code-named YAXPAPI (for Yet Another XML Parser API). The members of the XML-DEV mailing list included Tim Bray, the author of the Lark XML parser and one of the editors of the XML specification; David Megginson, the author of Microstar's Ælfred XML parser; Jon Bosak, the founder of XML; and many others who shared in the development of the Simple API for XML.

A large segment of the SAX design community comprised accomplished Java programmers, so it followed naturally that Java would be used to implement the event-based methods being proposed. More recently, SAX has been implemented in PERL, Python, Visual Basic, and other languages. In the next section, you will see how to instantiate a SAX parser and call methods on XML processing events using Java. You will create and compile a simple Java application to identify some of the events encountered during XML document parsing. Please note that this book is neither intended to teach you the Java programming language nor basic object-oriented programming techniques. If you would like a refresher on Java, please consider *Sams Teach Yourself Java in 21 Days, Second Edition (0-672-31958-6)*. You can also get a free implementation of Java and substantial Java documentation from the Sun Microsystems Web site at http://java.sun.com/j2se/1.3.

Java provides procedural, object-based (characterized by classes, encapsulation, and objects), and object-oriented (supporting inheritance and polymorphism) paradigms. In

**13**

this section, you will be able to write a Java program that deals with SAX events as objects and includes the reusable software components from standard SAX class libraries that you import into your program.

## Required Java Application Software

You will need to download and install several software packages to complete today's exercises. If you do not already have the Java 2 standard edition loaded on your computer, you can obtain a free copy from Sun Microsystems at `http://java.sun.com/j2se`. Install the distribution according to the instructions provided on the Web site.

You will also need to download and extract files from the archive for your SAX API. Many good options are available, but the examples today will use the JAXP parser from Sun Microsystems. You can obtain a free copy at `http://java.sun.com/xml/download.html`. Unpack or extract this distribution on your hard drive and keep track of the subdirectory into which it is expanded. You will need to set a `classpath` environment variable or use a `classpath` compiler option to point to this subdirectory at the time that you compile your Java program. The documentation distributed at `sun.com` regarding the JAXP distribution and its setup is comprehensive.

# A Java Application to List SAX Events

Writing Java applications is somewhat like creating structures from blocks of wood. The blocks might have different shapes and colors that contribute to the whole structure. You can create desired and predictable results by combining the qualities of the individual components. Java is somewhat like this because you can use the methods and interfaces from each of your imported or included classes to create a structure of objects that behave in predictable ways. For the application you write during this exercise, you will import classes and interfaces from several packages associated with the distributions noted earlier. You will create method calls for SAX parser methods like those listed in Table 13.2. Figure 13.1 depicts the methods that characterize the application you will write.

You can use a text editor and build this program as you read through the remainder of this section and learn about each section of the application. At the end of the section, a complete listing of the `EList` class will be detailed, along with comments to help identify each method called.

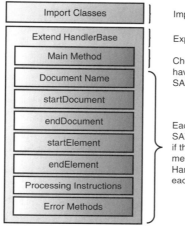

**FIGURE 13.1**

*The structure of the Java EList application.*

| | |
|---|---|
| Import Classes | Import Classes and Interfaces |
| Extend HandlerBase | Export and name the program |
| Main Method | Check that the proper arguments have been loaded and instantiate SAX parsers as needed |
| Document Name | |
| startDocument | |
| endDocument | Each event identified by the SAX processor will be reported if there is a corresponding method from the document's HandlerBase to call at the time each is encountered. |
| startElement | |
| endElement | |
| Processing Instructions | |
| Error Methods | |

## Import Classes

You will need to import the Java Input/Output (I/O) package to enable your program to manage data via input and output streams. You will do this by importing the `java.io` package from the Sun Microsystems Java 2 Standard edition. The classes of this package can be used with file processing and networking and provide a standard set of interfaces to other I/O types. The syntax of the import keyword is as follows:

```
import [package];
```

Like all reserved keywords in Java, `import` must be in lowercase letters. In addition to the `java.io` package, you will need the package that contains the classes and programmatic interfaces for SAX parsers, `org.xml.sax`. This includes the `HandlerBase` class that you will extend when you create your application.

To instantiate the classes for a SAX parser, you must also import the JAXP package `javax.xml.parsers`. This package actually includes classes for both SAX and DOM parsers, which can be instantiated as required for your application.

Additionally, you will require `javax.xml.parsers.SAXParserFactory` for instantiation of a SAX-based parser capable of validating an instance against a DTD; `javax.xml.parsers.ParserConfigurationException` to throw an error in the event that a parser cannot be properly instantiated; and `javax.xml.parsers.SAXParser` for instantiation of a SAX parser object. The complete import block in your application will look like this:

```
import java.io.*;
import org.xml.sax.*;
```

13

```
import javax.xml.parsers.SAXParserFactory;
import javax.xml.parsers.ParserConfigurationException;
import javax.xml.parsers.SAXParser;
```

## Extend the `HandlerBase` Class

The Java program you write will extend the `HandlerBase` class from the `org.xml.sax` package of the SAX 1 implementation. In the SAX 2 implementation, this is replaced by a `DefaultHandler`, rather than a `HandlerBase`. Accessing the `DefaultHandler` requires that you import `org.xml.sax.helpers.DefaultHandler`; otherwise, the two implementations are the same. For the purpose of this exercise, we will import the classes and make extensions on the original `HandlerBase` class. In this exercise, you will compile a class and name it `EList` (Event List) to produce a list of SAX events on the output stream. What you call your own class is not at all important, but you must be consistent throughout the Java program and ensure that you save the code with the class name, followed by a `.java` extension to ensure that the compilation succeeds. By convention, all class names—that is, Java class identifiers—begin with an uppercase alphabetic character and have an uppercase letter at the beginning of each unique word in the class name (for example, `MyOwnPersonalClassName`). The user-defined primary class extension statement will look like this:

```
public class EList extends HandlerBase
{
    [... all methods of the defined class]
}
```

All the methods of the user-defined class will be contained within the curly braces (`{...}`) following the declaration of the `EList` class. The `Handlerbase` class implements four interfaces from the `org.xml.sax` package. If you use the `DefaultHandler` implemented by SAX2, several different interfaces are imported. Table 13.3 summarizes these interfaces.

**TABLE 13.3**   Some of the Interfaces Implemented by the `HandlerBase`  Class of the `org.xml.sax` Package

| Interface | Description |
| --- | --- |
| DocumentHandler | Handles parsed events as they are encountered during the processing of a document |
| DTDHandler | Handles entities and unparsed entities defined by an associated Document Type Definition |
| EntityReference | Handles any external entities |
| ErrorHandler | Handles any errors encountered during parsing |

## Main Method

The first method to be executed in a Java application is the `main` method, a required method in Java. The `main` method of your application will perform several required functions. It will first establish the requirement that the user provide a filename for an XML document instance and will halt the application and produce an error report on the user's screen if this is not provided. Next, you will create a method that requires one argument in the form of a string to be provided on the command line when the program is invoked. The code for this portion of the `main` method looks like this:

```
1:    public static void main( String fname[] )
2:    {
3:      if ( fname.length != 1 ) {
4:          System.err.println( "Expected Syntax: java EList [filename]\n" );
5:          System.exit( 1 );
6:      }
```

**ANALYSIS**  Line 1 declares the `main` method, requiring a string argument, called `fname`. The keyword `static` declares that the `main` method is a class method. The `void` keyword indicates that this method will perform tasks, but not return information to the class after the task has been completed. All of the `main` method requirements adhere to the syntax for Java. Lines 3–4 test to ensure that exactly one argument is included on the command line when the `EList` class is invoked. If the syntax is not adhered to, the program will write a report to the screen (for example, `"Expected Syntax: java EList [filename]\n"`) and then halt processing and exit Java.

To start parsing an XML instance document, you will want to instantiate a `SAXParseFactory` object from the `javax.xml.parsers` package to obtain a SAX-based parser. You will pass the XML document instance obtained at the URL provided by the user on invocation, along with an instance of your `EList` class to a SAX parser object by calling a `newSAXParser` method. The parser will, in turn, read the XML document a character at a time and call the SAX methods you chose to encode in your `EList` class. You will see how to encode the individual parser methods shortly. Any errors or exceptions that the parser throws must be caught by your application and reported to the user. Any error in your `EList` class will cause the processor to halt and provide an immediate report, via the screen output stream, to the user.

**13**

The code that completes the `main` method looks like the snippet shown here:

```
1:        SAXParserFactory saxFactory = SAXParserFactory.newInstance();
2:
3:        saxFactory.setValidating( false );
4:
5:        try {
6:            SAXParser saxParser = saxFactory.newSAXParser();
```

```
 7:            saxParser.parse( new File( fname[ 0 ] ), new EList() );
 8:        }
 9:        catch ( SAXParseException spe ) {
10:            System.err.println( "Parse Error: " + spe.getMessage() );
11:        }
12:        catch ( SAXException se ) {
13:            se.printStackTrace();
14:        }
15:        catch ( ParserConfigurationException pce ) {
16:            pce.printStackTrace();
17:        }
18:        catch ( IOException ioe ) {
19:            ioe.printStackTrace();
20:        }
21:
22:        System.exit( 0 );
23:    }
```

**ANALYSIS**  Line 1 instantiates a SAXParserFactory object from the javax.xml.parsers package imported earlier. This provides the program with a SAX parser for event-based processing. Line 3 is a special instruction used to configure the SAXParserFactory object as a non-validating parser. You can change this value to true if you want to have the SAX parser validate your XML document instance against a properly associated Document Type Definition (DTD). Lines 6 and 7 instantiate a SAX parser object by calling the newSAXParser method and then passing the document named by the user along with an instance of the EList class to the parser. Lines 9–19 catch any parse exception errors (such as fatal XML syntax errors), SAX exception errors (such as a subclass of exceptions thrown when parsing errors occur), parser configuration errors (such as errors due to a failure to instantiate the parser objects), or I/O exception errors (such as problems encountered if an XML document instance is unavailable at the URL indicated or if the classpath environment is not properly defined) that are thrown by the SAX parser. Line 22 causes the application to halt and exit to the operating system if any of the errors noted are caught.

## SAX Methods

The first method in the next section of your application will override the HandlerBase method setDocumentLocator to report the URL of the document being processed by the SAX parser. This is the document that the user includes as an argument on the command line when you application is invoked. Create a reference for the filename and URL, called fname, and pass it to the getSystemId method. You will use the standard output object, System.output.println, to instruct the processor to print the string Name of Document: concatenated to the URL string contained by fname.getSystemId(). To do this, you will create the following method:

```
public void setDocumentLocator( Locator fname )
{
   System.out.println( "Name of Document: " + fname.getSystemId() );
}
```

Next, you will instruct the SAX parser to report when it has encountered the start of the document, or the document root node. You will override the `HandlerBase` method `startDocument`. This event happens only once in a single document instance. You will invoke the standard output object to report the fact that the SAX parser has encountered a document root node. The report will be in the form of a string—SAX Event - Start of Document presented to the user's screen. In each of the SAX methods you create, you will include `throws SAXException` to instruct the parser to throw any errors encountered. You will recall that the `main` method includes instructions to catch any errors, report them to the user, and halt the processing of the document. The complete method looks like this:

```
public void startDocument()
      throws SAXException
{
   System.out.println( "SAX Event - Start of Document" );
}
```

The end of the XML document is considered an event by a SAX parser, and a method can be included to report on the occurrence of this event. This is similar to the document start event already encoded, except that the `endDocument` method of the `HandlerBase` class is overridden in this case. This method looks like this:

```
public void endDocument()
      throws SAXException
{
   System.out.println( "SAX Event - End of Document" );
}
```

Next, you will override the `Handlerbase` method `startElement` to mark when the parser encounters an element start tag in the XML instance. The `startElement` method takes two arguments, each with a user-defined reference. The first argument holds the name of the element, and the second contains a list of the attributes on that element. Because you might encounter zero or more attributes on any element, you will need to provide a mechanism to report either none or any number of attributes on any element. Next, you will write a short loop to step through every attribute and send each, along with its corresponding value, to the screen via the standard output object.

In the case of multiple attributes on an element, you will iterate until each has been reported and no more remain. Additionally, you will format the output of the attribute name/value pairs with equal signs and double quotes that will require you to use escape

13

sequences for proper rendering. For instance, to print a double quote, you will use the escape sequence (\"). The backslash character (\) in a Java string is an escape character that causes the character immediately following the slash to be ignored by the Java interpreter and passed as part of the stream being created to represent the string. In Java, this is called a C-style escape sequence. The complete startElement method looks like this:

```
1:    public void startElement( String el_name, AttributeList attr )
2:      throws SAXException
3:    {
4:      System.out.println( "SAX Event - Element Start: " + el_name );
5:      if ( attr != null )
6:          for ( int i = 0; i < attr.getLength(); i++ )
7:              System.out.println( "SAX Event - Attribute: "
8:              + attr.getName( i )
9:              + "=\"" + attr.getValue( i )
10:             + "\"" );
11:   }
```

**ANALYSIS**   Line 1 overrides the Handlerbase method startElement when the SAX parser encounters an element. The name of the element, the first argument of this method, is referenced by el_name, and the list of attributes on the element is referenced by attr. Line 2 causes an exception to be thrown, which will be caught elsewhere, if a parsing error occurs. Lines 3 and 11 indicate the beginning and end of the method, respectively, by curly braces. The standard output device is invoked (line 4) to report the occurrence of a SAX event when this method is called. Lines 5–10 determine whether the element has attributes. If no attributes exist, then attr will possess a null value and the for loop will not be executed. Upon execution, each attribute name (getname) and its corresponding value (getValue) will be reported, with each couplet on a separate line. The AttributeList method getLength will provide you with a count of the attributes on any element, so that you can create a loop to iterate through all possible attributes, one at a time.

The end tag of an element is also considered an event by a SAX parser, so you will write a short method to report end tags encountered. This is identical to the start of document or end of document methods, except that you will override the endElement method of the HandlerBase class with a string containing the name of the element end tag encountered.

```
public void endElement( String el_name )
throws SAXException
{
    System.out.println("SAX Event - Element End: " + el_name );
}
```

The parsing of character data in an XML instance document is also considered an event by SAX. The characters method has variables for buffers, character offset value, and character string length. You will declare buf, offset, and len as char[], int, and int data types, respectively. The fully qualified string will be placed in a variable called stuff and reported via System.out.println as usual. This method will look like this:

```
public void characters( char buf [], int offset, int len )
    throws SAXException
{
  if ( len > 0 ) {
    String stuff = new String( buf, offset, len );

    System.out.println( "SAX Event - Characters: " + stuff );
  }
}
```

SAX can also report processing instructions as events. The processingInstruction method takes two arguments corresponding to the system name and value passed to an application by a processing instruction. For instance, a processing instruction in an XML instance document that looks like this:

```
<?message_reader incoming transactions?>
```

comprises a system name (message_reader) and a value (incoming transactions). The complete method is

```
public void processingInstruction( String part1,String part2 )
    throws SAXException
{
    System.out.println( "SAX Event - Processing Instruction: "
        + part1 + " " + part2 );
}
```

This is the last method you will include in your simple Java program. You will need to close the main method by adding a closing curly brace (}) to the end of the listing. The complete program is shown in Listing 13.2. Save your program as EList.

**LISTING 13.2**   The Complete EList Class Java Program—EList.java

```
 1: // Listing 13.2 - EList.java
 2:
 3: /*
 4:   compile with javac, ensure the CLASSPATH includes the appropriate
 5:   JAXP packages
 6: */
 7:
 8: import java.io.*;
 9: import org.xml.sax.*;
10: import javax.xml.parsers.SAXParserFactory;
11: import javax.xml.parsers.ParserConfigurationException;
```

13

**LISTING 13.2**  continued

```
12: import javax.xml.parsers.SAXParser;
13:
14: public class EList extends HandlerBase
15: {
16:     public static void main( String fname[] )
17:     {
18:         if ( fname.length != 1 ) {
19:           System.err.println( "Expected Syntax: java EList [filename]\n" );
20:           System.exit( 1 );
21:         }
22:
23:         SAXParserFactory saxFactory = SAXParserFactory.newInstance();
24:
25:         /*If you wish to have SAX validate an XML document against
26:            a DTD, you may change this value to true*/
27:           saxFactory.setValidating( false );
28:
29:         try {
30:           SAXParser saxParser = saxFactory.newSAXParser();
31:           saxParser.parse( new File( fname[ 0 ] ), new EList() );
32:         }
33:         catch ( SAXParseException spe ) {
34:             System.err.println( "Parse Error: " + spe.getMessage() );
35:         }
36:         catch ( SAXException se ) {
37:             se.printStackTrace();
38:         }
39:         catch ( ParserConfigurationException pce ) {
40:             pce.printStackTrace();
41:         }
42:         catch ( IOException ioe ) {
43:             ioe.printStackTrace();
44:         }
45:
46:         System.exit( 0 );
47:     }
48:
49:
50:     // print the document URL path and name
51:     public void setDocumentLocator( Locator fname )
52:     {
53:         System.out.println( "Name of Document: " + fname.getSystemId() );
54:     }
55:
56:     // SAX Event - Start of Document
57:     public void startDocument()
58:     throws SAXException
59:     {
60:         System.out.println( "SAX Event - Start of Document" );
61:     }
```

LISTING 13.2 continued

```
 62:
 63:    // SAX Event - End of Document
 64:    public void endDocument()
 65:    throws SAXException
 66:    {
 67:       System.out.println( "SAX Event - End of Document" );
 68:    }
 69:
 70:    // SAX Events for Elements and Attributes
 71:    public void startElement( String el_name, AttributeList attr )
 72:    throws SAXException
 73:    {
 74:       System.out.println( "SAX Event - Element Start: " + el_name );
 75:       if ( attr != null )
 76:          for ( int i = 0; i < attr.getLength(); i++ )
 77:             System.out.println( "SAX Event - Attribute: "
 78:             + attr.getName( i )
 79:             + "=\"" + attr.getValue( i )
 80:             + "\"" );
 81:
 82:    }
 83:
 84:    // SAX Event - Element End
 85:    public void endElement( String el_name )
 86:    throws SAXException
 87:    {
 88:       System.out.println("SAX Event - Element End: " + el_name );
 89:    }
 90:
 91:    // SAX Event - Character Data and Whitespace characters
 92:    public void characters( char buf [], int offset, int len )
 93:    throws SAXException
 94:    {
 95:       if ( len > 0 ) {
 96:          String stuff = new String( buf, offset, len );
 97:
 98:          System.out.println( "SAX Event - Characters: " + stuff );
 99:       }
100:    }
101:
102:    // SAX Event - Processing Instructions
103:    public void processingInstruction( String part1,String part2 )
104:    throws SAXException
105:    {
106:       System.out.println( "SAX Event - Processing Instruction: "
107:                      + part1 + " " + part2 );
108:    }
109: }
```

13

# Compiling and Executing EList

To compile EList, you will need to set the CLASSPATH environment variable or add the CLASSPATH option to the compiler command line instruction to ensure that you include the required JAXP packages. The JAXP documentation has complete instructions to accomplish this. In brief, you can set the in the CLASSPATH environment variable in Windows with the command line

```
Set CLASSPATH=[dir]\jaxp.jar;[dir]\parser.jar;
[dir]\crimson.jar;[dir]\xalan.jar;.
```

In this case, you replace [dir] with the path that points to the JAXP distribution that you installed earlier today. After this environment variable is set, you will compile the Java program with the command line instruction:

```
javac EList.java
```

For this to work requires that the classpath has been established correctly, the Java 2 Standard Edition (Java 2SE) distribution has been properly installed, and the bin subdirectory of that distribution is in the path for the executable files of your operating system. Complete instructions on setting path and class path environment variables are included with the documentation provided with the Java 2SE and JAXP distributions.

You could also include the -classpath option on the command line compile instruction. To do this in Windows, enter

```
javac -classpath [dir]\jaxp.jar;[dir]\parser.jar;
[dir]\crimson.jar;[dir]\xalan.jar;. EList.java
```

Because Java runs on multiple platforms, you can run this code on another operating system, such as UNIX. On UNIX systems, the compile instruction would look like this:

```
javac -classpath ${XML_HOME}/jaxp.jar:${XML_HOME}/parser.jar:
${XML_HOME}/crimson.jar:${XML_HOME}/xalan.jar:. EList.java
```

In this case, {XML_HOME} is the UNIX directory that contains the JAXP distribution files required by the application.

After the application is compiled, you can execute it by issuing the command line:

```
Java EList [file_name.xml]
```

When you have successfully compiled your application, execute it against the message01.xml file provided as Listing 13.1. The output should look something like this:

```
Name of Document: file:C:/SAX/message01.xml
SAX Event - Start of Document
SAX Event - Element Start: note
SAX Event - Characters:
```

```
SAX Event - Characters:
SAX Event - Element Start: message
SAX Event - Attribute: from="Kathy Shepherd"
SAX Event - Characters:

SAX Event - Characters:          Remember to buy milk on the way home from work
SAX Event - Characters:

SAX Event - Characters:
SAX Event - Element End: message
SAX Event - Characters:

SAX Event - Element End: note
SAX Event - End of Document
```

# SAX and Whitespace

In the previous exercise, you parsed an XML document that appeared to be quite simple. The XML document had two elements—one with an attribute, some character data, a comment, and an XML declaration. The XML document instance looked like this:

```
<?xml version = "1.0"?>
<!-- listing 13.1 - message01.xml -->
<note>
    <message from="Kathy Shepherd">
        Remember to buy milk on the way home from work
    </message>
</note>
```

Among other events, you chose to have a SAX parser report on any events, attributes, and character data. However, the output seemed to include more character reports than there were character data strings in the document instance. The document includes only one obvious character data string (Remember to buy milk on the way home from work). You might be wondering why there are multiple character event reports in the output generated by your EList Java application. This is because SAX counts the whitespace characters that it encounters as important, rather than normalizing them. Without a DTD, the parser is unable to determine whether an element, for instance, has mixed content. Because our document is not constrained by a DTD declaring and defining the content models for elements in the instance, all whitespace characters are considered by SAX to be significant; consequently, each whitespace character encountered fires an event that the parser has correctly reported back to the user.

Test this by removing the whitespace between elements in message01.xml and parse the resulting file again with your EList application. Save the modified XML document as message02.xml, which will look something like the run-on document instance shown as Listing 13.3.

**13**

**LISTING 13.3**  All Whitespace Characters Removed from a Simple XML Document—
`message02.xml`

```
<?xml version = "1.0"?><!-- listing 13.3 - message02.xml --><note><message from
="Kathy Shepherd">Remember to buy milk on the way home from work</message></not
e>
```

When you parse the document after removal of the whitespace characters, the result from
EList is quite a bit shorter:

```
Name of Document: file:C:/SAX/message02.xml
SAX Event - Start of Document
SAX Event - Element Start: note
SAX Event - Element Start: message
SAX Event - Attribute: from="Kathy Shepherd"
SAX Event - Characters: Remember to buy milk on the way home from work
SAX Event - Element End: message
SAX Event - Element End: note
SAX Event - End of Document
```

Note that the character events that formerly contained whitespace characters are no
longer present in the parser report.

# Parse Errors Reported by a SAX Processor

In the next exercise, you will purposely make a syntax error in the `message01.xml` document. In particular, change the case of one of the characters in the end tag of the note
element. The result is more interesting if you indeed make a modification near the end of
the document instance. You will recall that a SAX parser is an event-based processor.
Therefore, you would expect that the document would process correctly and report
expected results up until an error event is thrown and caught in your `main` method. If you
make a syntax error in the end tag of the last element, then everything up until that element should still process correctly, but the end tag will fire an error and no end of document event should be processed. Listing 13.4 shows the message document with an error
on the note end tag. Make a similar error and save your document as `message03.xml`.

**LISTING 13.4**  A Poorly Formed XML Instance for Use by Your SAX Processor—
`message03.xml`

```
1: <?xml version = "1.0"?>
2: <!-- listing 13.4 - message03.xml -->
3: <note>
4:    <message from="Kathy Shepherd">
5:       Remember to buy milk on the way home from work
6:    </message>
7: </Note>
```

When you process this document with EList, you should expect a result that looks like this:

```
Name of Document: file:C:/SAX/message03.xml
SAX Event - Start of Document
SAX Event - Element Start: note
SAX Event - Characters:

SAX Event - Characters:
SAX Event - Element Start: message
SAX Event - Attribute: from="Kathy Shepherd"
SAX Event - Characters:

SAX Event - Characters:      Remember to buy milk on the way home from work
SAX Event - Characters:

SAX Event - Characters:
SAX Event - Element End: message
SAX Event - Characters:

Parse Error: Expected "</note>" to terminate element starting on line 3.
```

Because of the nature of an event-based processor, the document was processed successfully right up until the error was encountered; then, in accordance with your programming instructions, the program halted and an error report was generated. In this case, the end tag </note> was expected; instead the document has an end tag </Note> (line 7 on listing 13.4).

# Parsing for Validation with SAX

The JAXP parser can be used to validate an XML instance against a schema. By setting the setValidating property on the saxFactory object to true, you can instruct JAXP to validate.

```
saxFactory.setValidating( true );
```

By instructing JAXP to validate, you can catch new errors that are specific to validation problems. For instance, you can catch warnings and minor validation problems that are issued by the parser by calling methods for minor and warn on the SAXParseException object. The code to create minor and warn methods looks like this:

```
public void error( SAXParseException minor )
throws SAXParseException
{
   throw minor;
}
```

13

```
public void warning( SAXParseException warn )
throws SAXParseException
{
    System.err.println( "Warning: " + warn.getMessage() );
}
```

More information about error types reported by SAX parsers is available at
`http://www.java.sun.com/xml/download.html`. The exercise at the end of the chapter
today will use error methods so that you can parse an XML document using its associated schema to test for validation.

# Summary

Today you explored the Simple API for XML (SAX), an XML API that allows developers to take advantage of event-driven XML parsing. Unlike the DOM specification, SAX
doesn't require the entire XML document instance to be loaded into memory. SAX notifies you when certain events happen as it parses your document. If your document is
large, using SAX will save significant amounts of memory when compared to using
DOM. This is especially true if you need only a few elements in a large document.

# Q&A

**Q** How does a programmer choose between a SAX and DOM API?

**A** DOM is excellent for a large variety of processing needs. You might prefer DOM
when you require random access to your document to implement complex searches. In cases where you need to resolve complex XPath filtering and may choose to
modify and save XML documents, the DOM offers superior capability.

SAX offers better performance when your XML documents are large. In cases
where you require a processor to abort when an error occurs, but otherwise process
normally, the SAX can be implemented under program control. If you need to
retrieve small amounts of information from large instances and cannot afford the
overhead required to instantiate the DOM, SAX is the answer.

**Q** How does a programmer use the SAX?

**A** You create an instance of an XML parser by instantiating a SAX object. You will
need to write a program to act as a SAX reader capable of trapping and reporting
on events encountered during processing.

# Exercise

The exercise is provided so that you can test your knowledge of what you learned today. The answer is in Appendix A.

Change your SAX-based `EList` application to validate XML instances against declared DTDs. Save the modified application as `EList2.java` and recompile it. Use the version of your `CD.xml` file with its associated `CD.dtd` file that you created on Day 4.

After everything is working as it should, purposely make a validation error, rather than an XML syntax error, by adding a new empty element that is not declared in the DTD. View the results as reported by SAX.

13

# WEEK 2

# DAY 14

# Adding Style to Content with Cascading Stylesheets (CSS)

The separation of style and content is a fundamental concept in XML. Style instructions can be associated with XML documents in several ways to permit presentation in a browser. One way is to link cascading stylesheets (CSS) to your XML documents, a method originally designed to enhance the presentation of HTML. Today, you will learn

- The components of a CSS rule set and the basic steps required to create a linked CSS document

- Several of the most useful CSS properties and how to assign values for those properties

- Some of the limitations of the CSS approach

# Style and Content

One of the principal design objectives of XML is the separation of content from any means of document display. You learned on Days 1 and 2 that this separation is one of the characteristic differences between XML and HTML. HTML mixes content and presentation in the same markup. For instance, the <H1> tag in HTML not only identifies data that is considered a heading, but also instructs the browser to render the data in a large font size. Likewise, the <I> tag in HTML tells the browser that the data it demarks is meant to be rendered in italic. XML, as you know, is markup that describes the data content, with no regard to how it might be rendered in a browser, on the printed page, or used by any other user agent.

 **Note**

A user agent is software that parses the characters of a document into data characters and markup according to predefined rules for each. Different user agents are implemented in different devices, such as computers, Web-enabled cell phones, Web browsers, and so on.

Because you can create your own element types in XML, a user agent has no built-in instruction set to determine how to display the data in those elements. If you choose to display your XML data in a browser, you will need to provide display instructions for the browser to use in rendering the data. You can do this in two ways: using cascading stylesheets (CSS) and the XML Stylesheet Language (XSL). Today, you will explore CSS, and tomorrow, you will be able to use and compare the XSLT approach.

## CSS and HTML

HTML was not originally intended to be a language for "rendering" on browsers, but rather for marking up data in a way that it could be shared across networks and disparate platforms. However, from its earliest revisions, special tags were included that had typographic meaning, such as italic <I>, bold <B>, line breaks <BR>, and so on. Even though these special purpose tags were included, HTML was never really able to completely control display of data. Prior to the development of CSS, Web developers had to use unorthodox means to accomplish some style effects. For instance, to indent at the beginning of a paragraph on a Web page, many developers inserted an inline "invisible gif image," which was an image file that had a desired horizontal length, but was zero pixels in height. The image was invisible to those who browsed the page, but it forced the text to move to the right to accommodate the horizontal size of the image.

**Tip**

If you are interested in reading about other such techniques, visit the "Stupid HTML Indent Tricks" Web site at `http://www.jbarchuk.com/indent/`.

Cascading stylesheets were created as a method to allow for robust formatting of HTML pages without constantly inserting information into the tags. Stylesheets can be written with a basic text editor such as Notepad, and saved with the `.css` file extension. Several versions of CSS are available. The W3C has defined a set of style conventions known as Cascading Stylesheets Level 1 (CSS1). CSS2, also defined by the W3C, is a newer version with many more features that is essentially a superset of CSS1. CSS3 is being developed, but is only minimally supported by user agents.

One of the fundamental features of CSS is that stylesheets cascade. Styles can be encoded within a document, within an element, or in an external document. In fact, for any given document instance, styles might exist in all three places. This flexibility of style location is provided for reasons of modularity and design flexibility. There are rules for how the various styles interact and, if in conflict, they will override another. Complete rules for overrides can be found at `http://www.w3.org/TR/REC-CSS1`. For instance, an external `.css` file (the extension given a CSS document) might style the content of an element in italic. Within the document, a global style encompassing this element might set the element to be bold. The bold setting would override the external italic setting in this cascade. In short, an inline style at the element level overrides any style set globally within a document, which in turn overrides any styles set in an external CSS file. Today, you will create external CSS documents to style XML instances.

If you have written HTML for the Web, you might already be familiar with CSS. CSS for XML is really no different; it provides a means of specifying style for elements to define how a user agent will handle those elements. Today, you will create and link cascading stylesheets to XML documents as one method of instructing a browser how to render each of the elements in your XML document.

## Web Browser Support for CSS

The use of a stylesheet to differentially render an element is strictly a client-side implementation. Not surprisingly, CSS has differential support by various browsers on different platforms. Table 14.1 summarizes support for CSS1 by specific browser implementations. Support for CSS2 and CSS3 is much more variable and is beyond the scope of today's practice. You can learn more about support for CSS2 and CSS3 at `http://www.w3.org/Style/CSS/`.

**14**

**TABLE 14.1** Browser Support for CSS1

| Platform | Browser | Versions |
|----------|---------|----------|
| Linux | Amaya | 2.0, 2.1, 2.2, 2.3, 2.4, 3.0, 4.0, 4.1, 4.2, 4.3.2 |
| Linux | Netscape Navigator | 4.7, Mozilla, 6 |
| Linux | Opera | 4a, 5.0 |
| Macintosh | ICab Internet Browser | 2.5 (partial) |
| Macintosh | Microsoft Internet Explorer | 3.0, 4.0, 5.0 |
| Macintosh | Netscape Navigator | 3.0 (partial), 4.06 (partial), 4.5, 4.74, 6 |
| Unix | Amaya | 2.0, 2.1, 2.2, 2.3, 2.4, 3.0, 4.0, 4.1, 4.2, 4.3.2 |
| Unix | Arena | 3 |
| Unix | Microsoft Internet Explorer | 4.01, 5.0 |
| Unix | Netscape Navigator | 4.6 |
| Windows | Amaya | 2.0, 2.1, 2.2, 2.3, 2.4, 3.0, 4.0, 4.1, 4.2, 4.3.2 |
| Windows | Microsoft Internet Explorer | 3.0, 4.0, 5.0, 5.5 |
| Windows | Netscape Navigator | 4.5, 4.7, 6 |
| Windows | Opera | 3.60, 4.02 |

Because the support for CSS is fairly widespread, albeit differential, some browsers can directly open an XML document with an attached stylesheet. The direct open method does not require an HTML page to render the data. However, this form of processing comes at a price. Because this approach is accompanied by uneven browser support, you will not be able to guarantee that your user will view the data in the fashion you intend with absolute certainty. You will learn more reliable approaches to presenting XML data on Day 16 when you use Extensible Stylesheet Language Transformations (XSLT) and on Day 17 when you build XML data islands on HTML pages.

## CSS and XML

With XML, as with HTML, the separation of style and content enhances the flexibility of the ultimate presentation of data and improves ease of maintenance. The XML data source does not need to be altered when it is necessary to change the look of the data presentation; you can simply adjust the linked CSS. Likewise, after you have created a CSS that presents data in the styling you require, you can add new XML documents that link to the same CSS, thereby ensuring presentation consistency on a Web site.

By creating multiple stylesheets, you can develop a system that delivers uniform data to different user agents. Imagine, for example, that you want to deliver the same XML data to all visitors of your Web site regardless of the browser they used to access your information. You can write a script that tests the user's browser to determine an appropriate CSS to produce optimal output results. This technique is known as *browser sniffing* and is used frequently on Web sites. You can determine the client's user agent in many ways, but perhaps the simplest approach is just to interrogate the `navigator.appName` property in JavaScript. A simple script using this approach, which can be placed almost anywhere on an HTML page, might look like this:

```
1: <script language="JavaScript">
2: <!--
3:    document.write("The browser detected is " + navigator.appName);
4: // -->
5: </script>
```

This simple JavaScript returns to the screen (`document.write`), via the default output stream, a concatenated string that includes the encoded name (`navigator.appName`) of the browser that executes the script. This, of course, assumes that the browser supports JavaScript, an increasingly safe assumption on the Web. If the browser does not support JavaScript, then it will ignore line 3 altogether due to the characteristic HTML comments (`<!-- -->`) placed around it (lines 2 and 4).

Many other client-side and server-side methods can programmatically determine the nature of the user agent being employed to access Web data. After the nature is determined, an appropriate stylesheet can be used to ensure that data is displayed as you want it to be.

The concept of multiple stylesheets being used to present similar data in a variety of renderings is important in Web design. Using these approaches, you can do the following:

- Selectively control different browsers.
- Produce data in different ways according to different context-sensitive controls. For example, from one XML source document, you might produce summary data for one presentation, selected subsets of data in tables for another purpose, and so on.
- Control the flow of data from XML documents into various applications.
- Format the data for use by a particular device, such as customizing views of data for use by Web-enabled wireless devices.

Tomorrow, you will create a simple script to permit a user to select an Extensible Stylesheet Language (XSL) stylesheet to view data in multiple views. You will see many similarities between CSS and XSL.

**14**

# Simple Stylesheet Creation

A cascading stylesheet is a text file, typically saved with a `.css` extension. It can be created by using a simple text editor or by using any editor with built-in support for CSS. The file contains rules that instruct the parsing application in a user agent how to display the elemental data. The rules comprise selectors and declarations that define how the data is to be displayed. Selectors typically refer to individual XML elements and the declarations determine how each selected element will be displayed. The declarations contain property/value pairs. Each property is assigned a defined value, such as block, 10pt, or bold. The syntax for a CSS rule is as follows:

```
Selector       { property:value; property:value; ...}
```

Using the familiar `message.xml` scenario developed over the past two weeks, start by creating an XML document instance that you will then style with a linked CSS file. Because CSS only allows you style elements and not attributes, create an XML instance that has several distinct elements, each with content that will be displayed in the rendered result. Create an XML document instance that looks something like the one in Listing 14.1. Save your document as `message01.xml`. You will use it with several stylesheets in the exercises that follow.

**LISTING 14.1**    XML Document to Be Styled—`message01.xml`

```
 1: <?xml version="1.0"?>
 2: <!-- listing 14.1 - message01.xml -->
 3:
 4: <note>
 5:     <msg>
 6:        <id>m1</id>
 7:        <from>Kathy Shepherd</from>
 8:        <message>Remember to buy milk on the way home from work</message>
 9:     </msg>
10:
11:     <msg>
12:        <id>m2</id>
13:        <from>Greg Shepherd</from>
14:        <message> I need some help with my homework</message>
15:     </msg>
16:
17:     <msg>
18:        <id>m3</id>
19:        <from>Kristen Shepherd</from>
20:        <message> Please play Scrabble with me tonight</message>
21:     </msg>
22: </note>
```

This XML document has a note root element that contains msg child elements. Each msg element contains id, from, and message child elements.

## Defining the Styles

Suppose you want to render the XML instance document with the content of each id element in italic, the content of from elements in bold, and the message text in blue. You can create CSS rules for each of the elements with declarations that contain the required property/value pairs to accomplish the desired result.

You need to know the names of the properties and their appropriate values for each of these effects. For this set of rules, you will need the following properties and values:

- font-style:italic: Displays the element's content in italic
- font-weight:bold: Displays the element's content in bold
- color:blue: Displays the element's content in blue

A more complete list of other useful properties will be provided shortly along with appropriate values for each. Recall the syntax presented earlier; the CSS to accomplish the effects described will look like Listing 14.2. Create a CSS file like the one shown and save it as style01.css.

**LISTING 14.2**    A Simple Cascading Stylesheet—style01.css

```
 1: /* listing 14.2 style01.css */
 2:
 3: id
 4:       {font-style:italic}
 5:
 6: from
 7:       {font-weight:bold}
 8:
 9: message
10:       {color:blue}
```

**ANALYSIS**    Line 1 shows the syntax of a comment in a CSS file. Comments in CSS are enclosed by /* and */ characters. The rule set for the id element (lines 3–4) declares that the content of the element will be displayed in italic ({font-style:italic}). The from element (line 6) will be rendered in bold ({font-weight:bold}). The message text will be displayed in blue ({color:blue}).

**14**

## Linking the CSS File

Now that you have a CSS file, you will need to link it to the XML document. You can do this by simply adding a processing instruction (PI) that includes the reserved keyword `xml-stylesheet` and two required attributes. The syntax of the PI is as follows:

```
<?xml-stylesheet type="text/css" href="myfile.css"?>
```

The `type` attribute is required to identify the type of Stylesheet that you are associating with the XML document. For a cascading stylesheet, the appropriate value of this attribute is always `"text/css"`. The `text` portion of the attribute value is known as a MIME or media type. Although the exact nature of a MIME type is beyond the scope of today's study, you should know that all of the stylesheets you create will be text, rather than another encoding type, such as application, multipart, message, and so on. The `css` portion is known as the subtype and, in this case, declares that you are creating a cascading stylesheet, as opposed to an Extensible Stylesheet Language (XSL) stylesheet, rich-text, tab-separated-values, or some other value.

You are also required to include an `href` attribute with a valid URL pointing to the associated CSS file as a value. The value of the `href` attribute can be a fully qualified URL pointing anywhere on the Internet, or it can simply be a partial URL indicating the relative location of a locally available CSS file. The syntax of the linking PI to associate the CSS file you created earlier is

```
<?xml-stylesheet type="text/css" href="style01.css"?>
```

Add this PI to your XML document just before the root element, and save the result as `mesasge02.xml`. Your XML document should now look like the one in Listing 14.3.

LISTING 14.3   XML Document with Processing Instruction Linking a CSS File—
`message02.xml`

```
 1: <?xml version="1.0"?>
 2: <!-- listing 14.3 - message02.xml -->
 3:
 4: <?xml-stylesheet type="text/css" href="style01.css"?>
 5:
 6: <note>
 7:     <msg>
 8:       <id>m1</id>
 9:       <from>Kathy Shepherd</from>
10:       <message>Remember to buy milk on the way home from work</message>
11:     </msg>
12:
13:     <msg>
```

**LISTING 14.3**    continued

```
14:        <id>m2</id>
15:        <from>Greg Shepherd</from>
16:        <message> I need some help with my homework</message>
17:     </msg>
18:
19:     <msg>
20:        <id>m3</id>
21:        <from>Kristen Shepherd</from>
22:        <message> Please play Scrabble with me tonight</message>
23:     </msg>
24: </note>
```

**ANALYSIS**    The processing instruction (`<?xml-stylesheet type="text/css" href="style01.css"?>`) has been added (line 4) to associate a stylesheet of type `text/css` located at `style01.css`, which is in the same subdirectory as the `message02.xml` file on your hard drive.

If you have followed along, you will be able to view `message02.xml` in a browser that supports CSS Level 1 and expect rendered output like that depicted by Figure 14.1.

**FIGURE 14.1**

`message02.xml` *styled according to rules in* `style01.xml` *as viewed in Netscape 6.*

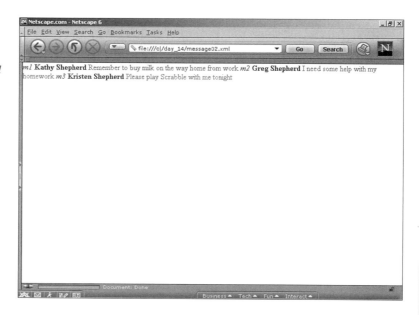

14

# CSS Properties

It is beyond the scope of this book to cover every possible CSS property; however, several of the most popular styles will be discussed and summarized in tables. For a complete list of properties, check out the many references available on the Web. An alphabetical listing can be found at `http://www.blooberry.com/indexdot/css/propindex/all.htm`. A complete list with a browser compatibility cross-reference can be found at `http://www.webreview.com/style/css1/charts/mastergrid.shtml`). The best way to learn to use these styles is to experiment with the properties and values. Try the examples that are described using the `message02.xml` document and modify the `style01.css` document as you read along. At the end of this section, compare your final CSS document and rendered output to the samples provided.

## Text Style Properties

The text style properties affect how text appears on a page. These properties affect alignment of text, line height, spacing between letters, and so on. Suppose, for instance, that you want the text in the `message` element to be left-aligned on the browser window and underlined. If you reuse the CSS file you created earlier, the `color` property will already be set for the `message` element; therefore, your new CSS rule will look like this:

```
message
      {color:blue;
        text-align:left;
        text-decoration:underline}
```

When you express multiple properties on an element using a CSS rule, you separate each declaration with a semi-colon. Table 14.2 summarizes a selection of useful CSS text styles.

**TABLE 14.2**    Selected CSS Text Style Properties

| Property | Purpose | Possible Values |
|---|---|---|
| letter-spacing | Controls the amount of space between each letter in a section of text. | normal (default) number of pixels |
| line-height | Controls the amount of vertical space between lines of text. | normal (default) number of pixels |
| text-align | Controls the alignment for a section of text. | browser decides (default) left right center |

**TABLE 14.2**    continued

| Property | Purpose | Possible Values |
|---|---|---|
| text-decoration | Controls what the text looks like. | none (default)<br>underline<br>overline<br>line-through<br>blink |
| text-indent | Controls the indentation of the first line in a section of text. | 0 (default)<br>number of pixels<br>percentage |
| text-transform | Changes the case of a section of text. | none (default)<br>uppercase<br>lowercase<br>capitalize |
| vertical-alignment | Controls the vertical alignment of a section of text. | baseline (default)<br>sub<br>super<br>top<br>text-top<br>middle<br>bottom<br>text-bottom |
| word-spacing | Controls the amount of space between words. This property does not work at the time of this writing. | normal (default)<br>number of pixels |

## Font Properties

The Font properties offered by CSS provide you with a rich set of controls over the look of characters used to render the content of selected elements. When you created your first CSS file, you used the `font-style` and `font-weight` properties. You set the `id` element content to render in an italic type and the content of the `from` element to be rendered in bold. Try changing your CSS file so that the `id` data is rendered in italic type that is 250% of the normal character height. To do this, you can use the following CSS rule for the `id` element:

```
id
        {font-style:italic;
         font-size:250%}
```

Table 14.3 summarizes some of the font properties available in CSS.

**14**

**TABLE 14.3**   Selected CSS Font Properties

| Property | Purpose | Possible Values |
|---|---|---|
| `font-family` | Controls the type of font shown on the page | browser decides (default) font family name, such as `Arial`) |
| `font-size` | Controls the size of the font | `medium` (default) number of pixels percentage |
| `font-style` | Controls the style of the font | `normal` (default) `italic` `oblique` |
| `font-variant` | Controls the variant of the font | `normal` (default) `small-caps` |
| `font-weight` | Controls the boldness of the font | `normal` (default) `lighter` `bold` `bolder` |

## Color and Background Properties

These properties provide you with controls for font colors, background colors, and the inclusion of images. When you created the CSS file in the first exercise today, you used the color property to render the message element content in blue. If you have not altered it, the from element data will be rendered in bold. Add to the from element a CSS rule to set the background color content to aqua. The new rule for the from element should look like this:

```
from
        {font-weight:bold;
          background-color:aqua}
```

Some of the other background and color properties are summarized in Table 14.4.

**TABLE 14.4**   Selected CSS Color and Background Properties

| Property | Purpose | Possible Values |
|---|---|---|
| `background-attachment` | Controls the scrolling of the background | `scroll` (default) `fixed` |
| `background-color` | Controls the color of the background | `transparent` (default) color name |
| `background-image` | Allows you to set a background image | `none` (default) image URL |

**TABLE 14.4**    continued

| Property | Purpose | Possible Values |
|---|---|---|
| background-position | Controls the position of the background on the page | 0% 0% (default) position in pixels, such as {20,20} percentage; for example, {5%,7%}<br>top<br>bottom<br>left<br>right<br>center |
| background-repeat | Allows different patterns of background repetition | repeat (default)<br>repeat-x<br>repeat-y<br>no-repeat |
| color | Controls the color of the text | browser decides (default)<br>color name |

## Border Properties

It is possible using CSS to have the browser draw visible borders around the content of selected elements. Add a CSS rule that renders a border around the content of the from element comprising double-lines. If you have followed along with the previous examples, the CSS rule for your from element will now look like this:

```
from
        {font-weight:bold;
         background-color:aqua;
         border-style:double}
```

Table 14.5 summarizes selected CSS Border Properties.

**TABLE 14.5**    Selected CSS Border Properties

| Property | Purpose | Possible Values |
|---|---|---|
| border-bottom-width | Controls the width of a border side | medium (default)<br>number of pixels<br>thin<br>thick |
| border-color | Controls the border color of a section | default text color (default) color name |

14

**TABLE 14.5**   continued

| Property | Purpose | Possible Values |
|---|---|---|
| `border-left-width` | Controls the width of a border side | medium (default)<br>number of pixels<br>thin<br>thick |
| `border-right-width` | Controls the width of a border side | medium (default)<br>number of pixels<br>`thin`<br>`thick` |
| `border-style` | Controls the style of a border | none (default)<br>`solid`<br>`double` |
| `border-top-width` | Controls the width of a border side | medium (default)<br>number of pixels<br>`thin`<br>`thick` |
| `border-width` | Controls the width of a border | undefined (default)<br>number of pixels<br>`thin`<br>`medium`<br>`thick` |
| `clear` | Defines whether a section prohibits other sections on its sides | none (default)<br>`left`<br>`right` |
| `float` | Controls the floating of a section | none (default)<br>`left`<br>`right` |
| `height` | Controls the height of a section | auto (default)<br>number of pixels<br>percentage |
| `margin-bottom` | Controls the width of a margin from the specified side | 0 (default)<br>number of pixels<br>percentage |
| `margin-left` | Controls the width of a margin from the specified side | 0 (default)<br>number of pixels<br>percentage |
| `margin-right` | Controls the width of a margin from the specified side | 0 (default)<br>number of pixels<br>percentage |

**TABLE 14.5**   continued

| Property | Purpose | Possible Values |
|---|---|---|
| margin-top | Controls the width of a margin from the specified side | 0 (default)<br>number of pixels<br>percentage |
| padding-bottom | Controls the amount of padding from the specified side | 0 (default)<br>number of pixels<br>percentage |
| padding-left | Controls the amount of padding from the specified side | 0 (default)<br>number of pixels<br>percentage |
| padding-right | Controls the amount of padding from the specified side | 0 (default)<br>number of pixels<br>percentage |
| padding-top | Controls the amount of padding from the specified side | 0 (default)<br>number of pixels<br>percentage |
| width | Controls the width of a section | auto (default)<br>number of pixels<br>percentage |

## Display Properties

These properties provide special instructions to the browser to control various aspects of spacing and display characteristics. The z-index property, for instance, is a special property used to control the order of elements when they are layered on top of one another. Layering can be accomplished by using relative and absolute positioning of elements in CSS. The concept of positioning is beyond the scope of today's exercises, but you can read about controlled positioning of element content using CSS at `http://www.w3.org/TR/REC-CSS2/`.

The `display:block` property value pair is useful in XML styling. The value `block` instructs the browser to insert a line break before and after the element's text. In your CSS file, create a rule that causes each `msg` element to display in a separate block with line feeds before and after each. Your new rule will look like this:

```
Msg
     {display:block}
```

14

**TABLE 14.6**    Selected CSS Display Properties

| Property | Purpose | Possible Values |
|---|---|---|
| white-space | Controls the whitespace formatting of a section | normal (default)<br>pre<br>nowrap |
| display | Controls the display of a section | block (default)<br>inline<br>list-item<br>none |
| visibility | Controls the visibility of an element | inherit (default)<br>visible<br>hidden |
| z-index | Controls the layering of an element | auto (default)<br>number |

## Resulting Style

If you have followed along with the examples described in this section, your CSS document will look like the one in Listing 14.4.

**LISTING 14.4**    The Complete Stylesheet Example—style03.css

```
 1: /* listing 14.4 style03.css */
 2:
 3: id
 4:         {font-style:italic;
 5:          font-size:250%}
 6:
 7: from
 8:         {font-weight:bold;
 9:          background-color:aqua;
10:          border-style:double}
11:
12: message
13:         {color:blue;
14:          text-align:left;
15:          text-decoration:underline}
16:
17: msg
18:         {display:block}
```

When this style sheet is associated with the XML message document created earlier today, the expected rendering will be similar to that depicted by Figure 14.2.

FIGURE 14.2

*Resulting message document with CSS styles rendered by Microsoft Internet Explorer 5.5.*

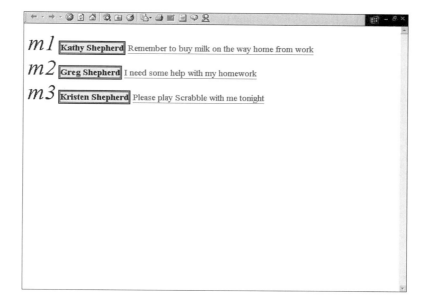

## Multiple Elements as Selectors

If you want to style several elements the same way, you can list all of the elements separated by commas as selector collection. For instance, if you want to color the `id` and `from` element content red, you can create a CSS rule set like this:

```
id, from
        {color:red}
```

# Limitations of CSS

You have seen that CSS can control many rendering properties and produce relatively simple, but effective results in a browser. Nonetheless, the CSS approach has some inherent limitations. For instance, Jon Bosak, a speaker at a W3C-sponsored meeting for Web Developers held on April 11, 1997, noted these limitations:

- CSS cannot grab an item—such as a chapter title—from one place and use it again in another place—such as a page header.

- CSS has no concept of sibling relationships. For example, writing a CSS stylesheet that will render every other paragraph in bold is impossible.

- CSS is not a programming language; it does not support decision structures and cannot be extended by the stylesheet designer.

**14**

- CSS cannot calculate quantities or store variables. This means, at the very least, that CSS cannot store commonly used parameters in one location that is easy to update.
- CSS cannot generate text, such as page numbers.
- CSS uses a simple box-oriented formatting model that works for current Web browsers but will not extend to more advanced applications of the markup, such as multiple column sets.
- CSS is oriented toward Western languages and assumes a horizontal writing direction.

  (source: http://www.webreview.com/1997/11_28/webauthors/11_28_97_5.
  shtml)

Many of these limitations have been addressed in XSL, the topic of Day 15.

# Summary

Today, you have created simple Cascading Style Sheets and used them to style XML for rendering in a browser. This is an approach that is supported by most of the major browsers and represents a client-side rendering option that is relatively flexible and easy to learn and maintain. You learned that CSS style rules are expressed as declarations comprising property/value pairs used to define how a user agent displays element content.

# Q&A

**Q  Does XML validity play a role with regard to the use of CSS?**

**A**  Cascading stylesheets will work to style any XML instance that is at least well formed. If a document instance includes a schema, that document must also be valid. This is not a requirement of CSS, but rather of the XML processor, or browser, that will attempt to validate a document if it includes a schema. Therefore, validity does not really play a role with regard to CSS, but it might be significant nonetheless.

**Q  How does use of a CSS for styling save effort in Web site management?**

**A**  If you have a Web site with multiple documents that all require a similar look, you can be a single stylesheet to style them all identically. When it comes time to change the overall style of the site, you can manipulate the stylesheets without having to touch the original data documents. All new documents that are added can be associated with the master stylesheet to ensure a consistent look across the entire site.

# Exercise

This exercise is provided so that you can test your knowledge of what you learned today. The answer is in Appendix A.

Using the properties that you learned today, style your `cd.xml` document so that it looks like the one depicted in Figure 14.3.

**FIGURE 14.3**

*Styled `cd.xml` document—`cd14.xml`—with an associated style sheet—`cd14.css`*

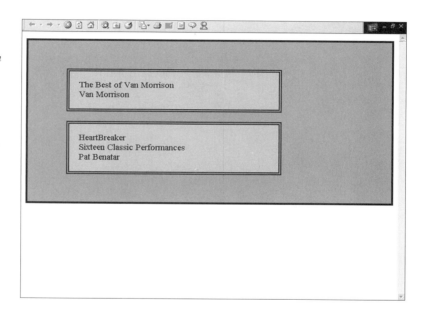

To achieve a result that is similar to that in Figure 14.3, you will need a few details. These are summarized in the following list:

- The Sams logo graphic is at `http://www.samspublishing.com/images/samslogo.gif`, but you do not have to download it.
- All of the text is in 14-point font.
- Sixty pixels of space exist between the outside border and the edge of the inner boxes.
- The color behind the Sams logo is HEX 999966.
- The color of the inner boxes is HEX 99cc99.
- The inner boxes occupy only three-quarters of the horizontal space available to them.

14

# PART III

# Putting XML to Work

# WEEK 3

# DAY 15

# Extensible Stylesheet Language (XSL) and Extensible Stylesheet Language Formatting Objects (XSL-FO)

The XML family of technologies includes the Extensible Stylesheet Language (XSL) that offers a richly featured formatting capability implemented as an XML vocabulary. XSL comprises a transformation programming language and a highly specialized dialect for the description of formatting objects. Today, you will learn

- The relationships among XSL, XSL-FO, and XSLT
- The operational process that works on XSL-FO

- The use of the Apache FOP XSL-FO interpreter
- The process used to create PDF files from XSL-FO documents

# Adding Format to Structure

The rich visual and multimedia tapestry of the Web has helped to promote the require-ments for industrial-strength presentation options for XML documents. The conceptual separation of the components of *style* from *structure* in XML maximizes the options for associating other markup vocabularies to provide semantic definition for elements. You explored one of these options yesterday when you created cascading stylesheets (CSS) to format XML output for use by compliant browsers. The Extensible Stylesheet Language (XSL) offers another means of associating style semantics with XML documents to for-mat output for the screen, for print media, and even for speech synthesis.

As suggested on Day 2, you might think of XML elements as being analogous to *nouns* in a spoken language, and attributes serving to qualify those elements like *adjectives* modifying nouns. By adding semantic definition in this metaphor, you might think of XSL instructions as *verbs* in XML markup. In fact, XSL is capable of more than just the expression of style-based formatting semantics. XSL can completely transform an XML instance document into a different markup structure.

XSL Version 1.0 is a candidate recommendation of the W3C that describes a language for expressing stylesheets. It consists of the following:

- A language for transforming XML documents, or Extensible Stylesheet Language Transformations (XSLT)
- A vocabulary for specifying formatting semantics, or Extensible Stylesheet Language Formatting Objects (XSL-FO)

Combined as a whole, this means an XSL stylesheet specifies the presentation of a class of XML documents. XSL uses a formatting vocabulary to describe how an instance of the class is transformed or changed into a new tree structure. However, the transforma-tion language (XSLT) can be used independently of the formatting semantics (XSL-FO), and this can seem confusing at first.

## XSL Naming Conventions

In the original proposal for XSL submitted to the W3C in August 1997, the authors (Microsoft Corporation, Inso Corporation, ArborText, University of Edinburgh, and James Clark) used the XSL acronym to describe the Extensible *Style* Language. At the time of its second draft recommendation, published in December of the same year, XSL came to mean the Extensible *Stylesheet* Language. The richness of the specification grew quickly and it became apparent that two distinct, but related processes typically characterized the styling of XML documents. The first of these involved a structural transformation, wherein elements were selected, grouped, and reordered. The second step often resulted in a formatting process that produced rendering semantics for specific user agents that presented the documents via screens, paper, speech, or other media. In April 1999, the logical separation of these two processes was formalized when the Extensible Stylesheet Language Transformation (XSLT) functionality was described in a separate document. In other words, XSL was said to comprise XSLT for defining transformations and XSL Formatting Objects (XSL-FO) to provide rendering instructions to a compliant processor.

The acronym XSL-FO is not mentioned in the official W3C recommendation suite, but it has become common in the XML industry at large and will be used today in the interest of clarity. You might want to pay particular attention to the context when reading about XSL on the Internet because the acronyms XSL, XSL-FO, XSL:FO, XSLFO, XSL/FO, and other variants are sometimes used interchangeably to refer to the same thing.

In July 1999, the XML Path Language (XPath), which you explored on Day 9, was separated from XSLT to describe a common syntax and the associated semantics for functionality that is shared between XSL Transformations (XSLT) and the XML Pointer Language (XPointer). You might recall from your reading on Day 11 that XPointer combines URIs with XPath expressions to expose fragments of remote XML documents to further processing.

## Formatting Object Creation and Interpretation

XSL Formatting Objects typically result from a transformation of an XML document that is destined to be used in print media. However, you can author XSL-FO code without transforming a document so that the syntax and semantics can be explored. This is not, however, typical of the process you would undertake in practice. Nonetheless, manual creation of Formatting Objects serves the task of learning FO syntax.

Today, you will explore XSL by manually creating and processing representative Formatting Objects (XSL-FO), and tomorrow you will learn about the Transformation language (XSLT) in more detail. Only a small portion of the more useful Formatting Objects will be described along with references to sources you can interrogate for information about other objects.

The Formatting Objects, therefore, are typically only one aspect of a multi-phase process that serves to modify the structure of an XML source tree. A result tree contains Formatting Objects after the transformation is complete. Therefore, XSLT, for the purpose of generating Formatting Objects, involves the transformation of an XML document tree structure into a Formatting Object result tree. XSLT can be thought of as a programming language that is expressed as an XML vocabulary, which details the transformation of a tree. XSL-FO is nothing more than another XML vocabulary, in which the objects described represent portions of a screen display or page layout and their properties.

## Operational XSL

So far you have read about several distinct processes and vocabularies used to modify an XML document for the purpose of styling the content. The individual components in a typical style transformation involving Formatting Objects include the following:

- An XML source document that appears to the XSLT process as a hierarchical node tree
- An XSL stylesheet, which is also a tree structure that carries the semantics for the transformation into Formatting Objects
- An XSLT processor that parses the source tree and stylesheet tree into memory and produces Formatting Objects
- An XSL-FO result tree that is a product of the transformation
- One or more Formatting Object Interpreters that read FO instances and produce output documents in a syntax, such as text, PDF (Portable Document Format), PCL (Printer Control Language), or MIF (Management Information Format), compliant with the needs of external user agents.

 **Note**

> In the future, it might be possible for user agents, such as Web browsers, cellular phones, and other client-side devices to support the interpretation of Formatting Objects. This would permit rich formatting possibilities for platform-independent content solutions.

Suppose that you have an XML document on your corporate intranet that contains the administrative policies for your organization. Perhaps this is a document that is updated regularly to reflect any changes to employee benefits, accounting practices, and other policies. You might want to periodically process that document to create a policy manual in PDF. The PDF captures formatting information so that documents distributed to different clients can be viewed as intended without requiring the originating application. In addition, most browsers will support the printing of PDF documents obtained from the Web by using a browser extension application, or plug-in. In this way, you can share data that does not rely on the often variable abilities of any one browser to print Web content.

The XSL-FO process works well for this purpose. An XML instance document (`corp.xml`) containing corporate policies and guidelines in appropriate elements might be associated with an XSL stylesheet (`corp.xsl`) that identifies formatting object semantics for the text size of headings, emphasized phrases, page margins, and so on. An XSLT engine would process the two XML documents (`corp.xml` and `corp.xsl`) as combined source trees in a transformation that would produce an FO output tree document (`corp.fo`). An FO interpreter would then process the FO result document, which is an XML instance, to translate the Formatting Objects into expressions saved as PDF output (`corp.pdf`). This would allow you to send electronic copies of the PDF file to employees regardless of the platforms supporting their client applications. In other words, whether an employee uses Unix, Linux, Macintosh, or Windows software, the PDF corporate policy file will appear and print the same. Each user will launch a client application supported by their own operating system that reads PDF files and renders and prints results identically. Figure 15.1 depicts this scenario.

**FIGURE 15.1**

*The XSL operation with transformation-producing formatting objects.*

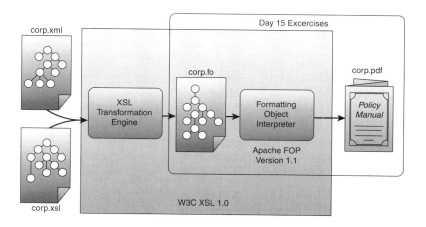

The FO result tree is just an XML document containing elements that belong to the FO namespace, which is identified by the URI `http://www.w3.org/1999/XSL/Format`. Today, rather than perform transformations to generate the FO result tree, you will create FO documents using an editor in the same way that you might when building any XML document. You are effectively skipping the transformation step. Then you'll process those documents with the FOP (Formatting Object Processor) engine, which is a print processor driven by XSL-FO. The section on Figure 15.1 entitled "Day 15 Exercises" shows the portion of the typical XSL operation that you will explore today.

## Apache FOP (Formatting Object Processor)

FOP is an open source Java application distributed freely on the Internet by the Apache Software Foundation (http://xml.apache.org/fop/). You can choose from several such processors, including the following:

- Renderx XEP, a commercial Java XSL-FO processor (http://www.renderx.com). A trial version is available.
- Arbortext Epic E-Content Engine (E3), a commercial product suite that includes FO processing support (http://www.arbortext.com).
- A more complete current list of processors is maintained by the W3C at http://www.w3.org/Style/XSL/.

 **Note**

> The FOP processor that you will use today does not support the entire W3C XSL 1.0 specification. Because, as of this writing, the specification is not yet a complete recommendation, but rather a candidate recommendation of the W3C, it is subject to considerable change in months to come. You can find the status of the recommendation and latest information about XSL at http://www.w3.org/Style/XSL/.

FOP is a Java application that reads a formatting object tree and then turns it into a PDF document. It also has the capability of delivering output in several other formats, including text, MIF, PCL, AWT, and output directly to a printer. FOP will accept FO result trees in the form of XML-FO documents that have been previously created by a text editor or an XSLT engine. FOP will also accept input directly from a DOM or SAX parser without requiring an intermediary operation to save an FO file. Today, you will generate the XML as XML-FO instance documents and process the result trees using FOP.

Download a copy of the release version of FOP from the Apache Project Web site (http://xml.apache.org/fop/) by following the links to download from the distribution directory. If you are a Java developer and prefer working with the latest development code, you can obtain a pre-release version of FOP by following the links to the CVS version. However, if you download the pre-release code, you must compile the FOP processor yourself with the Sun Microsystems Java 2 Standard Edition javac compiler. Regardless of the distribution that best suits your needs, you will have to have certain Java components installed on your computer prior to executing the FOP application. These versions are under constant change, so read the distribution notes that accompany the version you obtain carefully to ensure that you have all of the necessary components installed on your computer.

> **Note**
>
> The version used to process the examples shown today required installation of a Java virtual machine, obtained from the Sun Microsystems Java 2 Standard Edition at `http://www.java.sun.com/j2se`.

The release version of FOP distribution includes several helper libraries, including the following:

- Apache's Xerces-J XML parser that supports SAX and DOM
- Apache Xalan XSLT processor
- SVG (Scalable Vector Graphics) library w3c.jar corresponding to the SVG Candidate Recommendation (November 2, 2000)
- Jimi imaging library from Sun Microsystems

As with all Java applications, you need to concern yourself with the names of directories that hold your distribution and library files, the environment variables that define the path to libraries, and the program execution steps. Carefully follow the installation and program execution documentation provided with FOP for your operating system. In the exercises that follow, you will write FO XML documents and process them to create PDF output. The version of FOP available at the time of this writing, can be invoked by entering the following string on an operating system command line:

```
fop -fo myInputFile.fo -pdf myOutputFile.pdf
```

This string tells the processor that you are providing an FO document (`myInputFile.fo`) as input and expecting it to interpret the Formatting Objects to generate a PDF output file (`myOutputFile.pdf`).

However, the version of FOP you download might use a different command line string. For instance, the CVS version, available at the time of this writing, uses the following syntax:

```
java org.apache.fop.apps.CommandLine myInputFile.fo myOutputFile.pdf
```

> **Tip**
>
> New versions of Apache's FOP are released constantly. Carefully review the documentation accompanying the release you download for differences in command line execution instructions, environment variables, and foundational requirements.

To view your PDF output files, you need to have a PDF viewer installed on your computer. You can get a free copy of Adobe Acrobat Reader Version 5.0 or above from the Adobe Web site at `http://www.adobe.com/products/acrobat/readstep.html`.

If you decide to use the FOP integral viewer, you will not need a copy of Acrobat Reader. To invoke the viewer application, follow the directions in the *Running FOP* section of the documentation. As with other online FOP instructions, the syntax on the command line will depend on the version you download and install. The documentation will offer the current string for the release you obtain.

For instance, the Windows version of FOP uses the following syntax at the command line:

```
fop -fo myInputFile.fo -awt
```

The CVS version uses this:

```
java org.apache.fop.apps.AWTCommandLine myInputFile.fo
```

The result of entering this string is that the FO document (`myInputFile.fo`) is processed and the formatted results are displayed on the screen, using an FOP Java viewer, rather than being saved in a PDF file.

# Formatting Objects

Yesterday, you learned about the many options available with cascading stylesheets to format XML documents for rendering. The XSL-FO specification is a feature-rich collection of objects that surpasses the styles available with CSS.

Objects can control pagination and general document layout, such as the `root` object. The `root` object does not affect the formatting of the page, but it does identify the root element and provide a container for all of the remaining objects. Some formatting objects are placed inline with other objects. For instance, the `fo:external-graphic` object provides a referential link to a binary graphic that resides outside the FO result tree document. The page-number object is another example of an object that is encoded inline with other page layout objects. XSL-FO provides an extensive collection of objects used to format tables. Each table object can contain characteristics encoded as property attributes that control the appearance of an `fo:table-cell`, `fo:table-row`, `fo:table-column`, or an entire `fo:table`. Property attributes on a table element include formats for `padding`, `border`, `background-color`, and so on.

Table 15.1 summarizes Formatting Objects defined by the W3C XSL-FO specification (descriptive text source: `http://www.w3.org/Style/XSL/`) and indicates which of these objects is supported by version 1.1 of Apache's FOP (Apache FOP Features Documentation: http://xml.apache.org/fop/implemented.html). The specific objects that are not implemented in FOP version 1.1 are indicated by a notation "N/A" (N/A) in the FOP 1.1 column of the table. The list of properties available for these objects in the form of attributes is quite extensive.

You might want to familiarize yourself with the W3C documentation on XSL-FO if you intend to use it regularly. The properties for Formatting Objects can be found in section 5.3 of the specification at http://www.w3.org/TR/xsl/slice5.html#compcorr.

**TABLE 15.1**  W3C Formatting Objects Supported by FOP Version 1.1

| Formatting Object | Description | FOP 1.1 |
|---|---|---|
| fo:basic-link | Used to represent the start resource of a simple link | |
| fo:bidi-override | Used when it is necessary to override the default Unicode-bidirectionality algorithm direction for different (or nested) inline scripts in mixed-language documents | N/A |
| fo:block | Commonly used to format paragraphs, titles, headlines, figure and table captions, and so on | |
| fo:block-container | Used to generate a block-level reference-area | N/A |
| fo:character | Represents a character that is mapped to a glyph for presentation | |
| fo:color-profile | Used to declare a color profile for a stylesheet | N/A |
| fo:conditional-page-master-reference | Used to identify a page-master that is to be used when the conditions on its use are satisfied | |
| fo:declarations | Used to group global declarations for a stylesheet | |
| fo:external-graphic | Used for a graphic where the graphics data resides outside of the XML result tree in the fo namespace | |
| fo:float | Serves two purposes: It can be used so that during the normal placement of content, some related content is formatted into a separate area at the beginning of the page (or of some following page) where it is available to be read without immediately intruding on the reader. Alternatively, it can be used when an area is intended to float to one side, with normal content flowing alongside. | N/A |

**TABLE 15.1**  continued

| Formatting Object | Description | FOP 1.1 |
|---|---|---|
| fo:flow | Provides the flowing text content that is distributed into pages | |
| fo:footnote | Used to produce a footnote citation and the corresponding footnote | |
| fo:footnote-body | Used to generate the content of the footnote | |
| fo:initial-property-set | Specifies formatting properties for the first line of an fo:block | N/A |
| fo:inline | Commonly used to format a portion of text with a background or enclose it in a border | |
| fo:inline-container | Used to generate an inline reference-area | N/A |
| fo:instream-foreign-object | Used for an inline graphic or other "generic" object where the object data resides as descendents of the fo:instream-foreign-object | |
| fo:layout-master-set | A wrapper around all masters used in the document | |
| fo:leader | Used to generate leaders consisting either of a rule or of a row of a repeating character or cyclically repeating pattern of characters that may be used for connecting two text formatting objects | |
| fo:list-block | Used to format a list | |
| fo:list-item | Contains the label and the body of an item in a list | |
| fo:list-item-body | Contains the content of the body of a list-item | |
| fo:list-item-label | Contains the content of the label of a list-item; typically used to enumerate, identify, or adorn the list-item's body | |
| fo:marker | Used in conjunction with fo:retrieve-marker to produce running headers or footers | N/A |
| fo:multi-case | Used to contain (within an fo:multi-switch) each alternative sub-tree of formatting objects among which the parent fo:multi-switch will choose one to show and will hide the rest | N/A |
| fo:multi-properties | Used to switch between two or more property sets that are associated with a given portion of content | N/A |

**TABLE 15.1** continued

| Formatting Object | Description | FOP 1.1 |
|---|---|---|
| fo:multi-property-set | Used to specify an alternative set of formatting properties that, dependent on a user agent state, are applied to the content | N/A |
| fo:multi-switch | Wraps the specification of alternative sub-trees of formatting objects (each sub-tree being within an fo:multi-case) and controls the switching (activated via fo:multi-toggle) from one alternative to another | N/A |
| fo:multi-toggle | Used within an fo:multi-case to switch to another fo:multi-case | N/A |
| fo:page-number | Used to represent the current page number | |
| fo:page-number-citation | Used to reference the page number for the page containing the first normal area returned by the cited formatting object | |
| fo:page-sequence | Used to specify how to create a sub-sequence of pages within a document, such as a chapter of a report. The content of these pages comes from flow children of the fo:page-sequence | |
| fo:page-sequence-master | Specifies sequences of page-masters that are used to generate a sequence of pages | |
| fo:region-after | Defines a viewport that is located on the "after" side of the fo:region-body region | |
| fo:region-before | Defines a viewport that is located on the "before" side of the fo:region-body region | |
| fo:region-body | Specifies a viewport/reference pair that is located in the "center" of the fo:simple-page-master | |
| fo:region-end | Defines a viewport that is located on the "end" side of the fo:region-body region | |
| fo:region-start | Defines a viewport that is located on the "start" side of fo:region-body region | |
| fo:repeatable-page-master-alternatives | Specifies a sub-sequence consisting of repeated instances of a set of alternative page-masters; the number of repetitions can be bounded or potentially unbounded | |

**TABLE 15.1** continued

| Formatting Object | Description | FOP 1.1 |
|---|---|---|
| fo:repeatable-page-master-reference | Specifies a sub-sequence consisting of repeated instances of a single page-master. The number of repetitions may be bounded or potentially unbounded | |
| fo:retrieve-marker | Used in conjunction with fo:marker to produce running headers or footers | N/A |
| fo:root | Composed of formatting objects, this is the top node of an XSL result tree | |
| fo:simple-page-master | Used to generate pages and specify the geometry of the page, this page can be subdivided into up to five regions | |
| fo:single-page-master-reference | Specifies a sub-sequence consisting of a single instance of a single page-master | |
| fo:static-content | Holds a sequence or a tree of formatting objects that is to be presented in a single region or repeated in like-named regions on one or more pages in the page sequence; its common use is for repeating or running headers and footers | |
| fo:table | Used to format the tabular material of a table | |
| fo:table-and-caption | Used to format a table together with its caption | N/A |
| fo:table-body | Used to contain the content of the table body | |
| fo:table-caption | Used to contain block-level formatting objects containing the caption for the table only when using the fo:table-and-caption | N/A |
| fo:table-cell | Used to group content to be placed in a table cell | |
| fo:table-column | Specifies characteristics applicable to table cells that have the same column and span | |
| fo:table-footer | Used to contain the content of the table footer | |
| fo:table-header | Used to contain the content of the table header | |
| fo:table-row | Used to group table-cells into rows | |
| fo:title | Used to associate a title with a given document | |
| fo:wrapper | Used to specify inherited properties for a group of formatting objects; it has no additional formatting semantics | |

## Basic FO Construction

For the first exercise today, suppose you want to create a simple PDF file containing only a string of text—perhaps a page containing only a page title (My Messages) for the message and reminder system with which you have worked in recent days. You will create an FO file and choose PDF as an output format from the FOP interpreter.

You'll add other components to the page as we go, but a title will provide a good place to start. With this basic example, you'll save the output as an FO document instance and use FOP to create a PDF file. If you have Java 2 or Java Swing installed, you can also create output using the -awt option in the FOP processor command string. Both results will be shown shortly.

You will need to wrap your page heading text string in appropriate markup to create a PDF file. The markup steps to render a single string of text are few in number, but they provide a minimal template for more complex formats. Remember that an FO document is just an XML instance. You'll create it using your favorite text editor; however, be sure to save it with an .fo rather than an .xml file extension as good programming practice. You will also use the fo: prefix to serve as a proxy for the Formatting Object namespace (xmlns:fo=http://www.w3.org/1999.XSL/Format). The FOP application requires the use of this prefix.

The FO namespace is declared on the root element of the document. The root element of an XSL-FO document is always

```
<fo:root xmlns:fo="http://www.w3.org/1999/XSL/Format">
```

The root element is just a container. No style markup accompanies the root element, although it contains all of the other objects in the document.

If you leaf quickly through a few pages of this book, you might notice that the layout is consistent in terms of margins, the placement of headers, and other common page elements. In publishing, these overall page characteristics are set in elements known as *page masters*. Your favorite word processing software likely has a similar concept. Figure 15.2 depicts the Page Setup menu in Microsoft Word 2000, showing, for instance, margin dimensions and absolute positioning options for headers and footers. You can adjust the values in the fields to affect the layout of pages.

These settings that have a scope of the entire document are contained in XSL-FO by the fo:layout-master-set element. In other words, the fo:layout-master-set element is a container element, holding the properties of the master set. Within the fo:layout-master-set element are fo:simple-page-master elements, containers that define the layout in a fashion analogous to the definitions in a word processor. In XSL-FO, you might have multiple fo:simple-page-master elements so that you can control document format on a page-by-page basis if required.

**Figure 15.2**

*Page Setup controls in Microsoft Word 2000.*

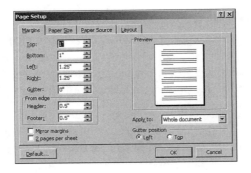

The `fo:simple-page-master` elements require a `master-name` attribute that you encode with a value of your own choosing. The name is required so that you can distinguish multiple masters from another. The syntax of the `fo:simple-page-master` element is as follows:

```
<fo:simple-page-master master-name="myPageName">
```

The `fo:simple-page-master` element defines five regions of a standard page: the header region, the footer region, the body of the document, and the margin regions on the left and right side of the body. The left margin area is known as the start region, and the area comprising the right margin is called the end region. Each of these regions has a corresponding XSL-FO element used to contain particular markup instructions.

The header region is known as the `fo:region-before` because it happens prior to the body in a sequential layout sense. The left margin region is called the `fo:region-start`; the body is `fo:region-body`; the right margin is `fo:region-end`; and the footer is `fo:region-end`. Figure 15.3 shows the relative positions of these regions on a page.

This orientation is specific to languages, such as English, that are laid out and read from left to right on a page. By way of contrast, Arabic or Hebrew pages created with Formatting Objects would require the `fo:region-start` to be on the right side of the page and the `fo:region-end` to be on the left side of the page.

Each of the regions might contain style markup, encoded as FO properties. For instance, if you want the text within the header to incorporate a left margin of two inches, you can place the appropriate attribute on the `fo:region-before` element. The element, in this case would look like this:

```
<fo:region-before element margin-left="2in"/>
```

**FIGURE 15.3**

*Formatting regions of
a page for languages
that are read from left
to right, like English.*

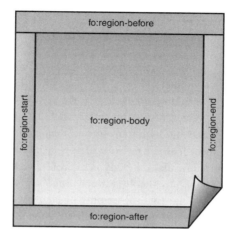

Suppose that you want to place the body of the output page you are about to create with
XSL-FO 1.5 inches from the left margin and 1 inch from the top, just as it is in the Word
document Page Setup shown in Figure 15.2. You can create an `fo:simple-page-master`
element that contains an `fo:region-body` element with appropriate attributes, namely
`margin-left` and `margin-top`. Assuming that you named the first page master `message-
page`, the complete `fo:layout-master-set` element will look like this:

```
<fo:layout-master-set>
  <fo:simple-page-master master-name="message-page">
    <fo:region-body margin-left="1.5in" margin-top="1in"/>
  </fo:simple-page-master>
</fo:layout-master-set>
```

You can see that the `fo:layout-master-set` element contains one child `fo:simple-
page-master` element with the `master-name` message-page. The `fo:simple-page-
master` element contains an `fo:region-body` element with attributes for page margins.

In XSL-FO, pages in a document are grouped into sequences with each sequence starting
from a new page. Sequences serve to explicitly define how pages will be presented. For
instance, you can instruct the processor to repeat a particular layout as long as needed
until all of the content is handled. You can do this by including an `fo:repeatable-page-
master-reference` element with an associated `master-name` attribute whose value is the
same as the named `simple-page-master` you want to have repeated for all of the content. You won't need to do this for the first exercise, but the technique will come in
handy with more complex Formatting Objects. For now, remember that sequences encoded with `fo:page-sequence` elements are important elements for complex page layouts.
In the first XSL-FO document, you will use an `fo:page-sequence` element to hold the
text content. It will look like this:

```
<fo:page-sequence master-name="message-page">
  other element content
</fo:page-sequence>
```

The *other element content* contained by the fo:page-sequence element will include an fo:flow container element. This is a special container object for all user text in the document. Everything contained by the fo:flow element will be formatted into regions on pages generated inside the page sequence. In your document, you will encode the flow-name attribute with the value message-page to link the flow to a specific region on the page. Specifically, the text will appear in the *body* because that is the referenced region. You know that the body is the referenced region because the fo:region-body element is contained by the fo:simple-page-master that has the master-name="my-page". By now, you might find the naming of elements confusing, but you have all of the component elements and attributes to create your first XSL-FO document. When these are all combined, you should have a document that looks like Listing 15.1. Enter this listing and save it as message01.fo.

**LISTING 15.1**    A First XSL-FO Document

```
 1: <?xml version="1.0"?>
 2: <!-- listing 15.1 - message01.fo -->
 3:
 4: <fo:root xmlns:fo="http://www.w3.org/1999/XSL/Format">
 5:
 6:   <fo:layout-master-set>
 7:     <fo:simple-page-master master-name="message-page">
 8:       <fo:region-body margin-left="1.5in" margin-top="1in"/>
 9:     </fo:simple-page-master>
10:   </fo:layout-master-set>
11:
12:   <fo:page-sequence master-name="message-page">
13:     <fo:flow flow-name="xsl-region-body">
14:       <fo:block>My Messages</fo:block>
15:     </fo:flow>
16:   </fo:page-sequence>
17:
18: </fo:root>
```

**ANALYSIS**    Line 4 contains the start tag of the root element (fo:root) with the namespace (xmlns:fo="http://www.w3.org/1999/XSL/Format") encoded. Lines 6–10 hold the fo:layout-master-set element that defines the layout structure for the entire document. The fo:layout-master-set element can contain any number of simple-page-master elements, but this instance has only one and it is named message-page. The body of this document will be set 1.5 inches from the left edge of the page and 1 inch from the top of the page (line 8). Lines 12–16 contain the `fo:page-sequence` element and its child elements, which provide formatting for the region that corresponds to the simple-page-master of the same master-name (message-page). The `fo:flow` element (lines 13–15) contains the text to be placed on the page in a `block`.

When you have entered and saved the `message01.fo` document, process it with FOP. To create a PDF file, enter the command line instruction appropriate for your version of FOP, such as

```
fop -fo drive:\path\message01.fo -pdf drive:\path\message01.pdf
```

To view the results on the screen instead, type the following, or type the equivalent as documented for the version of FOP you obtain:

```
fop -fo drive:\path\message01.fo -awt
```

If you look carefully at Figure 15.4, you will see that it shows both forms of output. In the background, the PDF file generated by FOP is seen as viewed in Adobe Acrobat. The foreground shows the resulting page as viewed in the FOP built-in Java viewer.

**FIGURE 15.4**

*Two views of the results generated by processing an XSL-FO document.*

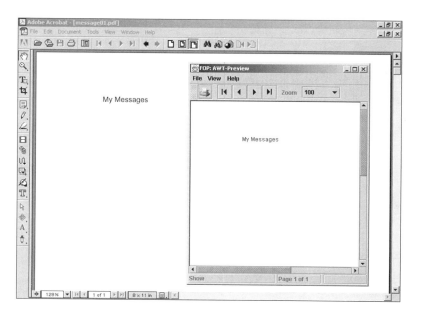

## Font Attributes

The rest of the formatting you might choose to do is largely a matter of combining style attributes and values with the elements they affect. You now know the basic structure of an XSL-FO document. This structure stays virtually the same no matter how complex the document becomes. By adding new page masters, sequences, and flows, you can create all regions of any page and create dramatic style effects. In this way, XSL-FO is similar to CSS. Many of the properties even map closely from one approach to the other. The W3C intended that XSL would be built on the prior work done to provide CSS.

In the next example, you will add a message that includes the sender's name and the text of the message. In addition, you'll add some text and font attributes to style the output. Start by moving the page heading `My Messages` to the center of the page by placing a `text-align="center"` attribute on the `fo:block` element containing the text. It will look like this:

```
<fo:block
    text-align="center">My Messages</fo:block>
```

Add appropriate attributes to make the text 28 points, in a sans-serif, bold, blue font. Your `fo:block` element will now look something like this:

```
<fo:block
   text-align="center"
   font-size="28pt"
   font-family="sans-serif"
   font-weight="bold"
   color="blue">My Messages
</fo:block>
```

Add two more `fo:block` elements within the same `xsl-region-body` of the page with the following text content:

```
From: Kathy Shepherd
Message: Remember to buy milk on the way home from work
```

Style both of these as 12 point, sans-serif fonts and save the results as `message02.xml`. Did you include blocks that look something like the following?

```
<fo:block
   font-size="12pt"
   font-family="sans-serif">From: Kathy Shepherd
</fo:block>

<fo:block
   font-size="12pt"
   font-family="sans-serif">Message:
      Remember to buy milk on the way home from work
</fo:block>
```

After you have made these additions and saved the document, process it with FOP and view the results. Did you get exactly what you expected? Take a look at the heading. Is it really in the center of the page, or does it appear to be too far to the right? One way of ensuring that the heading is truly in the center is to change the `fo:region-body` element to include a margin-right attribute that is the same as the margin-left attribute. You can encode it like this:

```
<fo:region-body margin-left="1.5in"
    margin-right="1.5in" margin-top="1in"/>
```

The final code will look something like Listing 15.2.

**LISTING 15.2**   An XSL-FO Example with Font Attributes—`message02.fo`

```
 1: <?xml version="1.0"?>
 2: <!-- listing 15.2 - message02.fo -->
 3:
 4: <fo:root xmlns:fo="http://www.w3.org/1999/XSL/Format">
 5:
 6:   <fo:layout-master-set>
 7:     <fo:simple-page-master master-name="message-page">
 8:       <fo:region-body margin-left="1.5in"
 9:           margin-right="1.5in" margin-top="1in"/>
10:     </fo:simple-page-master>
11:   </fo:layout-master-set>
12:
13:   <fo:page-sequence master-name="message-page">
14:     <fo:flow flow-name="xsl-region-body">
15:
16:       <fo:block
17:           text-align="center"
18:           font-size="28pt"
19:           font-family="sans-serif"
20:           font-weight="bold"
21:           color="blue">My Messages
22:       </fo:block>
23:
24:       <fo:block
25:           font-size="12pt"
26:           font-family="sans-serif">From: Kathy Shepherd
27:       </fo:block>
28:
29:       <fo:block
30:           font-size="12pt"
31:           font-family="sans-serif">Message:
32:               Remember to buy milk on the way home from work
33:       </fo:block>
34:
35:     </fo:flow>
36:   </fo:page-sequence>
37:
38: </fo:root>
```

15

The two new blocks begin on lines 24 and 29. Each contains a `font-size` and `font-family` attribute. Line 9 contains the `margin-right="1.5in"` attribute added to ensure that the `region-body` is centered on the page, and consequently that the `My Messages` text block is centered in the body region. The result is depicted in Figure 15.5.

**FIGURE 15.5**

*XSL-FO font styling.*

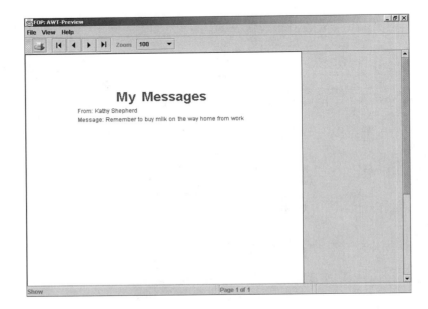

## Inline Styles

If you want to change the styling of the text string fragment `From:` so that it is different from the next part of the string `Kathy Shepherd`, you can wrap it in a new block. However, doing so also separates the two string fragments by a line feed. XSL-FO provides an easy way to encode inline styles using nested elements. The `fo:inline` element can be wrapped around an inline string fragment that you want to style separately from the rest of the string. Wrap an `fo:inline` element around the `From:` and `Message:` portions of the strings in your document. Make the text weighted bold and styled with italic. The markup for the `From:` string should look like this:

```
<fo:inline font-weight="bold"
font-style="italic" >From: </fo:inline>
```

Make the necessary modifications to your document and save it as `message03.fo`. Figure 15.6 depicts the result of these changes.

FIGURE 15.6

*XSL-FO inline styling.*

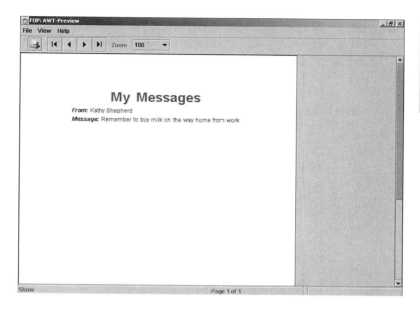

## XSL-FO Tables

Tables in XSL-FO comprise cells within rows. Next, you'll modify the message text so that it is placed into a table that is 2 columns by 2 rows. The basic syntax for a table is as follows:

```
<fo:table>

   <fo:table-column column-width="value" />
   <fo:table-column column-width="value" />
   ...any other columns

   <fo:table-body>

      <fo:table-row>
         <fo:table-cell>
            <fo:block>
               Cell Data
            </fo:block>
         </fo:table-cell>

         ...any other cells

      </fo:table-row>

      ...any other rows

   </fo:table-body>
</fo:table>
```

The specification requires that you define the rows and provide an `fo:table-column` element with a `column-width` attribute for each column in the table. For the purpose of this exercise, the left column will be 1-inch wide and the right column will be 4.5-inches wide.

```
<fo:table-column column-width="1in" />
<fo:table-column column-width="4.5in"/>
```

Padding of .05 inches (`padding=".05in"`) will be added to the cells so that the edges of the cells don't touch the table border. Just for interest, a background color with the value of aqua will be added to the blocks that contain `From:` and `Message:`. The code for the first cell should look like this:

```
<fo:table-cell padding=".05in">
   <fo:block background-color="aqua">
      From:
   </fo:block>
</fo:table-cell>
```

As always, any special styling attribute/value pairs that you want to apply—such as those for colors, cell or table borders, background colors, and so on—should be applied as attributes to the elements they directly modify. The complete document is shown as Listing 15.3 and saved as `message04.fo`. Yours might not have the comments; the comments have been added to help illustrate where each cell is encoded.

**LISTING 15.3**    XSL-FO Table Encoding—`message04.fo`

```
 1: <?xml version="1.0"?>
 2: <!-- listing 15.3 - message04.fo -->
 3:
 4: <fo:root xmlns:fo="http://www.w3.org/1999/XSL/Format">
 5:
 6:    <fo:layout-master-set>
 7:      <fo:simple-page-master master-name="message-page">
 8:        <fo:region-body margin-left="1.5in"
 9:                        margin-right="1.5in" margin-top="1in"/>
10:      </fo:simple-page-master>
11:    </fo:layout-master-set>
12:
13:    <fo:page-sequence master-name="message-page">
14:      <fo:flow flow-name="xsl-region-body">
15:
16:        <fo:block
17:            text-align="center"
18:            font-size="28pt"
19:            font-family="sans-serif"
20:            font-weight="bold"
21:            color="blue">My Messages
```

**LISTING 15.3** continued

```
22:          </fo:block>
23:
24:      <fo:table border-style="solid">
25:
26:          <!-- column-width is required -->
27:          <fo:table-column column-width="1in" />
28:          <fo:table-column column-width="4.5in"/>
29:
30:          <fo:table-body>
31:
32:            <!-- first row of table -->
33:            <fo:table-row>
34:
35:                <!-- upper-left cell -->
36:                <fo:table-cell padding=".05in">
37:                 <fo:block background-color="aqua">
38:                    From:
39:                 </fo:block>
40:                </fo:table-cell>
41:
42:
43:                <!-- upper-right cell -->
44:                <fo:table-cell  padding=".05in">
45:                 <fo:block>
46:                    Kathy Shepherd
47:                 </fo:block>
48:                </fo:table-cell>
49:            </fo:table-row>
50:
51:            <!-- second row of table -->
52:            <fo:table-row>
53:
54:                <!-- lower-left cell -->
55:                <fo:table-cell  padding=".05in">
56:                 <fo:block background-color="aqua">
57:                    Message:
58:                 </fo:block>
59:                </fo:table-cell>
60:
61:
62:                <!-- lower-right cell -->
63:                <fo:table-cell  padding=".05in">
64:                 <fo:block>
65:                    Remember to buy milk on the way home from work
66:                 </fo:block>
67:                </fo:table-cell>
68:
69:            </fo:table-row>
```

**LISTING 15.3**    continued

```
70:
71:        </fo:table-body>
72:      </fo:table>
73:
74:      </fo:flow>
75:    </fo:page-sequence>
76:
77: </fo:root>
```

**ANALYSIS**    Lines 1–22 are unchanged from the previous example. The table begins on line 24 and includes a border-style attribute designating a solid border around the entire table. The column widths for the left and right columns are set on lines 27 and 28 respectively. Line 33 begins the first table row. The elements belonging to the row are on lines 34–48. The upper-left cell of the table is encoded on lines 36–40. Each cell incorporates .05 inches of padding between the cell boundary and the boundaries of other cells or the border of the table. The cells in the left column only have an aqua background color (lines 37 and 56). The cell coding is repeated for each of the three other cells (starting on lines 44, 55, and 63 respectively). Lines 69–77 serve to close all open elements.

# Summary

Today, you created simple Extensible Stylesheet Language Formatting Objects (XSL-FO) and used them to style XML for rendering on a screen through a customized client. You also learned to generate PDF files for print and electronic distribution. You ran your code through an open-source Java FO interpreter from Apache, called FOP. This free processor runs on a number of different platforms and can be integrated into custom Java applications. You learned that XSL Formatting Objects are a subset of the XSL recommendation. XSL transformations (XSLT), which can operate separately from XSL-FO, form the remainder of the XSL specification. Tomorrow, you will learn about XSLT and use it to transform the structure of XML documents.

# Q&A

**Q What is the relationship between XSL, XSL-FO, and XSLT?**

**A** The W3C Extensible Stylesheet Language recommendation comprises a transformation portion (XSLT) and a language to describe Formatting Objects (XSL-FO). XSLT, which can transform the structure of an XML document into a new markup

15

structure, can function independently of XSL-FO. XSLT can transform an XML document into another XML document or into an HTML document, or for that matter into any other form of text document. XSL-FO is ideally suited to interpretation for use in print media and by a variety of user agents.

**Q   Where is the XML source file in an XSL-FO operation? How, for instance, do you get from an XML document to a PDF file?**

**A   ** The XSL-FO document is an XML instance document, but that is only a single document in an operation that typically has several steps. To get from an original XML source document to PDF output requires that the document be transformed from the XML source tree dialect in which it is written to an XSL-FO document. To do this, you associate an XML source document with an XSL stylesheet document for transformation by an XSLT processor. This association produces an XSL-FO result tree document. The XSL-FO result tree document is then passed through an interpreter that translates the XSL-FO into an output document in another vocabulary, such as PDF.

**Q   How can FOP be used as an embedded process within an application to generate output from Formatting Objects?**

**A   ** The FOP processor can be embedded in a Java application by instantiating the `org.apache.fop.apps.Driver` available from the FOP Web site. Considerable documentation is available at `http://xml.apache.org/fop/`. You can also integrate the FOP processor into the Apache Xerces SAX parser using the procedures documented on the same site. The Apache Xerces SAX parser is available at `http://xml.apache.org/` in versions for Java, C++, and PERL. This allows you to generate FOP results by firing SAX events to create FO output.

**Q   Can images be included in Formatting Object output?**

**A   ** External graphics files can be associated with an XSL-FO document using the `fo:external-graphics` element and an `src` attribute with a URI value. Using the `fo:external-graphic` element, the processor will embed the graphic in the output. The syntax of the `fo:external-graphic` element is as follows:

```
<fo:external-graphic src="URI"/>
```

# Exercise

The exercise is provided so that you can test your knowledge of what you learned today. The answer is in Appendix A.

Refer to the table of supporting Formatting Objects and use data from your `cd.xml` document to create a bulleted list of CD titles.

# DAY 16

# Extensible Stylesheet Language Transformations (XSLT)

The XSL Transformation Language (XSLT) converts an XML document tree into a new tree structure. The new tree can be another XML document, or it can be HTML or some other format. XSLT is a declarative, event-driven, rules-based programming language, written as a dialect of XML. Today, you will learn

- How XSLT transforms XML documents from one structure to another
- How to use the XT XSLT processor and the Architag XRay XML editor
- About a subset of the rich element set belonging to XSLT
- How to manipulate nodes, sort, and style output using XSLT

# Transforming from One Structure to Another

As you learned on Day 15, the Extensible Stylesheet Language (XSL) includes a transformation language (XSLT) and a formatting language (XSL-FO). A third component of the original XSL proposal, XPath, was moved into a separate specification, recognizing its utility to other XML technologies. Like XSL-FO, XSLT is an application of XML, thereby allowing you to create it easily with a simple text editor. Yesterday, you read that XSLT could operate separately from the rest of XSL. You will make use of this capability today by transforming XML documents into well-formed HTML pages without regard to XSL Formatting Objects.

Although you will use XSLT to transform XML into HTML, XSLT has a much broader application than that. XSLT can be used to transform XML into other forms of text and markup, even into other XML instances. XML to XML transformation is commonly used to modify XML documents for use by specific applications. For instance, businesses communicating with one another might use XSLT to transform XML provided by business partners to improve communication and compatibility. Imagine, for instance, a purchase order produced as an XML document instance that is transformed into an XML document employing a different structure for input into an order system. XSLT provides an easy and reliable means of making such a transformation.

Although XSL is, as of this writing, at the W3C Candidate Recommendation stage, XSL Transformations version 1.0 is actually a formal recommendation. The specification can be found at `http://www.w3.org/TR/xslt`. The fact that XSLT has matured more quickly than its XSL superset provides more support for the potential to operate XSLT independently of the rest of XSL. Even though you can use XSLT separately, which you will do today, the intent, according to the W3C, is that XSLT be used primarily for transformations that are part of an overall styling of XML data.

It is compelling in the field of Web development to use a transformation programming language. In some ways, the concept recognizes an unwritten programming rule that states you should use the tool that best suits the problem. Have you ever known someone so enamored by a single application that they insist on using it to solve all computing problems? If you used a spreadsheet application daily, would you expect to expand the first column to 80 characters wide and hit return at the end of each line to create your own word processor?

By using XML for intelligent data-aware storage and efficient, interoperable transmission of information, you are exploiting some of XML's inherent strengths. By transforming XML into HTML, for instance, you are able to present data in a format that can be used by virtually every modern browser. As you know, presentation of native XML is not fully implemented on most browsers, but HTML works well.

Transformation can also be built into applications as part of normal processing. Consider the way in which Internet Explorer *renders* the result when you load an XML page into the browser. As you know from your reading on Day 2, IE does not actually display the XML; rather, IE performs an XSL transformation using an stylesheet that is bundled into the IE distribution. When you install IE, you also install a number of companion products, including the MSXML parser and its associated libraries. A special stylesheet is included in that package. When you load an XML file into IE, it first checks to see if you have assigned a stylesheet to use for rendering. If you have not, IE uses its own default stylesheet—the one that gives you colored tags and a collapsible/expandable tree of markup and content. If you would like to view the default stylesheet, launch IE version 5 or greater and browse the following internal URI by entering it directly into the Address field:

```
res://msxml.dll/defaultss.xsl
```

You will be presented with the familiar tree view of a fairly complex XSL stylesheet, the analysis of which is beyond the scope of today's reading. Nonetheless, by the end of today, you will be able to view the stylesheet and identify its major rules and components.

## Operational XSLT

Transformations take place when an XSL transformation engine processes an XML document and an XSL stylesheet. You use the XSLT language to compose XSL stylesheets, which are also XML documents. An XSL stylesheet contains instructions for transforming XML source documents from one document type to another, such as XML or HTML. In structural terms, an XSL stylesheet specifies the transformation of one tree of nodes into another tree of nodes. Many transformation engines and editors exist with integral XSLT support.

## XSLT Processing Options

XSLT can occur in a variety of ways, and you will need to select tools that best suit your needs. For instance, you can perform local transformations using an engine that runs on your computer. In this scenario, you would invoke an engine and pass it the name of an XML document and the associated XSL document. The engine would process the transformation and generate a third document as output. Engines of this kind are readily available on almost every platform, and many include open-source code that can be integrated into other application programs. You can imagine that if you were to integrate the power of a transformation engine into your code, you could create sophisticated solutions incorporating XML data with other business processes. For a complete list of available XSLT engines, editors, and utilities, visit `http://www.xslt.com/xslt_tools_editors.html`. The W3C XSLT site (`http://www.w3.org/Style/XSL/`) also includes a listing of XSLT tools.

You will download and install a Java XSLT processor (XT) today from `http://jclark.com/xml/xt.html` to complete some of the transformation exercises. This XSLT processor will work in conjunction with a SAX parser. You installed a SAX parser on Day 13, so XT can make use of that.

Microsoft Internet Explorer supports client-side transformation of XML using XSL stylesheets. This is really only practical in environments where you can have complete control over browser deployment. Netscape browsers, for instance, do not support client-side transformation; you would need to guarantee that all of your users ran a compatible version of IE to make this style of transformation practical. Nonetheless, client-side transformations offer an easy way to quickly check your programming and render results. You will have an opportunity to use IE today to perform client-side XSLT if you choose.

Some text editors have integral support for XSLT that provides a workable environment for stylesheet development. You will have a chance to download a free editor today to try this approach (source: `http://www.architag.com/xray`).

You can also use server-side scripting to invoke a processor to transform XML into HTML prior to sending it to your Web server. This is an interesting technique that is valuable in some Web-centric applications.

## Corporate Procedures Manual: An XSLT Scenario

Yesterday, you considered the example of an XML corporate policy document being transformed into XSL Formatting Objects for presentation to an interpreter to generate a PDF version of a policy manual. By modifying the scenario slightly, eliminating the Formatting Objects and need for PDF output, consider the same XML source being transformed into HTML for presentation on a corporate intranet. You will still require several distinct processes and vocabularies to modify an XML document for the purpose of styling the content. The individual components in XSL transformation from XML to HTML include the following:

- An XML source document that appears to the XSLT process as a hierarchical node tree
- An XSL stylesheet, also a tree structure, which carries the semantics for the transformation
- An XSLT processor that parses the source tree and stylesheet tree into memory and produces a new tree structure as output

In the corporate policy scenario, you will still have an XML document on your corporate intranet that contains the administrative policies for your organization. As before, this is a document that is updated regularly to reflect any changes to employee benefits, accounting practices, and other policies. However, rather than producing a PDF document, you want to periodically process that document to create an HTML Web page that employees can reference at any time. By making this transformation a periodic process, you want to ensure that the Web content is kept up to date.

XSLT lends itself well to this scenario. Once again, an XML instance document (corp.xml) containing corporate policies and guidelines in appropriate elements will be associated with a stylesheet (corp.xsl). That stylesheet identifies matching rules and actions required to instruct the XSLT processor to make substitutions of XML elements with HTML tags for the text size of headings, emphasized phrases, page margins, and so on. An XSLT engine processes the two XML documents (corp.xml and corp.xsl) as combined source trees in a transformation that produces an HTML output tree document (corp.html). The entire operation has fewer steps than the process required for the creation of a PDF file using Formatting Objects. In this case, the transformation engine produces an HTML result tree, rather than an FO result tree. After the HTML result tree is created, the process is complete. The new HTML page will contain the desired content from the corporate policy document (corp.xml). Figure 16.1 depicts this scenario.

**FIGURE 16.1**

*XSL transformation process.*

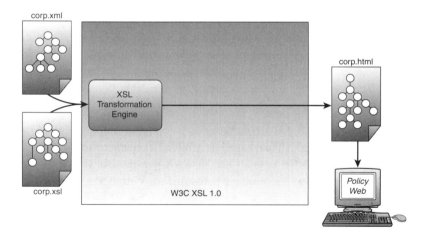

Today, you will create stylesheets and use the XSLT process, independently of the XSL-FO part of XSL. The XSL stylesheets you create will be used to transform XML document instances into instances of well-formed HTML for presentation on a browser. As noted earlier, you will have an opportunity to explore several engines.

## XSLT Tools Installation

Today, you will download and install several tools. The first is a Java XT processor. Several good alternatives exist:

- SAXON, a free Java processor (`http://users.iclway.co.uk/mhkay/saxon/instant.html`)
- Napa XSLT processor, written in C++ (`http://www.tfi-technology.com/xml/napa.html`)
- Apache Xalan (`http://xml.apache.org/xalan`)
- Fourthought 4Suite, written in Python (`http://4suite.org/`)
- Infoteria iXSLT, in C++ (`http://www.infoteria.com/`)

## XSLT Command Line Processor

The processor you will use today, called XT, is a free XSLT processor written in Java by James Clark, one of the authors of the XSLT specification. To download the application, browse to `http://jclark.com/xml/xt.html` and download the XT distribution files. You will want to follow the instructions carefully because, as with all Java programs, you will need to be aware of environment paths, such as the classpath and homepath, and ensure that you have established variables to represent the appropriate paths for the applications to function. In other words, because XT will require access to your SAX parser, the classpath environment variable on your system will necessarily require the path to the parser. The documentation provided with the distribution regarding setup will provide the necessary steps for your operating system; therefore, those specific instructions are not detailed here.

Alternately, if you are working on a computer running a Windows operating system, you can download XT packaged as a Win32 executable application. This is the simplest version to install. It includes the XP SAX parser, also written by James Clark, as part of the bundle. You will require a Microsoft Java Virtual Machine (VM) because the XT processor has been written to take advantage of that VM when executed on a Windows operating system. If you require a copy of the VM, go to `http://www.microsoft.com/java/vm/dl_vm40.htm`. However, if you have already installed Internet Explorer version 4.01 or higher on your computer, you will not need to install a new version of the VM; an adequate one was placed on your machine at the time VM was installed. This means that if you run a Windows OS and have IE already installed on your computer, you only need to download and install XT packaged as a Win32 executable. Users of other operating systems—such as Unix, Linux, and Macintosh—should obtain the full implementation of XT and read the installation instructions carefully.

After you have installed XT, you will be able to use it to perform XSL transformations. The command line syntax that you will use today to invoke the processor is as follows:

```
java -Dcom.jclark.xsl.sax.parser=your-sax-driver
     com.jclark.xsl.sax.Driver source.xml stylesheet.xsl result.html
```

Replace *source.xml* with the path and name of your source XML document. Replace *stylesheet.xsl* in the command line string with the fully qualified name of your XSL stylesheet, and *result.html* with the name of the output file you are creating. Most of the output files you create today will end in an .html extension because you will typically transform XML documents into HTML. However, XT can be used with a stylesheet programmed to return a different XML structure, if required.

If you installed the Win32 executable, you can use an abbreviated command line instruction to invoke XT:

```
xt source.xml stylesheet.xsl result.html
```

The same placeholder substitutions apply in this case.

## XSLT-Aware XML Editors

Several XML editors are capable of working with XSLT stylesheets. Some are able to perform the transformations using a built-in or locally referenced transformation engine and incorporate HTML viewers to demonstrate the transformed results. Some of the editors to consider include

- XMLwriter, a commercial XML editor with support for XSLT (http://xmlwriter.net/index.shtml)
- XML-Spy, a commercial product (http://www.xmlspy.com)
- IBM XSL Editor (http://www.alphaworks.ibm.com/tech/xsleditor)
- XSLDebugger (http://www.vbxml.com/xsldebugger/)

The editor you will use for exercise work today is called XRay XML Editor. It can be downloaded free from http://www.architag.com/xray. This editor has full support for well-formed XML and XML validating against DTDs, XDR, and XSD schemata. But today, you will use its engineered XSLT capabilities. You will be able to create an XML document in one window and an XSL stylesheet in another. Then you can perform the transformation in a third window and view the HTML or XML output in a fourth.

Download and set up XRay now, accepting all of the defaults during installation. You will use XRay later today to create and test XSLT stylesheets.

# XSLT Programming

When the XSLT processor is invoked, it begins to read the source XML document tree and the XSL document tree. The stylesheet contains sets of rules for transforming the original tree structure into a new result tree. The rules are expressed as a set of templates that are keyed on elements in the original XML document. Each template contains XPath matching expressions so that the XSLT processor can locate the target node in the source document. When a match occurs, the rules in the template are applied to the content of the element matched. This process continues until all of the templates and all of the matches have successfully been processed. XSLT is an event-driven process based on SAX parsing technology. The rules you construct inform the processor how to do things, such as

- Substitute XML markup for HTML markup
- Sort element content according to algorithms provided
- Hide and display information under program control
- Convert tables into graphics using, for instance, the XML Structured Vector Graphics Language

## XSLT Namespace Considerations

Because an XSLT document is XML, it is constructed of elements and attributes. The elements in XSLT are bound to the XSLT namespace:

```
http://www.w3.org/1999/XSL/Transform
```

As you will recall from Day 8, a namespace is just a label, but it is special because it is known to an XML processor. The processor associates programming expectations with the namespace provided. In this way, program behavior is linked to members of the element set encoded. This means that an XSLT processor, for instance, performs specific instructions on the basis of the elements encountered. Each element in an XSLT stylesheet corresponds to an event instruction passed to the processor, which in turn fires an event that performs a designated function. Unfortunately, not all processors implement the same set of events and functions. The W3C specification offers a means of coalescing the process suite, but differences exist. Sometimes other namespaces are employed to define alternative element sets. This provides you with a dilemma when it comes to coding XSLT. The W3C namespace will work with some processors, but not with all of them. For example, when you choose to perform client-side transformations in Internet Explorer, you will need to use a different namespace in your XSLT program:

```
http://www.w3.org/TR/WD-xsl
```

Luckily, for the majority of transformations you will work on today, the namespace is all you will need to change to select a client-side transformation, or a transformation using another engine.

## Rules-Based Event Processing

As discussed earlier, the process expressed by XSLT describes rules for transforming a source tree into a result tree. Each template rule is a stand-alone object that is idle until a match results in activating the rules it contains. As the XSLT engine processes the source tree a node at a time, it executes the rules when elements or other constructs are appropriately matched. When a match occurs, the instructions contained by the rule are performed.

You might think about the performance of each template rule as being analogous to execution of a sub-routine in another language. The sub-routines are stored in a collection, the XSL document, and are available to be called upon as needed. The order of the rules in the XSL document is insignificant. Each rule will be called if it is needed on the basis of a matched XPath expression. In other words, the XSLT processor will read the XML source document and pass element content to appropriate sub-routines when a match is found. The content of the element matched is passed to the XSLT sub-routine, or template rule, and processed. In the exercises you will work on today, this processing will typically involve the placement of HTML elements in the result tree.

The instantiation of the template, therefore, for a matched source element results in the creation of a portion of the result tree. The template might also contain special instructions that tell the processor how to deal with the content of the elements matched.

The sub-routine performs a number of standard functions. For instance, suppose you want to create HTML markup around the content of a particular element, such that it is part of a bulleted list on a Web page. This kind of process is performed well by an XSLT template. A match with that element would execute the instructions required to place an appropriate start tag on the result tree. At this point, the sub-routine typically provides possible exits. These exits are implemented as XSL elements. The elements provide functions to the XSLT language. Today, you will primarily use one of the following two template exits, or XSLT functions that provide an escape from the template:

- The content of the element being processed is exposed to all of the other rules in the XSL rule set (using an `xsl:apply-templates` element)
- The content is output directly onto the result tree being created (denoted by a `xsl:value-of` element).

Other functions are available in XSLT in addition to those discussed already. Table 16.1 summarizes XSLT functions.

The process is one of matching something and then doing something repeatedly until the entire source tree is transformed. What the template does is not restricted to producing element structure, such as creating HTML tags. The template could perform calculations and produce results on the basis of those calculations. It might also produce static content that could be placed on the result tree. What the template does is up to you. Regardless of the template's actions, you have the two exits, or functions described earlier. Of course other functions are available as well, but today you will focus on the `xsl:apply-templates` and `xsl:value-of` elements.

The XSLT language comprises elements and attributes like any XML document. The function attached to various elements is what makes XSLT special. The `xsl:apply-templates` and `xsl:value-of` elements are just two of the elements that belong to the XSLT dialect. Table 16.1 provides a list of XSLT elements and indicates the function (or exits) provided in each case.

**TABLE 16.1**   XSLT Elements

| Element | Description |
| --- | --- |
| xsl:apply-imports | Applies a template from an imported stylesheet |
| xsl:apply-templates | Applies a template to the current element |
| xsl:attribute | Adds an attribute to the nearest containing element |
| xsl:attribute-set | Defines a named set of attributes |
| xsl:call-template | Provides a way to call a named template |
| xsl:choose | Provides a way to choose between a number of alternatives based on conditions |
| xsl:comment | Creates an XML comment |
| xsl:copy | Copies the current node without child nodes and attributes to the output |
| xsl:copy-of | Copies the current node with child nodes and attributes to the output |
| xsl:decimal-format | Defines the character/string to be used when converting numbers into strings, with the format-number function |
| xsl:element | Adds a new element node to the output |
| xsl:fallback | Provides a way to define an alternative for instructions that are not implemented |
| xsl:for-each | Provides a way to create a loop in the output stream |
| xsl:if | Provides a way to write a conditional statement |
| xsl:import | Imports a stylesheet |
| xsl:include | Includes a stylesheet |
| xsl:key | Provides a way to define a key |

**TABLE 16.1**   continued

| Element | Description |
| --- | --- |
| xsl:message | Writes a message to the output |
| xsl:namespace-alias | Provides a way to map a namespace to another namespace |
| xsl:number | Writes a formatted number to the output |
| xsl:otherwise | Indicates what should happen when none of the `<xsl:when>` elements inside an `<xsl:choose>` element is satisfied |
| xsl:output | Provides a way to control the transformed output |
| xsl:param | Provides a way to define parameters |
| xsl:preserve-space | Provides a way to define the handling of whitespace characters by making them significant |
| xsl:processing-instruction | Writes a processing instruction to the output |
| xsl:sort | Provides a way to define sorting |
| xsl:strip-space | Provides a way to define the handling of whitespace characters by making them insignificant |
| xsl:stylesheet | Defines the root element of the stylesheet |
| xsl:template | Defines a template for output |
| xsl:text | Writes text to the output stream |
| xsl:transform | Defines the root element of the stylesheet |
| xsl:value-of | Creates a text node and inserts a value into the result tree |
| xsl:variable | Provides a way to declare a variable |
| xsl:when | Defines a condition to be tested and performs an action if the condition is true. This element is always a child element of `<xsl:choose>` |
| xsl:with-param | Provides a way to pass parameters to templates |

16

## XML to HTML Transformations

The best way to understand the nature of template rules is to write and test them. In this first exercise, you will take a simple XML document and apply an XSL transformation to produce an HTML result tree that can be rendered on a browser. The XML document follows the metaphor established earlier of a message and reminder system. After creating the XML document, you will create an XSLT document.

To link the two, use a stylesheet element on a processing instruction (PI) in the XML source document. This element has two attributes: type and href. The type attribute has two possible values: either text/xsl to denote a link to an XSL stylesheet, or text/css when a cascading stylesheet is being used. The `href` attribute provides a URI for the associated XSL document. The syntax of this PI is as follows:

```
<?xml-stylesheet type="text/xsl" href="myStyleSheet.xsl"?>
```

This PI is not used by all of the XSLT processors you might employ to perform transformations. A note about this PI can be found at `http://www.w3.org/TR/xml-stylesheet/` on the W3C Web site. You will sometimes see this element shown as `xml:stylesheet` (with a colon) rather than as `xml-stylesheet` (with a dash). The W3C recommends the use of the dash. When a parser that is capable of directly associating a stylesheet with an XML instance encounters this processing instruction, it makes the appropriate association. This association works in Microsoft Internet Explorer and Netscape 6.0. The W3C has supported the concept of stylesheet linking to promote use by the next release from major browser vendors.

Listing 16.1 shows the complete XML document. Create this document with a text editor and save it as `mesasge01.xml`.

**LISTING 16.1**    An XML Source Document—message01.xml

```
1: <?xml version="1.0"?>
2: <!-- listing 16.1 - message01.xml -->
3:
4: <?xml-stylesheet type="text/xsl" href="msg01.xsl"?>
5:
6: <note>
7:     <head>My Messages</head>
8:
9: </note>
```

**ANALYSIS**   The lining PI is on line 4. It associates an XSL stylesheet at `msg01.xsl`. The `note` root element (lines 6–9) contains a child `head` element (line 7) with text content.

The transformation in this first exercise will merely place the content of the `head` element (`My Messages`) into the `BODY` section of resulting HTML page. The root element of an XSL document is the `xsl:stylesheet` element, in which the `xsl` prefix binds the XSL elements to the namespace `http://www.w3.org/1999/XSL/Transform`, or another namespace depending on the intended processor. The `xsl:stylesheet` element contains the namespace attribute and a `version` attribute. XSLT comes in only one version so far: `version="1.0"`. The entire `xsl:stylesheet` element will look like this:

```
<xsl:stylesheet version = "1.0"
        xmlns:xsl = "http://www.w3.org/1999/XSL/Transform">
```

In this first exercise, you will need only one template rule. You will write a template rule that matches the note element and processes its content. The content of the note element is the head element. You will use the xsl:value-of element to choose (select) the content of the head element and place it directly on the output tree. You will need to include the standard HTML markup tags required to create an HTML page. The complete template rule should look like this:

```
<xsl:template match = "note">
        <HTML>
                <BODY><xsl:value-of select="head"/></BODY>
        </HTML>
</xsl:template>
```

**ANALYSIS** This rule is executed if the processor finds a match for the note element, which it does in this case. It then writes the tags <HTML> and <BODY> to the result tree. At this point, the processor encounters a xsl:value-of attribute. As noted earlier, this outputs the selected content directly to the result tree. The template then properly terminates the BODY and HTML tags. Listing 16.2 shows the complete XSL document, saved as msg01.xsl.

**LISTING 16.2**    XSL Transformation Document—msg01.xsl

```
 1: <?xml version="1.0"?>
 2: <!-- listing 16.2 - msg01.xsl -->
 3:
 4: <xsl:stylesheet version = "1.0"
 5:         xmlns:xsl = "http://www.w3.org/1999/XSL/Transform">
 6:
 7:     <xsl:template match = "note">
 8:             <HTML>
 9:                     <BODY><xsl:value-of select="head"/></BODY>
10:             </HTML>
11:     </xsl:template>
12:
13: </xsl:stylesheet>
```

**ANALYSIS** The root element (xsl:stylesheet) begins on line 4, with a version and xmlns attribute.

When you have both documents created and saved appropriately, process them using the XT XSLT processor to create an output tree as msg01.html. If you are using Windows, the command line instruction will be something like this:

```
xt message01.xml msg01.xsl msg01.html
```

If you are using another version of XT, your command line instruction will be similar to
this:

```
java -Dcom.jclark.xsl.sax.parser=your-sax-driver
com.jclark.xsl.sax.Driver message01.xml msg01.xsl msg01.html
```

If you received no errors, you should have produced the `msg01.html` file that will render
in a browser and look something like Figure 16.2. Because you have produced HTML, it
will render in almost any browser that supports HTML. You will see the results depicted
in several browsers today to illustrate this point.

Don't forget that XSLT is capable of producing a variety of text output formats. HTML
is only one of the possibilities. HTML is useful if you are producing output for the Web
that might be viewed by those using different browsers. However, you could also create
other XML dialects or text files using XSLT, as noted earlier. This could be beneficial if
you wanted to create, for instance, an XML document in the Wireless Markup Language
(WML) for rendering on Web-enabled wireless devices, such as cellular phones or personal digital assistants.

**FIGURE 16.2**

*The result of an XSL
transformation ren-
dered in Netscape 6.*

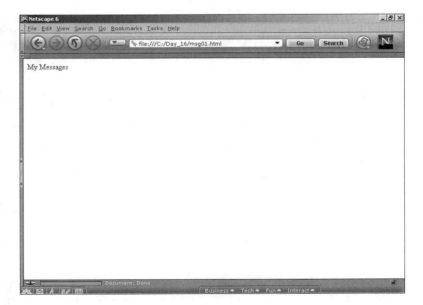

## XSLT Iterative Processing

Because the order of rules is insignificant, it is easy for XSLT to reuse a template rule.
All that is required for a rule to be processed is a successful match. If your XML document instance has repeated elements, a rule set can take care of processing all of them by

being applied multiple times. In the next exercise, you will have a chance to see the result of this iterative process.

Start by making the XML source document larger. You will need some data to use for the remaining exercises. The document should have a note root element containing several msg elements. Each msg element will contain a source, from, and message element with text content. The text content can be anything you want it to be, but ensure that your elements match the ones noted here so that the transformations work properly. Listing 16.3 shows a sample XML source document. Create one like it and save it as message02.xml.

**LISTING 16.3**   A More Complex XML Source Document—message02.xml

```
 1: <?xml version="1.0"?>
 2: <!-- listing 16.3 - message02.xml -->
 3:
 4: <?xml-stylesheet type="text/xsl" href="msg02.xsl"?>
 5:
 6: <note>
 7:     <msg>
 8:         <source>phone</source>
 9:         <from>Kathy Shepherd</from>
10:         <message>Remember to buy milk on the way home from work</message>
11:     </msg>
12:
13:     <msg>
14:         <source>e-mail</source>
15:         <from>Greg Shepherd</from>
16:         <message>I need some help with my homework</message>
17:     </msg>
18:
19:     <msg>
20:         <source>e-mail</source>
21:         <from>Kristen Shepherd</from>
22:         <message>Please play Scrabble with me tonight</message>
23:     </msg>
24:
25:     <msg>
26:         <source>pager</source>
27:         <from>Kathy Shepherd</from>
28:         <message>Buy a bottle of wine to take to the party tonight</message>
29:     </msg>
30:
31:     <msg>
32:         <source>phone</source>
33:         <from>Kristen Shepherd</from>
34:         <message>Can you drive me to my friend's house?</message>
35:     </msg>
36:
```

**LISTING 16.3**    continued

```
37:     <msg>
38:       <source>e-mail</source>
39:       <from>Greg Shepherd</from>
40:       <message>Meet me at the library</message>
41:     </msg>
42:
43:     <msg>
44:       <source>e-mail</source>
45:       <from>Kathy Shepherd</from>
46:       <message>Bob returned your phone call</message>
47:     </msg>
48:
49:     <msg>
50:       <source>pager</source>
51:       <from>Kathy Shepherd</from>
52:       <message>Pick up your shirts from the Dry Cleaners</message>
53:     </msg>
54:
55: </note>
```

**ANALYSIS** The XSL processing instruction on line 4 designates an XSL stylesheet at msg02.xsl. The root element, note, starts on line 6 and contains several msg elements. Each msg element contains a source, from, and message element with character data content.

In this exercise, you will create two match templates. One will match on the note element and produce the standard HTML tags to wrap around the content of the note element. You will need to use the xsl:template element with the match attribute set to note. Then you can place the standard HTML tags, such as HTML, HEAD, and BODY. Add a TITLE tag and an H1 tag with My Messages as content. The first template will look like this:

```
<xsl:template match="note">
  <HTML>
    <HEAD>
      <TITLE>Messages</TITLE>
    </HEAD>
    <BODY>
      <H1>My Messages</H1>
          <xsl:apply-templates/>
    </BODY>
  </HTML>
</xsl:template>
```

**ANALYSIS** When this rule executes, it will place <HTML>, <HEAD>, <TITLE>Messages</TITLE>, </HEAD>, <BODY>, and <H1>My Messages</H1> directly on the result tree. The result tree in this case is an HTML page you are creating. The next thing that happens is that the xsl:apply templates element is encountered. The xsl:apply-templates element exposes the content of the matched element, note to all other rules in the XSLT document. Because this is the root element, its content is element only. In particular, the msg elements are contained by the note element. Because the msg element has a match, the processor will exit this template and start processing the matched template. When it has finished, it will return here to complete the remaining steps, which are to place the terminating BODY and HTML elements on the result tree.

The second template will match on the msg element. This is the template that was jumped to by the processor when it encountered the xsl:apply-templates element in the first template. The rule in this template will create some HTML markup and permit the content of the msg element to pass to the result tree. You will refine this in later exercises. The rule will look like this:

```
<xsl:template match="msg">
    <P>Here is a message:<BR/>
      <xsl:apply-templates/>
    </P><BR/>
</xsl:template>
```

The xsl:apply-templates element in the second rule exposes the content of the msg element; because the child elements have no matching rules, the xsl:apply-templates element passes the content directly to the output tree. In some ways this is problematic.

The complete XSLT document is shown as Listing 16.4. Create this document and save it as msg02.xsl.

**LISTING 16.4**    Iterative Processing in XSLT—msg02.xml

```
 1: <?xml version="1.0"?>
 2: <!-- listing 16.4 - msg02.xsl -->
 3:
 4: <xsl:stylesheet version="1.0"
 5:     xmlns:xsl="http://www.w3.org/1999/XSL/Transform">
 6:
 7:     <xsl:template match="note">
 8:         <HTML>
 9:           <HEAD>
10:             <TITLE>Messages</TITLE>
11:           </HEAD>
12:           <BODY>
13:             <H1>My Messages</H1>
14:                 <xsl:apply-templates/>
15:           </BODY>
16:         </HTML>
17:     </xsl:template>
18:
19:     <xsl:template match="msg">
20:             <P>Here is a message:<BR/>
```

LISTING **16.4**    continued

```
21:              <xsl:apply-templates/>
22:            </P><BR/>
23:         </xsl:template>
24: </xsl:stylesheet>
```

**ANALYSIS**  The first template rule (lines 7–17) matches on the note element (line 7). A number of standard HTML tags are placed on the output tree (lines 8–13), then the xsl:apply-templates element exposes the content of the note element to all other rules in the document. The content of note is msg; therefore, the second template matches it. The second template now has control, and parsing includes the placement of the HTML tags on line 20. The xsl:apply-templates element exposes the content of the msg element to all other rules in the document. No other rules apply. The content of the child elements of the msg element is passed to the output tree at the same time that the xsl:apply-templates element triggers. When all of the msg elements have been processed, control returns to line 15 where the HTML tags are terminated.

After you have created this code example, use the XT processor to generate msg02.html and view it in a browser. As noted previously, because you are generating ordinary HTML, it can be processed by almost any browser. In fact, one of the reasons XSLT is used frequently to transform documents from XML into HTML is to create output that is independent of any single browser, platform, or operating system. Figure 16.3, for instance, shows the expected result of processing to generate msg02.html, as seen in a W3C Amaya browser. Amaya is a browser and editor provided by the W3C for use as a general-purpose Web tool (http://www.w3.org/Amaya/).

Some interesting logic is at work in the code represented by Listing 16.4, which might make XSLT processing seem confusing. The second rule passed the content of the msg element's child elements, even though you didn't expressly instruct it to do so. This approach works fine, but another, perhaps more intuitive, way exists to manage the passage of content directly to the output tree. That approach is to match for it and processes it explicitly.

Because XSLT allows you to use XPath expressions as the values of certain attributes, you can improve your control over the selection of nodes using the logic you learned on Day 9. For instance, you could select text nodes using the XPath expression text() or the *self* node with a period (.). These expressions would replace the explicit element names used previously as the values of match or select attributes.

In the current exercise, you could, and perhaps should, create a template that matches on all XPath text() nodes and pass the resultant text to the HTML page with the `xsl:value-of` element discussed earlier. By explicitly processing the text in this way, you are certain that the results will be as required, and you can add other formatting to the output as needed. If you were to create this rule, it could be as simple as this:

```
<xsl:template match="text()">
        <xsl:value-of select="."/>
</xsl:template>
```

**FIGURE 16.3**

*Result of iterative XSLT processing rendered by an Amaya browser.*

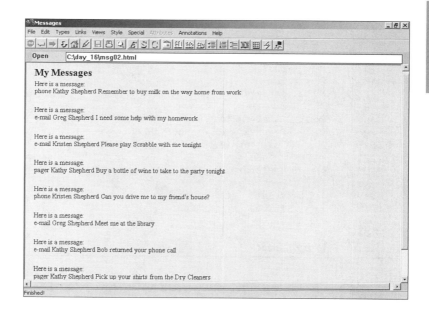

Add this template rule to your XSL document and save the result as `msg03.xsl`. To ensure that everything worked, transform the `message02.xml` document with XT using the `msg03.xsl` document to create `msg03.html` as output and browse the resulting HTML file. In your `message02.xml` document, change the `href` attribute (line 4, Listing 16.3) in the `xml-stylesheet` processing instruction to associate the `msg03.xsl` file. The revised PI will look like this:

```
<?xml-stylesheet type="text/xsl" href="msg03.xsl"?>
```

Listing 16.5 shows the complete `msg03.xsl` document.

**LISTING 16.5**    A Match on Text Nodes Is Added—`msg03.xsl`

```
1: <?xml version="1.0"?>
2: <!-- listing 16.5 - msg03.xsl -->
3:
4: <xsl:stylesheet version="1.0"
```

**LISTING 16.5** continued

```
 5:          xmlns:xsl="http://www.w3.org/1999/XSL/Transform">
 6:
 7:      <xsl:template match="note">
 8:         <HTML>
 9:           <HEAD>
10:             <TITLE>Messages</TITLE>
11:           </HEAD>
12:           <BODY>
13:             <H1>My Messages</H1>
14:                 <xsl:apply-templates/>
15:           </BODY>
16:         </HTML>
17:      </xsl:template>
18:
19:      <xsl:template match="msg">
20:             <P>Here is a message:<BR/>
21:               <xsl:apply-templates/>
22:             </P><BR/>
23:      </xsl:template>
24:
25:      <xsl:template match="text()">
26:             <xsl:value-of select="."/>
27:      </xsl:template>
28:
29: </xsl:stylesheet>
```

**ANALYSIS** A template that matches on text nodes (match="text()") is added to this listing on lines 25–27. The XPath expression text() returns child text nodes of the context node. The xsl:value-of with a select="." XPath expression instructs the processor to pass all text associated with the current node to the output tree (line 26). Recall from Day 9 that the period (.) refers to the current node of the XML tree.

## HTML Table Creation with XSLT

In the previous example, you transformed XML into HTML, but the result was not entirely pleasing. The text content of the source, from, and message elements ran together as a single string of characters. In this exercise, you will create template rules that match on those elements and place the content of each in cells on an HTML table. This is a useful process that can be employed effectively, even with large XML source documents to present data on an HTML page.

The first template will match on the root node. This time, instead of specifying the root element, use the XPath expression for the root node, which as you might recall from Day 9, is a forward slash (/). Whether you explicitly identify the root or use the XPath short-form version (/) is entirely up to you. Both work the same way and produce identical results. The alternative is shown here merely to familiarize you with the options. Although you will see both approaches in use, the short-form version is beginning to gain in popularity. In the first template, add HTML tags to create a table, with the border attribute set to 1 and width attribute set to 100%. The first template should look like this:

```
<xsl:template match="/">
  <HTML>
    <HEAD>
       <TITLE>Messages</TITLE>
    </HEAD>
    <BODY>
       <H1>My Messages</H1>
       <TABLE BORDER="1" WIDTH="100%">
          <xsl:apply-templates/>
       </TABLE>
    </BODY>
  </HTML>
</xsl:template>
```

The only new elements are the TABLE tags and the selection of the root node using a forward slash. Next, you will create a template for the table rows that will correspond to the msg element. It will look like this:

```
<xsl:template match="msg">
   <TR>
      <xsl:apply-templates/>
   </TR>
</xsl:template>
```

The next rule will effectively populate the table cells with the content of source, from, and message. You might be wondering why you only need one template rule to handle the content for three elements. Thanks to the integration of XPath expressions in XSLT, you can use the pipe (|) as a Boolean "or" between the names of elements to which you want to apply the same template. The final rule will look like this:

```
<xsl:template match="source | from | message">
   <TD>
      <xsl:apply-templates/>
   </TD>
</xsl:template>
```

Putting these together results in Listing 16.6.

**LISTING 16.6**    Creating Tables with XSLT—msg04.xsl

```
1: <?xml version="1.0"?>
2: <!--listing 16.6 - msg04.xsl -->
3:
4: <xsl:stylesheet version="1.0"
5:     xmlns:xsl="http://www.w3.org/1999/XSL/Transform">
```

16

---

**LISTING 16.6** continued

```
 6:
 7:    <xsl:template match="/">
 8:       <HTML>
 9:          <HEAD>
10:             <TITLE>Messages</TITLE>
11:          </HEAD>
12:          <BODY>
13:             <H1>My Messages</H1>
14:             <TABLE BORDER="1" WIDTH="100%">
15:                <xsl:apply-templates/>
16:             </TABLE>
17:          </BODY>
18:       </HTML>
19:    </xsl:template>
20:
21:    <xsl:template match="msg">
22:       <TR>
23:          <xsl:apply-templates/>
24:       </TR>
25:    </xsl:template>
26:
27:    <xsl:template match="source | from | message">
28:       <TD>
29:          <xsl:apply-templates/>
30:       </TD>
31:    </xsl:template>
32:
33: </xsl:stylesheet>
```

---

**ANALYSIS** Line 7 matches on the root node of the XML document to apply the first template to the entire XML instance. The TABLE tags on lines 14 and 16 wrap the rest of the result tree. The template on lines 21–25 establish the table rows, selecting the msg container elements. Line 27 shows how to use a single rule to match on three different elements.

**Tip**

Some of the examples today use XT, whereas others use Architag's XRay XML editor. You can follow along and use the tools depicted, or you can select your own. For instance, XRay works only on Windows systems, but Unix users have options for XSLT, including XT, Apache Xalan, and others. Whichever XSLT engine you choose, the code for the examples shown today will port directly without major modification. Nonetheless, check the documentation accompanying the engine you select to determine any runtime options and version-specific idiosyncrasies.

If you want to follow along with the example, use the XRay XML editor to process this example, using the following procedure:

1. After you have both documents saved, launch XRay and open the `message02.xml` document. It will appear in a window in the application.

2. Open the `msg04.xsl` document; it will open in a new window.

3. With both documents open, select `New XSLT Transform` from the File menu in XRay. A third window will appear with a large blank field in the body of the screen and two single line entry fields near the top of the window. The top single line field is titled XML Document.

4. Pull down the selections for the XML Document field by clicking on the arrow at the extreme right of the field. Select `message02.xml` as the `XML Document`.

5. Following the same procedure, fill the XSL Stylesheet field by pulling down and selecting the `msg04.xsl` document. After you fill the second field, the XSLT processor will fill the large text field on this window with the results of the transformation.

6. Select `New HTML View` from the File menu and pull down the field to select Transform 1. Note, however, that your number might be different, such as Transform 2 or Transform 3. Each time you execute a transformation, XRay increments the Transform number. It is just a reference number. You should now see a display that is similar to the view you would have in an IE 5 browser. Figure 16.4 shows the table result in XRay.

7. From the Window menu, select one of the Tile options. You should now be able to see all four screens at once. The screens are dynamically linked; if you make a change on one screen that affects another display, you will see the results immediately. This kind of dynamic editor offers an excellent environment for development.

## XSLT Sorting

XSLT offers rich sorting capability so that you can order selected nodes by ascending or descending order. In addition, you can order either by uppercase characters first or by lowercase characters first. You can also order by data types. In the next exercise, you will arrange the rows of the table on the basis of the `from` column in ascending alphabetical order. To do this, add one template to the existing XSLT program. This template will match on the root element `note`. Next, use the `xsl:apply-templates` elements, but add an attribute to select the `msg` element. This tells the XSLT engine that it should process only the selected child nodes. In this particular document, `msg` is the only child of `note`, but this handy attribute is being shown so that you know how to apply it in other instances. By not encoding a selection, the default action is to process all child nodes.

The `xsl:sort` element will be included as content of the `xsl:apply-templates` element. On the `xsl:sort` element, you will encode two attributes: `select` and `order`. The `select` attribute indicates which element will be sorted, and `order` determines whether it will be an ascending or descending sort. A complete list of all of the allowable attributes for each element is available from the W3C at `http://www.w3.org/TR/xslt`. The complete new rule is as follows:

```
<xsl:template match="note">
        <xsl:apply-templates select="msg">
                <xsl:sort select="from" order="ascending"/>
        </xsl:apply-templates>
</xsl:template>
```

Add this rule to your `msg04.xsl` document in XRay and save the modified file as `msg05.xsl`. The complete new document is shown as Listing 16.7.

**FIGURE 16.4**

*XSLT transformation resulting in a table and shown via the XRay XML editor.*

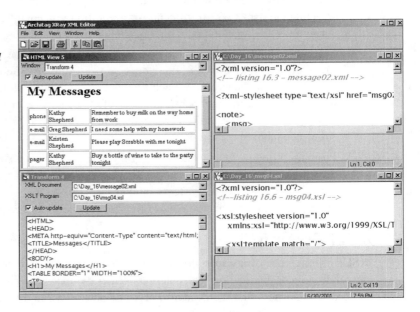

**LISTING 16.7**    Sorting Table Rows with XSLT—`msg05.xsl`

```
1: <?xml version="1.0"?>
2: <!--listing 16.7 - msg05.xsl -->
3:
4: <xsl:stylesheet version="1.0"
5:      xmlns:xsl="http://www.w3.org/1999/XSL/Transform">
6:
```

**LISTING 16.7** continued

```
 7:    <xsl:template match="/">
 8:       <HTML>
 9:         <HEAD>
10:            <TITLE>Messages</TITLE>
11:         </HEAD>
12:         <BODY>
13:            <H1>My Messages</H1>
14:            <TABLE BORDER="1" WIDTH="100%">
15:               <xsl:apply-templates/>
16:            </TABLE>
17:         </BODY>
18:       </HTML>
19:    </xsl:template>
20:
21:    <xsl:template match="msg">
22:       <TR>
23:            <xsl:apply-templates/>
24:       </TR>
25:    </xsl:template>
26:
27:    <xsl:template match="note">
28:            <xsl:apply-templates select="msg">
29:                <xsl:sort select="from" order="ascending"/>
30:            </xsl:apply-templates>
31:    </xsl:template>
32:
33:    <xsl:template match="source | from | message">
34:       <TD>
35:            <xsl:apply-templates/>
36:       </TD>
37:    </xsl:template>
38: </xsl:stylesheet>
```

**ANALYSIS** The new template rule is shown on lines 27–31. The rule matches the root element note (line 27). The template is applied only to the msg child of the matched node. The child msg elements will be handled in ascending alphabetical order as the XSLT process continues. The rest of this example remains the same.

Did you notice that as you entered characters in XRay, your display changed in all four windows? The parser attempts to validate the XML instance documents on every keystroke. When you have finished, your table will be re-ordered, as shown in Figure 16.5.

FIGURE 16.5

*Table sorted in ascending order on the* from *column.*

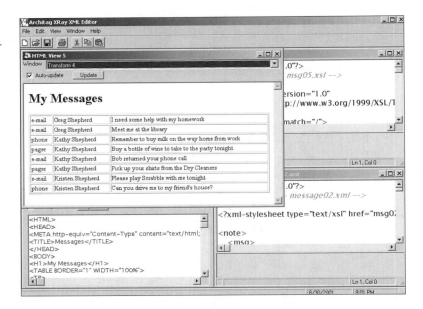

## Style Attribute Additions with XSLT

In the next example, you'll add color, size, and face attributes to an HTML FONT tag to style messages in one column of the table. This example serves to show how you can use the xsl:attribute-set element in XSLT. This special element should be an immediate child of the root element and can contain xsl:attribute elements used to define attributes. The xsl:attribute approach offers the developer rich opportunities for developing extensive relationships between elements and attributes in the result tree.

Each xsl:attribute element has a required name attribute that serves to name the attribute being created. For instance, suppose you want the message text in your table to be colored red. You could create an attribute for the color and attach it where needed in the transformation. The xsl:attribute-set element in your example would look like this:

```
<xsl:attribute-set name="message-attributes">
  <xsl:attribute name="size">+1</xsl:attribute>
  <xsl:attribute name="color">blue</xsl:attribute>
  <xsl:attribute name="face">Verdana</xsl:attribute>
</xsl:attribute-set>
```

The name="message-attributes" attribute on the xsl:attribute-set element is a reference that will be called in the next step. The three xsl:attribute elements create three attributes with associated values. These will be passed on to an element on the result tree during the transformation process. In this case, the attributes are HTML FONT attributes and should be associated with a FONT tag in the transformation. A new template rule will be generated to associate the attributes with the FONT element. Because you are styling only the message elements in the original XML, the match will be on the message element. Here is what the new template rule will look like:

```
<xsl:template match="message">
    <TD>
        <FONT xsl:use-attribute-sets="message-attributes">
            <xsl:apply-templates/>
        </FONT>
    </TD>
</xsl:template>
```

As you see, the `<FONT xsl:use-attribute-sets="message-attributes">` tag establishes the encoding of the attributes on the result tree FONT tag. You will need to do one more task for this to work properly: remove the message element from the match attribute on the previous template. The final code for this example is presented as Listing 16.8.

**LISTING 16.8**    Applying Attribute Styles with XSLT—`msg06.xsl`

```
 1: <?xml version="1.0"?>
 2: <!--listing 16.8 - msg06.xsl -->
 3:
 4: <xsl:stylesheet version="1.0"
 5:     xmlns:xsl="http://www.w3.org/1999/XSL/Transform">
 6:
 7:    <xsl:template match="/">
 8:        <HTML>
 9:          <HEAD>
10:            <TITLE>Messages</TITLE>
11:          </HEAD>
12:          <BODY>
13:            <H1>My Messages</H1>
14:            <TABLE BORDER="1" WIDTH="100%">
15:                <xsl:apply-templates/>
16:            </TABLE>
17:          </BODY>
18:        </HTML>
19:    </xsl:template>
20:
21:    <xsl:attribute-set name="message-attributes">
22:      <xsl:attribute name="size">+1</xsl:attribute>
23:      <xsl:attribute name="color">blue</xsl:attribute>
24:      <xsl:attribute name="face">Verdana</xsl:attribute>
25:    </xsl:attribute-set>
```

16

**LISTING 16.8**  continued

```
26:
27:      <xsl:template match="message">
28:         <TD>
29:            <FONT xsl:use-attribute-sets="message-attributes">
30:               <xsl:apply-templates/>
31:            </FONT>
32:         </TD>
33:      </xsl:template>
34:
35:      <xsl:template match="msg">
36:         <TR>
37:            <xsl:apply-templates/>
38:         </TR>
39:      </xsl:template>
40:
41:      <xsl:template match="note">
42:            <xsl:apply-templates select="msg">
43:               <xsl:sort select="from" order="ascending"/>
44:            </xsl:apply-templates>
45:      </xsl:template>
46:
47:      <xsl:template match="source | from ">
48:         <TD>
49:            <xsl:apply-templates/>
50:         </TD>
51:      </xsl:template>
52: </xsl:stylesheet>
```

**ANALYSIS**  Lines 21–25 are the attribute set (xsl:attribute-set) with the reference name message-attributes. Lines 22, 23, and 24 establish attributes for size, color, and face respectively. The new template is on lines 27–33 with a match on the message element in the XML source document. The referential name message-attributes is called by the xsl:use-attribute-sets attribute on the FONT tag. The message element has been removed from the xsl:template element on line 47. Figure 16.6 depicts the post-transformation result rendered on the IE browser.

**FIGURE 16.6**

*Styling selective content with XSLT.*

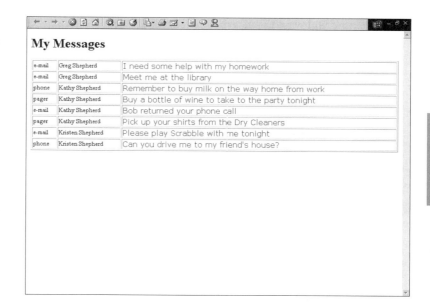

## Advanced XSLT Programming

As is the case with most programming languages, XSLT provides elements that can be used for conditional testing, looping on a given set of nodes, and switches among alternative branches of logic. Although these are beyond the scope of today's exercises, several of the most useful elements used to provide these constructs are discussed in this reference section. All of these elements are listed in Table 16.1 and further details on their use can be found at http://www.w3.org/TR/xslt.html.

### xsl:for-each

The xsl:for-each element permits a form of simple looping in XSLT for a given node set. This instruction is useful for processing repetitive nodes. The syntax of the xsl:for-each element is as follows:

```
<xsl:for-each select="node">
    template body
</xsl:for-each>
```

The value of the select attribute can be any XPath expression. You could, for instance, select each of the msg elements in your message02.xml document (Listing 16.3) with an xsl:for-each element that looked like this:

```
<xsl:for-each select="msg">
```

Suppose you want to place the contents of the source, from, and message elements from
each msg parent element into cells of an HTML table. You could create a template with
xsl:for-each, such as this:

```
<xsl:for-each select="msg">
  <TR>
      <TD><xsl:value-of select="source"/></TD>
      <TD><xsl:value-of select="from"/></TD>
      <TD><xsl:value-of select="message"/></TD>
  </TR>
</xsl:for-each>
```

The xsl:for-each element provides a means to functionally map the input nodes
to desired output nodes. For instance, on the basis of each msg element in the
message02.xml document, the code snippet will create a table row containing cells
populated with content from the source, from, and message elements.

### xsl:if

The xsl:if element in XSLT allows an instruction to be executed if a conditional test
returns a Boolean true value. Unlike the if statement in most languages, the xsl:if
statement does not include a corresponding else statement. When the condition tested
returns a true value, the instruction is executed. The syntax of the xsl:if element is as
follows:

```
<xsl:if test=expression>
    template body
</xsl:if>
```

For instance, if you want to select only those msg elements from the message02.xml document that had source child elements with the content e-mail, you could write this:

```
<xsl:for-each select="msg" >
    <xsl:if test="source='e-mail'">
        <xsl:value-of select="message"/><br/>
    </xsl:if>
</xsl:for-each>
```

If you included this snippet in a template that matched the note element in your document, it would return the content of the message elements, for which source contained
e-mail, or this:

```
I need some help with my homework
Please play Scrabble with me tonight
Meet me at the library
Bob returned your phone call
```

## xsl:choose, xsl:when, xsl:otherwise

The xsl:choose element in XSLT defines a conditional template with choices among alternatives. The xsl:choose element provides functionality similar to switch, if-then-else, or select statements in other languages. The xsl:choose element has no attributes. It is a container element that has one or more xsl:when child elements and might have an xsl:otherwise child element. There can be any number of xsl:when elements, but at least one must be contained by every xsl:choose element. The xsl:otherwise element is optional, but it must be the last element contained by the xsl:choose element if it is present.

```
<xsl:choose>

    <xsl:when test=expression>
        template body
    </xsl:when>

    <xsl:otherwise>
        template body
    </xsl:otherwise>

</xsl:choose>
```

The xsl:when element allows an instruction to be executed if a conditional test returns a Boolean true value, similar in fashion to the operation and criteria of the xsl:if element. The test attribute can take any XPath expression as a value. Because the xsl:otherwise is the choice made if the xsl:when elements are not satisfied, it does not require a Boolean test.

For example, if you want to treat the content of your message elements differently depending on the content of the source element, you can write an xsl:choose element to test for each of the possible values of the source element. Perhaps you need to provide a label that indicates the source of each message. For msg elements that have a source child element containing e-mail, you might provide the label E-Mail Message: and so on. The code for the xsl:choose element would look something like the following snippet:

```
<xsl:choose>

    <xsl:when test="source='e-mail'">
        <P>E-Mail Message:
            <xsl:value-of select="message"/><br/>
        </P>
    </xsl:when>

    <xsl:when test="source='phone'">
        <P>Phone Message:
```

```
            <xsl:value-of select="message"/><br/>
        </P>
    </xsl:when>

    <xsl:otherwise>
        <P>Pager Message:
            <xsl:value-of select="message"/><br/>
        </P>

    </xsl:otherwise>

</xsl:choose>
```

In the case of the `message02.xml` document, you could use XPath expressions to test for two of the three values of the `source` element. The third value, all that is left over after testing for the other two, could be selected using the `xsl:otherwise` element. If you included this snippet in a template that selected each `msg` child element of the `note` element in your document, it would return labeled messages, such as this:

```
Phone Message: Remember to buy milk on the way home from work
E-Mail Message: I need some help with my homework
E-Mail Message: Please play Scrabble with me tonight
Pager Message: Buy a bottle of wine to take to the party tonight
Phone Message: Can you drive me to my friend's house?
E-Mail Message: Meet me at the library
E-Mail Message: Bob returned your phone call
Pager Message: Pick up your shirts from the Dry Cleaners
```

Because an XSL stylesheet is an XML instance that follows the general syntax rules of XML, you might expect to be able to nest other elements as needed. For instance, if you want to sort the output on the basis of the different sources, you might add an `xsl:sort` element to the XSLT document that looks something like this:

```
<xsl:sort select="source" order="ascending"/>
```

However, `xsl:choose` does not permit child elements other than `xsl:when` and `xsl:otherwise`; therefore, you will need to place the sort outside of the `xsl:choose` collection.

# Summary

Today, you used the XSL Transformation Language (XSLT) to transform XML into HTML. You saw that XSLT could operate independently of the rest of XSL. To process XSLT requires an XSLT processor. You used XT, a freely available Java processor, with a command line interface and also a processor built into the XRay XML Editor. XSLT uses the concept of template matching to enforce rule sets. XSLT relies on XPath to locate nodes in a source tree for matching. XSLT is a powerful technology that is best characterized as an event-driven, rules-based programming language.

# Q&A

**Q  What is the relationship between XPath and XSLT?**

**A**  XPath is used in XSLT match templates to locate elements to be processed by a template rule set. XPath was originally a component technology. It was later separated from XSLT so that it could be used readily with other XML technologies.

**Q  What are the hardware and operating system limitations of XSLT?**

**A**  XSLT operates on many systems. All that XSLT requires is a SAX-based parser and libraries of common procedure calls. Versions of XSLT engines have been written in most major languages for almost all popular computer platforms.

**Q  The Apache Project has an XSLT engine called Xalan that came with the Formatting-Object Processor downloaded for yesterday's exercises. How can Xalan be used to transform XML into HTML?**

**A**  Xalan is an XSLT processor from the Apache XML Project group for transforming XML documents into HTML, text, or other XML document types. You can, for instance, use Xalan in place of XT. You will first need to decide which version of the Xalan engine you will use. At the time of this writing, the FOP distribution, for instance, included Xalan 1.2.2 and Xalan 2.1.0, both written in Java. You can always download new versions of Xalan or other Apache project software from `http://xml.apache.org/`. Refer to the online documentation for the version you choose to use. As with most Java applications, you will need to establish appropriate environment variables and set the `classpath` to include the application and any required helpers. In this case, you will need to include the `Xerces.jar` files for the Xerces parser, or substitute the parser of your choice. You can call Xalan from the command line with an instruction something like this:

```
java org.apache.xalan.xslt.Process -IN myfile.xml -XSL myfile.xsl
        -OUT myfile.out
```

However, you should check the documentation for the syntax that is appropriate for the version you are using because the command structure might be different for the version you download. At the time of this writing, twenty-two flags and arguments could be set at the command line to control traces, linefeeds, HTML formatting, and so on. Refer to the documentation for more details.

16

# Exercise

The exercise is provided so that you can test your knowledge of what you learned today. The answer is in Appendix A.

XSLT has an element, xsl:number, that automatically numbers matched elements. Write XSLT code that uses xsl:number to index the title of the CDs in your CD.xml document. If you get stuck, check the W3C site for examples of xsl:number.

# DAY 17

# Binding XML Data to HTML Elements

Using data binding techniques, you can incorporate XML data on HTML pages for flexible rendering of data. You can use a variety of approaches to accomplish this via the creation of data islands with standard HTML elements bound to XML elements. Today, you will learn

- How to create simple data islands
- How to bind HTML elements to specific XML elements
- How to control the flow of bound data with JavaScript
- How to invoke an XML Data Source Object as a Java applet to pass XML data to an HTML page

## Creating Simple Data Binding Instances

Data binding comes in many types. Some involve complex mapping of a data model onto a data-specific object model internal to a computer program. In this manner, for instance, it is possible to bind XML data on objects created in Java or other languages. Some forms of data binding can effectively convert generalized structures into specific structures for purposes of secondary processing by applications that require highly structured data. In its simplest form, as it pertains to XML, data binding involves the extraction of character data from elements under selective program control to associate those data with different elements in other markup languages. Today, you will employ simple data binding to create accessible links between data stored in XML and rendering tags native to HTML. In this way, you will be exploiting the intelligent data storage of XML and the efficient display capabilities of HTML.

Using simple data binding, you can process XML documents to display XML data directly on a conventional HTML page. Even though in some sense this is another form of data transformation, you will find simple data binding to be more limiting than the very rich XSLT language you learned on Day 16. You will also find that many of the techniques discussed today will only work in Microsoft Internet Explorer browsers version 4 and higher. Nonetheless, the creation of simple data islands, particularly in conjunction with client-side scripting, enables you to quickly and efficiently create specialized tools for evaluation of XML data, troubleshooting, or fast perusal of symmetric XML datasets. Mastering these techniques can save you time and effort when it comes to perfecting or maintaining complex XML data collections.

Today, you will create a XML dataset that will serve as a data source. You will link the dataset to an HTML page and then bind the HTML elements to fields in the dataset, such as elements in the XML document. You will also explore the use of Data Source Object (DSO) programming employing a number of different technologies, such as direct DSO loading and XMLDSO Java applets. Then you will combine data binding with scripting to control the flow of XML data on the HTML page. These approaches, as they are shown today, use Microsoft software techniques that are not available from other vendors. However, because the tools are free of charge and available on multiple platforms, they provide an excellent opportunity to explore data binding.

## XML Document Structure

To follow along with the simple data binding examples today, you can create or modify one of the message XML documents used on previous days. Use a document that is structured symmetrically to control the flow of data onto the HTML page. Symmetry in document structure is characteristic of a flat-file database, where you have records with predefined fields in a static order. Using the metaphor of the messaging system developed over the past few weeks, each unique msg will constitute a record. The note root element will contain any number of these records, such as child elements. Each msg element will contain source, from, and message child elements—such as the fields on the records—which, in turn, contain character data. Figure 17.1 depicts this structure as a document tree.

**FIGURE 17.01**

*Structure of the XML message source document.*

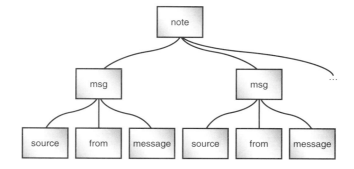

You can see that the pattern repeats in a predictable fashion and that the root contains any number of msg elements that all contain the same child element structure. Using this structure and ensuring that the element types in your document are labeled exactly like those in the diagram, create an XML instance document and save it as message01.xml. If you follow along with the examples provided, you will reuse this document several times. It will be very useful to have multiple records in your dataset; therefore, either create new ones, or copy and paste several so that you have at least six child msg elements, each with a source, from, and message child. Listing 17.1 provides an example of the XML dataset required. Yours might have different character data, but ensure that the element names are identical, including case.

**LISTING 17.1** A Hierarchical XML Dataset—message01.xml

```
 1: <?xml version="1.0"?>
 2: <!-- listing 17.1 - message01.xml -->
 3:
 4: <note>
 5:    <msg>
 6:       <source>phone</source>
 7:       <from>Kathy Shepherd</from>
 8:       <message>Remember to buy milk on the way home from work</message>
 9:    </msg>
10:
11:    <msg>
12:       <source>e-mail</source>
13:       <from>Greg Shepherd</from>
14:       <message>I need some help with my homework</message>
15:    </msg>
16:
17:    <msg>
18:       <source>e-mail</source>
19:       <from>Kristen Shepherd</from>
20:       <message>Please play Scrabble with me tonight</message>
```

**LISTING 17.1**    continued

```
21:        </msg>
22:
23:        <msg>
24:          <source>pager</source>
25:          <from>Kathy Shepherd</from>
26:          <message>Buy a bottle of wine to take to the party tonight</message>
27:        </msg>
28:
29:        <msg>
30:          <source>phone</source>
31:          <from>Kristen Shepherd</from>
32:          <message>Can you drive me to my friend's house?</message>
33:        </msg>
34:
35:        <msg>
36:          <source>e-mail</source>
37:          <from>Greg Shepherd</from>
38:          <message>Meet me at the library</message>
39:        </msg>
40:
41:        <msg>
42:          <source>e-mail</source>
43:          <from>Kathy Shepherd</from>
44:          <message>Bob returned your phone call</message>
45:        </msg>
46:
47:        <msg>
48:          <source>pager</source>
49:          <from>Kathy Shepherd</from>
50:          <message>Pick up your shirts from the Dry Cleaners</message>
51:        </msg>
52:
53: </note>
```

**ANALYSIS**  The note root element contains msg child elements with element-only content. Each msg element contains one each of a source, from, and message child element. The source, from, and message elements contain character data.

You can see that in the message01.xml document, the msg elements are like records or rows in a conventional database, and the source, from, and message child elements are like fields or columns on those records. In the next section, you will be able to link this document to an HTML page and then bind standard HTML elements to the fields in the dataset. Establishing the link is the next task you will do.

# Linking an XML Document to an HTML Page with a Data Island

Associating an XML document with an HTML page requires that a link be established. To do this, you will use a special HTML element called <XML>. This element, supported by Microsoft Internet Explorer 4.0 and above, is an HTML element, not an XML element. <XML> can take several attributes, but you will typically use two that are necessary for data binding. The source attribute (src) provides a valid URI to locate the XML data source being linked. An id attribute will provide you with a named reference to be used elsewhere on the HTML page so that you can incorporate the data from the XML document in programming. The syntax of the HTML <XML> element is as follows:

```
<XML src="[URI]" id="[name]"/>
```

Interestingly, some versions of the Microsoft Internet Explorer (IE) browser do not support this tag in the form shown. Early builds of IE that do not fully support HTML version 4.01, or XHTML 1.0 might not accept the short form version of this empty element. If you find that you are unable to make one of the examples in the exercises that follow work as it should and you are sure that you have used the code precisely as it is shown, it is possible that your browser version might need to be updated. As a compromise to upgrading, you should always be able to use the longer form of the HTML element:

```
<XML src="[URI]" id="[name]"></XML>
```

Note the closing tag, despite the fact that this is an empty element. Some versions of IE do not support the self-terminated HTML empty tag. This is true even of some of the early builds of version 5.0 of IE on some platforms. Microsoft recommends that you update to the latest free version of IE to ensure compatibility with evolving programming techniques like this. In addition, as with all software, many of the older builds have errors and security exposures that have been corrected in newer versions.

The use of the <XML> tag produces a link that is known as a data island. A *data island* is an XML document imbedded within an HTML page. The XML document might be imbedded in a virtual sense through the use of the <XML> tag with an src attribute that provides a URI to an external XML document, or it might be imbedded by including the XML document inline with the HTML page code. In the latter case, a less practical approach, the XML document will be wrapped in <XML> tags.

**Note**

Although an XML document can be imbedded directly inline with HTML code, this is not particularly practical and is contrary to the general philosophy of good XML programming, which aims to keep content and style separate. All of the code you write today will involve external XML data source documents.

Relying on an external link to the `message01.xml` document you created earlier today, the link might look something like this:

```
<XML id="myMsg" src="message01.xml"/>
```

The value of the `id` attribute (`"myMsg"`) provides a unique name, assigned by you, that can be referenced elsewhere in the HTML using the pound sign (#) HTML convention. In other words, a reference to this data island will be encoded as `#myMsg` on any element that requires that association.

If required, the `src` attribute can have a fully qualified URI as a value. Therefore, the data source can be located anywhere on the Internet, or, as in this example, locally on the same domain or host.

## Placing an XML Link in an HTML Page

Now that you know the syntax of an XML data island linking element, create an HTML page that includes the tag. For the purpose of the exercises today, it is assumed that you already know how to write HTML pages. You will need the typical HTML elements, such as `HTML`, `HEAD`, `BODY`, and so on, and you will place the new `<XML>` tag, with appropriate attributes, in the body section of your HTML page. Listing 17.2 shows one possible HTML page with the new data island included. Create a similar page and save it as `island01.html`.

**LISTING 17.2** An HTML Page Including an XML Data Island—`island01.html`

```
 1: <!DOCTYPE HTML PUBLIC "-//W3C//DTD HTML 4.01 Transitional//EN"
 2:  "http://www.w3.org/TR/html4/loose.dtd">
 3: <!-- listing 17.2 island01.html -->
 4:
 5: <HTML>
 6: <HEAD>
 7: <TITLE>XML Data Island</TITLE>
 8: </HEAD>
 9:
10: <BODY>
11: <XML id="myMsg" src="message01.xml"/>
12:
13: </BODY>
14: </HTML>
```

**ANALYSIS** Lines 1–2 provide the standard `DOCTYPE` declaration for an HTML version 4.01 document that adheres to the `Transitional` DTD for HTML. Line 11 is the element (`<XML id="myMsg" src="message01.xml"/>`) that links the `message01.xml` data source, known by the reference `myMsg`, to the HTML document.

After you have created `island01.html`, load it into IE and view the results. Why do you think that nothing much seems to happen at this stage?

You have created a data island that links the `message01.xml` document to the `island01,html` page, but you haven't yet bound the data from the XML document to elements in HTML that are capable of rendering. Consequently, nothing has been exposed to display. You will need to use binding HTML data elements to place the XML document data on an HTML page.

## Binding HTML Elements to XML Elements

To effect any form of rendering will require you to bind HTML elements to specific XML elements in the XML dataset. Some of the elements in HTML that have data binding capability include the following:

- A
- APPLET
- BUTTON
- DIV
- FRAME
- IMG
- INPUT
- LABEL
- MARQUEE
- SELECT
- SPAN
- TEXTAREA

Today, you will primarily use DIV and SPAN as containers for XML data that can be placed within other HTML elements to control the display of data on the browser. When you bind an HTML element to an XML element, the browser will display the character data content of the XML element. The syntax of the DIV or SPAN element to accomplish this binding is as follows:

```
<DIV datasrc="#[reference] datafld="[XML Element Type]"></DIV>
```

or

```
<SPAN datasrc="#[reference] datafld="[XML Element Type]"></SPAN>
```

17

The `datasrc` attribute provides the source of the data to be bound to the element. The `datafld` attribute identifies the component source field that will be bound, obtained from the `datasrc`. To bind an HTML SPAN element to the `from` element in the `message01.xml` document, you might encode the SPAN element as follows:

```
<SPAN datasrc="#myMsg" datafld="from"></SPAN>
```

This would bind the SPAN to the `from` element in the named (#myMsg) referenced Data Source Object (`message01.xml`).

Although DIV and SPAN are both container elements that can hold data, styles, or other HTML elements for use on an HTML page, they behave differently. The DIV element is a block element that forces the contents to be displayed discreetly from other elements by adding breaks before and after its contents. The SPAN element is an inline container element that is often used to add style to an existing element. SPAN does not produce line breaks before and after its contents, but rather integrates its contents inline with the elements around it. You will typically choose to use the SPAN element when you want to incorporate data from an XML document into existing HTML structures.

## Creating HTML Tables Containing XML Data

Suppose that you want to take the data from `message01.xml` and render it via a table on an HTML page. You could use a SPAN inside the Table Data (TD) cell elements of the table. You will need to do this because the TD element is not one of the binding HTML elements. Nonetheless, creating a table of bound elements using SPAN is one of the easiest ways to display XML data on an HTML page because the HTML TABLE element is capable of recursion during the dynamic presentation of data. In other words, you can create a full table of XML data on an HTML page, with a row for each record in the dataset, by writing only one row of HTML table code. The table will dynamically create enough rows to accommodate all of the data that is passed during processing of the linked data source. The syntax for the HTML table element will be as follows:

```
<TABLE datasrc="#[reference]">
  <TR>
    <TD><SPAN datafld="[element name]"></SPAN></TD>
    [... another <TD> for every additional field]
  </TR>
</TABLE>
```

If the SPAN element is contained within another HTML element, you can use the short form version for an empty element:

```
<TD><SPAN datafld="[element name]"/></TD>
```

However, due to variable support by different versions of the browser, you might want to stick with the longer version.

In the case of the `message01.xml` document, the TABLE element might look something like this:

```
<TABLE datasrc="#myMsg">
  <TR>
    <TD><SPAN datafld="source"></SPAN></TD>
    <TD><SPAN datafld="from"></SPAN></TD>
    <TD><SPAN datafld="message"></SPAN></TD>
  </TR>
</TABLE>
```

Add some typical table attributes to dress up your own table and include a header row to provide labels for the columns in your table. One possible approach to this is shown in Listing 17.3. Create a similar HTML document and save it as `island02.html`.

**LISTING 17.3**   HTML Table Cells Bound to an XML Data Source—`island02.html`

```
 1: <!DOCTYPE HTML PUBLIC "-//W3C//DTD HTML 4.01 Transitional//EN"
 2:  "http://www.w3.org/TR/html4/loose.dtd">
 3: <!-- listing 17.3 island02.html -->
 4:
 5: <HTML>
 6: <HEAD>
 7: <TITLE>XML Data Island</TITLE>
 8: </HEAD>
 9:
10: <BODY>
11: <XML id="myMsg" src="message01.xml"/>
12: <H1>My Messages</H1>
13:   <TABLE id="table" border="6" width="100%"
14:        datasrc="#myMsg" summary="messages">
15:      <THEAD style="background-color: aqua">
16:            <TH>Source</TH>
17:            <TH>From</TH>
18:            <TH>Message</TH>
19:      </THEAD>
20:      <TR valign="top" align="center">
21:            <TD><SPAN datafld="source"/></TD>
22:            <TD><SPAN datafld="from"/></TD>
23:            <TD><SPAN datafld="message"/></TD>
24:      </TR>
25:   </TABLE>
26: </BODY>
27: </HTML>
```

**17**

ANALYSIS    Line 11 establishes the data island with the HTML XML element. The id="myMsg" attribute provides a reference (myMsg) that is used on line 14 to indicate the data source for the table. The XML document that is being bound is indicated by the src attribute value. The table start tag (lines 13–14) contains the datasrc attribute, indicating the named reference (#myMsg) of the data island. The table start tag also contains other attributes used for identification—id and summary—or formatting—border and width— of the table output. A table head section is included (lines 15–19) to provide a header row that labels the table columns. The only TR is encoded on lines 20–24. Lines 21–23 bind to the XML source, from, and message elements by using SPAN elements.

When you load this document into the Microsoft Internet Explorer browser version 5.0 or higher, you can expect output like that depicted by Figure 17.2.

**FIGURE 17.2**

*XML data displayed as an HTML table.*

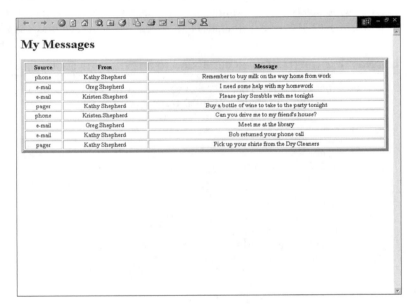

As you can see from this example, even though only one data row is encoded on the HTML page, the table continues to dynamically create rows until all of the XML data is expended. This provides a simple, efficient, and useful technique for loading XML data on an HTML page.

## Adding JavaScript Data Flow Controls

If you use these techniques to display large XML datasets, you might want to control the flow of data in page-at-a-time snapshots. To demonstrate this kind of control, set the datapagesize attribute on the TABLE element to a value of 3. You can use any value you want to establish the maximum number of data rows to display at one time. In the case of your island02.html page, encoding the new attribute will result in a table start tag that looks something like this:

```
<TABLE id="table" border="6" width="100%"
       datasrc="#myMsg" summary="messages"
       datapagesize="3">
```

JavaScript provides a means of navigating through multi-page documents on a Web page with methods on some objects. To navigate through the records in this case, you can call standard JavaScript paging methods, such as firstPage(), lastPage(), nextPage(), and previousPage() on the Data Source Object. You will simply append the paging methods to the value of the id attribute on the TABLE start tag to create fully qualified method calls. For instance, to display the first page of the #myMsg data source, you will use the firstPage() method:

```
table.firstPage()
```

The value of the id attribute on the TABLE element is table. Therefore, the fully qualified method to load the first page is table.firstPage(). Other JavaScript paging methods include previousPage(), nextPage(), and lastPage().

One of the easiest ways to invoke one of these method calls is to assign the method call to the onClick attribute of an HTML BUTTON element. For instance, you can use the following lines to create four buttons:

```
<BUTTON onClick="table.firstPage()">&lt;&lt;
</BUTTON>

<BUTTON onClick="table.previousPage()">&lt;
</BUTTON>

<BUTTON onClick="table.nextPage()">&gt;
</BUTTON>

<BUTTON onClick="table.lastPage()">&gt;&gt;
</BUTTON>
```

Modify your HTML page by adding the datapagesize attribute on the TABLE element and incorporating the BUTTON calls. Save your modified page as island03.html. Listing 17.4 shows the complete HTML page with the changes required.

**LISTING 17.4**   JavaScript Paging Controls Added to an HTML Table Containing Bound XML Data—island03.html

```
1: <!DOCTYPE HTML PUBLIC "-//W3C//DTD HTML 4.01 Transitional//EN"
2:  "http://www.w3.org/TR/html4/loose.dtd">
3: <!-- listing 17.4 island03.html -->
```

**17**

**LISTING 17.4**    continued

```
 4:
 5: <HTML>
 6: <HEAD>
 7: <TITLE>XML Data Island</TITLE>
 8: </HEAD>
 9:
10: <BODY>
11: <XML id="myMsg" src="message01.xml"/>
12: <H1>My Messages</H1>
13:    <TABLE id="table" border="6" width="100%"
14:          datasrc="#myMsg" summary="messages"
15:          datapagesize="3">
16:        <THEAD style="background-color: aqua">
17:               <TH>Source</TH>
18:               <TH>From</TH>
19:               <TH>Message</TH>
20:        </THEAD>
21:        <TR valign="top" align="center">
22:               <TD><SPAN datafld="source"/></TD>
23:               <TD><SPAN datafld="from"/></TD>
24:               <TD><SPAN datafld="message"/></TD>
25:        </TR>
26:    </TABLE>
27:    <BR/>
28:    <BUTTON onClick="table.firstPage()">&lt;&lt;
29:    </BUTTON>
30:
31:    <BUTTON onClick="table.previousPage()">&lt;
32:    </BUTTON>
33:
34:    <BUTTON onClick="table.nextPage()">&gt;
35:    </BUTTON>
36:
37:    <BUTTON onClick="table.lastPage()">&gt;&gt;
38:    </BUTTON>
39:
40: </BODY>
41: </HTML>
```

**ANALYSIS**    The start tag of the TABLE element (lines 13–15) contains a `datapagesize` attribute, set to 3 data rows. The buttons used to make the paging calls are on lines 28–38. The button created on lines 28–29 loads the first page of the data when it is activated by a user's click. The text on the button comprises two less than signs (<<), appropriately encoded as entities (&lt; and &gt;) to avoid any problems with parsing markup characters, to symbolically indicate a jump to the first record in the dataset.

The button created on lines 31–32 loads the previous page of the data when it is activated by a user's click. If the table is already displaying the first page of data, then a click on the previous page button is ignored. The button created on lines 34–35 loads the next page of the data when it is activated by a user's click. If the table is already displaying the last page of data, then a click on the next page button is ignored. The button created on lines 37–38 loads the last page of the data when it is activated by a user's click.

After you have created and saved your new HTML page, load it into the Internet Explorer browser. You should expect a result similar to that depicted by Figure 17.3.

**FIGURE 17.3**

*XML data in an HTML table with JavaScript paging controls.*

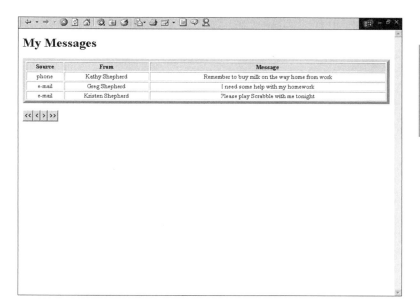

**17**

## Browsing Single Record Data

Suppose you would like to present the data from the XML dataset a record at a time. You could generate a single listing of the fields without binding to a table and then use JavaScript controls to move backward and forward through the data. The XML data comprises multiple records, as you discovered earlier today. Those records can be accessed individually using the Data Source Object (DSO) recordset member object. The DSO is part of a standard access technology that Microsoft calls the ActiveX Data Objects (ADO). ADOs exist for many forms of data including database, plain text, and XML, but you will use the DSO methods that belong to the XMLDSO (XML Data Source Object) technology.

Start by establishing the list of fields using a simple SPAN combination in place of the TABLE created in the last exercise. It could be as simple as this:

```
<BODY>
<XML id="myMsg" src="message01.xml"/>
<H1>My Messages</H1>
 <SPAN datasrc="#myMsg" datafld="source"></SPAN><BR/>
 <SPAN datasrc="#myMsg" datafld="from"></SPAN/><BR/>
 <SPAN datasrc="#myMsg" datafld="message"></SPAN/><BR/>
</BODY>
```

Next, add the HTML buttons needed to control the DSO recordset methods. The methods you can use include those that are summarized in Table 17.1.

TABLE 17.1  DSO Recordset Methods

| Method | Accesses | Call Syntax |
|---|---|---|
| move | The specified record in the dataset by its ordinal value (#) | myMsg.recordset.move([#]) |
| moveFirst | The first record in the dataset | myMsg.recordset.moveFirst() |
| moveLast | The last record in the dataset | myMsg.recordset.moveLast() |
| moveNext | The next record in the dataset | myMsg.recordset.moveNext() |
| movePrevious | The previous record in the dataset | myMsg.recordset.movePrevious() |

For instance, to move to the last record in the dataset, you can write a button script like this:

```
<BUTTON onClick="myMsg.recordset.movelast()">
     &gt;&gt;
</BUTTON>
```

This button, when activated by the user, will call the DSO recordset method to change the current record to the last record in the dataset referred to as myMsg. The JavaScript methods you called previously protected against end of file and start of file errors by ignoring calls to records that were beyond the scope of the document. The DSO methods do not provide for such protection, so you will have to script around errors that might occur if you are at the first or last record and try to access a non-existent previous or next record. The recordset object has a BOF (Beginning of File) and EOF (End of File) property that will help in this regard. You can simply test for the EOF or BOF with an if statement on the button script. For instance, the movePrevious button will test to see if the recordset is at the Beginning of File (BOF). If it is, then the script will call a moveNext() method rather than a movePrevious() method. The script will look like this:

```
<BUTTON onClick="myMsg.recordset.moveprevious();
              if (myMsg.recordset.BOF)
                  myMsg.recordset.movenext()">
```

Using these techniques, the complete button script snippet might look like this:

```
<BUTTON onClick="myMsg.recordset.movefirst()">
     &lt;&lt;
</BUTTON>
<BUTTON onClick="myMsg.recordset.moveprevious();
                  if (myMsg.recordset.BOF)
                      myMsg.recordset.movenext()">
     &lt;
</BUTTON>
<BUTTON onClick="myMsg.recordset.movenext();
                  if (myMsg.recordset.EOF)
                      myMsg.recordset.moveprevious()">
     &gt;
</BUTTON>
<BUTTON onClick="myMsg.recordset.movelast()">
     &gt;&gt;
</BUTTON>
```

Put all of this together and create an HTML page that resembles Listing 17.5 and you will be able to step through the XML-bound dataset, one record at a time.

**Note**

> The Microsoft Developers Network Web site at `http://msdn.microsoft.com/library/default.asp?url=/library/en-us/xmlsdk30/htm/`
>
> `xmconadditionaldatabindingandxmlresources.asp` contains additional information on XML Data Source Object Methods, Data Binding Architectures, and Event Model Support for Data Binding.

**LISTING 17.5**    Single Record Browsing—island04.html

```
 1: <!DOCTYPE HTML PUBLIC "-//W3C//DTD HTML 4.01 Transitional//EN"
 2:  "http://www.w3.org/TR/html4/loose.dtd">
 3: <!-- listing 17.5 island04.html -->
 4:
 5: <HTML>
 6: <HEAD>
 7: <TITLE>XML Data Island</TITLE>
 8: </HEAD>
 9:
10: <BODY>
11: <XML id="myMsg" src="message01.xml"/>
12: <H1>My Messages</H1>
13:   <SPAN datasrc="#myMsg" datafld="source"></SPAN><BR/>
14:   <SPAN datasrc="#myMsg" datafld="from"></SPAN><BR/>
15:   <SPAN datasrc="#myMsg" datafld="message"></SPAN/><BR/>
```

17

**LISTING 17.5**     continued

```
16:
17:    <BR/>
18:
19:    <BUTTON onClick="myMsg.recordset.movefirst()">
20:        &lt;&lt;
21:    </BUTTON>
22:    <BUTTON onClick="myMsg.recordset.moveprevious();
23:                      if (myMsg.recordset.BOF)
24:                          myMsg.recordset.movenext()">
25:        &lt;
26:    </BUTTON>
27:    <BUTTON onClick="myMsg.recordset.movenext();
28:                      if (myMsg.recordset.EOF)
29:                          myMsg.recordset.moveprevious()">
30:        &gt;
31:    </BUTTON>
32:    <BUTTON onClick="myMsg.recordset.movelast()">
33:        &gt;&gt;
34:    </BUTTON>
35:
36:    </BODY>
37:    </HTML>
```

**ANALYSIS**    Line 11 establishes the data island using the HTML element XML. Lines 13–15 render a single record using SPAN elements to bind to the XML source, from, and message elements. The button scripts, calling the DSO recordset methods discussed earlier, are encoded on lines 19–34.

# Instantiating XMLDSO Via a Java Applet

When you install Internet Explorer on your computer, the com.ms.xml.dso Java common library package is included in the distribution. This package includes an applet called XMLDSO that can be used to provide XML data to an HTML page in conjunction with the data-binding techniques you have studied already today. In the next exercise, you will invoke this applet to provide a pathway for data that will be bound to XML elements on an HTML table.

The DSO applets were originally created as part of an overall strategy to make structured information available to HTML pages via objects. The first such objects were designed to provide relational database records to HTML pages. Later, an XML DSO was created to bind XML data sources to HTML elements.

The syntax that you will use for invoking the XMLDSO applet in an HTML page is this:

```
<APPLET code="com.ms.xml.dso.XMLDSO.class"
        width="100%" height="50" id="[reference]">
   <PARAM NAME="url" VALUE="[URI]">
</APPLET>
```

The APPLET start tag includes a code attribute. The value of the code attribute is the fully qualified class name and package identifier for the XML DSO. The width and height attributes provide a report window of the designated dimensions, used to return error messages or load success indicators. The id attribute provides a reference that can be used elsewhere on the HTML page for data binding. The APPLET element contains one required child element (PARAM), which indicates the URL for the XML document instance that is serving as a dataset.

Use the APPLET element in place of the <XML> element in the next exercise to bind HTML TD elements to elements in the XML document, message01.xml. You will need to modify your HTML page to look like Listing 17.6. When you have made the necessary changes, save your page as island05.html and browse the results.

**LISTING 17.6**    XML Data Island Created with a Java XMLDSO Applet—island05.html

```
 1: <!DOCTYPE HTML PUBLIC "-//W3C//DTD HTML 4.01 Transitional//EN"
 2:  "http://www.w3.org/TR/html4/loose.dtd">
 3: <!-- listing 17. island05.html -->
 4:
 5: <HTML>
 6: <HEAD>
 7: <TITLE>XML Data Island</TITLE>
 8: </HEAD>
 9:
10: <BODY>
11: <applet code="com.ms.xml.dso.XMLDSO.class"
12:         width="100%" height="50" id="myMsg">
13:    <PARAM NAME="url" VALUE="message01.xml">
14: </applet>
15: <H1>My Messages</H1>
16:    <TABLE id="table" border="6" width="100%"
17:           datasrc="#myMsg" summary="messages">
18:        <THEAD style="background-color: aqua">
19:               <TH>Source</TH>
20:               <TH>From</TH>
21:               <TH>Message</TH>
22:        </THEAD>
23:        <TR valign="top" align="center">
24:               <TD><SPAN datafld="source" /></TD>
25:               <TD><SPAN datafld="from" /></TD>
```

17

---

**LISTING 17.6** continued

```
26:                        <TD><SPAN datafld="message"/></TD>
27:               </TR>
28:          </TABLE>
29:     </BODY>
30: </HTML>
```

---

**ANALYSIS** Lines 11–14 include the applet that instantiates the XMLDSO. The created object is referred to as myMsg (line 12). The source of the XML document instance is at message01.xml (line 13). The TABLE (lines 16–28) is unchanged from previous exercises.

Figure 17.4 depicts the results of loading this page in the browser.

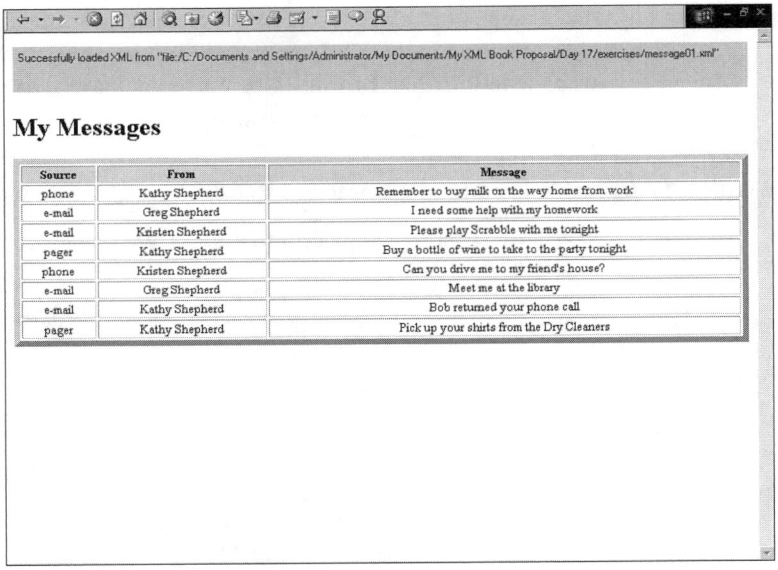

**FIGURE 17.4**

*An XML data island created on an HTML page using the XMLD-SO Java applet.*

Successfully loaded XML from "file:/C:/Documents and Settings/Administrator/My Documents/My XML Book Proposal/Day 17/exercises/message01.xml"

**My Messages**

| Source | From | Message |
|---|---|---|
| phone | Kathy Shepherd | Remember to buy milk on the way home from work |
| e-mail | Greg Shepherd | I need some help with my homework |
| e-mail | Kristen Shepherd | Please play Scrabble with me tonight |
| pager | Kathy Shepherd | Buy a bottle of wine to take to the party tonight |
| phone | Kristen Shepherd | Can you drive me to my friend's house? |
| e-mail | Greg Shepherd | Meet me at the library |
| e-mail | Kathy Shepherd | Bob returned your phone call |
| pager | Kathy Shepherd | Pick up your shirts from the Dry Cleaners |

## Reporting Errors

The report window that you created by encoding a height and width on the XML DSO APPLET start tag is used to return messages from the applet. If you followed the previous example closely, then you saw a small green window that returned a report of successful loading of the XML DSO. To become familiar with error reporting, change the URI in the PARAM element to a non-existent file and load the HTML page. You will be presented with an XML DSO Parse Exception error, reported on a red background. These error messages can often tell you how to fix common problems. Because the XML DSO uses an XML parser, you can expect parser errors as well under certain error scenarios. The most common errors you will encounter include simple parsing errors and file exception errors. In other words, if the XML document you are attempting to bind is not well formed, binding will not work. Also, if it is not located at the URL you provide, an error will occur. The errors that are reported by the XMLDSO applet include those available using the MSXML parser. An overview of XMLDSO error handling can be obtained at `http://msdn.microsoft.com/library/default.asp?url=/library/en-us/ xmlsdk30/htm/xmconusingxmldatasourceobject.asp`.

# Summary

Today, you explored a number of different approaches to creating XML data islands on HTML pages. You were able to combine the intelligent storage of data in XML with the rendering capabilities of HTML. You learned several techniques for binding HTML elements to specific XML elements. You created JavaScript controls to manage the flow of data from the XML source dataset a page and a record at a time. Finally, you used an XML DSO Java applet to source data from an XML document instance for use with HTML. These techniques can be used quite effectively to build tools for maintenance and interrogation of symmetrically structured XML document instances.

The data binding approaches examined today are interesting and simple to implement, but they are somewhat limited to a small subset of available Microsoft technologies. Because the tools are free, they certainly might warrant investigation, particularly if you are looking for a simple means to manipulate symmetric XML data. The requirement that the data be symmetrical, however, is also a limitation of this approach. Nonetheless, using data binding as described today can provide you with additional tools to add to your XML arsenal.

# Q&A

**Q In what ways can XML be like a database when it comes to simple data binding?**

**A** XML document instances can act like flat-file databases if they are symmetrically structured. The immediate child elements of the root element are analogous to records in a database, and the child elements of the records are like fields in a database.

**Q How do DIV and SPAN differ with regard to data binding?**

**A** Both DIV and SPAN are container elements for styles or data. SPAN works inline with other elements, whereas DIV produces a line feed before and after its content when browsed.

Q **If someone tries to view an XML data island created in this way using Netscape Navigator, what happens?**

A Because Netscape browsers do not support the Microsoft XML Data Source Objects, no data will be shown. Remember that the exercises you worked on today are only useful with the Microsoft tools indicated.

# Exercise

The exercise is provided so that you can test your knowledge of what you learned today. The answer is in Appendix A.

Use the method of your choice to create a bound HTML table containing the data from your CD XML dataset.

# DAY 18

# XBase and XInclude

Several emerging technologies are worthy of consideration for future XML implementations. The XML Base (XBase) recommendation by the W3C describes a facility for defining base URIs for parts of XML documents. XML Inclusions 1.0 (XInclude) provides a processing specification for general-purpose inclusion of XML documents, or fragments of documents, in a merge process. Today, you will learn

- The details of the proposed XBase facility and the syntax to be used for specification of Base URIs
- How XInclude is proposed as a means of providing general-purpose inclusion
- The differences between XInclude and other forms of combining XML documents

## XML Base

The XML Base proposal became a recommendation of the W3C on June 27, 2001. XBase describes a single, namespace-aware attribute (`xml:base`) meant to indicate a base URI that is used to resolve a fully qualified relative URI in an

XML document. HTML programmers will recognize the similarity between XBase and the HTML BASE element, which is used to provide a qualification URI for resolving URIs in HTML links to images, stylesheets, applets, and so on.

The XBase recommendation specifies an attribute that you ideally place on an XLink element. However, in the future, it might also be suited to use with other XML technologies that could benefit from resolution of a fully qualified URI. As of this writing, the xml:base attribute does not have much support at the browser and application level, although Netscape 6 will resolve a URI qualified in this manner. Because the xml:base attribute uses the xml: prefix, it is automatically bound to the http://www.w3.org/XML/1998/namespace URI.

## The xml:base Attribute

A document has a base URI by virtue of the host on which it is located. In other words, when you specify a relative URI, the processor is able to resolve the fully qualified URI by assuming that the host is the implied, although unspecified, domain to be included in the URI. For instance, suppose that you place a simple XLink on a message element in an XML document, as you did on Day 10. The link might look something like this:

```
1:      <message xlink:type="simple"
2:              xlink:href="ks.html">
3:          Remember to buy milk on the way home from work
4:      </message>
```

In this example, a simple link is established to a document at ks.html (lines 1–2). It is assumed that the resource being linked to is locally available on the same domain or server as the XML instance document.

You could rewrite this XLink using an xml:base attribute to fully qualify the location of the link. Suppose, for instance, that you want to establish a base URI of http://www.architag.com/devan/ for the link. The syntax of the xml:base attribute is this:

```
xml:base="[URI]"
```

The URI you encode will be concatenated to the relative URI used—in this case on the Xlink—to provide a fully qualified URI. In other words, the http://www.architag.com/devan portion of the URI will be added to the start of the ks.html resource URI. The resulting, fully qualified URI for the link will, therefore, become resolved to http://www.architag.com/devan/ks.html.

You would encode this by adding the xml:base attribute on the message element to look like this:

```
1:        <message xml:base="http://www.architag.com/devan/"
2:                 xlink:type="simple"
3:                 xlink:href="ks.html">
4:           Remember to buy milk on the way home from work
5:        </message>
```

**ANALYSIS** The `xml:base` attribute on the `message` element (line 1) establishes the base URI as `http://www.architag.com/devan`. The `xlink:href` attribute has a value of `ks.html`. Therefore, the fully qualified resource URI for this XLink is resolved to `http://www.architag.com/devan/ks.html`.

One of the advantages of the XBase approach is that you can specify a base URI and it can remain with the document when the document is moved to a new host. You might also use an XBase technique to provide a simple means of modifying relative URIs in a large XML document instance by simply changing an XBase URI, rather than having to edit each instance of the URI throughout the document.

## Multiple XBase Attributes

Because the `xml:base` attribute is placed on an element, it is possible to have as many such encodings as required in an XML instance document. The scope of the `xml:base` attribute is the element on which it is encoded and any child elements it contains.

Therefore, the base URI of an element is the base URI specified by an `xml:base` attribute on the element if one exists. If the element does not have a base URI, it inherits the base URI of the parent element if one exists. Otherwise, the base URI of an element is the base URI for the document containing the element. Consider, for instance, the following XML snippet:

```
 1:        <message xml:base="http://www.architag.com/devan/"
 2:                 xlink:type="simple"
 3:                 xlink:href="ks.html">
 4:                 Remember to buy milk on the way home from work
 5:                 <Reference xml:base="http://www.architag.com/"
 6:                            xlink:type="simple"
 7:                            xlink:href="index.html">
 8:                            home page
 9:                 </Reference>
10:        </message>
```

**ANALYSIS** The `Reference` element is bound to the base URI `http://www.architag.com` on line 5. Therefore, the `index.html` hypertext reference is resolved as the fully qualified URI `http://www.architag.com/index.html`. If the `xml:base` attribute on line 5 were removed from this document instance, the `index.html` hypertext reference would be bound to the base URI of its parent element message and would resolve as

18

`http://www.architag.com/devan/index.html`, a completely different address location. Consequently, if the `xml:base` attributes on lines 1 and 5 were removed, the hypertext references on lines 3 and 7 would resolve to the base URI of the XML instance document. This would typically result in a resolution to the server on which the document resided.

# XML Inclusions

The XInclude 1.0 specification is at the W3C working draft, in last call stage. The recommendation includes a processing model and proposed syntax for inclusion of separate XML documents in a single instance. You might recognize the idea of reusable components merged into a whole from object-oriented computing. Languages such as C++ and Java allow you to implement classes of methods and imports as components. XInclude promises to offer a means of taking the same modular building approach with complex XML document instances. Using XInclude, you can build a document by combining other documents referenced by a URI.

The inclusion processing that is undertaken at the time of parsing is a limited form of transformation. You studied XSLT transformations on Day 16. This is a much simpler form of transformation and only serves to merge the referenced documents into an output document. However, the resulting document does represent a new tree structure comprising the content added during the inclusion. Prior to the inclusion process, the output document is called the *source infoset* in the language of the W3C proposal. After the inclusion, the output document is known as the *result infoset*.

Each document that is merged into the result infoset is referenced by its respective URI. The result infoset, therefore, is the source infoset after the content of each of the included infosets has replaced its referencing XInclude element. A required `href` attribute on an XInclude element declares the URI of the referenced XML document to be merged into the result infoset. The `include` element belongs to the XInclude namespace (`http://www.w3.org/199/XML/xinclude`) and is typically referenced by an `xinclude:` prefix that serves as a proxy to the namespace. It follows that the simplest syntax for the XInclude element with an `href` attribute is this:

```
<xinclude:include href="[URL]"/>
```

Suppose, for example, that you are working on a corporate policy manual and several different departments contribute the sections of that manual. Each department might provide an XML document containing specific policies to be merged into the final document. Perhaps the Human Resources department would provide details of policies pertaining to vacation time and health care claims (`HR.xml`). The Finance department might

contribute policies about purchasing and travel reimbursement procedures
(Finance.xml). The Administration department might add mission statements and corporate objectives (Admin.xml). You could establish a master document (policy.xml) to
hold the final complete manual and *include* the contributions of each department in composing the final product. Figure 18.1 depicts this scenario.

**FIGURE 18.1**

*Document merging
with XInclude.*

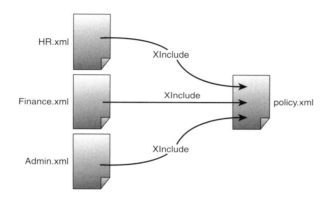

Your policy.xml document would have XInclude elements with href attributes corresponding to HR.xml, Finance.xml, and Policy.xml. Listing 18.1 shows a possible
encoding of a policy.xml document that incorporates XInclude.

**18**

**LISTING 18.1**    A Source Infoset with XInclude Elements—policy.xml

```
1: <?xml version="1.0"?>
2: <!-- listing 18.1 - policy.xml -->
3:
4: <manual xmlns:xinclude="http://www.w3.org/1999/XML/xinclude">
5:     <prolog>Corporate Procedure Manual</prolog>
6:     <section><xinclude:include href="HR.xml"/></section>
7:     <section><xinclude:include href="Finance.xml"/></section>
8:     <section><xinclude:include href="Admin.xml"/></section>
9: </manual>
```

**ANALYSIS**    The manual root element includes an xmlns:xinclude attributed that declares
the XInclude namespace ("http://www.w3.org/1999/XML/xinclude"). Each
section child element of the root element (lines 6–9) contains an xinclude:include
element with an href value corresponding to one of the referenced XML documents
(HR.xml, Finance.xml, or Admin.xml) to be merged into policy.xml.

## XML Parsing During Inclusion

An optional `xinclude:parse` attribute can be included on the XInclude element to declare whether the referenced document is to be considered XML or plain text. If this attribute is given a value of `xml`, the referenced document will be considered to be XML and entity substitution, validation, XInclude, and other normal parsing tasks will be performed prior to inclusion. The other possible value for this attribute is `text`, which results in the included document being considered as plain text character data that is not parsed.

## XPointer Expressions

The `href` attribute can include XPointer expressions to include a fragment from a referenced document rather than the entire document. You learned all about XPointer fragments on Day 11. Suppose that you know the structure of the `HR.xml` file described earlier and that it contains a number of paragraph child elements in various sections, such as `introduction`, `policy_1`, and `policy_2`. If you wanted, for instance, to include the `paragraph` child elements of the `introduction` element, you could use XInclude with XPointer. The inclusion portion of the source infoset might look something like this:

```
<section>
<xinclude:include href="HR.xml#xpointer(introduction/paragraph)"/>
</section>
```

## Support for XInclude

As of this writing, XInclude does not have much application support. Browsers do not perform XInclude transformations; you need to build your own logic for processing inclusions. This is something that can be done in Java, for instance, to meet a specific need. XInclude will have browser-level support as it matures and progresses through the formal W3C recommendation process.

It might seem that XInclude is very much like XLink when the `show` attribute is given the value `embed`, but in fact, they are different. The XLink/embed approach does not create a new tree structure. XML inclusions using a transformation approach result in a completely different result infoset. In other words, XLink with the `show="embed"` attribute does not result in the creation of a new XML tree structure.

# Summary

Today was a relatively short day during which you learned about two evolving technologies: XBase and XInclude. You learned that XBase provides a means of specifying base URIs for relative links in an XML document. This is similar in intent to the HTML BASE element. You also explored XInclude, a means of incorporating data from multiple documents into a transformed result infoset. When an XInclude-aware processor parses a source infoset document and `xinclude` elements are encountered, data substitutes the element at the referenced URI. You can optionally parse the referenced document as an XML instance. Although XInclude is not yet well supported by browsers, it is anticipated that more processors will be developed as the W3C formalizes the proposal.

# Q&A

**Q How is a base URI affected by the relocation of an XML document to a new host domain?**

**A** The base URI at the document level will reflect the new host. However, if you have encoded an XBase URI for use by some of the relative links in your document, those can remain the same even if the document moves.

**Q Is there any limit to the number of documents that can be included using XInclude?**

**A** The number of documents included using XML Inclusion is limitless. It is possible to construct a large and complex XML instance that uses the XInclude modularity extensively.

**Q What are some of the limitations of XInclude?**

**A** The single greatest limitation for XML Inclusions is the lack of processor support. When browsers are able to support XInclude, modular XML might become a reality.

**Q Are processors available that currently support XInclude?**

**A** At the time of this writing, the Apache XML Project Software known as Cocoon supports XInclude. Cocoon is a publishing framework that is implemented as an open source Java suite. Cocoon uses several W3C technologies, such as XML, XSL, DOM, and XInclude, to provide Web content.

**18**

DAY **19**

# XML Integration with Corporate Business Models

Traditional corporate computer applications are using XML technologies more frequently. A variety of enterprise systems designed to manage the distribution and dissemination of information, provide data and application integration, or maximize knowledge and workflow management is particularly well suited to XML solutions. The use of XML as a means of improving business processes and creating new opportunities has become a strategic objective for many organizations. Today, you will learn

- The basics of document analysis
- The role of XML in enterprise applications
- The significance of the three-tier architecture for Web applications
- Some simple middle-tier scripting techniques to move information from corporate databases to dynamic Web pages using XML

# Business Modeling with XML Technologies

This book has shown you many of the individual technologies that comprise XML and how they provide a means of exchanging structured information. You are aware of the standards and proposals that characterize XML. You have investigated the mechanisms behind XML and have used a variety of approaches for manipulation and display of XML data. Today, you will be able to explore the ways in which XML can be used in the delivery of integrated business applications. A number of application scenarios will be presented along with the challenges to be met from a business perspective, the benefits offered by XML, architectural considerations, and discussion of how you might proceed to create solutions based on XML technologies. Later today, you will have an opportunity to create a working data exchange solution using server-side scripting—such as Active Server Pages (ASP)—to extract information stored in a database and present it as an XML dataset. Then, you will write server-side scripts to move data from the database into a virtual XML structure that can be bound to table elements on an HTML page for browser-side rendering.

## Basic Document Analysis Considerations

One of the typical steps in creating XML applications is the analyzing documents to determine how best to mark them up. You might want to transform a paper document, or more likely a class of documents—such as procedures, memoranda, legal briefs, contracts, or restaurant menus)—into XML instances. Sometimes this transformation will involve using an existing schema that defines the structure of a document, and other times it will require you to start from scratch with no predefined element types from which to draw. Either way, you will need to thoroughly analyze samples of each document class you are encoding to understand their structure and composition.

Document analysis is the act of examining the parts, purposes, and requirements for one or more classes of documents to design a detailed and definitive description for each. In practice, that description is often expressed as a Document Analysis Report and a corresponding set of schemata statements that serve to define the structure of documents. Applying a public domain or commercially available schema to the definition of a particular document class might be possible, but analysis is still required to ensure that the "fit" is ideal. If it is not, the very nature of XML schemata permits you to extend as you need.

The most important factor in producing an accurate and useful description of a document class is collecting accurate and useful information about the documents that comprise the class. The best source of that information is often not obtained by reviewing the documents, but rather by tapping the knowledge possessed by the persons responsible for the creation, production, and maintenance of the documents. Without the awareness of purposes and requirements for the documents, the structures you identify might be arbitrary and inaccurate.

In simpler terms, only document owners typically know what is useful and important in their documents. If you take on the role of the document analyst, you might find yourself trying to elicit that information from individuals rather than from real examples of the class. A sample of documents is incomplete and inconclusive. In addition, the analysis of documents alone seldom provides all of the information you need. It is essential that you understand the data components, or entities of data, and how they relate to best design a system to use that data.

With or without the assistance of document owners, analysis involves the identification and definition of the component parts of a document class in sufficient granularity to encode, through the application of structured tag sets, the data that you want to represent. In fact, the degree of granularity you choose might be one of the most difficult decisions to make in the early stages of document analysis. Too little detail might result in questionable value, and too much might involve effort that overshadows any benefit. As with any software development project, the analysis stages are critical to success, timeliness, and cost efficiency of the effort.

The result of careful analysis will be the adoption or creation of a markup vocabulary to describe a class of documents. Because author-generated element types characterize XML, any collaborative efforts to create a markup vocabulary should be carefully directed. Suppose, for instance, that you are working on the creation of a corporate accounting system markup language as a member of a team. If each member of your team creates a different tag for purchase order numbers—such as Ponum, Purchase_order_number, PO_number, PON, and P_O_numb—and then creates disparate element type names for other components of your accounting system, the effort of eventually unifying the system under a common vocabulary might be prohibitive. Therefore, the full analysis should be complete before markup begins and a vocabulary should be defined (or adopted) and described by an associated schema before document conversion.

To ensure effective markup, you will need to know a great deal about the ultimate objectives of the system you are creating. If, for instance, the goal is for efficient retrieval, reuse, and interchange of information, you must determine, with a high degree of precision, the element names, element data composition, and definition of validation errors on any element type.

You might find that a group approach is effective in a majority of XML document analysis projects, but again, beware of effort duplication and the potential for proliferation of disparate element types to describe the same data. In the case of a common-interest group, company, or industry, the goal might be to create a single valid vocabulary for data interchange outside the realm of your immediate control. If you are working in an industry that has been through this process before, you might be able to adopt an existing schema. Sources and repositories on the Internet for industry-specific schemata include the following:

19

- Biztalk.org (with 300+ schemata searchable in 11 industry categories from more than 75 organizations)
- Xml.org (with links to more than 200 schema-producing organizations listed in 80+ categories)
- Schema.net (with schemata in major commercial categories, contributed by special-interest groups and industry organizations)

If you are unable to adopt an industry schema, you might find the creation of a new schema based on document structure a familiar task. You will, of course, need to know the tag set, the information that is contained by the elements, and the relationship of elements to one another with regard to occurrence, order, and so on.

## XML Analysis Steps

You can adopt several formal approaches to analysis and some proprietary systems that provide a road map to the process. Most of these approaches have certain qualities in common and aim to satisfy similar needs. Analysis helps to formalize the collection of relevant and useful data for modeling. By authoring a schema or analysis report, you are effectively creating a framework or basic infrastructure for the hierarchy of data components and the capabilities of data interchange.

You might find that one of the side benefits of all of this effort is the creation of extraordinarily detailed meta data that can improve context and precision searching on your documents. Placing information in structures—such as conclusions, ingredient lists, procedures, authors, purpose, and location—allows you to create context data references.

### Requirements Definition

Defining requirements is one of the most important steps in the analysis process. Requirements drive decisions for the architecture, analysis, and design of systems. A clear understanding of the requirements allows you to determine the appropriate granularity for element definition. Requirements allow you to establish acceptable tradeoffs, if required, between design and implementation efforts if a conflict exists. When you express the requirements, you can set the following:

- Application goals: Why do you need/want to use XML, and who uses the information that is stored, created, or processed? What are the requirements for interchange, searching, security, and reuse of data? What do you want to do that you can't do currently?
- Application non-goals: What are the real limits to what you are trying to accomplish? What, by design, is purposely being omitted from this application and why?

- Typical/desired output from the system: Will the output be in the form of electronic books, Web pages, enterprise shared data, hard copy, search service data, alternative formats, or multimedia?

- Organizational requirements: What are the marketing considerations? Is the effort well supported?

- Existing document standards: What are the corporate style guides and policy statements regarding public and private data?

- Existing application standards: What are the related schema, industry or special-interest group activities, or government or corporate oversight authorities?

## Determination of Scope

Of equal important to defining the requirements, determining the scope will help to establish the information universe that defines the boundaries of your markup. In many cases, the purpose of a project will be to increase or decrease an existing scope. You will need to understand the impact associated with those modifications. For instance, will a class of marketing documents be expanded to include coverage of newly developed products? If so, how will this business plan affect your application? Do you have room in the design for extensibility as an expectation?

## Identification of Element Set

The process of establishing the element set can be quite complex. You might need to consider, for instance, whether existing document types are appropriate for your proposed application. Sometimes paper documents are created on the basis of convenience rather than with consideration to optimal structure. Perhaps, by way of example, you will end up with an XML instance that encapsulates several paper documents and the routing information that is known to the users of the data.

After you establish the granularity of the information set, you will be able to name the elements on the basis of what is meaningful, reusable, searchable, and so on. This can be a tricky objective to satisfy. How do you decide how much is too much detail? A particular markup problem might have no ideal solution; however, storing and maintaining data that you might never use is wasteful and expensive.

Identifying elements requires that you establish a selectivity and sensitivity to the data and its structure. For instance, a memorandum might contain sections, headings, paragraphs, words, and punctuation from a purely structural standpoint. The same document might be described as comprising "To," "From," "Subject," "Date," "Regarding," and "Body" components when analyzed on the basis of content.

19

## Establishment of Information Relationships

Part of the analysis phase requires that you understand the relationships among information components. You might need to be aware, for instance, whether your elements have hierarchical expectations. Elements are containers, so be sure to fully understand what it is that each contains. For instance, suppose that you are creating an XML file to hold data passed in a bookkeeping report application. An accounting transaction container might contain a descriptor, such as a journal number, and one or more actions. An action might, in turn, contain an account number, an amount, and an attribute with values of either debit or credit.

You will recall from your work with schemata that the element order, enumeration of attribute values, and determination of whether elements and attributes are required might also be significant. Dependencies can also become apparent during analysis. In accounting system transactions, for example, a credit must exist for every debit in matched couplets for a ledger to be in balance. Knowing this required relationship will help you to better define the system.

## Other Forms of Information Analysis

You have read about some techniques that can be used to help analyze static information, such as paper documentation. If you are creating XML on the basis of an existing database, don't overlook the use of a data dictionary as a source of structural detail. In the sections that follow, you will read about several typical business problems that might be suited to solutions that employ XML technologies. In most cases, these systems are characterized by one or more databases that contain information that could be exchanged as XML documents.

# Business Applications

The use of XML technologies in applications for enterprises is growing in popularity. The powerful combination of schemata for validation, XSL for styling, and XML storage for the intelligence it offers lends itself to the creation of efficient enterprise solutions that represent operating benefits for corporations. The introduction of these technologies often leads to increased efficiency of the business process, improvements in execution of transaction-based procedures, and the facilitation of new business paradigms. With these objectives in mind, the use of XML technologies has become a strategic consideration for many businesses. In the section that follows, you will have an opportunity to consider the business impacts and advantages that can be realized using XML in several specific scenarios. These are just samples of applications that can be derived using XML. Read through these examples and evaluate how XML and the technologies you have explored add to the utility of application classes described. Then, imagine how you might use similar approaches to solve business problems in your organization. For each enterprise application scenario, you will be presented with the following:

- A review of the business problems to be addressed
- The potential benefits offered by XML
- Architectural and development process issues

# Information Dissemination and Aggregation Applications

Suppose you want to use data exchange technologies to manage and coordinate an elaborate process in your company. Perhaps you are creating a new product or marketing a new service. Maybe you need to share engineering data with various departments in your company to allow decisions to be made about manufacturing, marketing, and so on. Depending on the size of your project, you will likely need a system to establish, monitor, and maintain the flow of data. Your partners on a project can be internal or external, thereby requiring a flexible means of data exchange. You will want to ensure that the handling of this important data is reliable.

Earlier today, you reviewed some of the steps typically used to analyze documents during conversion to XML structures. It might have occurred to you that the information in those documents has asset value and that the implicit worth of the information is often the justification for the effort it takes to integrate that data in XML-based solutions. For a growing number of companies, information has become the product that is manufactured and sold to customers. At the very least, the dissemination of information is often a companion co-process in traditional product delivery. The effective, timely, accurate, and efficient delivery of information can provide a competitive advantage to almost any organization in the modern economy. The distribution channel of choice for information exchange has become the Web, which offers efficiency and global access. The Web works as well to reach customers and employees internally as it does to exchange relevant information with business partners and clients across the street or around the world.

## XML Benefits

As discussed on Days 1 and 2, HTML, although successful by virtue of its pervasive omnipresence and platform neutrality, suffers from inadequacies. Where structured data is required, particularly data deriving from dynamic access to disparate originating sources, HTML is cumbersome at best. By building a systematic gestalt from the suite of XML technologies you have read about over the past eighteen days, you can overcome these limitations and broker data-centric information in new ways.

19

The separation of style and content in XML is one factor that leads to a more successful implementation of dynamic data content on Web pages. For HTML to be used in data delivery applications requires that you alter the text in standard markup tags to reflect data components. HTML cannot provide sufficient service to do this without relying on a variety of other Web technologies. By comparison, XML and XSL add efficiencies of scale and control that surpass almost anything you can accomplish with HTML. In addition, as you learned on Day 16, you can still convert the product of any XML technology to HTML for unconditional presentation to the vast array of user agents that offer native support for HTML. As you saw on Day 15, you can even provide a means for users of your information assets to apply personal preferences to the presentation of the data brokered in your application.

Local users can select stylesheets to apply to data stored in XML, and applications can be created to access the data directly without using stylesheets. Later today, you will create a server-side script that takes XML data and places it in an HTML table that can be pushed over the Web to almost any browser. These strengths help to characterize XML as a superlative technology for information dissemination rather than merely a page publishing technology.

## Architectural and Development Considerations

Information aggregation and dissemination is ideally suited to Web-based architectures. In a typical scenario, users, or customers, of the information make requests to a server that retrieves or constructs a response based on source information. The result document can be associated with a stylesheet, perhaps transformed, and ultimately delivered to the client-side user agent. Because universal support for XML does not exist at the browser level, most XML-based information dissemination and aggregation systems rely on server-side pre-processing prior to delivery.

You can see that either static content or dynamically generated content can be served in this manner. Static content might originate in a repository of pre-packaged documents. Dynamic content might be aggregated and constructed using a data integration server. Either way, XML offers significant advantages over HTML-based solutions, or for that matter, over solutions that are based entirely on proprietary mechanisms for data construction, such as databases. This is not to say that you shouldn't use HTML or databases. In fact, both might have a role in an ultimate solution. You might find that using those technologies to do what they are ideally suited to do—such as paint browser pages or efficiently store indexed data—and adding appropriate XML technologies results in an optimum solution.

When you create this kind of application, you typically decide the nature and classes of documents and data to disseminate and then build templates for delivery. In practical terms, a template can consist of a schema and one or more stylesheets. For static content documents, human authors can use applications to create XML documents. Dynamic document creation can be automated by applications that draw on database and delivery information stored electronically. In addition, business partners can provide portions of content electronically, or via Web access, that this process can also accommodate. As you have seen already, the extensibility and interoperability of XML technologies provide you with an efficient means of merging vendor or business partner schemata with those that you develop in-house.

## Application Integration Solutions

In many organizations, a variety of packaged and custom-built applications characterize the environmental software suite. Order Fulfillment, Enterprise Resource Planning (ERP), Human Resources, Accounting and Finance, Sales Force Automation, and so on are typically based on disparate application software that might even reside on multiple platforms. This is not poor design or the result of bad business planning; it is just an artifact of the nature of business applications. Typically, a business application is highly specialized to address selected aspects of the business process. To fulfill all of its needs, a company might rely on several distinct packaged solutions. The problem arises when it comes time to integrate data from one application with data from another. Traditional methods of customized integration are expensive, slow, and labor intensive, often requiring the services of external consultants specializing in business application integration, sometimes called Enterprise Application Integration (EAI).

## XML Benefits

Because XML deals in data that is stored as text, it offers integration capabilities that can be easily scripted and combined for a large variety of uses. The nature of intelligent storage of data provides you a means of ensuring that metadata are part of the transfer infrastructure. Several specialized XML applications are designed expressly to provide a translation service between applications. For instance, server solutions from WebMethods (http://www.webMethods.com) and BizTalk (http://www.biztalk.org) do the work of translating business logic among applications. Although these are somewhat beyond the scope of today's reading, you should know that these XML-based solutions accomplish sophisticated application integration even when those applications reside over the Internet in different enterprises. Tomorrow, you'll read about the Simple Object Access Protocol (SOAP) and learn how a completely platform-independent solution can provide a means of invoking remote objects via method calls wrapped in XML containers.

19

## Architectural and Development Considerations

Architecture for application integration using XML involves the transfer of XML encoded data from one program to another over a local network, or indeed, over the Internet. Later today, you will build an HTML application that resides on a Web server. When that application is loaded, it will launch a separate server-side script written in VBScript. The server script will interrogate a Microsoft Access database by using a Structured Query Language (SQL) expression and will return an XML stream of data. The HTML application will bind to the XML elements by using simple object data binding and will render in a table on a Web page. This is just one example of the nature of interoperable integration that is easily facilitated by XML.

As with the application you will build later, the process for development of integration involves several systematic steps. You essentially need to develop a protocol engine, or use one that is readily available, which can format a request instruction. The request should be capable of establishing a connection to a Web server to execute an application residing on the host. The host application will process and generate a response that is shipped back to the requesting application. Next, you will create a mapping layer that translates the data contained in the response into structures that can be processed by the local application.

# Data Integration Applications

Sometimes the data that you require will not be in a single database. It might reside in several databases, and these might not necessarily be located in the same enterprise. A class of applications known as data integration applications can fill the requirement of collecting data and providing a unification of output. This kind of integration can save time and effort for employees that need to consolidate data from different sources to complete complex business transactions. The cost of running individual applications might be considered the sum of all the processing conducted independently plus the manual steps required to consolidate the results or produce a report of a collaborative nature. Automation of these processes often makes good business sense.

## XML Benefits

The centralized synthesis of complex business data characterizes a viable solution for data integration applications. In practical terms, the application will likely require multi-directional access to a variety of component processes; it is in this regard that the benefits of XML become immediately apparent. In other words, the resulting synthesis might be required as input or feedback to component applications in the data integration loop. The abilities of XML technologies to provide interoperable data exchange might, in some cases, make it the de facto format for business transactions. Much of this has relevance on the client side, where support for XML is still weak, but developing quickly. Until then, synthesis can be accomplished on servers and pushed in a variety of formats through universal means to user agents.

## Architectural and Development Considerations

Typically, data integration solutions are built on an architecture that is characterized by an integration server that sits between a variety of client applications on one side and several databases or data sources on the other. The data sources might be database records, files in a file system, or applications. The only requirement is that they be remotely accessible. The integration server takes data from these sources, composes them into XML data streams, and passes them on to client applications in a form that is usable. It might also accept updated information from a client application, disassemble it into component parts, and store it away in the appropriate data facility. Access to the data sources can happen using native XML mechanisms or via other database and file system transports, such as Java Database Connectivity (JDBC), Open Database Connectivity (ODBC), and proprietary APIs.

# Three-Tier Web Architecture

Today, you have read about architectures that are typically deployed on a *three-tier client-server model*. This architecture is a special type of client/server architecture consisting of three well-defined and separate processes, each running on a different `platform`.

## Client Tier

The user interface that runs on the user's computer (that is, the client) is often characterized by a browser application. Any other client-side user agent, such as a Web-enabled wireless device, cellular phone, or personal digital assistant, might also represent this tier. This is the first of the three tiers, often called the user tier or client tier.

## Middle Tier

The middle tier contains the functional modules that actually process data. This middle tier runs on a server, or several servers, one of which is the application server. Another class of servers, Web servers, are also housed on the middle tier and often serve as portals to other middle tier applications. The information dissemination and aggregation application you read about earlier is an example of an application that would reside on the middle tier. Server-side scripting is maintained and executed on middle-tier servers. Suppose you visit an online bookstore and upon access, the Web site greets you by name and suggests newly available books that might be of interest to you based on your past purchases. Perhaps you typically buy books like this one about computer programming.

19

The personalization application will execute on the middle tier. It will likely read stored records in a database on the data tier to determine your purchasing preferences, process the results in the middle tier, look up new listings that "match" your preferences, and report back to you on the client tier its suggestions for similar titles that you might want to purchase. This is a classic example of a three-tier Web application.

## Data Tier

As mentioned, the third tier is known as the data tier and most often includes a database management system (DBMS) that stores the data required by the middle tier. This tier runs on a second server, the database server. Subscriber profiles and online catalogs, like those used by your online bookstore, are typically stored in databases on the data tier.

You will find that XML can live on or between any of the tiers. The application scenarios you read about earlier today offer examples of how XML can be used at all layers of this popular architecture. In the exercises that follow, you will build XML-based applications that communicate between and operate on all three of the tiers. This best-practices model of development corresponds to the approach promulgated by the W3C and by Web developers.

# XML Use Across the Tiers

In the exercises that follow, you will use middle-tier programming to access data that is stored on a database. Then you will move the data through the creation of XML structures to a browser for client-side rendering. The examples use the following technologies:

- Extensible Markup Language version 1.0 (XML) for data transport between tiers
- Hypertext Markup Language (HTML) for rendering of data on a client-side browser
- Microsoft Access 2000 to store database records and represent the data tier
- Microsoft Internet Information Services (IIS) version 5.0 to provide a local Web server for testing and execution of the applications
- Microsoft Windows 2000 as an operating system
- ODBC Data Source Administrator version 3.5 to set a System Data Source Name (DSN) for an object describing how to connect to the database
- Structured Query language (SQL) to extract data from the database under the control of a middle-tier script
- Visual Basic Script (VBScript) to create Active Server Pages for server-side scripting

To follow along and create the application, you can use the specified component technologies, although the exact versions are not critical. You might want to substitute other familiar components—such as an alternative database or middle-tier scripting language—and base your design on the functionality of the models offered. However, other than the XML employed, it is beyond the scope of this book to teach the syntax or detailed usage of the component technologies listed. A brief discussion of each functional part of the exercise code examples will be offered, but you might want to turn to more extensive references for in-depth discussion of SQL, IIS, VBScript, HTML, and the ODBC API or Microsoft Access. Sams, the publisher of this book, offers excellent tutorial-based materials on all of these technologies.

**Note**

In addition, you should know that the choice of Microsoft products is for illustration purposes. You can certainly substitute other products for Web servers and supporting products. For instance in place of the suite described, you might choose to install Apache, Tomcat, and MySQL.

## Data Tier

Continuing the metaphor of an XML-based messaging and reminder system, you will create a database with individual messages as records. The fields will correspond to message components that should be familiar from work on previous days, namely id, from, source, and message. The id field will be an autonumber key field on the database. All other fields will have a text data type. Remember that although this exercise shows a Microsoft Access database, you can use any ODBC-compliant database that supports SQL.

To create your database using Access, launch the application and select Create a New Database Using Blank Access Database from the from the pop-up window that is displayed when the application opens. Figure 19.1 shows this selection.

**FIGURE 19.1**

*Creating a new Access database.*

**19**

A dialog will appear asking you to save your new database. For all of the remaining steps to work as described, create a new directory, c:\day_19, and save your database in this new directory as message.mdb. You could, of course, choose any directory you want to, but you will need to remember your choice and make appropriate substitutions along the way. If you do choose c:\day_19 as your directory, the fully qualified path to your new database will be as follows:

```
C:\day_19\message.mdb
```

After you have saved your new database, you will be presented with the main Access database design window. Select the option Create Table in Design View from the Tables object. This should be the option that is already highlighted. Figure 19.2 shows the option you need to choose.

**FIGURE 19.2**

*Selecting Design View in Microsoft Access.*

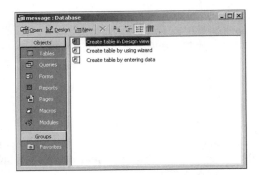

On each of the lines of the table provided, you will enter details about one of the fields in your new table. On line 1, enter id for the Field Name and tab to the Data Type column. From the pull-down list that appears when you click on the down arrow in that cell of the table, choose AutoNumber. Before moving on to the next field, make this field the primary key by clicking the small key icon on the toolbar at the top of the screen, or by choosing Primary Key from the Edit pull-down menu. Tab or place your cursor in the next row down on this table, which corresponds to the next field of the table you are creating. Enter from as the Field Name and Text as the Data Type. Repeat this to create the source and message fields, both of which have text data types. Your completed Design View window should now look like the one in figure 19.3.

From the File pull-down menu, select Save As and name your table msg. From the View pull-down menu, select Datasheet View and you can now enter data directly into your database. You will not put data in the id field because the AutoNumber function in Access will take care of this for you. Use the Tab key to place your cursor in the first from cell and enter a name. Continue to enter data in each of the fields to create several records. You don't need to use the same data as is shown in Figure 19.4, nor must you limit yourself to only three records if you would like to enter more.

**FIGURE 19.3**

*Creating access database fields in Design View.*

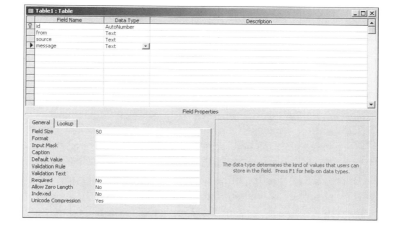

**FIGURE 19.4**

*The* msg *table populated with data.*

You can now close the database. You have created a database of messages that can be accessed via scripting in a subsequent step. The database contains records corresponding to individual messages or reminders, similar to the way you represented these in XML on previous days.

As you know, a database offers a convenient and efficient means of storage, complete with indexing, database security, and all of the other features that organizations rely on from this technology. Most enterprises keep some data assets on databases. Often this represents the legacy data that you might require when you are creating dynamic Web content or when you are establishing connectivity between applications. Ultimately, you will want to move the data from a database in the form of an XML stream so that it can be easily incorporated into other applications or styled for delivery to a client.

## Setting an ODBC Data Source Name

The Open Database Connectivity (ODBC), like Java Database Connectivity (JDBC) tools are types of database access facilities that are provided through the instantiation of special client and server driver software. ODBC provides you an Application Programming Interface (API) that allows for data extraction from a database through a unified source.

19

You will use ODBC by creating a named source with the Windows Data Source Name (DSN) Administrative Tool. This will provide a conceptual connection between the application and the database that can be traversed by an object call in a middle tier script. The DSN establishes a named reference and a link to the database driver (in your case for Microsoft Access) that is associated with a particular database. By setting this DSN, you will provide a direct pipeline to your database through the operating system that effectively incorporates the path through the file system. In other words, when you create an object that connects to your DSN, the object will use ODBC to access the database so that you can pass SQL statements to work with the data. The database object will provide a connection to the database with its own set of methods. The connection will survive until you close it with a `Close` method in the API.

To create the DSN, you will need to use the Data Sources (ODBC) administrative tool. The assumption is that you are using Windows 2000 for this exercise. Open the Windows 2000 Control Panel by clicking the Start button on your Windows toolbar and choosing the Settings submenu, followed by the Control Panel option. In the Control Panel, open the Administrative Tools folder and launch the Data Sources (ODBC) tool. When the Data Sources (ODBC) tool window is presented, click on the System DSN tab. Be especially careful to select the System DSN tab and not the User DSN or File DSN tab.

**Tip**

You can either set up a System DSN or a User DSN. The User DSN, however, only allows the creator of the DSN to access the database through the data source. For multiple users on the machine to access a particular database, either multiple User DSNs or a System DSN must be configured. A System DSN allows all the users of a machine to access the database through that data source.

You will be presented with a window containing existing DSNs, if any. Click on the Add button and you will be given a new window that lists all of the database drivers installed on your computer. As long as Microsoft Access 2000 is properly installed as a part of the Office 2000 suite on your system, you should have an appropriate driver available to you in this list. Select the Microsoft Access Driver (*.mdb) and click the Finish button. You will be presented with a window called ODBC Microsoft Access Setup. In the Data Source Name field, enter messageDB, paying careful attention to the spelling and case.

You will want the DSN to be identical to the one shown here to ensure that the scripts you create in subsequent steps function. Click the Select button on this screen and use the Select Database File dialog box to locate your database at c:\day_19\message.mdb. At this point, your screen should be similar to the one depicted by Figure 19.5.

**FIGURE 19.5**

*Creating a data source name with the ODBC administrative tool.*

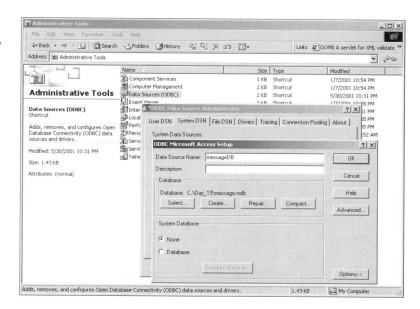

Close all of the dialog boxes by selecting OK in each case.

## Establishing the Web Server

In the exercises that follow, you will use IIS as a Web Server, accessible via your Web browser. IIS provides an excellent means of testing server-side programming on a local host. Often, programmers develop applications on a local host, such as IIS, and then promote them to an external host as production Web sites. You can accomplish this in other ways, but IIS offers a simple alternative that works well.

To use Microsoft Internet Information Services (IIS) as your Web server in subsequent steps, you will need to register your c:\day_19 directory as a *Web share* directory. To this, use the Windows Explorer facility to locate your c:\day_19 directory. With the directory visible in an Explorer window, right-click it and select the Sharing option from the pop-up menu. Click on the Web Sharing tab, being careful not to use the Sharing tab by mistake. Select the Share this folder radio button on the Web Sharing option screen. A new window will appear, named Edit Alias. You don't need to change anything on this

**19**

screen; the default choices provide sufficient IIS support to complete the remaining exercises. Note that the system assigns the alias `day_19` automatically to this Web share. You will use that alias as part of the URL you enter into your browser when you access programs stored in that particular Web share directory on the Web Server. The syntax that is required to load a program, such as an HTML page or server script, stored in this Web share directory is as follows:

```
http://localhost/day_19/myfile.asp
```

The `localhost` portion of this URL replaces the standard `www.domain.ext` addressing that you use when browsing Web sites on the Internet with HTTP. The address instruction `localhost` refers to the internal Web server provided by IIS and the alias `day_19` is a proxy for the directory on which you created a Web share earlier. `myfile.asp` is the filename of a document, an HTML application, or Active Server Page (ASP) script you want to launch via the server.

## Accessing a Database with a Server-Side Script

In the next exercise, you will create an Active Server Page (ASP) that will generate HTML to render data obtained via SQL from the DSN you created earlier. In other words, now that you have a database that is available through your ODBC API, you can create a connection object that allows you to pass SQL statements to the database, which will return results to your server-side script. By wrapping the results of your query in HTML statements, you can render the results—such as database records—on a browser. Suppose, for instance, that you would like to use the script to query the database and return all of the fields of each record in a bulleted list. The objective of this exercise is to produce output that looks something like that depicted by Figure 19.6.

**FIGURE 19.6**

*HTML output generated by a server-side script accessing a database.*

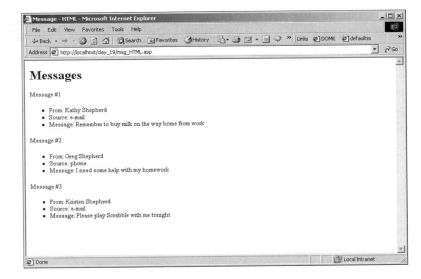

You might want to launch your favorite text editor and begin creating the script as you read through the steps that follow. The Active Server Page will comprise VBScript and HTML. VBScript is natively readable and interpreted by Web browsers on the IIS Web server. You will start by setting up the ASP to be a VBScript-based page with the language declaration statement, using the following syntax:

```
<%@ Language = "VBScript"%>
```

Then you can create the beginning of the HTML page with standard <!DOCTYPE ...>, <HTML>, <HEAD>, and <BODY> sections. These sections will all require closure, like they would on any traditional HTML page. However, within the <BODY> section of the page, you will place the logic required to open the ODBC connection, pass the SQL statements to the database, and format the response within HTML statements.

To connect with the database you referenced with your DSN earlier, you will create a new server object that instantiates the Connection ActiveX Data Object (ADO), along with an open method to which you pass the DSN as an argument. The syntax for this object call and its associated method is as follows:

```
set oMyObject = Server.CreateObject("ADODB.Connection")
oMyObject.open("myDSN")
```

Specifically, you will use the following code:

```
set oMsg = Server.CreateObject("ADODB.Connection")
oMsg.open("messageDB")
```

The new object will be called oMsg and the messageDB DSN is encoded as the argument passed via the open method to the ADO. This serves, literally, to open a connection between this ASP script and your message.mdb database. The connection will remain open until you close it using the Close property on the Connection object, which looks like this:

```
OMsg.Close
```

The Close property will follow any other logic that you want to execute while the ODBC is open, such as executing SQL statements and formatting responses from the query. To execute SQL, you can use the Execute method on the Connection object. The result will be a RecordSet object that is returned by the Execute method. The syntax used to pass SQL to a database via these object calls is as follows:

```
Set myRecordSetVariable = oMyObject.Execute("SQL statement")
```

To select all of the records (*) from the msg table in your message.mdb database, you will use a simple SQL statement like this:

```
SELECT * FROM msg;
```

19

If you then label the resulting `RecordSet` as `msgRS`, the complete object call will become this:

```
Set msgRS = oMSG.Execute("SELECT * FROM msg;")
```

If you want to return only the first record of the database, you can print to the default output device, or screen, all of the fields required. However, because in this case you want to report all of the records on your database, you will need some facility to iterate through the records and report each until you run out. The easiest approach would be to program a loop that reads a record, produces output, and then proceeds to the next record for processing. VBScript do loops work well for this. You will start your loop with a statement that instructs the interpreter to loop until no more records exist, which is indicated when the script reaches an End of File (EOF) marker. Within the loop, you will write the fields you want to report from each record to the screen and then move on to the next record and loop through the process again. The syntax for this loop is as follows:

```
do until myRecordSetVariable.EOF
    Response.Write (myRecordSetVariable("field_name"))
    ...
    myRecordSetVariable.MoveNext
Loop
```

The loop required in this exercise looks like this:

```
do until msgRS.EOF
    Response.Write ("<P>Message #" & _
        msgRS("ID") & "<UL>")
    Response.Write ( _
        "<LI>From: " & msgRS("from") & "</LI>" & _
        "<LI>Source: " & msgRS("source") & "</LI>"& _
        "<LI>Message: " & msgRS("message") & "</LI>" )
    Response.Write ("</UL>")
    msgRS.MoveNext
Loop
```

After this loop, you will close the connection using `oMsg.Close` as described earlier. Then you will release the object by setting the `oMsg` variable to null, with the following:

```
Set oMSG = nothing
```

All that remains is for you to terminate the `BODY` and `HTML` elements. The complete application is provided as Listing 19.1. Save your script as `msg_HTML.asp`.

**LISTING 19.1**  An ASP Script to Extract Records from a Database—msg_HTML.asp

```
1: <%@ LANGUAGE = "VBScript"%>
2: <%' listing 19.1 - msg_HTML.asp
3: %>
4:
```

**LISTING 19.1** Continued

```
5: <!DOCTYPE HTML PUBLIC "-//W3C//DTD HTML 4.01 Transitional//EN"
6:   "http://www.w3.org/TR/html4/loose.dtd">
7: <!-- HTML file generated by ASP -->
8:
9: <HTML>
10:     <HEAD>
11:         <TITLE>Message - HTML</TITLE>
12:     </HEAD>
13:     <BODY>
14:         <H1>Messages</H1>
15:         <%
16:         set oMsg = Server.CreateObject("ADODB.Connection")
17:         oMsg.open("messageDB")
18:
19:         set msgRS = oMsg.Execute("SELECT * FROM msg;")
20:
21:         do until msgRS.EOF
22:             Response.Write ("<P>Message #" & _
23:                 msgRS("ID") & "<UL>")
24:             Response.Write ( _
25:                 "<LI>From: " & msgRS("from") & "</LI>" & _
26:                 "<LI>Source: " & msgRS("source") & "</LI>"& _
27:                 "<LI>Message: " & msgRS("message") & "</LI>" )
28:             Response.Write ("</UL>")
29:             msgRS.MoveNext
30:         Loop
31:         oMsg.Close
32:         set oMsg = nothing
33:         %>
34:     </BODY>
35: </HTML>
```

19

**ANALYSIS**  Line 1 establishes the scripting language for the Active Server Page as VBScript. Lines 5–6 provide the DOCTYPE declaration for the HTML page being generated by the script. Lines 9–14 provide typical HTML tags for the generated page. Lines 15–33 contain the remainder of the VBScript. The ADO is created on line 16 and named oMsg. The Connection object is provided with the messageDB DSN using the open method (line 17). Line 19 passes the SQL query to the database with the Execute method on the Connection object. Lines 21–30 contain the loop that prints the results of the query to the screen. The loop iterates until the end of the database file is encountered (line 21). Each of the fields of the first record encountered is reported to the default output device (Response.Write) and wrapped in appropriate HTML tags (lines 22–28). On line 29, the MoveNext property on the RecordSet object instructs the process to move one record ahead on the database. Line 30 instructs the script to loop back to the do statement on line 21. If the last record has not yet been processed, the loop continues until it has. Line 31 instructs the connection to close, and line 32 sets the oMsg variable to null. The script is terminated on line 33 and the remaining lines terminate open HTML elements with close tags.

To execute your server script and produce the results shown by Figure 19.1, you will need to point your browser at the copy of the ASP that resides on your Web host. To do this, enter the following URL in the Address field of your Microsoft Internet Explorer browser:

```
http://localhost/day_19/msg_HTML.asp
```

## Creating XML from a Database with a Server-Side Script

The previous example produced output in HTML for rendering in a browser. If you examine the code closely, you will see that the result is also well-formed XML, but it is expressed in the HTML vocabulary. By making only minor modifications to the script, you can have it generate XML that looks like the examples you created on previous days.

In the next example, you will make all of the same object calls and use the same SQL statement, but you will wrap the results in XML tags, rather than HTML. In other words, rather than starting with <!DOCTYPE ...>, <HTML>, <HEAD> and <BODY> sections, you will encode an XML declaration and the required root element:

```
<?xml version="1.0"?>
<note>
    ...VBScript
</note>
```

The loop code will be slightly different as well, reflecting the XML tags to be used instead of HTML. The loop code should look like this:

```
do until msgRS.EOF
    Response.Write ("<msg id='" & _
        msgRS("ID") & "'>")
    Response.Write ( _
        "<from>" & msgRS("from") & "</from>" & _
        "<source>" & msgRS("source") & "</source>" & _
        "<message>" & msgRS("message") & "</message>" )
    Response.Write ("</msg>")
    msgRS.MoveNext
Loop
```

Note that the HTML list items are now the familiar XML elements from, source, and message. Note also that the value from the database id field is being used as an attribute value in the XML result.

The complete program is shown as Listing 19.2. Make the necessary changes to your first script and save the new code as msg_XML.asp, being careful to ensure that you name yours exactly as shown because it will be called by another program in the next exercise.

**LISTING 19.2**   An ASP Script to Extract Records from a Database and Return the Result as Well-Formed XML—msg_XML.asp

```
 1: <%@ LANGUAGE = "VBScript"%>
 2: <%' listing 19.2 - msg_XML.asp
 3: %>
 4:
 5: <%Response.ContentType="text/xml"%>
 6: <?xml version="1.0"?>
 7: <!-- XML file generated by ASP -->
 8:
 9: <note>
10:     <%
11:     set oMsg = Server.CreateObject("ADODB.Connection")
12:     oMsg.open("messageDB")
13:
14:     set msgRS = oMsg.Execute("SELECT * FROM msg;")
15:
16:     do until msgRS.EOF
17:         Response.Write ("<msg id='" & _
18:             msgRS("ID") & "'>")
19:         Response.Write ( _
20:             "<from>" & msgRS("from") & "</from>" & _
21:             "<source>" & msgRS("source") & "</source>" & _
22:             "<message>" & msgRS("message") & "</message>" )
23:         Response.Write ("</msg>")
24:         msgRS.MoveNext
25:     Loop
26:     oMsg.Close
27:     set oMsg = nothing
28:     %>
29: </note>
```

**ANALYSIS**   Line 1 establishes the scripting language for the Active Server Page as VBScript. Line 6 provides the XML declaration for the document being generated by the script. Line 9 provides the start tag for the root element (note) for the generated page. Lines 10–28 contain the remainder of the VBScript. The ADO is created on line 11 and named oMsg. The Connection object is provided with the messageDB DSN using the open method (line 12). Line 14 passes the SQL query to the database with the Execute method on the Connection object. Lines 16–25 contain the loop that prints the results of the query to the screen. The loop iterates until the end of the database file is encountered (line 16). Each of the fields of the first record encountered is reported to the default output device (Response.Write) and wrapped in appropriate XML tags (lines 17–23). On line 24, the MoveNext property on the RecordSet object instructs the process to move one record ahead on the database. Line 25 instructs the script to loop back to the do statement on line 16. If the last record has not yet been processed, the loop continues until it has.

19

Line 26 instructs the connection to close, and line 27 sets the oMsg variable to null. The script is terminated on line 28 and the end tag of the root element (</note>) is provided on line 29.

You can execute this script by entering the following URL via your browser:

```
http://localhost/day_19/msg_XML.asp
```

Execution of this script should produce output that looks like the result depicted by Figure 19.7.

**FIGURE 19.7**

*XML output generated by a server-side script accessing a database.*

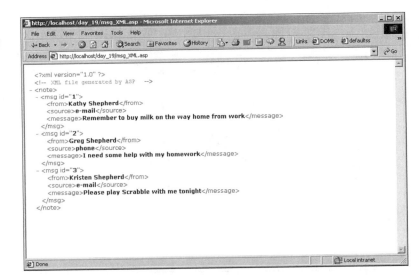

## Processing Downstream

The previous example produced output in XML from your database, but it doesn't lend itself to rendering on a browser as is. You could create a stylesheet and associate it to style the output. However, instead of this approach, you will create an HTML page that establishes an XML data island and binds HTML elements to corresponding XML data elements. You made extensive use of this technique on Day 17. The difference here is that rather than access a static XML document as you did then, your data island in the next exercise will call the msg_XML.asp script to generate what might be best thought of as *virtual XML*. In this case, the XML data is transient, residing in memory, but never stored permanently on disk.

If you kept a copy of the island02.html page created on Day 17, you might want to edit it now. It is similar to the page required to fulfill this exercise. The major difference is that the data island in the current example draws from an ASP program rather than from a static XML document. In the current exercise, the HTML <XML> tag, therefore, will look like this:

```
<XML src="msg_XML.asp" id="myMSG"/>
```

Note that the source for the data island is the ASP. Because of this, you will only be able to execute this page by passing it through the IIS Web Server. In other words, you cannot browse this page as you might with a traditional HTML page. The Web server, to ensure that the ASP code is executed, must first process it.

The rest of the page contains standard HTML markup and the data required to build the table of bound elements. The table code portion of the HTML page will look like this:

```
<TABLE id="table" border="6" width="100%"
        datasrc="#myMsg" summary="messages">
    <THEAD style="background-color: aqua">
            <TH>From</TH>
            <TH>Source</TH>
            <TH>Message</TH>
    </THEAD>
    <TR valign="top" align="center">
            <TD><SPAN DATAFLD="from"/></TD>
            <TD><SPAN DATAFLD="source"/></TD>
            <TD><SPAN DATAFLD="message"/></TD>
    </TR>
</TABLE>
```

The value of the data source attribute on the table tag corresponds to the id attribute value provided in the data island tag (<XML src="msg_XML.asp" id="myMSG"/>). Each of the <TD> cells contains a SPAN element bound to one of the from, source, or message elements in the XML instance document. The complete program is shown as Listing 19.3.

**LISTING 19.3**  An ASP Data Island Using Transient XML Data from a Database—ASP_isle.html

```
 1: <!DOCTYPE HTML PUBLIC "-//W3C//DTD HTML 4.01 Transitional//EN"
 2:    "http://www.w3.org/TR/html4/loose.dtd">
 3: <!-- listing 19.3 - ASP_isle.html -->
 4:
 5: <HTML>
 6:     <HEAD>
 7:          <TITLE>XML Data Binding</TITLE>
 8:     </HEAD>
 9:     <BODY>
10:          <H1>Messages</H1>
11:     <XML SRC="msg_XML.asp" ID="myMsg"/>
12:     <TABLE id="table" border="6" width="100%"
```

19

LISTING **19.3**   Continued

```
13:            datasrc="#myMsg" summary="messages">
14:         <THEAD style="background-color: aqua">
15:            <TH>From</TH>
16:            <TH>Source</TH>
17:            <TH>Message</TH>
18:         </THEAD>
19:         <TR valign="top" align="center">
20:            <TD><SPAN DATAFLD="from"/></TD>
21:            <TD><SPAN DATAFLD="source"/></TD>
22:            <TD><SPAN DATAFLD="message"/></TD>
23:         </TR>
24:       </TABLE>
25:     </BODY>
26: </HTML>
```

**ANALYSIS**  Line 11 establishes the data island as coming from msg_XML.asp using the HTML XML element. The id="myMsg" attribute provides a reference (myMsg) that is used on line 13 to indicate the data source for the table. The XML document that is being bound to is indicated by the src attribute value. The table start tag (lines 12–13) contains the datasrc attribute, indicating the named reference (#myMsg) of the data island. A table head section is included (lines 14–18) to provide a header row that labels the table columns. The TR is encoded on lines 19–23. Lines 20–22 use SPAN elements to bind to the XML from, source, and message elements, respectively.

You will execute this page by browsing with the following URL:

```
http://localhost/day_19/ASP_isle.html
```

The result should look like Figure 19.8.

# Summary

Today, you learned about integrating XML into business models via enterprise applications. Most of the models reviewed include some reliance on databases. The three-tier architecture of the Web provides databases in the data tier. Middle-tier scripts can access data stored in databases, process and manipulate it, and push it to the client. Downstream processes can access middle-tier applications to perform the work required to extract data. You used a number of technologies to accomplish data and application integration, but at the core of these technologies, XML provided data exchange capabilities.

FIGURE 19.8

*A downstream Web application accessing a middle-tier script.*

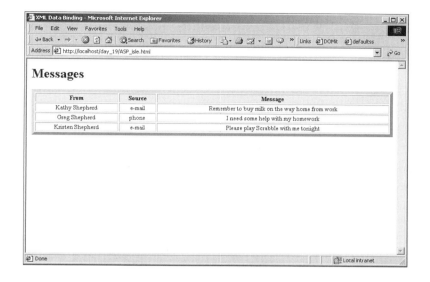

# Q&A

**Q  What is document analysis?**

**A**  Document analysis is the act of examining the parts, purposes, and requirements for one or more classes of documents to design a detailed and definitive description for each.

**Q  What is the three-tier Web architecture?**

**A**  It is a special type of client/server architecture consisting of three well-defined and separate processes, each running on a different platform. The client tier, comprising browsers or other user agents, accesses applications via a Web server on the middle tier. Data is stored on the data tier, traditionally in databases, file systems, or other formal structures.

19

# Day 20

# XML e-Commerce

E-business represents a significant opportunity for companies wanting to improve the management of their operations through the automation of business-to-consumer and business-to-business data exchange. A number of protocols for collaborative data use, remote invocation of objects, and XML messaging have been developed, but they are still in the early stages of development. Final and formalized standards have yet to be developed, but a great deal of work has gone into development of methodologies to date. Today, you will learn

- Some of the advantages of XML in e-business applications
- Representative uses of XML in business-to-consumer (B2C) and business-to-business (B2B) applications
- XML protocols for structured business messaging

## The Business Use of XML

Yesterday, you read about applications that were particularly beneficial to enterprises. Each scenario described a system that used and benefited from XML, resulting in enhanced internal operations of typical businesses. Today, you will read about advantages associated with the use of XML technologies by those who sell products and services on the Web. The trend toward prefixing almost any common word with *e-* has lead to some confusion about just what e-commerce and e-business really refer to. Think of e-business or e-commerce as almost any regular business transaction conducted between companies and individuals (business-to-consumer) or companies and other businesses (business-to-business). Business-to-consumer transactions are typically referred to by the acronym B2C, and business-to-business is shortened as B2B. You might also have heard of business to government (B2G) and perhaps other acronyms. Today, you will focus first on the ways in which XML can offer benefits for B2C systems, and then on several exciting new technologies in the B2B arena.

## The Cost of Doing e-Business

According to IBM (source: `http://www-7.ibm.com/nz/e-business/overview.html`), consumers are expected to spend in excess of $130 billion in 2001 via online transactions. Other industry analysts forecast the largest revenue growth within the B2B sector. E-commerce between businesses is expected to grow to $1.3 trillion by 2003, or ten times the amount predicted for consumer e-commerce. This amount is roughly equivalent to 9% of all U.S. trade, and more than the gross domestic product (GDP) of Britain or Italy, twice that of Canada, and one third that of Japan (source: `http://www.oecd.org/std/gdp.htm`). In 2004, e-commerce is expected to top $7.3 trillion according to analysis by The Gartner Group as reported by the Business Technology Network (`http://content.techweb.com/wire/story/TWB20000217S0002`). To ensure that these investments offer suitable returns, the best technical solutions will be required. Not surprisingly, XML plays a significant role in many of these solutions.

E-business and e-commerce are no longer technologies of the future. Most companies are investing heavily in the integration of business processes on the Web *now*. Sales on the Web began with consumer goods and spread rapidly to include such things as supply chain management, electronic marketplace trading, and instantaneous electronic product and service procurement models. These initiatives are driving huge network expansion efforts around the world, moving economies, and even influencing national elections. According to studies conducted by PricewaterhouseCoopers (PWC) (`http://www.pwcmoneytree.com/`), "Those companies that use e-business [technologies] can leapfrog the competition and achieve sustained competitive advantage. Today's and tomorrow's e-executives need to know how they can achieve similar results."

**Note**

E-business is the integration of core business systems with Web technology. In the most general terms, e-business means conducting business over intranets, extranets, or the Internet. E-commerce typically refers to buying and selling over the Web.

A primary component of any e-business strategy is the integration of the supply chain: business-to-business (B2B). You will soon see a great deal of focus on this e-segment with affordable XML-based technical solutions that offer key platforms for the small/medium business space. B2B is the area most likely to have significant financial impact on the greatest number of e-businesses over the next few years. According to PricewaterhouseCoopers, "The business-to-business component is what twenty-first century executives need to understand in order to win over the long term."

# B2C Applications

The business-to-consumer model includes the online automation of a number of transaction-based applications. Many of these are suited to use XML technologies that offer enhanced functions and improved efficiency. In the next section, you will read about two representative examples of these applications and how XML can be incorporated. Similar to the approach used to present enterprise application scenarios yesterday, today you will be offered the following:

- A short review of the business problems to be addressed
- The potential benefits offered by XML
- Architectural and development process issues

## Online Personalization Applications

Perhaps you have visited a Web portal site and provided your address, zip code, or postal code to obtain weather reports for your location. At the time that you received the local weather report, you might also have been presented with local news stories, and certainly focused advertising. In fact, the advertising might have paid for the seemingly free information you were provided. After all, why would a portal content provider deliver you free news, sports, weather, and other services, if not to generate revenue? Typically you have not paid money, as such, to view these sights. However, an advertiser might see value in your being exposed to banner advertisements or pop-up windows while you catch up on sports scores or local news.

This kind of personalization is really only the beginning of what is possible on the Web using XML in conjunction with other technologies. Some online bookstores, for instance, provide a customized recommendation of books related to those that you typically buy if you are a frequent purchaser. An online bookstore might write a cookie on your machine when you visit. The cookie, if programmed efficiently, is nothing more than a number that is keyed to a record on a server-side database. That record could contain information such as your name, the details of your previous purchases, the topics that typically entice your purchase, and the frequency of your buying habits. Perhaps a profile document stored in XML might look something like the one shown in Listing 20.1.

**20**

**LISTING 20.1** Personalization Profile Mockup—`profile.xml`

```
 1: <?xml version="1.0"?>
 2: <!-- Listing 20.1 - profile.xml -->
 3:
 4: <profile>
 5:     <cookie id="6233265454"/>
 6:     <first_name>Devan</first_name>
 7:     <last_name>Shepherd</last_name>
 8:     <last_purchase date="07-01-01" frequency="6"/>
 9:     <interests>
10:         <category>technical</category>
11:         <sub_category>computer</sub_category>
12:         <topic>XML</topic>
13:         <topic>Web Development</topic>
14:         <topic>C#</topic>
15:         <topic>E-Commerce</topic>
16:     </interests>
17: </profile>
```

Businesses other than online bookstores are offering customized content. Customized content has become a common model for generating advertising revenues by attracting viewers with information services. Customization increases traffic, particularly for sites that struggle to retain visitors.

HTML-based customization technologies are limited and best suited to delivery of only a few static content pages, or of dynamic content that is generated from pre-specified models. Dynamic content using these techniques is more challenging. As the complexity of site management grows, the expense of maintaining custom delivery of content with HTML tools typically increases.

## XML Benefits

XML offers a smoother integration of disparate content and increased flexibility to customize delivery to individuals. This is due in part to XML's inherent capabilities in structuring text data. Individual structures can be generated as needed. Typically, these will be drawn from legacy data sources using technologies similar in concept to those presented yesterday.

## Architectural and Development Considerations

Typically, a Web site using this form of customized content delivery identifies the customer and passes the identification to a database. The database provides records that are analyzed by a customization engine that determines patterns and selects the information to present. A customization engine might choose a schema to define the data structures and associate an XSL stylesheet to transform the data for presentation as required. The schema helps to determine which data elements are pulled from the information repository. The XSL styles or transforms the output according to the user's specific needs. These steps can be made dynamic so that each presentation of data is unique. In this way, customized data can be delivered each time the application is launched.

The design of a profile with such a system is one of the most important requirements for success. Analysis of user requirements and content desires maximizes the returns on the effort involved in storing and delivering information.

Some portal systems are able to pool their profile collections such that an application starting out as a B2C delivery system comes to include components that characterize B2B transactions. The more you know about a visitor to your portal Web site, the more able you are to provide interesting and valuable content. By sharing profile data with compatible content providers, customization can be based on increased information about the visitor. If your partners use the same XML vocabulary for profiling, the task becomes even simpler and more effective.

Some interesting implications are associated with this kind of Web data with regard to document persistence. These implications help to distinguish these sites from those that contain static information. The data documents that comprise the profiles, for instance, should be stored so that preference information is available over time. On the other hand, the content created by a customization engine is ideally transient. The content persists only until the visitor to the site consumes it. Static Web sites often contain information that is used again and again that is not dynamically generated. The requirements by consumers of data on portal sites require dynamic data creation. Retaining individual documents is unnecessary if they can be generated easily at any time in a custom fashion. After the data is created and consumed, it is released. If needed again, the data can always be regenerated.

Another reason for releasing the generated information is that typically these kinds of data are meant to be perpetually updated. If, for instance, your site delivers weather forecasts or stock values, you want that data to be current. After the data is consumed, it becomes outdated and can be released. A new call for stock values or weather forecasts should return more recent results.

## Data Aggregation Sites

Information Aggregation applications on the Web are ideally suited to XML. These applications consolidate information from disparate sources into a single presentation. In the same way that distributors moving material goods consolidate ordering, shipments, and delivery, aggregators offer consolidation via the Web. Sometimes consolidation is done to move material goods and products through electronic distribution channels. In other cases, consolidation brokers digital information.

**20**

Suppose that you sell home theater systems on a Web site that helps consumers select individual components by providing comparisons, audio quality statistics, and pricing. The aggregation of data on the components could be offered as a service. Consumers might not want to read entire specifications on every individual component, and the rate at which individual components change is increasing. The aggregation application could ensure that final system combinations are compatible. Pricing could be used as a variable for section. In other words, given a budget amount, an optimum solution could be designed depending on whether the consumer was more interested in sound quality or video quality, or perhaps on the basis of a media preference for CD, MP3, or video disc. A distributor could also offer this kind of information aggregation such that a number of super stores, video specialty shops, and department stores, in addition to consumers, could benefit from the aggregated information. The aggregation could be offered as part of the supply chain, such that orders placed with the distributor would be assembled in accordance with customized package requirements prior to delivery.

## XML Benefits

Information aggregation on a large scale is difficult due to the proliferation of incompatible systems at all points in the information chain. For instance, the specifications, details, and order transaction data provided by component manufactures in the home theater example are likely to be on a variety of platforms in diverse formats. Extracting just the important facts from all of these sources in a machine-readable structure might prove quite difficult. Making the data not only machine readable but also human intelligible makes it more complicated. The proprietary formats associated with each supplier make it difficult to aggregate the data. After the aggregation is accomplished, an aggregator must ensure that the information is presented in a format that is useful and usable to retailers and consumers over the Web. Perhaps it is necessary to provide multiple output formats based on a single collection of aggregated information.

Using XML to gather the information from a variety of sources, consolidate it into a single source, and serve the aggregation in multiple formats makes sense. As you know, XML is machine readable and human intelligible. Input can be consolidated easily into an intelligent data set with markup that preserves the structure of the information. Then, using XSLT in conjunction with schemata, you can deliver aggregated information in a variety of formats without compromising the integrity of the data or having to create multiple collections of the source. In fact, the schemata become assets in an aggregation and, when tied to marketing data, can provide an organization with a competitive advantage. Capturing the information requirements of consumers, solution providers, or even those providing home stereo solutions can maximize an organization's returns by stressing combinations and options that attract the greatest interest. Tracked over time, these patterns can become salable assets with value to retailers on the output side of aggregation and to manufacturers on the input side.

## Architectural and Development Considerations

By accessing the data available from a variety of source providers, an aggregator can add value by creating a set of information combinations. In some cases, data might be sourced from providers who are able to deliver information in XML format. In those cases, the provider is given a schema or obtains it from an industry-specific repository, and then creates output in the structure dictated. Other providers of data might use different formats, which the aggregator can accept and manipulate prior to aggregation. The processing and aggregation steps offer unique value and ultimately lead to trade. After the repository is built, a Web-based electronic inquiry, either from a consumer or originated by a retailer, can cause the application to access the necessary documents, produce a dynamic set of data, and apply an XSL stylesheet appropriate for the needs of the requestor.

Other examples of information aggregators on the Web include the following:

- Services that aggregate travel information from a variety of sources and provide consumers with the lowest airfare, hotel packages, car rentals, and restaurant specials for selected destinations.
- Web sites that offer to find the lowest price for electronics, consumer goods, and so on. These sites are often called Web shopping robots. They source and aggregate a selection of cameras, computers, sporting goods, jewelry, and other goods and deliver price comparisons for Web consumers to evaluate.
- Financial aggregators that search for the lowest mortgage rates, loan rates, or insurance policies.

In all of these cases, the key to success is in building a reliable and highly automated stream of data that flows from an information provider through an aggregator to an information consumer. At each step in the process, the information aggregator adds value to the information being brokered. On the input side, the aggregator collects only the valuable data that is required to meet specific needs. By eliminating the noise of unneeded marketing and specification detail, the aggregator can focus a response set of data precisely to the needs of the information consumer.

**20**

Development of this type of application requires that you analyze and map a variety of information provider data to the needs and desires of information consumers. After you determine what is available and how you can package it for those who require it, you can draft schemata to define the structures involved and publish those for information providers that choose to subscribe to your services. For instance, in the case of consumer goods shopping robots on the Web, manufacturers that choose to participate often do so by subscription to the service. Industries sometimes provide their own focused aggregation. For instance, in June 2001, an agreement was signed between United, Delta,

Continental, Northwest, and American Airlines to create `http://www.orbitz.com` to sell seats on flights directly to consumers, in direct competition with independent travel aggregation sites, such as `http://www.travelocity.com` and `http://www.expedia.com/`. According to a CNN story on the agreement (`http://www.cnn.com/2001/TECH/internet/06/05/orbitz.travel.idg/index.html`) the $50 million startup cost of the operation will be funded by the airlines that will use a distributed architecture and promise to deliver superior content.

## Supply Chain Integration

Related to aggregation is the relatively new trend toward XML-based supply chain integration. Electronic connectivity in marketplaces is making it easier for businesses to communicate with one another to exchange commerce transactions. Suppose that you sell computers to large electronic superstores, computer chains, and discount warehouse outlets. You might have a supply chain to provide you with component parts, such as computer circuit boards, monitors, keyboards, printers, cases, and other components. This supply chain is a marketplace to you. You are also a provider of computers in a marketplace that serves the outlets that retail your goods. In such a scenario, price change information can be communicated from each supplier to a number of retailers, and each retailer in turn might want to place orders for items at the new price. XML allows developers to create well-formed documents describing the transactions.

Suppose, for instance, that you need to buy memory cards to place in your computers. You might want to approach your supply chain and request bids on prices for the quantity of memory cards you require. You could then do business with the supplier who met your requirements for quantity, quality, and price.

Automation is intended to help data originators, whether retailer or supplier, to encode exchange documents in formats that can be transmitted easily over the Web. Solutions must track the sending and receiving of transactions with precision. Ideally, all messages should be electronically acknowledged upon receipt, so that transport is guaranteed despite technical problems associated with Internet connectivity. Without acknowledgement, automated systems should retransmit critical transactions until they have been transported successfully. Furthermore, solutions should provide for authentication, security, and data integrity at all points throughout the exchange network.

# From Data Taxonomy to Data Exchange

When developers first considered the issues related to sharing business data over the Web to transact commerce electronically, the design often centered on vocabularies and dialects. The analysis typically resolved precisely what information was to be exchanged and determined a format, or schema, for that exchange. Many of the early aggregation efforts, for instance, followed that model. It worked for the delivery of a variety of solutions, but suffered from being highly customized to meet a specific need. If the business data structure evolved over time, the transactions needed to be re-created in adherence with continuously modified schemata. What has been needed is a shift from the issues of data taxonomy to the fundamental question of how to transfer XML between parties as part of a meaningful, reliable exchange. In this section, you will review the leading protocols for XML data exchange and the problems they are meant to address. It is assumed that as a programmer, you are familiar with scripting languages and the basics of HTTP and Web protocols. Therefore, this discussion is specific to the protocol issues themselves and not the underlying constructs.

The W3C provides an overview of a variety of XML data exchange protocols at `http://www.w3.org/2000/03/29-XML-protocol-matrix`. Although dozens of protocols have been offered for consideration by the W3C, XML-RPC, SOAP, WDDX, and ebXML have emerged as the most likely to be adopted or combined into a final solution for XML transport.

## XML HTTP Object Calls

Many of the business transactions involved in E-business are passed over the Internet on the HTTP protocol. It is relatively simple to simulate such a transaction through the use an XML HTTP object to retrieve a remotely located XML source document. Suppose, for instance, that you want to write a quick Web page that is capable of retrieving any XML document from a Web server by providing it a URL. You could use the XML HTTP object provided by Microsoft with a small amount of JavaScript to do this quite simply. In practice, you might not use this Microsoft-dependent technology unless you could guarantee that it was usable by all those who needed to access Web pages in this manner. This is offered for descriptive purposes to show just one approach to accomplishing this form of connectivity.

Using JavaScript, the object could be instantiated as a new ActiveX object in the same way you invoked the Document Object Model `Microsoft.XMLDOM` object on Day 12. The syntax would be as follows:

```
var myVariable = new ActiveXObject("Microsoft.XMLHTTP")
```

After the object is instantiated, you could use method calls on your variable to perform standard HTTP methods, such as GET or POST. A GET method could be used to retrieve an XML document from a remote server or any other content desired, and a POST could be used to send an XML document to a server-side script for processing. The GET would look something like this:

```
myVariable.open("GET", (URL), false)
myVariable.send()
myReponseVariable = myVariable.responseText
```

**20**

The open method establishes an HTTP GET method to the URL you designate. The false parameter indicates that the method is synchronous; therefore, it must therefore finish executing before another method can execute. The send() method passes the GET method over HTTP, and the response of the call is stored in the variable you designate as *myResponseVariable*.

After you have the response, in this case the full text of the XML file you are retrieving, you can print it on the screen by sending it to the default output device. To complete a simple example of this approach, you will need to wrap it in HTML tags that prevent the markup from being parsed, such as <XMP>. This wrapper would look like this:

```
document.write("<XMP>" + myReponseVariable + "</XMP>");
```

A complete HTML program using this approach is shown as Listing 20.2. Enter this example and save it as httpGetXML.html.

**LISTING 20.2**    A File Retrieve Program Using the XMLHTTP Object—httpGetXML.html

```
 1: <!DOCTYPE XHTML PUBLIC "-//W3C//DTD HTML 4.01 Transitional//EN"
 2:   "http://www.w3.org/TR/html4/loose.dtd">
 3: <!-- Listing 20.2 httpGetXML.html -->
 4:
 5: <HTML>
 6: <BODY>
 7: <SCRIPT language="JavaScript">
 8:
 9:         var URL=prompt("Please enter the URL of an XML file to retrieve",
10:         "Enter XML File URL");
11:
12:         var xmlHttp = new ActiveXObject("Microsoft.XMLHTTP")
13:         xmlHttp.open("GET", (URL), false)
14:         xmlHttp.send()
15:         xmlDoc=xmlHttp.responseText
16:
17:         document.write("<XMP>" + xmlDoc + "</XMP>");
18: </SCRIPT>
19: </BODY>
20: </HTML>
```

**ANALYSIS** Lines 9–10 create a simple JavaScript prompt, asking the user to provide a URL to a page containing the content to be retrieved. Lines 12–15 instantiate an XML HTTP object (line 12) and make a synchronous GET method string (line 13) that is sent over HTTP (line 14). On line 15, the response is stored in a variable (xmlDoc). The content of that variable is reported to the screen on line 17.

Try loading this page into a browser and entering the URL for an XML page stored on a remote Web server. For instance, you could retrieve the XML Schema document that defines W3C namespaces at `http://www.w3.org/XML/1998/namespace`. If you are using the IIS Web Server on your computer, you could also retrieve a document created on a previous day and stored locally, provided it is stored in a virtual Web directory.

## XML-RPC and SOAP

XML-RPC is a protocol for Remote Procedure Calls whose conversation over TCP port 80 (HTTP) is encoded into XML. XML-RPC implementations are written in many languages for many platforms. Every XML-RPC application comprises two distinct parts. The first part makes an XML-RPC request to some Web service and is consequently known as a client call. If your script is answering XML-RPC requests, it is referred to as a *listener*. Several implementations of XML-RPC are in use today. These implementations—based on such diverse technologies as PERL, Tcl, Python, PHP, and AppleScript—offer proof that the mechanism is as platform- and language-neutral as its designers intended. Programming languages such as Java, C++, C#, and VB offer means of accomplishing this as well.

The direct descendent of XML-RPC is the Simple Object Access Protocol (SOAP), a means of invoking a remote object with the passage of simple parameters over HTTP in XML wrappers. SOAP, like XML-RPC, is a Web-based abstraction of distributed client/server object communication. The complete SOAP 1.1 recommendation is currently qualified by the W3C as a note, which has been submitted for review and discussion. The text of the note can be found at `http://www.w3.org/TR/SOAP/`. Soap is an XML dialect that is meant to be a lightweight protocol for exchange of data required to invoke a remote object and to return the results of that invocation to the originating requestor. The W3C note defines SOAP as "an XML based protocol that consists of three parts: an envelope that defines a framework for describing what is in a message and how to process it, a set of encoding rules for expressing instances of application-defined datatypes, and a convention for representing remote procedure calls and responses."

**20**

**Note**

SOAP is well positioned to provide sophisticated applications for remote object invocation. The support by major industry leaders will help to ensure the development of platform-neutral solutions. At the time of this writing, the technology is still somewhat immature and tools will need to develop further for widespread use to be practical.

SOAP provides you a way to make remote calls on object methods or functions. In traditional customized XML applications, the client-side and server-side applications must know what the message format is to exchange data. SOAP provides the following:

- A standard mechanism for representing the procedure call interface
- A mechanism for querying to determine what functionality is available
- The syntax of each call

SOAP, therefore, can replace the explicit XML conversations that occur in custom XML implementations. To make this process truly seamless, services or tools must be available to provide the SOAP XML packaging and unpackaging and perform the data exchange operations.

SOAP accomplishes this generic passing of object call parameters by packaging the calls in a standardized electronic envelope structure. Think of SOAP envelopes as analogous to postal envelopes. You place the information you want to pass to the object in the envelope and mail it over the Internet via HTTP. This is called the *SOAP request* document. At the receiving end, the SOAP server opens the envelope, removes the content, and passes it on to the remote object in the form of an object invocation call. The response received from the object is placed back in the envelope and returned over the Internet, via HTTP, to the originating client. This is called the *SOAP response* document. A SOAP request document is an XML instance document that contains a SOAP envelope, an optional SOAP header, and a required SOAP body. The body of the SOAP document contains the remote object invocation parameters. A SOAP message complies with the following syntax rules:

- It must be encoded using XML.
- It must have a SOAP envelope.
- It can have a SOAP header.
- It must have a SOAP body.
- It must use the SOAP envelope namespaces.
- It must use the SOAP encoding namespace.
- It must not contain a DTD reference.
- It must not contain XML processing instructions.

The syntax of a SOAP request document is as follows:

```
<?xml version="1.0"?>
<SOAP-ENV:Envelope
      xmlns:SOAP-ENV="http://schemas.xmlsoap.org/soap/envelope/"
      xmlns:SOAP-ENC=http://schemas.xmlsoap.org/soap/encoding/>
   <SOAP-ENV:Header>
```

```
    ...optional header information
    </SOAP-ENV:Header>

    <SOAP-ENV:Body>
    ...object invocation parameters
    </SOAP-ENV:Body>

</SOAP-ENV:Envelope>
```

This SOAP request document contains a `SOAP-ENV:Envelope` root element that is bound to the `http://schemas.xmlsoap.org/soap/envelope/` namespace. The `SOAP-ENV:Header` is an optional element. The `SOAP-ENV:Body` is required and contains the parameters that are passed to the remote object.

The syntax of a SOAP response document is as follows:

```
<?xml version="1.0"?>
<SOAP-ENV:Envelope
        xmlns:SOAP-ENV="http://schemas.xmlsoap.org/soap/envelope/"
        xmlns:SOAP-ENC=http://schemas.xmlsoap.org/soap/encoding/>
    <SOAP-ENV:Header>
    ...optional header information
    </SOAP-ENV:Header>

    <SOAP-ENV:Body>
    ...object invocation response
    </SOAP-ENV:Body>

</SOAP-ENV:Envelope>
```

This SOAP response document contains a `SOAP-ENV:Envelope` root element that is bound to the `http://schemas.xmlsoap.org/soap/envelope/` namespace. The `SOAP-ENV:Header` is an optional element. The `SOAP-ENV:Body` is required and contains the response from the remote object.

Imagine that you have access to a remote object that returns the current trading value of a stock or traded fund as a price quotation. You might be required to merely pass the object the symbol for the stock or fund you want to be quoted. The object would then return to you the current or last traded price. Listing 20.3 shows the complete SOAP request document sent to an imaginary stock quotation object.

20

**LISTING 20.3**    SOAP Request Document for a Price Quotation—SOAP_req.xml

```
1: <?xml version="1.0"?>
2: <!-- Listing 20.3 SOAP_req.xml -->
3:
4: <SOAP-ENV:Envelope
5:     xmlns:SOAP-ENV="http://schemas.xmlsoap.org/soap/envelope/"
6:     xmlns:SOAP-ENC="http://schemas.xmlsoap.org/soap/encoding/">
```

**LISTING 20.3**    continued

```
 7:
 8:    <SOAP-ENV:Header>
 9:      <SOAPsrvr>123</SOAPsrvr>
10:    </SOAP-ENV:Header>
11:
12:    <SOAP-ENV:Body>
13:      <q:getQuote xmlns:q="urn:Devan's-delayed-quotes">
14:       <symbol>ssefx</symbol>
15:      </q:getQuote>
16:    </SOAP-ENV:Body>
17:
18: </SOAP-ENV:Envelope>
```

**ANALYSIS**  In this example, the SOAP-ENV:Envelope root element (lines 4–18) contains a SOAP-ENV:Header element (lines 8–10) and a SOAP-ENV:Body element (lines 12–16). The required namespaces for the envelope and for any SOAP encoding are provided on lines 5 and 6. The header of this SOAP document contains a SOAPsrvr that holds content used by the SOAP server to manage the package being passed. The body contains a q:getQuote element that is bound to the urn:Devan's-delayed-quotes namespace. The symbol element contains the name of, in this case, a mutual fund, ssefx (The Shepherd Street Equity Fund), for which the remote object will return a last traded price.

Listing 20.4 shows the complete SOAP response document sent from the SOAP server following the completion of the object call. The SOAP response envelopes the output from the object.

**LISTING 20.4**    SOAP Response Document for a Price Quotation—SOAP_resp.xml

```
 1: <?xml version="1.0"?>
 2: <!-- Listing 20.4 SOAP_resp.xml -->
 3:
 4: <SOAP-ENV:Envelope
 5:     xmlns:SOAP-ENV="http://schemas.xmlsoap.org/soap/envelope/"
 6:     xmlns:SOAP-ENC="http://schemas.xmlsoap.org/soap/encoding/">
 7:
 8:    <SOAP-ENV:Header>
 9:      <ProcessID mustUnderstand="0">0</ProcessID>
10:    </SOAP-ENV:Header>
11:
12:    <SOAP:Body>
13:      <q_resp:getQuoteResponse xmlns:qres='urn:Devan's-delayed-quotes'>
14:       <return>14.59</return>
15:      </q_resp:getQuoteResponse>
```

**LISTING 20.4**    continued

```
16:  </SOAP:Body>
17:
18:  </SOAP-ENV:Envelope>
```

**ANALYSIS**    In this example, the SOAP-ENV:Envelope root element (lines 4–18) contains a SOAP-ENV:Header element (lines 8–10) and a SOAP-ENV:Body element (lines 12–16). The required namespaces for the envelope and for any SOAP encoding are provided on lines 5 and 6. The header of this SOAP document contains a SOAPsrvr that holds content used by the SOAP server to manage the package being passed. The body contains a q_resp:getQuoteResponse element that is bound to the urn:Devan's-delayed-quotes namespace. The return element contains the price at which the mutual fund, ssefx (The Shepherd Street Equity Fund), last traded.

For these SOAP messages to function, you would need to create a SOAP client application to send and receive them. On the server-side, a SOAP server would interpret the messages and pass the parameters to the remote object. The SOAP server would also receive the results from the object and place them back into the SOAP response document for return transmission to the SOAP client application. Figure 20.1 shows a simple SOAP client created using the IBM Sash Weblications development environment. The client, created by xmethods.com, provides a number of small applications that use SOAP messages to invoke remote objects.

**FIGURE 20.1**

Xmethods.com—*IBM Sash SOAP client.*

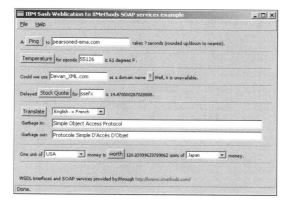

**20**

**Note**    IBM Sash is a highly configurable development system used to create network applications. Some developers use Sash to build e-business applications and hook them up to back-end systems and HTTP servers, using existing resources and infrastructure. You can use Sash to turn Web pages into fully functional Windows applications featuring content downloaded off the Web.

You can create your own SOAP client and server programs to access objects using one of the many SOAP development kits available on the Web. These distributions include client-side and server-side tools as well as examples. Some of these are available from the following:

- IBM SOAP for Java, now a part of the Apache XML Project: `http://xml.apache.org/soap/`
- Lucin SOAP Toolkit: `http://www.soaptoolset.com/`
- Microsoft SOAP Toolkit: `http://msdn.microsoft.com/xml/general/soap1and2.asp`

SOAP supports all data types found in the "Built-in Datatypes" section of the W3C working draft XML Schema Part 2: Datatypes. It also supports many structure and array-based compound types (`http://www.w3.org/TR/2001/REC-xmlschema-2-20010502/`).

## Web Distributed Data Exchange (WDDX)

The WDDX, developed by Allaire (`http://www.allaire.com/handlers/index.cfm?ID=5624&Method=full`), provides a mechanism for exchanging complex data structures over HTTP, as an alternative to SOAP. According to Allaire documentation, WDDX is meant "to provide a more Web-like way to transmit structured data objects between network entities without changing the programmatic approach to developing Web applications from page-based to object-based."

WDDX differs from XML-RPC and SOAP in two fundamental ways. First, its approach to serialization is structure-based rather than object-based. In addition, WDDX is not fundamentally based on RPC semantics. The WDDX DTD and a serialization module that performs the transformation from native language data structures into XML and vice versa characterize WDDX. A WDDX packet is created when an application converts data structures into WDDX. These packets can be validated against the WDDX DTD. Listing 20.5 shows a simple WDDX document comprising a single packet that, similarly to the SOAP example, is sent to determine the price of a mutual fund.

**LISTING 20.5**    WDDX XML Packet to Obtain a Mutual Fund Price—`WDDX_stock.xml`

```
1: <?xml version='1.0'?>
2: <!-- Listing 20.5 WDDX_stock.xml -->
3:
4: <!DOCTYPE wddxPacket SYSTEM 'Stock_check.dtd'>
5: <wddxPacket version='0.9'>
6:      <data>
7:          <struct>
8:              <var name='getQuote'>
9:                  <value>SSEFX</value>
```

**LISTING 20.5**    continued

```
10:                    </var>
11:                </struct>
12:            </data>
13: </wddxPacket>
```

**ANALYSIS**    The `wddxPacket` root element (lines 5–13) contains a `data` child element. The `data` element (lines 6–12) contains a `struct` element (lines 7–11). In turn, the `struct` element contains a `var` element (lines 8–10) that passes parameters to a host-based application.

Allaire has released the WDDX specification to the general developer community. WDDX has been implemented in ColdFusion and an SDK with support for the Java language, JavaScript, PERL, and COM/ASP.

## ebXML

The acronym ebXML stands for electronic business XML, a joint initiative of the United Nations body for Trade Facilitation and Electronic Business (UN/CEFACT) and the Organization for the Advancement of Structured Information Standards (OASIS). The ebXML initiative is meant to provide "an open XML-based infrastructure enabling the global use of electronic business information in an interoperable, secure and consistent manner by all parties" (source: `http://www.ebxml.org/`). Currently, ebXML has very little vendor support.

The ebXML is organized into teams responsible for different aspects of e-business that employ XML technologies. The team responsible for transport, routing, and packaging has developed recommendations for a message envelope specification, an overall requirements document, and a message-header specification.

The message envelope is an XML document that consists of a header envelope and a payload envelope. The header envelope contains the message header, routing information. Listing 20.6 shows a sample header envelope.

**20**

**LISTING 20.6**    ebXML Header Envelope—`ebXML_header.xml`

```
1: <?xml version="1.0" encoding="UTF-8"?>
2: <!-- Listing  20.6, ebXML_header.xml -->
3:
4: <ebXMLMessageHeader>
5:     <Version>1.0</Version>
6:     <MessageType>Request</MessageType>
7:     <ServiceType>Stock Quote</ServiceType>
8:     <Intent>Last Trading Price</Intent>
9: </ebXMLMessageHeader>
```

[ic:Analysis]The ebXMLMessageHeader root element (lines 4–9) contains Version, MessageType, ServiceType, and Intent child elements. These provide routing information, instructions, and digital signatures to the receiving applications.

The payload envelope might contain one or more body segments. Listing 20.7 shows a sample message body fragment. The document is not complete, but it is enough to show a mock-up of a payload.

LISTING 20.7    Sample ebXML Document—ebXML payload.xml

```
1: <!-- Listing  20.7, ebXML_payload.xml -->
2:
3:  <Control>
4:   <Session Identity="Quote">
5:    <Value>SSEFX</Value>
6:   </Session>
7:  </Control>
```

**ANALYSIS** This snippet of code provides a sample of a message body. The Control element (lines 3–7) contains a Session (lines 4–6) and Value element (line 5) that pass information to an application that returns stock pricing.

At the time of this writing, ebXML is nearly two years old, although the first specification is dated May, 2001. It seemed, for some time, that ebXML would diverge completely from the SOAP efforts because SOAP 1.0 does not provide complete handling of binary data, a desire expressed by the ebXML workgroups. The ebXML approach was created to enable the global use of electronic business information in an interoperable, secure, and consistent manner by all parties.

Even though ebXML and SOAP have many qualities in common, the standards committee responsible for ebXML felt that SOAP was not entirely open and non-proprietary. Therefore, ebXML could not implement SOAP and retain its own interoperable design. Nonetheless, the similarities are uncanny. Both approaches provide a transport framework within which business documents can be securely and reliably transferred. Both are built on industry standard MIME technologies and use XML header and routing functionality. These two standards are so very similar that developers often wonder why two standards exist at all. As a consequence of peer review, the ebXML committees have agreed to adopt a portion of the SOAP specification to save the industry the confusion of two competing standards. This means that over time, ebXML will develop into a complementary, rather than a competitive technology. It will incorporate SOAP messages as payload for document exchange. It is likely that ebXML vendor offerings will be developed in the near future to take ebXML from the planning stage into full-scale implementations.

# Summary

Today, you learned about various e-business metaphors that employ XML technologies. Most of these provide a means for commerce transactions to be packaged and exchanged over the Internet on the HTTP protocol. Several scenarios were presented for B2C and B2B applications and the motivations discussed for each. Businesses anticipate being able to make significant investments in the use of XML technologies for e-commerce in the future.

# Q&A

**Q  How is XML useful for data aggregation sites?**

**A**  XML offers structural controls and intelligent storage of data. XML is suited for environments where the formats of originating data are different and must be combined into a structured output, requiring variable formats for user agents and information consumers.

**Q  How does XML-based supply chain management improve business models?**

**A**  Electronic controls in a marketplace for management of the supply chain enhance the speed and accuracy of conducting business. The flow of business transaction can be monitored and improved through automation.

**Q  Where can I get more information about SOAP implementations for B2B transaction processing?**

**A**  You can find many good sources of information on the Web, such as the following:

- `http://www.soapware.org/directory/4/calendarhttp://www.soapware.org/http://www.soapware.org/`. This site provides specification information, service directories, tutorials, implementation examples, articles, and news on SOAP.

- `http://soap.weblogs.com/http://soap.weblogs.com/`. This site summarizes all of the newsgroup information about SOAP, with content from the Apache XML project, interviews with SOAP experts, and documentation.

- `http://www.xmlrpc.com/http://www.xmlrpc.com/`. This site provides information, opinions, and news about simple cross-platform distributed computing.

- `http://blogspace.com/rss/http://radio.userland.com/http://radio.userland.com`. This site offers a Web application server to run on your desktop that is effectively a powerful XML-based news aggregator, supporting XML-RPC and SOAP 1.1 right out of the box.

**20**

**Q  On what standards does SOAP rely?**

**A**  SOAP relies on HTTP 1.0 or greater and can take advantage of the HTTP extension framework (`http://www.w3.org/Protocols/HTTP/ietf-http-ext`). SOAP
also relies on the core W3C XML recommendation (`http://www.w3.org/TR/
1998/REC-xml-19980210`). SOAP supports (but does not mandate) the W3C XML
namespace recommendation (`http://www.w3.org/TR/REC-xml-names`). SOAP
payloads must be well-formed XML, but no validation (via DTDs or otherwise) is
required. The use of XML Schema (`http://www.w3.org/TR/xmlschema-1/`) to
describe SOAP endpoints is being considered as of this writing, but that is not for-
mally part of the SOAP/1.0 specification.

**Q  Why would a developer choose to use SOAP over a custom XML/HTTP
solution?**

**A**  SOAP offers significant benefits over a custom-developed proprietary XML vocabulary. The growing support for SOAP by vendors offering full-scale solutions is
improving the overall implementation of these technologies. Client and server
applications are quickly becoming available for most industries, and "best-
practices" models are emerging that offer technical and efficiency advantages.

**Q  What are the limitations of SOAP?**

**A**  SOAP does not say anything about bi-directional communication, although it is
possible to layer these semantics on top of a SOAP implementation. The current
SOAP spec describes how SOAP payload can be transmitted via HTTP, but does
not address other protocols.

**Q  Because SOAP travels over HTTP, it can pass through most firewalls. Does
this provide new security threats?**

**A**  SOAP is merely a payload that can be carried via HTTP. Therefore, it is not less
secure than any other HTTP transmission. In addition, the designers of SOAP have
disallowed the inclusion of programming instructions in the SOAP protocol to prevent potential security problems. Because SOAP packets include HTTP headers
data, firewalls could, in the future, be enhanced to filter transmissions on the basis
of header data. As with other HTTP transmissions, SOAP will support the use of
Secure Socket Layers (SSL) and similar schemes of authentication.

**Q  How do B2B transactions translate into improvements for downstream busi-
ness operations?**

**A**  In many cases, the B2B transaction model replaces paper processes. Replacing
these processes with electronic interactions that are faster, more accurate, and more
flexible allows all players in the marketplace to benefit.

DAY **21**

# Building an XML Web Application

XML is well suited to use on Web sites, particularly when XSL transformations and scripting and other forms of programming are performed on the server, rather than on the client. Tying together many of the technologies discussed on previous days, you will create a small Web application today. Today, you will learn

- To create a Web application based on XML files
- To perform server-side XSLT
- To use the XML Document Object Model to create nodes on an XML tree

## The Web Application Design

Today, you will build a Web site application that allows wine enthusiasts to enter tasting notes about the wines they have tried. The data collected will include the name of the wine, the house that produced the wine, the region it comes from, the wine type or varietal, the vintage, and tasting notes. The records could be stored and extracted from a database, similar to the way you accessed message records on Day 19. Today, however, you will use native XML as a means of storing the data. In particular, the data will reside in an XML file hosted on the server, and you will instantiate an XML Document Object Model object to create new nodes on the stored document tree. Server-side scripts written as Active Server Pages will be used to perform an XSL transformation of the XML source document into HTML for presentation of a table of all of the tasting notes presented.

The application will comprise a number of related documents. In the exercises that follow, you will create each of those documents and then place them on a Web server for execution. To build this application in the manner specified, you will need to use some Microsoft-specific tools. You could just as easily build a similar application using other server-side and client-side applications if you wanted to.

The structure of the application will include a home page (`index.html`) with links to a form for data entry (`wine_notes.html`) and a server-side script (`view_notes.asp`) that will list all of the records in the dataset (`wine_notes.xml`). An optional cascading stylesheet (`wine_notes.css`) can provide a consistent look to the entire application by styling all of the HTML pages in a similar fashion. When a user completes the form (`wine_notes.html`), a server-side script (`add_notes.asp`) will process the entry and append it to the `wine_notes.xml` document. A second server-side script is provided to allow users to view the complete set of wine tasting notes (`view_notes.asp`). Figure 21.1 depicts the architecture described.

**FIGURE 21.1**

*Architecture of the wine tasting notes Web application.*

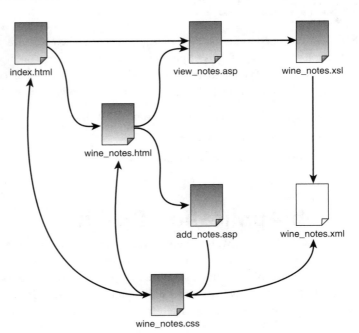

## Storage of Note Records in `wine_notes.xml`

The data for this application will be stored in an XML file with a `wine_notes` root element. Each `wine` element will be like a record on a hierarchical database structure. A `wine` element will contain `house`, `region`, `type`, `vintage`, and `notes` child elements. The `notes` element will be encoded as a CDATA section to ensure that anything entered by the user will be recorded, but not parsed by the XML processor. A `date` attribute on the `wine` element will hold a date and time stamp used to indicate when each record is added to the dataset. A server-side script will automatically generate the date and time stamp when a new record is saved. Listing 21.1 shows a sample `wine_notes.xml` file with several records included. You will need to enter at least one record manually at the time you create this document, so that a structure is in place on the file. Create a document like the one shown and save it as `wine_notes.xml`.

**LISTING 21.1**    A Wine Notes Dataset—`wine_notes.xml`

```
 1: <?xml version="1.0"?>
 2: <!-- Listing 21.1 - wine_notes.xml -->
 3:
 4: <wine_notes>
 5:     <wine date="6/9/2001 10:40:01">
 6:             <house>Chateau de La Chaize</house>
 7:             <region>Brouilly, France</region>
 8:             <type>Beaujolais</type>
 9:             <vintage>1998</vintage>
10:             <notes><![CDATA[Full of berries and firm enough to hold its own
11: with a variety of foods, particularly aged hard cheeses]]></notes>
12:     </wine>
13:     <wine date="6/9/2001 11:20:08">
14:             <house>Chateau d'Epire</house>
15:             <region>Savennieres, France</region>
16:             <type>Cuvee Speciale</type>
17:             <vintage>1998</vintage>
18:             <notes><![CDATA[Firm, flinty acid, with a late spiciness that
19: is reminiscent of the soft, lactic tingle of a Berlinerweisse]]></notes>
20:     </wine>
21: </wine_notes>
```

**ANALYSIS**    The `wine_notes` root element (line 4–20) contains `wine` child elements with `date` attributes on them (lines 5 and 13). Each `wine` element contains a `house`, `region`, `type`, `vintage`, and `notes` element. The notes element is encoded as a CDATA section (lines 10 and 18).

**21**

## Creation of a Web Form as `wine_notes.html`

The file `wine_notes.html` is an HTML page that provides a form for entering details about a particular wine. The form you build in this exercise will provide entry fields, as summarized in Table 21.1. The fields on the form will correspond directly to elements in the XML file (`wine_notes.xml`).

**TABLE 21.1**    Form Fields and Corresponding XML Elements

| HTML Field Label | XML Element | Description |
|---|---|---|
| House/Label | house | This field will be used to enter the name of the winemaker, or the label name of the wine. |
| Region/Location | region | The region, locale, country, or some other geographic indicator will be entered in this field. |
| Type/Varietal | type | The type of wine, or the variety of grape used, will be provided in this field. |
| Vintage | vintage | The year of harvest will be indicated by entries in this field. |
| Tasting Notes | notes | Free-form text will be allowed here for tasting notes. These notes will describe each wine's qualities and characteristics. The data will be placed in the XML document as a CDATA section preserving whitespace and special characters. |

Each of the fields, except the Tasting Notes field, will be created with a standard HTML INPUT child element of the FORM element. Each of these INPUT elements will use the following syntax:

```
<INPUT TYPE=TEXT NAME="REFEERENCE" MAXLENGTH="VALUE">
```

The free-form text field for the tasting notes will use a TEXTAREA element like this:

```
<TEXTAREA NAME="REFERENCE" COLS="VALUE" ROWS="VALUE">
```

Most of the HTML pages in this application will use an external cascading stylesheet (CSS) to ensure a consistent presentation of the entire site. The CSS file will be called `wine_notes.css` and will be associated with the current page via the LINK element, like this:

```
<LINK rel = "stylesheet" type = "text/css"
      href = "wine_notes.css"/>
```

The FORM created on this page will use the POST method to pass the information collected from the user to the add_notes.asp script that will append the data to the wine_notes.xml document created in the previous step. Listing 21.2 shows the complete page. Create this document and save it as wine_notes.html.

**LISTING 21.2**    An HTML Form to Collect Wine Tasting Notes—wine_notes.html

```
 1: <!DOCTYPE HTML PUBLIC "-//W3C//DTD HTML 4.01 Transitional//EN"
 2:  "http://www.w3.org/TR/Html4/loose.dtd">
 3: <!-- Listing 21.2 - wine_notes.html -->
 4:
 5: <HTML>
 6:   <HEAD>
 7:     <TITLE>Online Wine Testing Notes</TITLE>
 8:     <LINK rel = "stylesheet" type = "text/css"
 9:           href = "wine_notes.css"/>
10:   </HEAD>
11:   <BODY>
12:     <H1>Online Wine Tasting Notes</H1>
13:     <H3>Add Your Wine Tasting Notes:</H3>
14:     <FORM METHOD=POST ACTION="add_notes.asp">
15:       <TABLE border ="1">
16:         <TR>
17:           <TD>
18:             <TABLE cellspacing="3" cellpadding="3">
19:               <TR>
20:         <TD ALIGN="RIGHT">House/Label:</TD>
21:         <TD ><INPUT SIZE="40" TYPE=TEXT NAME="HOUSE" MAXLENGTH="60">
22:         </TD>
23:         </TD>
24:       </TR>
25:       <TR>
26:         <TD ALIGN=RIGHT>Region/Location:</TD>
27:         <TD><INPUT SIZE="40" TYPE=TEXT NAME="REGION" MAXLENGTH="60">
28:         </TD>
29:       </TR>
30:       <TR>
31:         <TD ALIGN=RIGHT>Type/Varietal:</TD>
32:         <TD><INPUT SIZE="40" TYPE=TEXT NAME="TYPE" MAXLENGTH="60">
33:              
34:             <INPUT TYPE="RESET" VALUE="Clear the Form">
35:         </TD>
36:       </TR>
37:       <TR>
38:         <TD ALIGN=RIGHT>Vintage:</TD>
39:         <TD><INPUT SIZE="40" TYPE=TEXT NAME="VINTAGE" MAXLENGTH="20">
40:              
41:             <INPUT TYPE="SUBMIT" VALUE="Add Notes To Collection">
42:         </TD>
```

21

**LISTING 21.2**    continued

```
43:        </TR>
44:        <TR>
45:          <TD ALIGN=RIGHT VALIGN=TOP>Tasting Notes:</TD>
46:          <TD><TEXTAREA NAME="NOTES" COLS="60" ROWS="5"></TEXTAREA>
47:        </TR>
48:
49:      </TABLE>
50:
51:        </TD>
52:      </TR>
53:    </TABLE>
54:      <UL>
55:        <LI><A HREF="index.html">Return to Home Page</A></LI>
56:      </UL>
57: </FORM>
58:
59: </BODY>
60:
61: </HTML>
```

**ANALYSIS**    Lines 14–57 contain the FORM that is created to accept data from users. House (line 21), region (line 27), type (line 32), and vintage (line 39) are assigned a text entry field. The free-form text notes are collected with a TEXTAREA tag (line 46). A LINK to a cascading stylesheet is made on lines 8 and 9. A reset button (<INPUT TYPE="RESET" VALUE="Clear the Form" SIZE="40">) is encoded on line 34 so that users can clear the fields of the form. A submit button <INPUT TYPE="SUBMIT" VALUE="Add Notes To Collection">) is encoded on line 41 so that users can process the form. The process is a POST method (<FORM METHOD=POST ACTION="add_notes.asp">) that passes the data collected on the form to the add_notes.asp file. The <A> tag on line 55 provides a link to the home page of this Web application.

## Styling the Web Site with `wine_notes.css`

The use of a cascading stylesheet is strictly optional. In fact, if you omit the CSS file, you can ensure that your application is not exclusive of browsers that do not provide full support for CSS. If you omit the CSS file, remember to remove the <LINK> tags from the HTML pages in this application, although most browsers that do not support CSS will likely just ignore the <LINK> tag.

The advantage of having a CSS file is that it can be used to provide a consistent look on all of the pages of the application. That is how it is used in this case. To that end, a CSS file is offered as a model if you choose to apply styles in your application. Choose your own styles, or use the ones provided in Listing 21.3.

**LISTING 21.3**   Optional Styles Applied to the Application—`wine_notes.css`

```
 1:  <!-- Listing 21.3 - wine_notes.css -->
 2:
 3:         BODY       {display:block; background-color:#999966;
 4:                     background-image:URL(http://www.samspublishing.com/images/
 5:                     samslogo.gif);
 6:                     background-repeat:no-repeat}
 7:
 8:         H1         {text-align:center;padding:6px;font-weight:bold;
 9:                     color:#99cc99;font-style:bold;
10:                     font-family:verdana,arial,sans-serif;}
11:
12:         H3         {padding:6px;font-size:12pt;
13:                     font-family:verdana,arial,sans-serif;}
14:
15:         P          {font-family:verdana,arial,sans-serif;}
16:
17:         TD         {font-family:verdana,arial,sans-serif;
18:                     background-color:#99cc99;}
19:
20:         A:link     {color:#99cc99;font-size:14pt;text-decoration:none;}
21:
22:         A:visited  {color:#99cc66;font-size:14pt;text-decoration:none;}
23:
24:         A:hover    {text-decoration:underline; color:red;font-weight:bold;}
25:
26:         .head      {background-color:99cc99;
27:                     font-family:verdana,arial,sans-serif;font-size:14pt;}
28:
29:         SPAN       {font-family:verdana,arial,sans-serif;font-size:12pt;}
30:
31:         TR         {font-family:verdana,arial,sans-serif;}
32:
33:         LI         {font-family:verdana,arial,sans-serif;}
```

**ANALYSIS**   Each of the markup elements to which unique styles are to be applied are listed in the CSS file along with the styles chosen. On lines 4 and 5, the CSS refers to a graphics image stored on an external Web server. You could point this at a local graphic instead, if desired.

## Construction of a Home Page as `index.html`

Create a home page for the application and call it `index.html`. The home page requires only two links and some marked up text. One link should be provided to the `wine_notes.html` page you created earlier. Another link should be provided to the `view_notes.asp` page that lists all of the notes in the `wine_notes.xml` document.

**21**

Listing 21.4 shows a possible `index.html` page. If you chose to use a CSS file, then you can link that file to this page with a LINK tag.

LISTING 21.4    Wine Tasting Notes Web Application Home Page—`index.html`

```
 1: <!DOCTYPE HTML PUBLIC "-//W3C//DTD HTML 4.01 Transitional//EN"
 2:  "http://www.w3.org/TR/Html4/loose.dtd">
 3: <!-- Listing 21.4 - index.html -->
 4:
 5: <HTML>
 6:  <HEAD>
 7:   <TITLE>Wine Tasting Notes</TITLE>
 8:   <LINK rel = "stylesheet" type = "text/css" href = "wine_notes.css">
 9:  </HEAD>
10:  <BODY>
11:   <H1>Online Wine Tasting Notes</H1>
12:   <HR/>
13:   <H3>Navigation</H3>
14:   <H3>Please select one of the following:</H3>
15:   <UL>
16:    <LI><A HREF="view_notes.asp">View all of the Wine Note Records</A></LI>
17:    <LI><A HREF="wine_notes.html">Add a new Wine Tasting Note</A></LI>
18:   </UL>
19:  </BODY>
20: </HTML>
```

ANALYSIS    This home page has links to the `wine_notes.html` page (line 17) and the `view_notes.asp` page (line 16). A LINK to associate the `wine_notes.css` stylesheet is provided on line 8.

## Server-Side Wine Note Management with `add_notes.asp`

An Active Server Pages (ASP) server-side script will be used to append the notes offered by users to the `wine_notes.xml` document. Document Object Model objects will be instantiated to do this, similar to those used on Day 12. You can start by establishing variables to hold the values passed from the form for each of the element nodes in the dataset. The elements that will be populated include `wHouse`, `wRegion`, `wType`, `wVintage`, and `wNotes`. Therefore, the variables can be established with the following:

```
Dim wHouse
Dim wRegion
Dim wType
Dim wVintage
Dim wNotes
```

You will also need to establish variables to hold individual content passed via the DOM to the node types in the XML instance. You will create a variable for the document node, the root node, and the notes nodes. You will also need an attribute node to hold the time/date stamp values. These can be established with the following:

```
Dim oWineNotesDOM
Dim oWineNotesRootNode
Dim oDateStamp
Dim oWineNotesNodes
```

Because you will be passing data directly from the HTML form fields, you can trap the HTTP values directly and encode the captures by name, as in the following:

```
wHouse=Request("HOUSE")
wRegion=Request("REGION")
wType=Request("TYPE")
wVintage=Request("VINTAGE")
wNotes=Request("NOTES")
```

To instantiate a DOM object for the wine notes, you can use the server-side create object syntax that you have used on previous days. In this case, the syntax will look like this:

```
Set oWineNotesDOM = Server.CreateObject("Microsoft.XMLDOM")
oWineNotesDOM.async = false
```

The XML document can be loaded into the DOM with the following command:

```
oWineNotesDOM.load server.mappath("wine_notes.xml")
```

You will need to trap any parser errors, such as a non-existent XML document or any related I/O errors, with the following:

```
If oWineNotesDOM.parseError.ErrorCode <> 0 Then
```

If an error occurs, the script will create an empty XML document with the following:

```
oWineNotesDOM.loadXML "<wine_notes/>"
End If
```

The script can issue a time/date stamp when a record is saved by adding code that includes a date attribute associating the now() method call:

```
Set oDateStamp = oWineNotesDOM.documentElement.AppendChild
(oWineNotesDOM.createElement("wine"))
oDateStamp.setAttribute "date", now()
```

For each of the element nodes (*elementNameXML*) in the XML document, you will pass the form data to a newly created element node (*oMyObjectName*) in the result tree. The syntax in each case will look like this:

```
Set oMyObjectName = oMyDateStampObjectName.appendChild
(oMyObjectName.createElement("elementNameXML"))
oMyObjectName.Text = MyElementName
```

**21**

You will need to repeat this for each of the new nodes you are creating—in this case, house, region, type, vintage, and notes. In the case of the notes element, you will add the createCDATASection() method on the notes object. The complete script is shown as Listing 21.5.

**LISTING 21.5**    Server-Side ASP Script to Add Records—add_notes.asp

```
 1: <HTML>
 2:   <link rel = "stylesheet" type = "text/css"
 3:    href = "wine_notes.css">
 4: <%
 5: ' Listing 21.5 - add_notes.asp
 6:
 7:   Dim wHouse
 8:   Dim wRegion
 9:   Dim wType
10:   Dim wVintage
11:   Dim wNotes
12:
13:   Dim oWineNotesDOM
14:   Dim oWineNotesRootNode
15:   Dim oDateStamp
16:   Dim oWineNotesNodes
17:
18:   wHouse=Request("HOUSE")
19:   wRegion=Request("REGION")
20:   wType=Request("TYPE")
21:   wVintage=Request("VINTAGE")
22:   wNotes=Request("NOTES")
23:
24:   Set oWineNotesDOM = Server.CreateObject("Microsoft.XMLDOM")
25:   oWineNotesDOM.async = false
26:
27:   oWineNotesDOM.load server.mappath("wine_notes.xml")
28:
29:   If oWineNotesDOM.parseError.ErrorCode <> 0 Then
30:
31:     oWineNotesDOM.loadXML "<wine_notes/>"
32:   End If
33:
34:   Set oDateStamp = oWineNotesDOM.documentElement.AppendChild
35:   (oWineNotesDOM.createElement("wine"))
36:   oDateStamp.setAttribute "date", now()
37:
38: ' Build a new 'house' element node in the wine_notes.xml document
39:   Set oWineNotesNodes = oDateStamp.appendChild
40:   (oWineNotesDOM.createElement("house"))
41:   oWineNotesNodes.Text = wHouse
42:
```

**LISTING 21.5**    continued

```
43: ' Build a new 'region' element node in the wine_notes.xml document
44:    Set oWineNotesNodes = oDateStamp.appendChild
45:    (oWineNotesDOM.createElement("region"))
46:    oWineNotesNodes.Text = wRegion
47:
48: ' Build a new 'type' element node in the wine_notes.xml document
49:    Set oWineNotesNodes = oDateStamp.appendChild
50:    (oWineNotesDOM.createElement("type"))
51:    oWineNotesNodes.Text = wType
52:
53: ' Build a new 'vintage' element node in the wine_notes.xml document
54:    Set oWineNotesNodes = oDateStamp.appendChild
55:    (oWineNotesDOM.createElement("vintage"))
56:    oWineNotesNodes.Text = wVintage
57:
58: ' Build a new 'notes' element node in the wine_notes.xml document
59: ' wrap the text in CDATA markup to preserve spaces entered by users
60:    Set oWineNotesNodes = oDateStamp.appendChild
61:    (oWineNotesDOM.createElement("notes"))
62:    oWineNotesNodes.appendChild oWineNotesDOM.createCDATASection(wNotes)
63:
64: ' Save the modified wine_notes.xml document
65: '    You must have write permissions enabled for the directory!
66:    oWineNotesDOM.Save Server.MapPath("wine_notes.xml")
67: %>
68: <BR/><BR/><BR/>
69: <H1>Thank You</H1>
70:
71: <P>
72: <B>Your Wine Notes about : <%= sWine %></B><BR/>
73: </P>
74: <PRE>
75: <%= wNotes %>
76: </PRE>
77:
78: <P><B>Have been entered</P>
79:
80: <P>Click <A href="view_notes.asp">Here</A> To View Wine Notes</P>
81:
82: </HTML>
```

**ANALYSIS** Lines 7–16 establish the variables required in the rest of this script. The HTTP header variables are passed via the requests on lines 18–22. The DOM object (oWineNotesDOM) is created on line 24 and the XML document (wine_notes.xml) is passed to this object on line 27. The time and date stamp is established, upon successful execution of this script. The stamp is encoded as a date attribute on the wine element by

**21**

the code on lines 34–36. Each of the new XML element nodes (house, region, type, vintage, and notes) is created starting on lines 38, 43, 48, 53, and 58, respectively. The notes element is further qualified with the createCDATASection(wNotes) method on line 62. The save property of the DOM object is executed on line 66 to save the modified wine_notes.xml result document. Lines 69–82 provide a minimal HTML report of successful transfer to the screen.

## Provision of Wine Notes Using view_notes.asp

To produce a listing of all the notes contained in the wine_notes.xml file, a script will execute a server-side XSL transformation (wine_notes.xsl). You can do this by instantiating two XML DOM objects: one for the XML document and one for the XSL document. Then you will write the resulting transformation result tree to the screen with a command that looks like this:

Response.Write *oMyXMLDOMObject*.TransformNode(*oMyXSLDOMObject*)

Listing 21.6 shows the complete script.

**LISTING 21.6**    Perform a Server-Side XSLT—view_notes.asp

```
 1: <%
 2: ' Listing 21.6 - view_notes.asp
 3:
 4:    Dim oWineNotesXML        ' XML document
 5:    Dim oWineNotesXSL        ' XSL document
 6:
 7: ' Instantiate the XML DOM Object for the wine_notes.xml file
 8:    Set oWineNotesXML = Server.CreateObject("Microsoft.XMLDOM")
 9:    oWineNotesXML.async = False
10:
11: ' Load the wine_notes.xml file into the DOM object
12:    oWineNotesXML.Load Server.MapPath("wine_notes.xml")
13:
14: ' Create the XML DOM Object for the wine_notes.xsl Stylesheet
15:    Set oWineNotesXSL = Server.CreateObject("Microsoft.XMLDOM")
16:    oWineNotesXSL.async = False
17:
18: ' Load the wine_notes.xsl file into the Style DOM object
19:    oWineNotesXSL.load Server.MapPath("wine_notes.xsl")
20:
21: ' Write the transformed document out to the browser
22:    Response.Write oWineNotesXML.TransformNode(oWineNotesXSL)
23: %>
```

**ANALYSIS** The required new object variables are declared on lines 4 and 5. The first DOM object is created on the server on line 8 for the oWineNotesXML object. This object is loaded with the contents of `wine_notes.xml` on line 12. The process is repeated for the XSL file on lines 15 and 19. On line 22, the result of the transformation is printed to the screen.

## Transformation of Content with `wine_notes.xsl`

The transformation referred to in the discussion of the `winenotes.asp` script is defined by the `wine_notes.xsl` document. For the most part, this XSLT places the content of XML elements and attributes in appropriate HTML markup for presentation on a browser.

If you chose to use a CSS, you can do so again here with the LINK tag:

```
<LINK rel = "stylesheet" type = "text/css"
      href = "wine_notes.css"/>
```

The XSLT will use a single template match on the root node of the XML document and place appropriate HTML tags on the output tree. The template match statement with its XPath expression will look like this:

```
<xsl:template match="/">
```

Create an HTML table with a heading row that contains a single cell (<TD>) the width of the table.

Using an `xsl:for-each` element to select each wine container element in the XML instance will create the second row of the table. You can also add an `order-by` attribute to sort the records. In this case, sort by the time and date stamp allied by the previous script. The selection statement will look like this:

```
<xsl:for-each select="wine_notes/wine" order-by="-wine[@date]">
```

The complete XSLT document is shown as Listing 21.7. Create this document and then save it as `wine_notes.xsl`.

**LISTING 21.7**    A Wine Notes Application XSLT—wine_notes.xsl

```
1: <?xml version="1.0"?>
2:
3: <!-- Listing 21.7 - wine_notes.xsl -->
4:
5: <xsl:stylesheet xmlns:xsl="http://www.w3.org/TR/WD-xsl">
6:
7:    <xsl:template match="/">
8:
9:    <HTML>
```

21

**LISTING 21.7**    continued

```
10:        <HEAD>
11:         <TITLE>Online Wine Testing Notes</TITLE>
12:         <LINK rel = "stylesheet" type = "text/css"
13:               href = "wine_notes.css"/>
14:        </HEAD>
15:        <BODY>
16:         <H1>Online Wine Tasting Notes</H1>
17:        <TABLE border = "1" width="100%">
18:         <TR class="head">
19:           <TD class="head">Tasting Notes</TD>
20:         </TR>
21:         <TR>
22:           <TD>
23:             <TABLE width="100%">
24:
25:             <xsl:for-each select="wine_notes/wine" order-by="-wine[@date]">
26:                <TR>
27:                  <TD width = "100%">
28:                    <B>Entered: </B> <xsl:value-of select="@date"/><BR/>
29:                    <B>House:    </B> <xsl:value-of select="house"/><BR/>
30:                    <B>Region:   </B> <xsl:value-of select="region"/><BR/>
31:                    <B>Type:     </B> <xsl:value-of select="type"/><BR/>
32:                    <B>Vintage: </B> <xsl:value-of select="vintage"/><BR/>
33:                    <B>Notes:    </B> <PRE><SPAN>
34:                        <xsl:value-of select="notes"/></SPAN></PRE><BR/>
35:                    <HR/>
36:                  </TD>
37:                </TR>
38:             </xsl:for-each>
39:
40:             </TABLE>
41:           </TD>
42:         </TR>
43:        </TABLE>
44:        </BODY>
45:       </HTML>
46:
47:      </xsl:template>
48:
49: </xsl:stylesheet>
```

**ANALYSIS**    Line 7 establishes a template match on the root node (`<xsl:template match="/">`). Typically, HTML statements are placed on the output tree on lines 9–23. The CSS is associated with the HTML being generated by the XSLT on lines 12 and 13. Each of the records is selected and sorted by date and time on line 25 (`<xsl:for-each select="wine_notes/wine" order-by="-wine[@date]">`). The content of each attribute and element node of the source tree is passed to the result tree on lines 28–34. The `notes` content is placed in HTML preformatted tags (`<PRE>`).

## Creation of the Web Site

After you have created all of the component files, save them in a directory on a Web server. If you are working on IIS, you can create a virtual "Web Share" for the directory holding the files, as you have done on previous days. Execute the `index.html` page on the Web server. On IIS, the command would look like this:

```
http://localhost/myVirtualDirectory/index.html
```

The HTML data entry form should look something like the one depicted by Figure 21.2, and the list of all notes should look something like Figure 21.3.

**FIGURE 21.2**

*The online wine tasting notes application data entry form.*

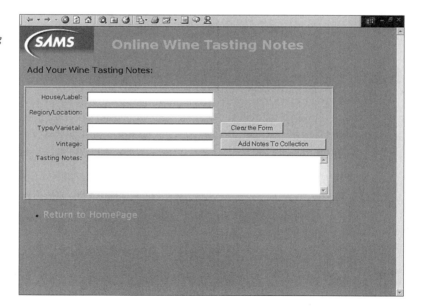

21

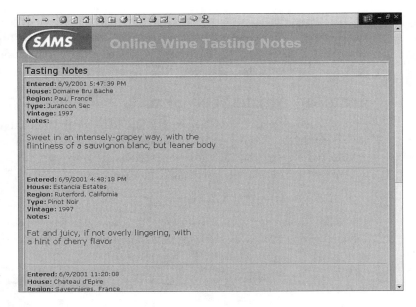

**FIGURE 21.3**

*A listing of all the wine tasting notes stored in the XML dataset.*

# Summary

Today, you created an entire application from start to finish that relied on XML, XSLT, server-side scripting, CSS, the XML DOM, and related technologies. The application provides a form that can be used to append information to an existing XML document. This demonstrates the integration of several complementary technologies.

# Q&A

**Q** **What would be required to make this Wine Note Storage and Retrieval application browser neutral?**

**A** You would have to change the cascading stylesheet and use only CSS style supported by the browsers accessing the site. The XML and XSL would function on any browser that supports them without modification.

**Q** **What are some other application types that could be created using a similar architecture?**

**A** A number of aggregation applications could be constructed using the kind of transformations and objects shown in the examples today. You could, for instance, create a research aggregation site where scientists provide findings to be shared with other investigators.

# Exercise

The exercise is provided so that you can test your knowledge of what you learned today. The answer is in Appendix A.

Enhance the wine application by creating a search capability using JavaScript or VBScript and an XML data island. Search the names of the Producers' House/Label field for any matching string of characters and then report back to the screen the full record of any located entry.

# PART IV

# Appendixes

# APPENDIX A

# Answers to the Questions

## Possible Solution to Exercise on Day 1

```
<exercise day="1">
  <name>Devan Shepherd</name>
  <address>123 any street</address>
  <email>me@whatever.com</email>
  <dob month="August" year="1958" day="11"/>
</exercise>
```

## Possible Solution to Exercise on Day 2

The instance presented in Listing 2.4 has several serious problems. Some of these include

- The reserved word XML in the declaration line must be in lowercase.

- The value of 1.0 for the attribute version in the declaration programming instruction must be in quotes.

- There is no unique root element in this document.

- Several examples of attribute values are not properly quoted.

- The first <cd> element has no closing tag.
- The <tracks...> elements are empty and require termination.
- Some of the tags require an angle bracket to be added.
- Several start and end tag pairs are not case matched.

The document could be made well formed by correcting the problems to produce code like that shown in Listing A.1.

**LISTING A.1**    A Solution to the Day 2 Exercise

```
 1: <?xml version="1.0"?>
 2: <music>
 3:     <cd number="432">
 4:     <title>The Best of Van Morrison</title>
 5:     <artist>Van Morrison</artist>
 6:     <tracks total="20" />
 7:     </cd>
 8:     <cd number="97">
 9:     <title>HeartBreaker</title>
10:     <subtitle>Sixteen Classic Performances</subtitle>
11:     <artist>Pat Benatar</artist>
12:     <tracks total="16" />
13:     </cd>
14: </music>
```

# Possible Solution to Exercise on Day 3

Figure A.1 depicts a possible tree diagram for the MCML.

**FIGURE A.1**

*A possible solution to the Day 3 exercise: A tree diagram for the Music Collection Markup Language (MCML).*

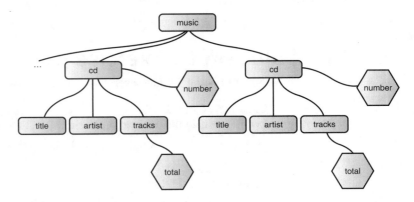

The content or business rules that might be applied to MCML include

- The root element is called `music` and it contains one or more `cd` elements.
- The `cd` element contains one each of `title`, `artist`, and `tracks` in that order.
- The `cd` element contains a required attribute called `number`, which must contain an integer value.
- The `tracks` element contains a required attribute called `total`, which must contain an integer value.

# Possible Solution to Exercise on Day 4

Listing A.2 shows a DTD that could be used to validate the MCML instance.

**LISTING A.2**   MCML DTD—`cd.dtd`

```
<!ELEMENT music     ( cd+ ) >
<!ELEMENT cd        ( artist | subtitle | title | tracks )* >
<!ELEMENT artist    ( #PCDATA ) >
<!ELEMENT subtitle  ( #PCDATA ) >
<!ELEMENT title     ( #PCDATA ) >
<!ELEMENT tracks    EMPTY >
<!ATTLIST cd
          number    NMTOKEN   #REQUIRED >
<!ATTLIST tracks
          total     NMTOKEN   #REQUIRED >
```

# Possible Solution to Exercise on Day 5

Listing A.3 shows an XDR schema that could be used to validate the MCML instance.

**LISTING A.3**   XDR Schema for the MCM Language

```
 1: <?xml version="1.0" encoding="UTF-8"?>
 2: <Schema
 3:     name="Untitled-schema"
 4:     xmlns="urn:schemas-microsoft-com:xml-data"
 5:     xmlns:dt="urn:schemas-microsoft-com:datatypes">
 6:     <ElementType name="music" model="closed" content="eltOnly" order="seq">
 7:             <element type="cd" minOccurs="1" maxOccurs="*"/>
 8:     </ElementType>
 9:     <ElementType name="cd" model="closed" content="eltOnly" order="one">
10:             <AttributeType name="number" dt:type="string" required="yes"/>
11:             <attribute type="number"/>
12:             <group minOccurs="0" maxOccurs="*" order="one">
```

**LISTING A.3** continued

```
13:                    <element type="artist" minOccurs="1" maxOccurs="1"/>
14:                    <element type="subtitle" minOccurs="1" maxOccurs="1"/>
15:                    <element type="title" minOccurs="1" maxOccurs="1"/>
16:                    <element type="tracks" minOccurs="1" maxOccurs="1"/>
17:            </group>
18:        </ElementType>
19:        <ElementType name="artist" model="closed"
                        content="textOnly" dt:type="string"/>
20:        <ElementType name="subtitle" model="closed"
                        content="textOnly" dt:type="string"/>
21:        <ElementType name="title" model="closed"
                        content="textOnly" dt:type="string"/>
22:        <ElementType name="tracks" model="closed"
                        content="empty">
23:            <AttributeType name="total" dt:type="number"
                        required="yes"/>
24:            <attribute type="total"/>
25:        </ElementType>
26: </Schema>
```

# Possible Solution to Exercise on Day 6

Listing A.4 shows an XDR schema that could be used to validate the MCML instance.

**LISTING A.4** XSD Schema for the MCM Language

```
1: <?xml version="1.0" encoding="UTF-8"?>
2: <xsd:schema xmlns:xsd="http://www.w3.org/2000/10/XMLSchema">
3:     <xsd:element name="artist" type="xsd:string"/>
4:     <xsd:complexType name="cdType">
5:         <xsd:sequence>
6:                <xsd:element ref="title"/>
7:                <xsd:element ref="subtitle" minOccurs="0"/>
8:                <xsd:element ref="artist"/>
9:                <xsd:element name="tracks" type="tracksType"/>
10:        </xsd:sequence>
11:        <xsd:attribute name="number" use="required">
12:                <xsd:simpleType>
13:                        <xsd:restriction base="xsd:NMTOKEN">
14:                                <xsd:enumeration value="432"/>
15:                                <xsd:enumeration value="97"/>
16:                        </xsd:restriction>
17:                </xsd:simpleType>
18:        </xsd:attribute>
19:    </xsd:complexType>
20:    <xsd:element name="music">
21:            <xsd:complexType>
```

A

```
22:                     <xsd:sequence>
23:                         <xsd:element name="cd" type="cdType"
                                      maxOccurs="unbounded"/>
24:                     </xsd:sequence>
25:                 </xsd:complexType>
26:         </xsd:element>
27:         <xsd:element name="subtitle" type="xsd:string"/>
28:         <xsd:element name="title" type="xsd:string"/>
29:         <xsd:complexType name="tracksType">
30:             <xsd:attribute name="total" use="required">
31:                     <xsd:simpleType>
32:                         <xsd:restriction base="xsd:NMTOKEN">
33:                             <xsd:enumeration value="16"/>
34:                             <xsd:enumeration value="20"/>
35:                         </xsd:restriction>
36:                     </xsd:simpleType>
37:             </xsd:attribute>
38:         </xsd:complexType>
39: </xsd:schema>
```

# Possible Solution to Exercise on Day 7

Listing A.5 shows the MCML XML document with the required changes in each cd element. Listing A.6 provides a DTD that validates the XML document and declares and defines an entity for substitution of a text string.

**LISTING A.5** The MCML Instance with an Entity Substitution—cd07.xml

```
1: <?xml version="1.0"?>
2: <!-- listing 7.3 - cd07.xml-->
3:
4: <!DOCTYPE music SYSTEM "cd.dtd">
5: <music>
6:     <cd number="432">
7:         <title>The Best of Van Morrison</title>
8:         <artist>Van Morrison</artist>
9:         <tracks total="20"/>
10:        <style>&style;</style>
11:    </cd>
12:    <cd number="97">
13:        <title>HeartBreaker</title>
14:        <subtitle>Sixteen Classic Performances</subtitle>
15:        <artist>Pat Benatar</artist>
16:        <tracks total="16"/>
17:        <style>&style;</style>
18:    </cd>
19: </music>
```

**LISTING A.6**    A DTD for the MCML Instance with an Entity Declaration—cd.dtd

```
 1: <!-- listing 7.4 - cd.dtd-->
 2:
 3: <!ELEMENT music (cd+)>
 4: <!ELEMENT cd (artist | subtitle | title | tracks | style)*>
 5: <!ELEMENT artist (#PCDATA)>
 6: <!ELEMENT subtitle (#PCDATA)>
 7: <!ELEMENT title (#PCDATA)>
 8: <!ELEMENT tracks EMPTY>
 9: <!ELEMENT style (#PCDATA)>
10: <!ATTLIST cd
11:     number NMTOKEN #REQUIRED
12: >
13: <!ATTLIST tracks
14:     total NMTOKEN #REQUIRED
15: >
16: <!ENTITY style "This CD is a compilation
17:     of the artist's top hits and is characteristic
18:     of the style we have come to enjoy."
19: >
```

# Possible Solution to Exercise on Day 8

Listing A.7 shows a possible solution to the exercise. The new namespace is declared on line 5 with a URI of urn:myoldies:LPs. Lines 17–21 show the new class of data, including a vinyl namespace prefix.

**LISTING A.7**    MCML with a vinyl Namespace—cd08.xml

```
 1: <?xml version="1.0"?>
 2: <!-- Listing 8.7 - cd08.xml -->
 3:
 4: <music
 5:     xmlns:vinyl="urn:myoldies:LPs">
 6:   <cd number="432">
 7:       <title>The Best of Van Morrison</title>
 8:       <artist>Van Morrison</artist>
 9:       <tracks total="20"/>
10:   </cd>
11:   <cd number="97">
12:       <title>HeartBreaker</title>
13:       <subtitle>Sixteen Classic Performances</subtitle>
14:       <artist>Pat Benatar</artist>
15:       <tracks total="16"/>
16:   </cd>
17:   <vinyl:record number="105">
```

**LISTING A.7** continued

```
18:        <vinyl:title>King of Blue</vinyl:title>
19:        <vinyl:artist>Miles Davis</vinyl:artist>
20:        <vinyl:tracks total="11"/>
21:    </vinyl:record>
22: </music>
```

# Possible Solution to Exercise on Day 9

Table A.1 shows potential solutions for the Exercise on Day 9.

**TABLE A.1** Possible Solutions

| Problem | Possible Solution |
| --- | --- |
| Select all elements subordinate to the root node. | `//*` |
| Select all track elements that have a `total` attribute with a value of 16. | `//tracks [@total="16"]` |
| Select all elements that contain the letter "`i`" in their names. | `//*[contains (name(),"i")]` |
| Select any elements that have names with greater than 11 characters. | `//*[string-length(name ())>11]` |
| Select all of the peers of the first `cd` element. | `/music/cd/ following-sibling::*` |

# Possible Solution to Exercise on Day 10

Listing A.8 shows a possible result. You need to have a document called `shelf.xml` to satisfy this simple link.

**LISTING A.8** Possible Solution to Exercise on Day 10—`cd10.xml`

```
1: <?xml version="1.0"?>
2: <!-- Listing 10.9 - cd10.xml -->
3:
4: <music
5:    xmlns:vinyl="urn:myoldies:LPs"
6:    xmlns:xlink="http://www.w3.org/1999/xlink'>
7:   <cd number="432" xlink:type="simple"
8:                           xlink:href='shelf.xml'
```

LISTING A.8     continued

```
 9:                                    xlink:show="replace"
10:                                    xlink:actuate="onRequest">
11:       <title>The Best of Van Morrison</title>
12:       <artist>Van Morrison</artist>
13:       <tracks total="20"/>
14:    </cd>
15:    <cd number="97">
16:       <title>HeartBreaker</title>
17:       <subtitle>Sixteen Classic Performances</subtitle>
18:       <artist>Pat Benatar</artist>
19:       <tracks total="16"/>
20:    </cd>
21:    <vinyl:record number="105">
22:       <vinyl:title>King of Blue</vinyl:title>
23:       <vinyl:artist>Miles Davis</vinyl:artist>
24:       <vinyl:tracks total="11"/>
25:    </vinyl:record>
26: </music>
```

Listing A.9 shows an XML document accessed by the simple link activation.

**LISTING A.9**     A Document at the End of the CD XLink—`shelf.xml`

```
1: <?xml version="1.0"?>
2: <!-- Listing 10.10 - shelf.xml -->
3:
4: <shelf>
5: This CD is located on the third shelf
6: </shelf
```

# Possible Solution to Exercise on Day 12

Listing A.10 shows code to return the `title` and `artist` elements for the first CD in your collection.

**LISTING A.10**     DOM Script for the MCML—`DOM_12a.html`

```
1: <!DOCTYPE HTML PUBLIC "-//W3C//DTD HTML 4.01 Transitional//EN">
2: <!-- Day 12 Exercise 1 - DOM_12a.html -->
3:
4: <html>
5: <head>
6: <title>DOM Scripting</title>
7: </head>
```

**LISTING A.10** continued

```
 8: <body>
 9: <script language="javascript">
10: <!--
11:
12:     var oMystuff = new ActiveXObject("Microsoft.XMLDOM")
13:     oMystuff.async="false"
14:     oMystuff.load("cd12.xml")
15:
16:
17:     document.write
18:        ("Title:")
19:     document.write
20:        (oMystuff.getElementsByTagName("title").item(0).text)
21:
22:     document.write
23:        ("<br/>Artist:")
24:     document.write
25:        (oMystuff.getElementsByTagName("artist").item(0).text)
26:
27:
28: -->
29: </script>
30:
31: </body>
32: </html>
```

**ANALYSIS**  A script, beginning on line 9, contained within the <body> section (lines 8–31) of an HTML page. Line 9 declares the script language (language="javascript") with a language attribute on the script element. Line 10 begins a comment that effectively hides the entire script from early browsers that are not JavaScript aware. Lines 12–14 are the document object creation and XML load steps. Lines 17–18 print text on the screen for the title element. Line 20 selects the text (text) contained by the first (item(0)) title element (getElementsByTagName("title")) in the object that contains the document (oMystuff). In a similar fashion, line 25 selects the text of the first artist element in the XML document. Lines 28–30 terminate the comment, script, and body section.

# Exercise—Part 2

To select the second title and artist elements from the XML document, you need to change the number of the item() methods on lines 20 and 25 to 1. The completed code looks like this:

**LISTING A.11**    DOM Script for the MCML—DOM_12b.html

```
 1: <!DOCTYPE HTML PUBLIC "-//W3C//DTD HTML 4.01 Transitional//EN">
 2: <!-- Day 12 Exercise 1 - DOM_12b.html -->
 3:
 4: <html>
 5: <head>
 6: <title>DOM Scripting</title>
 7: </head>
 8: <body>
 9: <script language="javascript">
10: <!--
11:
12:     var oMystuff = new ActiveXObject("Microsoft.XMLDOM")
13:     oMystuff.async="false"
14:     oMystuff.load("cd12.xml")
15:
16:
17:     document.write
18:       ("Title:")
19:     document.write
20:       (oMystuff.getElementsByTagName("title").item(1).text)
21:
22:     document.write
23:       ("<br/>Artist:")
24:     document.write
25:       (oMystuff.getElementsByTagName("artist").item(1).text)
26:
27:
28: -->
29: </script>
30:
31: </body>
32: </html>
```

**ANALYSIS**    The values passed to the item() methods on lines 20 and 25 are set to 1 to select the second instance of each element. The text content of the selected items is returned to the screen.

# Possible Solution to Exercise on Day 13

You will need to modify the validation value on line 27 of Listing 13.2 to true and recompile the instance.

```
27:          saxFactory.setValidating( true );
```

Because you are changing the name of the class to EList2.java, you will also have to change the references to the class name on lines 14, 19, and 31 for the program to compile properly.

To trap validation errors as they occur, you will need to override the error method of the HandlerBase class and force the processor to halt and report an error, rather than continue processing the remainder of the document instance.

The two new methods are

```
1:    public void error( SAXParseException minor )
2:    throws SAXParseException
3:    {
4:        throw minor;
5:    }
6:    public void warning( SAXParseException warn )
7:    throws SAXParseException
8:    {
9:        System.err.println( "Warning: " + warn.getMessage() );
10:   }
```

**ANALYSIS** The first new method (lines 1–5) throws any minor parsing errors to be caught by the error handlers in your main method. The second method (lines 6–10) reports any warning messages generated by the SAX parser.

When you compile these changes and modify your CD XML document by adding a new empty element near the end of the instance, you can expect a result that is something like this:

```
Name of Document: file:C:/SAX/cd13_bad.xml
SAX Event - Start of Document
SAX Event - Element Start: music
SAX Event - Element Start: cd
SAX Event - Attribute: number="432"
SAX Event - Element Start: title
SAX Event - Characters: The Best of Van Morrison
SAX Event - Element End: title
SAX Event - Element Start: artist
SAX Event - Characters: Van Morrison
SAX Event - Element End: artist
SAX Event - Element Start: tracks
SAX Event - Attribute: total="20"
SAX Event - Element End: tracks
SAX Event - Element End: cd
SAX Event - Element Start: cd
SAX Event - Attribute: number="97"
SAX Event - Element Start: title
SAX Event - Characters: HeartBreaker
SAX Event - Element End: title
SAX Event - Element Start: subtitle
SAX Event - Characters: Sixteen Classic Performances
SAX Event - Element End: subtitle
SAX Event - Element Start: artist
SAX Event - Characters: Pat Benatar
```

```
SAX Event - Element End: artist
SAX Event - Element Start: tracks
SAX Event - Attribute: total="16"
SAX Event - Element End: tracks
SAX Event - Element End: cd
Parse Error: Element "music" does not allow "empty" here.
```

The error (a new empty element that is not permitted according to the associated DTD) is reported on the last line and then the parser terminates.

Note that the processor traps no superfluous character events. This is because the DTD serves to define character data, and ignorable whitespace is not reported.

# Possible Solution to Exercise on Day 14

You can use several methods to accomplish the effects in Figure 14.3. A possible CSS file to solve this challenge is shown as Listing A.12.

**LISTING A.12**　　Possible Solution to Exercise on Day 14

```
 1: /* Exercise, Day 14, cd14.css */
 2:
 3: music
 4:    {display:block;
 5:     font-size:14pt;
 6:     padding:60px;
 7:     border-style:solid;
 8:     background-color:#999966;
 9:     background-image:URL(http://www.samspublishing.com/images/samslogo.gif);
10:     background-repeat:no-repeat}
11:
12: title, artist
13:    {display:block}
14:
15: cd
16:    {display:block;
17:     padding:20px;
18:     border-style:double;
19:     border-width:thick;
20:     width:75%;
21:     margin:20px;
22:     background-color:#99cc99}
```

**ANALYSIS**　　Lines 3–10 provide a rule set for the music root element. The content of the music element is displayed as blocks with leading and trailing line feeds (line 4).

The size of content text is set at 14 points (line 5). Sixty pixels of padding exist between the inner border and the outside edges of the inner boxes (line 6). The outside border is rendered as a solid line (line 7). The background color is set at HEX 999966, which matches the coloration of the Sams logo (line 8). The graphic is accessed via the Web at the designated URL (line 9). The background-repeat property is set to no-repeat (line 10) to avoid the graphic tiling over the entire surface of the outer box. Lines 12–13 ensure a line feed between the title and artist element content. The cd element content is styled by the rule set on lines 15–22. To ensure space between the words and each of the inner boxes, 20 pixels of space is provided as padding (line 17). The inner boxes are bordered by a thick, double line (lines 18–19). Line 20 establishes the 75% horizontal space relationship between the outer box and the inner boxes. The background color of the inner boxes is set at HEX 99cc99 on line 22.

# Possible Solution to Exercise on Day 15

The easiest way to create a bulleted list is by establishing an fo:list-block element containing list items. Each list item is encoded in a label/body pair. The label defines the bullet and the body gives the text data that resides next to the bullet. Listing A.13, cd15.fo, shows one way to create the desired effect.

**LISTING A.13**    Possible Solution to Exercise on Day 15

```
 1: <?xml version="1.0"?>
 2: <!-- Day 15 Challenge - cd15.fo -->
 3:
 4: <fo:root xmlns:fo="http://www.w3.org/1999/XSL/Format">
 5:
 6:   <fo:layout-master-set>
 7:     <fo:simple-page-master master-name="CD">
 8:       <fo:region-body margin-left="1.5in"
 9:           margin-right="1.5in" margin-top="1in"/>
10:     </fo:simple-page-master>
11:   </fo:layout-master-set>
12:
13:   <fo:page-sequence master-name="CD">
14:     <fo:flow flow-name="xsl-region-body">
15:
16:       <fo:block
17:           text-align="center"
18:           font-size="28pt"
19:           font-family="sans-serif"
20:           font-weight="bold"
21:           color="blue">CD Titles
```

**LISTING A.13**    continued

```
22:            </fo:block>
23:
24:        <fo:list-block>
25:
26:          <fo:list-item>
27:
28:              <fo:list-item-label>
29:                 <fo:block>*</fo:block>
30:              </fo:list-item-label>
31:
32:              <fo:list-item-body>
33:                 <fo:block start-indent=".25in">
34:                       The Best of Van Morrison</fo:block>
35:              </fo:list-item-body>
36:
37:          </fo:list-item>
38:          <fo:list-item>
39:
40:              <fo:list-item-label>
41:                 <fo:block>*</fo:block>
42:              </fo:list-item-label>
43:
44:              <fo:list-item-body>
45:                 <fo:block start-indent=".25in">
46:                       HeartBreaker</fo:block>
47:              </fo:list-item-body>
48:
49:          </fo:list-item>
50:
51:        </fo:list-block>
52:
53:      </fo:flow>
54:    </fo:page-sequence>
55:
56: </fo:root>
```

**ANALYSIS**    The fo:list-block element begins on line 24. Each list item element (fo:list-item) contains two child elements: fo:list-item-label and fo:list-item-body. The fo:list-item-label elements define the blocks containing the bullets (asterisks). The fo:list-item-body elements contain the titles of the CDs. On the fo:list-item-body elements is a start-indent attribute that leaves a space between the bullet and the body of the list item. Figure A.2 shows the result of interpreting this code with FOP.

FIGURE A.2

*XSL-FO list items.*

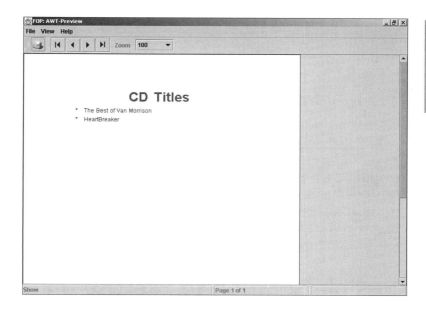

A

# Possible Solution to Exercise on Day 16

One way of solving this exercise is to write two simple templates. The first template would handle the typical HTML tags. This template would match on the root element (music) or the root node (/). The second template would match on the cd element and use the xsl:number element with a directed xsl:apply-templates for the element to be counted (title). Listing A.14 shows the complete listing.

**LISTING A.14** Possible Solution to Exercise on Day 16—cd16.html

```
1: <?xml version="1.0"?>
2: <!-- Day 16 - Exercise - cd16.xsl -->
3:
4: <xsl:stylesheet xmlns:xsl="http://www.w3.org/1999/XSL/Transform"
5:                 version="1.0">
6:
7:     <xsl:template match="music">
8:         <HTML>
9:         <HEAD>
10:        <TITLE>CD Collection</TITLE>
11:        </HEAD>
12:        <BODY>
13:            <xsl:apply-templates/>
14:        </BODY>
15:        </HTML>
```

**LISTING A.14**     continued

```
16:        </xsl:template>
17:
18:        <xsl:template match="cd">
19:                <xsl:number/>. <xsl:apply-templates select="title"/><br/>
20:        </xsl:template>
21:
22:
23: </xsl:stylesheet>
```

**ANALYSIS**     Lines 18–20 contain the template that performs the element counting. This template matches on the cd element (line 18). The xsl:number element will increment sequentially for each execution of the template. Because the template will iterate for each cd element, this action will count the CDs. Only the title element is included along with the count in the output tree, due to the select (line 19).

# Possible Solution to Exercise on Day 17

One possible solution involves the use of the XML DSO applet. Listing A.15 shows the code to complete the challenge in this manner.

**LISTING A.15**     Possible Solution to Exercise on Day 17—cd17.html

```
 1: <!DOCTYPE HTML PUBLIC "-//W3C//DTD HTML 4.01 Transitional//EN"
 2:  "http://www.w3.org/TR/html4/loose.dtd">
 3: <!-- listing 17.7 cd17.html -->
 4:
 5: <HTML>
 6: <HEAD>
 7: <TITLE>XML Data Island</TITLE>
 8: </HEAD>
 9:
10: <BODY>
11: <applet code="com.ms.xml.dso.XMLDSO.class"
12:         width="100%" height="50" id="CDs">
13:    <PARAM NAME="url" VALUE="cd17.xml">
14: </applet>
15: <H1>My Messages</H1>
16:    <TABLE id="table" border="6" width="100%"
17:           datasrc="#CDs" summary="messages">
18:        <THEAD style="background-color: aqua">
19:               <TH>Title</TH>
20:               <TH>Artist</TH>
21:        </THEAD>
22:        <TR valign="top" align="center">
```

LISTING A.15    continued

```
23:                    <TD><SPAN datafld="title"/></TD>
24:                    <TD><SPAN datafld="artist"/></TD>
25:          </TR>
26:     </TABLE>
27:  </BODY>
28:  </HTML>
```

A

# Possible Solution to Exercise on Day 21

Start by creating an XML data island for the wine_notes.xml document. You will recall from Day 17 that the syntax looks like this:

```
<XML ID="oMyDSOObjectName" SRC="mySource.xml"/>
```

Get the search string from users by opening an input button to collect characters. Store the entered string in a variable that you can feed into a search function. Use VBScript or JavaScript to search through the house element content of the wine_notes.xml document and return the entire record to a new variable when a match is found. Format the output of the variable. One possible search function in JavaScript might look like this:

```
function fSearchNotes ()
  {
  strHouse = SearchText.value.toUpperCase();
  if (strHouse == "")
     {
     strSearchResult.innerHTML = "&ltPlease enter "
                    + "a search string into "
                    + "'Title text' box.&gt";
     return;
     }

  oWineNotesDSO.recordset.moveFirst();

  RSSearchResultOutput = "";
  while (!oWineNotesDSO.recordset.EOF)
     {
     RSstrHouse = oWineNotesDSO.recordset("house").value;

     if (RSstrHouse.toUpperCase().indexOf(strHouse)
        >=0)
        RSSearchResultOutput += "<P><B>"
                    + oWineNotesDSO.recordset("house")
                    + "</B>, "
                    + oWineNotesDSO.recordset("region")
                    + ", <I>"
```

```
                              + oWineNotesDSO.recordset("type")
                              + "</I>, "
                              + oWineNotesDSO.recordset("vintage")
                              + ", <BR/>"
                              + oWineNotesDSO.recordset("notes")
                              + "</P>";

                oWineNotesDSO.recordset.moveNext();
                }

        if (RSSearchResultOutput == "")
            strSearchResult.innerHTML = "&ltSorry, no Wine "
            + "Tasting Notes were found&gt";
        else
            strSearchResult.innerHTML = RSSearchResultOutput;
        }
```

A complete page is shown as Listing A.16.

**LISTING A.16**   A Search Function for the Online Wine Notes Application That Uses an XML Data Island—wine_search.html

```
 1: <!DOCTYPE XHTML PUBLIC "-//W3C//DTD HTML 4.01 Transitional//EN"
 2:   "http://www.w3.org/TR/html4/loose.dtd">
 3:
 4: <!-- Day 21 Exercise - wine_search.html -->
 5:
 6: <HTML>
 7:
 8: <HEAD>
 9:
10:     <TITLE>Book Finder</TITLE>
11:     <LINK rel = "stylesheet" type = "text/css"
12:           href = "wine_notes.css"/>
13:
14: </HEAD>
15:
16: <BODY>
17:
18:     <XML ID="oWineNotesDSO" SRC="wine_notes.xml"/>
19:
20:     <H1>Online Wine Tasting Notes</H1>
21:     <H3>Search For Notes By Producer's House/Label</H3>
22:
23:     Enter characters from the Producer/House Name: <BR/>
24:     <INPUT TYPE="TEXT" ID="SearchText" SIZE="50"> 
25:     <BUTTON ONCLICK='fSearchNotes()'>Search</BUTTON>
26:     <HR>
27:     Results:<P>
28:     <DIV ID=strSearchResult></DIV>
29:
```

**LISTING A.16**    continued

```
30:     <SCRIPT LANGUAGE="JavaScript">
31:        function fSearchNotes ()
32:           {
33:           strHouse = SearchText.value.toUpperCase();
34:           if (strHouse == "")
35:              {
36:              strSearchResult.innerHTML = "&ltPlease enter a search "
37:                                 + "string into "
38:                                 + "'Produce/House Name' box.&gt";
39:              return;
40:              }
41:
42:           oWineNotesDSO.recordset.moveFirst();
43:
44:           RSSearchResultOutput = "";
45:           while (!oWineNotesDSO.recordset.EOF)
46:              {
47:              RSstrHouse = oWineNotesDSO.recordset("house").value;
48:
49:              if (RSstrHouse.toUpperCase().indexOf(strHouse)
50:                 >=0)
51:                 RSSearchResultOutput += "<P><B>"
52:                                 + oWineNotesDSO.recordset("house")
53:                                 + "</B>, "
54:                                 + oWineNotesDSO.recordset("region")
55:                                 + ", <I>"
56:                                 + oWineNotesDSO.recordset("type")
57:                                 + "</I>, "
58:                                 + oWineNotesDSO.recordset("vintage")
59:                                 + ", <BR/>"
60:                                 + oWineNotesDSO.recordset("notes")
61:                                 + "</P>";
62:
63:              oWineNotesDSO.recordset.moveNext();
64:              }
65:
66:           if (RSSearchResultOutput == "")
67:              strSearchResult.innerHTML = "&ltSorry, no Wine Tasting"
68:                                 + "Notes were found&gt";
69:           else
70:              strSearchResult.innerHTML = RSSearchResultOutput;
71:           }
72:     </SCRIPT>
73:     <UL>
74:       <LI><A HREF="index.html">Return to Home Page</A></LI>
75:     </UL>
76:
77: </BODY>
78:
79: </HTML>
```

**ANALYSIS**   Line 18 establishes a data island on the HTML binding the wine_notes.xml document as a source. Lines 23–25 create a data entry field for the user to enter a search string. The string entered is called SearchText. When the user submits the string, the fSearchNotes() function is called (line 31). The search function interrogates the content of the house element (line 47) and returns the entire record, as a record set (line 44), when a match on the SearchText string is found. The result string is formatted (lines 51–61) and sent to the browser as output. If the user fails to enter characters before submitting the form, lines 34–40 report an error message. If the search returns no records, lines 66–68 report an error. Line 74 provides a means for the user to return to the home page of the application.

# APPENDIX B

# Resources

Despite the extensive research and the timely nature of this book, some standards will have changed by the time you read it. Others will be developed that are not available at the time of this writing. Therefore, you will find that the following Web sites offer excellent reference material for the major topics covered in *Sams Teach Yourself XML in 21 Days, Second Edition*.

## Selected W3C Recommendations

The World Wide Web Consortium follows a specific process for review and promotion of technology based on consensus and testing. The recommendation track process is published at http://www.w3.org/Consortium/Process-20010208/tr. A new technology begins life as a NOTE that is issued to the W3C for review by its members. After the note stage, each of the following progressively more mature phases are completed:

- Working Draft: The working draft provides a detailed plan of action for the working committee to follow in exploring and expanding the description of a new technology.

- Last Call Working Draft: This phase provides other W3C committees and the public an opportunity to review the working draft and offer comments for improvement or consensus.
- Candidate Recommendation: The candidate recommendation provides outside investigators and users a chance to implement the new technology according to the working draft document.
- Proposed Recommendation: This phase recognizes successful implementation experience and satisfaction of the charter created for the working group.
- W3C Recommendation: A recommendation is the result of extensive investigation and consensus from internal and external reviewers.

## XML 1.0 Recommendation

This is the official W3C Recommendation for XML version 1.0. It is relatively short and quite readable.

```
http://www.w3.org/TR/REC-xml
```

## XML Schema: Part 0, Primer

Now that the W3C XML Schema language is at the recommendation stage, this is a particularly useful document. Part 0, Primer provides a readable overview of the specification, which describes how you may add constraints to XML instance documents to enforce structural validity.

```
http://www.w3.org/TR/xmlschema-0/
```

## XML Schema: Part 1, Structures

The XML Schema: Part 1, Structures documentation describes the concepts and syntax of the XML Schema definition language.

```
http://www.w3.org/TR/xmlschema-1/
```

## XML Schema: Part 2, Datatypes

The XML Schema: Part 2, Datatypes documentation defines XML datatypes for use in XML Schemata and other XML vocabularies.

```
http://www.w3.org/TR/xmlschema-2/
```

## XSL Transformations (XSLT) Version 1.0

The XSLT syntax and semantics are described in detail in this recommendation. It describes how you can use XSLT to transform documents expressed in one markup language into a new structure in the same language or into a different markup language.

http://www.w3.org/TR/xslt

### XML Path Language (XPath) Version 1.0

XPath is an expression-based language used to define the location of fragments of XML documents. Documentation is provided on using XPath in XSLT and XPointer.

http://www.w3.org/TR/xpath

### Document Object Model (DOM)

The following references are to a variety of sites that specify various aspects of the DOM, used to expose the nodes of an XML document to further programming.

- Document Object Model (DOM) Level 1 Specification:
  http://www.w3.org/TR/REC-DOM-Level-1/
- Document Object Model (DOM) Level 2 Core Specification:
  http://www.w3.org/TR/DOM-Level-2-Core/
- Document Object Model (DOM) Level 2 Views Specification:
  http://www.w3.org/TR/DOM-Level-2-Views/
- Document Object Model (DOM) Level 2 Events Specification:
  http://www.w3.org/TR/DOM-Level-2-Events/
- Document Object Model (DOM) Level 2 Style Specification:
  http://www.w3.org/TR/DOM-Level-2-Style/
- Document Object Model (DOM) Level 2 Traversal and Range Specification:
  http://www.w3.org/TR/DOM-Level-2-Traversal-Range/

### Namespaces in XML

The specification for the use of namespaces in XML is described in detail at this site.

http://www.w3.org/TR/REC-xml-names/

### XML Base

A recommendation for describing a base URL for relative URLs is defined at this site:

http://www.w3.org/TR/xmlbase/

### XML Linking Language (XLink) Version 1.0

XLink provides hypertext functionality in an XML document that far surpasses anything available in HTML. The recommendation for the XLink language is provided at this site:

http://www.w3.org/TR/xlink/

B

### XML Information Set

In the case where other specifications need to refer to XML version 1.0 in some form, this document describes a set of definitions that can be employed. This document serves almost as a Glossary for XML-critical concepts and terminology.

```
http://www.w3.org/TR/xml-infoset/
```

### Extensible Stylesheet Language (XSL) Version 1.0

The text of the XSL recommendation is at this site. It describes how XSL can be used to create a stylesheet to define the formatting vocabulary employed to present a class of XML document instances.

```
http://www.w3.org/TR/xsl/
```

# Selected W3C Working Drafts

### XML Inclusions (XInclude) Version 1.0

This draft descibes an approach for the inclusion of XML documents or portions of XML documents in merged XML instances.

```
http://www.w3.org/TR/xinclude/
```

### XML Pointer Language (XPointer) Version 1.0

By pairing URIs with XPath descriptions, you can locate specific content in a document using the XPointer language described in this draft document.

```
http://www.w3.org/TR/xptr
```

### XPath Requirements Version 2.0

Additional information on XPath can be found here:

```
http://www.w3.org/TR/xpath20req
```

### XSLT Requirements Version 2.0

Additional information on the next version of XSLT can be found here:

```
http://www.w3.org/TR/xslt20req
```

### Document Object Model (DOM) Level 3 Core Specification

The DOM Level 1 and Level 2 are well defined. This draft provides details on a proposal for a Level 3 version of the DOM. Level 3 extends—but aims to include—all of the description provided by Level 2 and Level 1.

```
http://www.w3.org/TR/DOM-Level-3-Core/
```

### Simple Object Access Protocol (SOAP) 1.2

SOAP, as it is proposed here, is a minimal protocol for transaction-based exchange of information in a decentralized, distributed environment, through the invocation of remote objects.

```
http://www.w3.org/TR/2001/WD-SOAP12-20010709
```

B

## Selected W3C Notes

### Web Services Description Language (WSDL) 1.1

This documentation defines WSDL as an XML format used to define network services. WSDL can be used in conjunction with SOAP, HTTP GET/POST, and other communication protocols.

```
http://www.w3.org/TR/wsdl
```

## Highly Recommended General XML Information Web Sites

### Tim Bray's Annotated Version of the XML 1.0 Recommendation

Tim Bray is a co-author of the XML recommendation. His annotated version of specification is readable and authoritative.

```
http://www.xml.com/axml/axml.html
```

### The XML Cover Pages (by Robin Cover)

This is one of the most extensive sites of its kind on the Internet. It includes links to software and the current versions of all XML-related specifications. It is frequently updated and quite complete.

```
http://www.oasis-open.org/cover/xml.html
```

### Apache XML Project

The Apache XML Project provides high-quality open source software for XML application development. Many of the solutions offered have been ported from Java into C++, PERL, or COM. You will find Xerces XML parsers; Xalan, an XSLT stylesheet processor; Cocoon, an XML-based Web publishing engine; FOP, an XSL-FO engine; Xang, a rapid development environment for dynamic server pages; support for XML SOAP; Batik, a toolkit for Scalable Vector Graphics; and Crimson, a full-featured XML parser.

```
http://xml.apache.org
```

### IBM XML Developer Works

The IBM Developer Works Web site provides extensive information about XML products and technologies. You will find tutorials, free software, and support dialog.

```
http://www-106.ibm.com/developerworks/xml/
```

### Microsoft Developers Network (MSDN)

The MSDN Web site provides access to information about all forms of development using Microsoft tools. The XML sections include free parsers, toolkits for SOAP, Web service development and customization utilities, SDKs, technical documentation, and tutorials.

```
http://msdn.microsoft.com/library/default.asp?url=/nhp/Default.asp?con-
tentid=28000438
```

### SAX 2.0: The Simple API for XML

SAX is a standard interface for event-based processing of XML instance documents. It was developed as a collaborative effort of the XML DEVelopers mailing list (XML-DEV).

```
http://www.megginson.com/SAX/
```

### XML-DEV Mailing List

The XML-DEVelopers mailing list is primarily for those who are developing applications using XML technologies. You can subscribe by sending an e-mail to `majordomo@ic.ac.uk`. The body of the message should read `subscribe xml-dev`. You can view hypertext archives of the XML-DEV mailing list at the site listed.

```
http://lists.xml.org/archives/xml-dev/
```

# Useful XML Editors

This section contains some recommended software for developing XML applications.

### Architag XRay XML Editor

The XRay XML Editor by Architag International provides a comprehensive work environment for the editing of XML documents, schemata, XSL, XSLT, HTML, and DHTML. A real-time error-checking capability gives instantaneous feedback and updates with each keystroke. The XRay XML Editor is available as a free download from the Architag.com Web site:

```
http://www.architag.com/xray/
```

**XML Spy by Altova, Inc.**

XML Spy offers an Integrated Development Environment (IDE) for XML. Editing, validation, and transformation are built into the IDE along with a powerful capability to create DTDs, XSD, XDR, and other schemata from an XML instance document. Given a schema in one language, XML Spy can convert it into another language. A single user license for XML Spy costs $199.

http://www.xmlspy.com/

**Turbo XML by Tibco Extensibility**

Turbo XML version 2.0, formerly XML Authority, is a full-featured commercial editor. Turbo XML offers an IDE with support for the W3C XSD and tools for creation, conversion, and validation of schema instances. A time-limited trial version is available for evaluation.

# Other XML Software

It is impossible to provide a comprehensive and completely accurate listing of all available software for XML development because it's always changing. For a complete and current list of free and commercial software products available to XML developers, visit the XML software site. You will find listings for all types of software, such as object serialization tools, conversion tools, database interfaces, content management systems, schema editors, APIs, tools, utilities, Web service programs, browsers, editors, parsers, and engines for all XML technologies.

http://www.xmlsoftware.com/

# INDEX

# X

# Other Related Titles